INTERNATIONAL ARCHITECTURE & INTERIORS
Series directed by Matteo Vercelloni

NEW
RESTAURANTS
IN USA
& EAST ASIA

MATTEO VERCELLONI
EDITED BY SILVIO SAN PIETRO
PHOTOGRAPHS BY PAUL WARCHOL

EDIZIONI L'ARCHIVOLTO

IDEAZIONE E CURA DEL PROGETTO
Silvio San Pietro
Matteo Vercelloni

TESTI
Matteo Vercelloni

FOTOGRAFIE
Paul Warchol

REDAZIONE
Matteo Vercelloni

PROGETTO GRAFICO
Morozzi & Partners

REALIZZAZIONE GRAFICA E IMPAGINATO
Marcella Bonacina
Albina Bonacina
Silvio San Pietro

TRADUZIONI
Andrew Ellis

SI RINGRAZIANO
Gli architetti e gli studi di progettazione per la cortese collaborazione e per aver fornito i disegni dei loro archivi.
We are grateful to the architects and designers who have kindly contributed to this project and have provided drawings from their files.

[ISBN 88-7685-098-8]

A norma della legge sul diritto d'autore e del codice civile è vietata la riproduzione di questo libro,
di parti di esso, di disegni, planimetrie e fotografie con qualsiasi mezzo, elettronico, meccanico, per mezzo di fotocopie,
microfilms, registrazioni o altro. L'Editore preseguirà ogni violazione dei propri diritti esclusivi in sede giudiziaria.

© Copyright 1998
EDIZIONI L'ARCHIVOLTO
Via Marsala, 3 - 20121 Milano
Tel. 02/2901.0424 - 2901.0444
Fax 02/2900.1942 - 659.5552

I edizione febbraio 1998

INDICE GENERALE
CONTENTS

PREFACE / PREFAZIONE Matteo Vercelloni	6
150 WOOSTER RESTAURANT NEW YORK,NY, USA. Diana Agrest e Mario Gandelsonas Architects	14
ALL STARS CAFE NEW YORK, NY, USA. David Rockwell Archietct	18
AMBERJACK'S RESTAURANT SOUTH NORWALK, CT, USA. Haverson Architecture and Design	22
AMERICA RESTAURANT LAS VEGAS, NV, USA. Ark Restaurant Corp. - Turett Collaborative Architects	25
BAANG RESTAURANT GREENWICH, CT, USA. David Rockwell Architect	29
BEN'S CUISINE NEW YORK, NY, USA. Haverson Architecture and Design	33
BOHEMIA JAZZ CLUB TOKYO, JP. Branson e Coates Architecture	37
BRYANT PARK GRILL NEW YORK, NY, USA. Hardy Holzman Pfeiffer Associates	42
CAFFE' BONGO TOKYO, JP. Branson e Coates Architecture	50
CAN RESTAURANT NEW YORK, NY, USA. Stomu Miyazaki Es Studio Inc, Wys & Partners	55
CHINA GRILL MIAMI SOUTH BEACH, FL, USA. Jeffrey Beers Architects	60
CHRISTER'S RESTAURANT NEW YORK, NY, USA. David Rockwell Architect	65
FISH DANCE RESTAURANT KOBE, JP. Frank Gehry Architect	69
MARKET AT NEWPORT RESTAURANT NEW YORK, NY, USA. Turett Collaborative Architects	78
METROPOLE TOKYO, JP. Branson e Coates Architecture	84
MIREZI RESTAURANT NEW YORK, NY, USA. Gene S. Park, Min Yang Architects	89
MONKEY BAR NEW YORK, NY, USA. David Rockwell Architect	93
MOONSOON RESTAURANT SAPPORO, JP. Zaha M Hadid Architect	99
MOTOWN CAFE LAS VEGAS, NV, USA. Haverson Architecture and Design	109
MOTOWN CAFE NEW YORK,NY, USA. Haverson Architecture and Design	118
NOBU RESTAURANT NEW YORK, NY, USA. David Rockwell Architect	124
PLANET HOLLYWOOD ORLANDO, FL, USA. David Rockwell Architect	129
POIRET RESTAURANT NEW YORK, NY, USA. Ark restaurant Corp. - Nancy Mah Weinstein Architect	138
SAVANNAH RESTAURANT MIAMI BEACH, FL, USA. Afuture Company - Alex Locadia, Giusi Mastro Architects	142
SCALINI RESTAURANT KUALA LUMPUR, MY. Tony Chi Architect & Associates	146
SEQUOIA RESTAURANT CHARLOTTE, NC, USA. Ark Restaurant Corp. - Bill Lalor Architect	152
SI PIAZZA RESTAURANT NEW YORK, NY, USA. Haverson Architecture and Design	157
SPIGA RESTAURANTS SCARSDALE e BEDFORD, NY, USA. Haverson Architecture and Design	162
SYMPHONY CAFE' NEW YORK, NY, USA. Jeffrey Beers Architects	168
TAPIKA RESTAURANT NEW YORK, NY, USA. David Rockwell Architect	173
TATOU RESTAURANTS BEVERLY HILLS, CA e NEW YORK, NY, USA. David Rockwell Architect	179
TORRE DI PISA RESTAURANT NEW YORK, NY, USA. David Rockwell Architect	185
VILLAGE EATERIES RESTAURANT LAS VEGAS, NV, USA. Hardy Holzman Pfeiffer Associates	194
VONG RESTAURANT NEW YORK, NY, USA. Haverson Architecture and Design, David Rockwell Architect	200
ZIP CITY RESTAURANT NEW YORK, NY, USA. Fradkin Pietrzak Architect	205
ZOE RESTAURANT NEW YORK, NY, USA. Jeffrey Beers Architects	210
TECHNICAL DATA / SCHEDE TECNICHE	215
BIOGRAPHIES / BIOGRAFIE	229

PREFACE

Third in the series "International Architecture & Interiors," this book focuses on restaurant design, offering a broad and stimulating array of thirty-six designs realized over the last decade in the United States, Japan, and Malaysia. The restaurants we have chosen are nearly all by North American architects, except for a number of local ones in Japan by the British designer Nigel Coates and the Iraqi architect Zaha Hadid, who completed his studies in London, where he now lives and works. The book offers a comparative overview of new western architecture, particularly of the kind emerging in the U.S., where, unlike in Europe, restaurant design involves not just the interiors but the building's entire setting, sometimes allowing total freedom to experiment new languages and imaginative layout solutions.

The previous two books in this series took a sweeping look at "domestic" architecture in the United States, covering both apartment design and the characteristically American single-family home. In this book we delve deeper into the new offering of U.S. interior design, moving from the private to the public sector, a field in which restaurants have become of major interest, and which leaves the architect a free rein for innovative and imaginative design solutions for hospitality and comfort. In addition to following the same line of inquiry explored in the previous two books on aspects of U.S. architecture, this third book in the series is once again illustrated with the photography of Paul Warchol, an artist of world renown, whose work testifies to the many architectural solutions, the lighting and colors, the atmosphere, and details of each of the restaurants under study.

The idea of flanking the Americans with a number of British architects allows us to compare the different poetics employed, endorsing the values expressed by interior design in the West and exported to Japan and Malaysia, where together with Gehry's renowned "Fish Dance" at Kobe, an unmistakable landmark of the cityscape, we find the famous "Monsoon" restaurant by Zaha Hadid at Sapporo, the "Bohemia," the "Metropole," and the "Café Bongo" by Nigel Coates in Tokyo, and not least the recent addition, "Scalini," by Tony Chi in Kuala Lumpur.

Our study of the chosen designs from the architectural and stylistic point of view has prompted us to also consider the symbolic aspects of today's restaurant *per se*, and the new sociological trends tied to the habit of "eating out." Given that the latest statistics from the United States show that an estimated two out of three meals will be bought and eaten outside the home, and given that the entrenched custom of eating lunch and dinner out shows no signs of waning, then restaurants, with all their myriad variations of food, style, and architecture are undoubtedly one of the frontiers of design to keep an eye on from both the sociological and marketing point of view. Their success lies perhaps more in their overall image and design than in the culinary offerings they serve. At first sight, most people would presume that the choice of where to eat is based entirely on the quality of the food, and yet what propels the public to choose one place over another is the architectural impact, which is therefore more than merely accessory to the food itself. If the truth were told, it is the restaurant itself that is being sold, and is designed to address the client's needs at behavioral and psychological level, over and above the fare on the menu. Eating out is hardly a question of survival. Going to a restaurant transforms the act of consuming food into a social event, ennobled by the setting, by the style and image of the place, whether this be the local branch of the family diner, a check tablecloth Italian-style trattoria, or some new "in" venue fitted out by a designer or architect of renown, as in the case of those presented here in this book. To put it briefly, the physical pleasure of eating out cannot be severed from the psychological needs fulfilled by the atmosphere of the restaurant. As pointed out by Joanne Finkelstein in her in-depth sociological study *Dining Out. A Sociology of Modern Manners* (Cambridge 1989), eating out is enjoyed as a form of entertainment, in which human interchange is mediated by the visuals and the atmosphere created by the individual's imagination. This has nothing to do with the quality of the food served. The impressions of pleasant social exchange and luxury aroused by the restaurant environment are iconically represented through its atmosphere, the style of furnishings, and illumination, the plates and cutlery, and so forth. In this respect, we might compare the restaurant environment with stage design for a theater (not for nothing Philippe Starck has dubbed his successful design for a Madrid restaurant "Teatriz," slotted into a defunct theater), where in a paroxysmal and indirect Brechtian attitude the guests become actors, each one the star of his or her own set piece, with roles that vary from table to table, restaurant to restaurant. Think of the rules of etiquette observed in the more luxurious restaurants, where a tie is obligatory and people speak in hushed voices over candle-lit tables. In contrast are the family diners with a large group of people around a table, where everyone has to shout over the noise of the others, with hackneyed jokes and trite remarks made over a bottle of red wine or pint of chilled beer. Another recent alternative is the Japanese-style karaoke eatery.

Whatever the case, the design of the setting is of paramount importance in this "public theater." The objects, the pictures on the walls, the furnishings, fabrics, and colors – everything conspires to make the spectacle more engaging, to aid the recital of the actor-guest. It goes without saying, in their role as theaters, as wholly artificial stage sets, restaurants tend to follow and endorse the latest trends in the movies, in architecture, in the "minimalist" or "decorative" currents in vogue. Despite this, in the limitless range of ideas, contemporary restaurants often provide fertile soil in which to try out new expression and idiom, to assay new combinations of materials and fittings beyond the possibilities of the standard domestic environment. The examples chosen here have the shared characteristic of being valid experiments within the bounds of the various styles currently in vogue, ranging from the classic formulation typical of the golden age of restaurants, to the studied and elaborate modern projects involving imaginative forays into the world of museum and set design.

In the style of eating out there are various trends that follow one another, trends that become the going fashion: high-class restaurants, provincial diners in rustic style, postmodern and minimalist restaurants, beach bars, fast-food joints, Thai and Indian restaurants, and so on. The way these places are fitted out are a projection of human feelings. They sum up the mood we hope to have as we consume our food when we eat out, and at the same time they are the means for creating the hoped-for mood. Richly upholstered chairs and plush wallpaper fuel the sense of luxury and good taste. Conversely, plastic seating in strong colors communicate a sense of cheerfulness, fostering conversation and socialization. The material impression that we receive from the restaurant, its atmosphere and its furnishings, when we eat out, are just as important was the things we eat.

Besides defining themselves as forms of "architecture of desire," restaurants are also made to arouse certain feelings and forms of behavior between table-companions. To some extent the setting prescribes the rules for dress, speech, and manners, materializing personal desires and making human emotions tangible. For instance, both McDonald's and the Italian trattoria try to convey the image of a family setting; while a romantic atmosphere with soft lighting is more typical of the fashionable bistro; sophistication and luxury are the characteristics of an evening reception, often staged in a plush hotel or in a hall tricked out for the occasion. In a certain sense, if we think of the swanky, exclusive type of restaurant, we notice certain traits of behavior that hark back centuries even. The restaurant as a place to dine came into being after the French Revolution, owing to the glut of unemployed chefs from the royal kitchens, who constituted a kind of subspecies of the aristocracy in their own way, emulating their masters' lifestyle. Luxury and extravagance, artifice and theatrical flair were the ingredients that turned the new taverns into chic gathering places, irrespective of the food served therein. Together with the grand hotels built in the 1800s, the *restaurants à la mode* were basically a middle-class simulation of the banquets staged in the manors and palaces of the nobility. As if on a culinary stage, open to all and sundry (or to whoever could pay to take part), the actor-guests rehearsed the gestures and mannerisms of the waning gentry.

In her essay, Joanne Finkelstein draws up a list of types of eating place, classifying each one with a certain set of behaviors. The list includes, therefore, such restaurant genres as the "spectacular informal," the "formal," the "parody," the "bistrot mondain," the "café mundane," the fast-food joint, the local "ethnic" place. In each case, the architecture and interiors play a vital role; in some the fittings are fundamental, in others of secondary importance, though always present and significant.

From this point of view, we only need to study the examples given in this book to realize the essential task fulfilled by the architectural setting. While astute dissonances and strong volumetric and chromatic contrasts characterize the "Monsoon Restaurant" of Zaha Hadid in Sapporo, an uncontainable compositive and figurative creativity typical of the theater and musical inform the David Rockwell's designs for "Planet Hollywood," the elegant "Nobu," the

"All Stars Café," and the exclusive reconstruction of the "Monkey Bar" in New York. Closely tied to the world of music – and particularly the musical – are the "Motown" restaurants in downtown New York and Las Vegas by the Haverson Architecture studio. Softer atmospheres and more unusual environments, aiming to create exclusive ambiances through a sapient synthesis of materials and composition are the principle assets of "Scalini" in Kuala Lumpur, the "Si Piazza" and the "Mirezi" in New York, the very recent "Savannah" in Miami, to name but a few. Snatched straight from the film studio lot is the recent "Village Eateries," built by Hardy Holzman Pfeiffer Associates in Las Vegas inside the "New York New York" Hotel-Casino enclave. In a class of its own is "Fish Dance" by Frank Gehry, a restaurant slotted into the downtown fabric of Kobe, Japan, a unmissable landmark consisting of a huge vertical fish in metal netting, its head pointing skyward.

The tradition of giving an eye-catching exterior to a restaurant in both architectural and figurative senses has its origins in Adolf Loos's "Café Museum" in Vienna (1899), progressing toward the three-dimensional ad sign typical of the American diner (from "White Towers" and "McDonald's" to "Denny's" to "Kentucky Fried Chicken," to the blue obelisk of the "Howard Johnson's" outlets). Basically a sales outlet in the broadest sense, with its lights and colors the restaurant stands out in the urban landscape in which it has been studiously inserted, proposing an architectural alienation in the process of reformulating a different and pervasive reality. The restaurants contained in this book offer a highly qualified range of diversified architectural spaces, places characterized by varied and multiple spatial solutions and settings, each one with its own distinct atmosphere, but all linked by their common ambition to be spaces of desire, spaces in which the guests act out their roles at social level. As Finkelstein points out, in a restaurant we can pretend to be rich, successful, sophisticated, and urbane. We can play the passionate lover, the affectionate friend, the generous parent, the grateful spouse, or exciting partner. The restaurant is a theater of sorts, in which fiction rules, and the truth is immaterial.

Matteo Vercelloni

PREFAZIONE

Terzo volume della collana "International Architecture & Interiors", questo libro affronta il tema del ristorante offrendo un ricco e stimolante confronto tra trentasei progetti realizzati in America, Giappone e Malesia nell'ultimo decennio. I ristoranti selezionati sono firmati nella quasi totalità da progettisti americani, a esclusione di alcuni locali realizzati in Giappone dal designer inglese Nigel Coates e dall'architetto Zaha Hadid, di origine irachena, ma formatasi a Londra, città dove oggi vive e lavora. Si tratta quindi di un confronto tra progetti appartenenti alla cultura occidentale e a quella americana in particolare, dove, a differenza che in Europa, l'architettura del ristorante si spinge oltre il semplice progetto d'interni, per abbracciare la dimensione scenografica e spettacolare, in cui sperimentare, a volte in totale libertà, nuovi linguaggi e brillanti soluzioni compositive.

Dopo avere proposto nei primi due volumi della collana una ricca rassegna di architetture domestiche americane, dagli appartamenti alle grandi case unifamiliari, con questo libro ci proponiamo di offrire un ulteriore approfondimento sull'architettura d'interni americana, spostandoci però dalla dimensione privata a quella pubblica, dove il ristorante è una delle categorie di maggiore interesse, in cui architettura e immaginazione sono chiamate a esprimere figure sempre innovative e inedite soluzioni di ospitalità e comfort. Oltre al comune tema di analisi dell'architettura d'interni americana, ciò che accomuna questo terzo libro ai primi due della collana, sottolineando un percorso di consolidata continuità d'immagine, é la lettura fotografica anche in questo caso condotta con il consueto rigore da Paul Warchol, fotografo di fama internazionale impegnato in questo caso nel testimoniare al meglio soluzioni architettoniche, luci e colori, atmosfere e dettagli dei ristoranti selezionati.

L'avere affiancato alla serie dei progettisti americani alcuni protagonisti inglesi ha significato arricchire il confronto tra le diverse poetiche e ha testimoniato il valore del progetto d'interni occidentale, esportato in questo caso in Giappone e in Malesia, dove insieme al "Fish Dance" di Kobe progettato da Frank Gehry come vero e proprio *landmark* urbano troviamo il famoso ristorante "Monsoon" di Zaha Hadid a Sapporo, il "Bohemia", il "Metropole" e il "Caffé Bongo" di Nigel Coates a Tokyo e il recentissimo "Scalini" di Tony Chi a Kuala Lumpur.

Esaminare i progetti selezionati dal punto di vista architettonico e stilistico ha comportato anche riflettere sul significato simbolico del ristorante contemporaneo e sulle nuove tendenze sociologiche legate al fenomeno del 'mangiare fuori'. Se le ultime statistiche americane prevedono che intorno alla fine del secolo due pasti su tre saranno comprati e consumati fuori casa e se l'abitudine di consumare pranzi e cene fuori appare inarrestabile, il ristorante, nelle sue molteplici varianti alimentari, figurative e architettoniche, appare senza dubbio uno degli spazi pubblici da osservare con maggiore attenzione sia dal punto di vista sociologico, sia da quello di mercato, ricercandone il successo forse più nella sua immagine e nelle sue sorprendenti soluzioni compositive che nella sua sostanza culinaria. Certo di primo acchito chiunque affermerebbe che la scelta di un ristorante è dettata dalla qualità del cibo offerto, ma molte volte ciò che spinge il pubblico in un locale piuttosto che in un altro è la scena architettonica, che solo in apparenza fa da contorno ai cibi, ma che in realtà si rivela come il vero prodotto venduto destinato a soddisfare il cliente a livello comportamentale e psicologico prima che culinario e gastronomico. Anzitutto il 'mangiare fuori' non può essere ridotto a un semplice fatto di sopravvivenza; andare al ristorante trasforma l'atto di consumazione del cibo in un evento sociale nobilitato dalla ricchezza della scenografia, dalla perfezione dell'immagine, sia che essa si limiti a quella riconoscibile e familiare delle catene *fast food,* sia che offra le tovaglie a quadretti della classica trattoria all'italiana, sia che si tratti di uno stucchevole 'localino alla moda' o di un esclusivo ristorante firmato da designer e architetti di successo come quelli presentati in questo libro. In poche parole il piacere fisico del 'mangiare fuori' si presenta in uno stretto e inscindibile legame con la dimensione psicologica soddisfatta dall'aura del locale. Come ha sottolineato in un approfondito studio sociologico Joanne Finkelstein[1] : "L'evento viene goduto come forma di divertimento e parte del moderno spettacolo in cui relazioni sociali sono mediate attraverso immagini visuali e un'atmosfera creata dall'immaginazione. Ciò non ha niente a che vedere con il piacere dell' ingestione del cibo.[...] le immagini di ricchezza, felicità, lusso e le relazioni sociali piacevoli evocate all'interno del ristorante sono rappresentate iconicamente attraverso la sua atmosfera, lo stile d'arredamento, la mobilia, l'illuminazione, le stoviglie e via dicendo". Da questo punto di vista possiamo paragonare il ristoran-

1. Joanne Finkelstein, Dining Out. A Sociology of Modern Manners, Cambridge 1989, trad. It. "Andare a pranzo fuori - Sociologia delle buone maniere" Il Mulino, Bologna 1992.

te a una sorta di palcoscenico teatrale (anche per questo Philippe Starck ha chiamato "Teatriz" un suo fortunato progetto per un ristorante madrileno costruito all'interno di un teatro in disuso) dove in un parossistico e indiretto atteggiamento brechtiano i commensali si trasformano in attori più o meno protagonisti, con ruoli che variano da tavola a tavola, da locale a locale. Si pensi alle regole di etichetta dei ristoranti lussuosi dove è d'obbligo la cravatta si parla sottovoce a lume di candela accompagnati da musiche di sottofondo e da luci soffuse; o viceversa a quelle cene di gruppo in ristoranti più alla buona dove invece si fa a gara a chi parla più forte, per emergere con grevi battute scaldate da bottiglioni di vino rosso o da generose pinte di birra gelata; oppure alla più recente pratica del canto dei dilettanti che caratterizza i ristoranti-karaoke di importazione nipponica.

In tutti i casi appare di grande importanza il ruolo svolto dalla scena in questi palcoscenici pubblici; oggetti e quadri, soluzioni architettoniche e d'arredamento, materiali e colori, tutto concorre a far funzionare al meglio lo spettacolo, a soddisfare pienamente l'ospite-attore. Ovviamente, in quanto sorta di luogo teatrale, artificiale e scenografico, il ristorante segue e traduce le mode del momento dettate dal cinema, dall'architettura, dalle correnti 'minimal' o 'decorative', ma nello sterminato ed eclettico scenario del ristorante contemporaneo non mancano esempi dove il tema architettonico è occasione per sperimentare nuove espressioni e linguaggi, per azzardare accostamenti materici e disegni di arredi che sarebbero impensabili ad esempio nel mondo degli interni domestici. Gli esempi selezionati cercano di cogliere la comune caratteristica di valida sperimentazione all'interno di diverse tendenze che dalla rivisitazione del ristorante classico della *Golden Age*, passano alla definizione di spazi scanditi da rigorose e raffinate modernità per spingersi sino alle dimensioni di reinvenzione museale e cinematografica.

Ecco allora che "nello stile del pranzare fuori si notano ondate diverse in cui si succedono, diventando volta a volta di moda, ristoranti raffinati, ristoranti di provincia di tipo rustico, ristoranti postmoderni e minimalisti, ristoranti da spiaggia, fast food, ristoranti thailandesi, indiani ecc. Gli oggetti d'arredamento diventano rappresentazioni delle emozioni umane; riassumono lo stato d'animo che ci prospettiamo di godere mangiando fuori e in quanto tali ci paiono essere al tempo stesso gli strumenti che creano emozioni desiderate. Sedie rivestite sontuosamente di pelle o di tappezzeria sono testimonianza evidente di lusso e di buon gusto; i rigidi mobili di plastica vivacemente colorata trasmettono un senso di allegria e di libertà dalle convenzioni. L'impressione materiale che si riceve dal ristorante, la sua atmosfera e il suo arredamento, quando ci si trova a pranzare e cenare fuori, rivestono altrettanta importanza quanta ne hanno le cose che si mangiano"[2].

Oltre a definirsi come 'architettura del desiderio', quella espressa dal ristorante possiede anche la funzione di stimolare determinate emozioni e particolari comportamenti nel commensale. In un certo senso la scena detta le regole di come vestirsi, di come parlare, di come agire, materializzando desideri personali e trasformando le emozioni umane in oggetti tangibili. Ad esempio l'impressione di ambiente familiare viene venduto sia nel Mc Donald's, sia nella trattoria italiana; l'atmosfera romantica con i toni soffusi è propria del bistrot alla moda; la sofisticazione, la mondanità, il lusso tipiche di una grande cena da ricevimento serale, consumata ad esempio in un grande albergo o in un salone personalizzato. In un certo senso, se pensiamo al ristorante di lusso ed esclusivo, possiamo rintracciare fenomeni d'uso e di comportamento di origine antica. In effetti inizialmente il ristorante, nato dopo la Rivoluzione Francese per la disponibilità di cuochi sulla piazza non più impegnati nelle cucine reali, costituì per molti aspetti un'imitazione degli stili di vita dell'aristocrazia. Lusso e stravaganza, artificio e scenografia erano gli ingredienti che promuovevano il successo di questi locali prima ancora dei cibi più o meno buoni che venivano offerti. Insieme ai grandi alberghi ottocenteschi, i ristoranti 'alla moda' divennero la riproposizione in chiave borghese dei pranzi nei grandi palazzi dell'aristocrazia, dove in una sorta di palcoscenico culinario offerto a tutti (o meglio a chi poteva pagare) si riproducevano gesti e messe in scena di un'aristocrazia in declino.

Nel suo saggio Joanne Finkelstein definisce anche una tipologia dei ristoranti, una tabella di classificazione che fa corrispondere a ogni tipo di locale un diverso comportamento; tra i vari ristoranti troviamo il "ristorante spettacolare informale" e "formale", il "parodic restaurant", il "bistrot mondain", il "café mundane" le catene fast food e il ristorante "etnico locale". Per tutti i tipi l'architettura svolge un ruolo determinante; in alcuni il peso dell'arredamento e della scenografia appare fondamentale, in altri rimane in secondo piano, anche se in realtà è sempre presente e rilevante.

Da questo punto di vista basta analizzare gli esempi selezionati nel libro per rendersi conto del fondamentale ruolo svolto dalla scena architettonica. Se abili dissonanze e forzature volumetrico-cromatiche caratterizzano il "Monsoon Restaurant" di Zaha Hadid a Sapporo, un'inarrestabile creatività compositiva e figurativa, più legata al mondo del teatro e del musical che a quello dell' architettura in senso canonico, caratterizza la produzione di David Rockwell dal "Planet Hollywood" al raffinato "Nobu", dall'"All Stars Café" all'esclusiva ricostruzione del "Monkey Bar" newyorkese. Appartengono al mondo della musica, quasi dei teatri per improbabili musicals, i ristoranti "Motown" di New York e Las Vegas di Haverson Architecture. Atmosfere più soffuse e meno inconsuete, tese verso la creazione di ambienti esclusivi attraverso una sapiente sintesi materico-compositiva caratterizzano lo "Scalini" a Kuala Lumpur, il "Si Piazza" e il "Mirezi" a New York, il recentissimo "Savannah" a Miami, solo per citarne alcuni. Mentre rubato al mondo del set cinematografico appare il recentissimo "Village Eateries" costruito da Hardy Holzman Pfeiffer Associates a Las Vegas all'interno del grande Hotel-Casinò "New York New York". Un discorso a parte merita il "Fish Dance" di Frank Gehry, un ristorante che si propone nella città di Kobe in Giappone come un 'segno urbano' inequivocabile, segnalato dal grande pesce verticale in maglia metallica con la testa rivolta verso il cielo. Questa tradizione di caratterizzare anche l'aspetto esterno dei ristoranti, dal punto di vista architettonico e figurativo, parte da esempi illustri come il loosiano "Café Museum" viennese (1899), per arrivare al segno grafico tridimensionale e pubblicitario con le catene dei *diners* americani (dalle "White Towers" ai "Mc Donalds", da "Denny's" al "Kentucky Fried Chicken" all'obelisco blu dell'"Howard Johnson's"). Il ristorante, come lo spazio commerciale in senso lato, emerge con le sue luci e i suoi colori nel paesaggio urbano, in cui si innesta con studiata regia proponendo uno straniamento architettonico nel processo di riformulazione di una diversa e pervasiva realtà.

I ristoranti che compongono questo libro si propongono come qualificati e diversificati spazi architettonici, luoghi caratterizzati da varie e molteplici soluzioni ambientali e scenografiche, e da atmosfere diverse fra loro, ma legate dal comune carattere di essere *spazi del desiderio* e della *recitazione sociale* : "al ristorante possiamo fingere di essere ricchi, persone di successo, alla moda, sofisticate e urbane. Possiamo assumere il ruolo dell'ardente innamorato, dell'amico affezionato, del genitore generoso, del coniuge riconoscente o del compagno eccitante. E' un teatro in cui il falso non viene scoperto e l'onestà non è necessaria"[3].

Matteo Vercelloni

*2-3 Joanne Finkelstein,
Op. cit.*

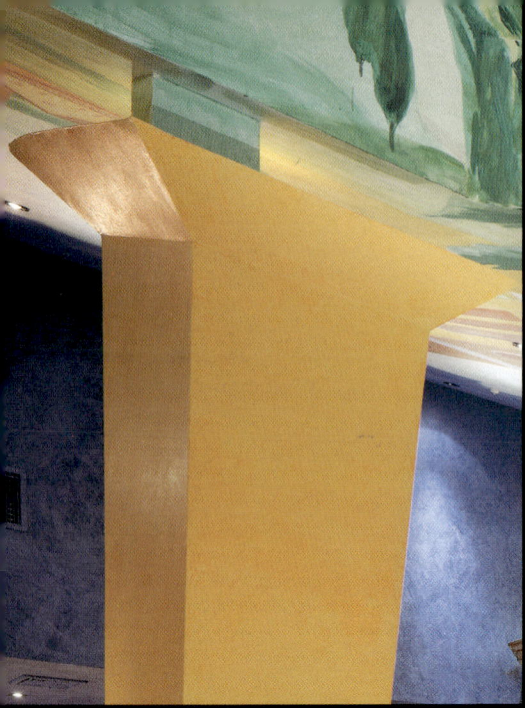
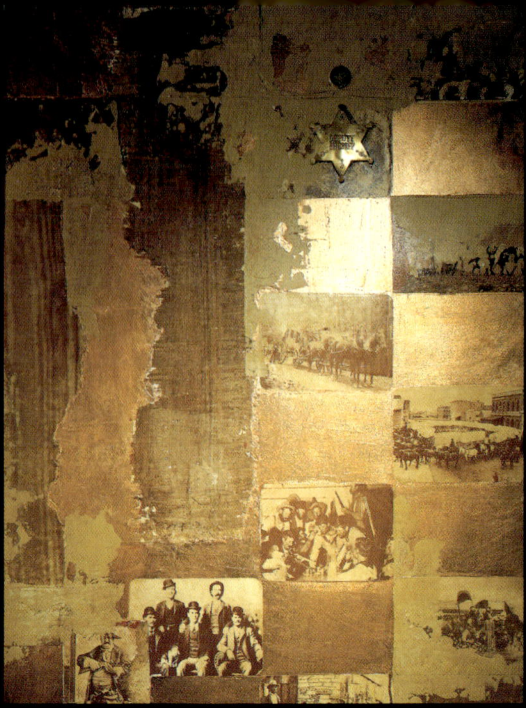
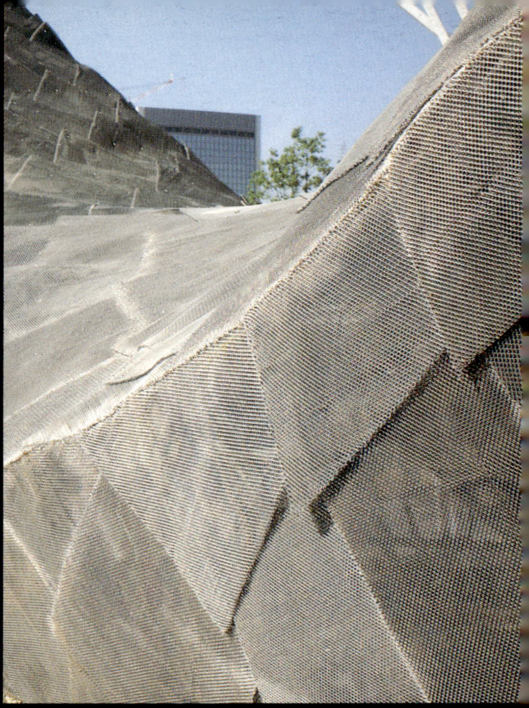
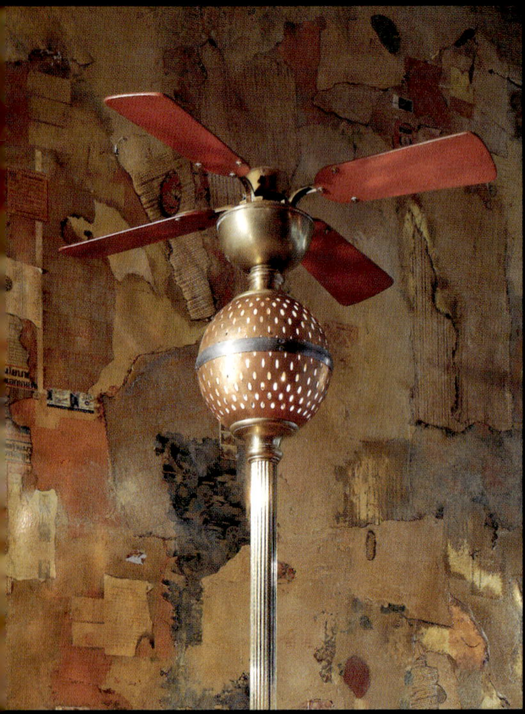
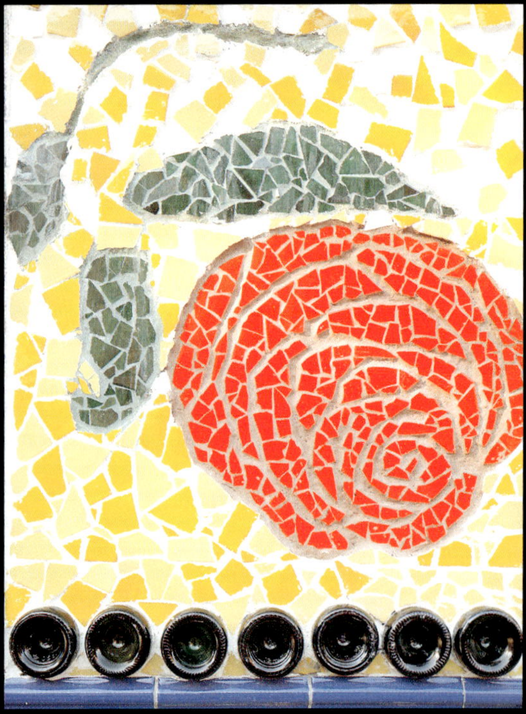
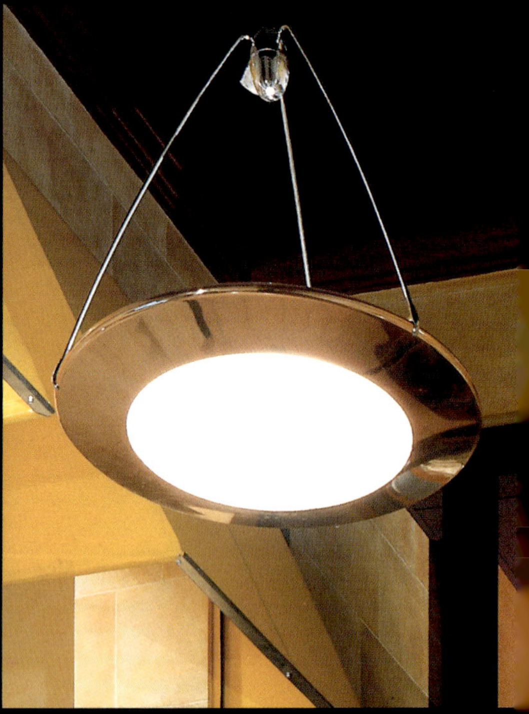
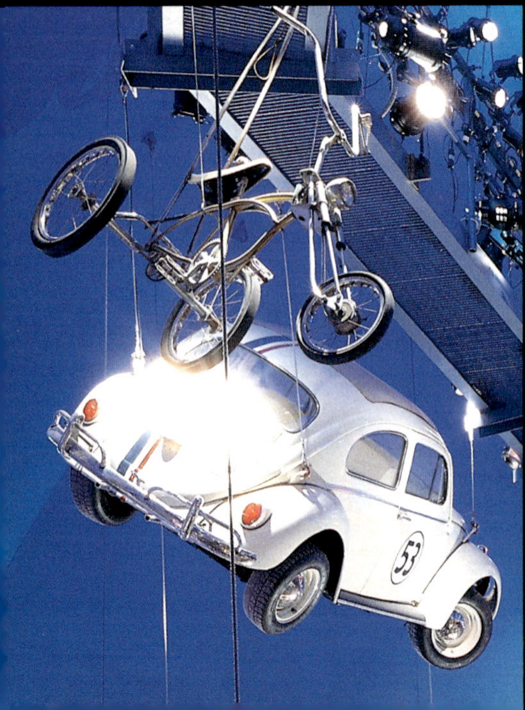
53
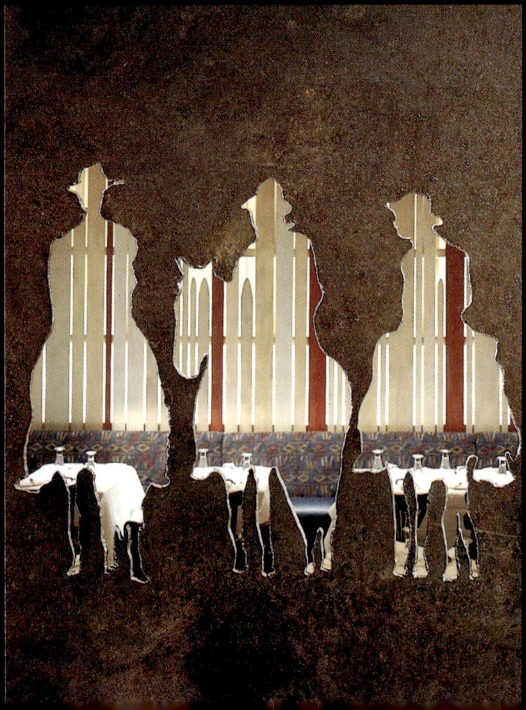
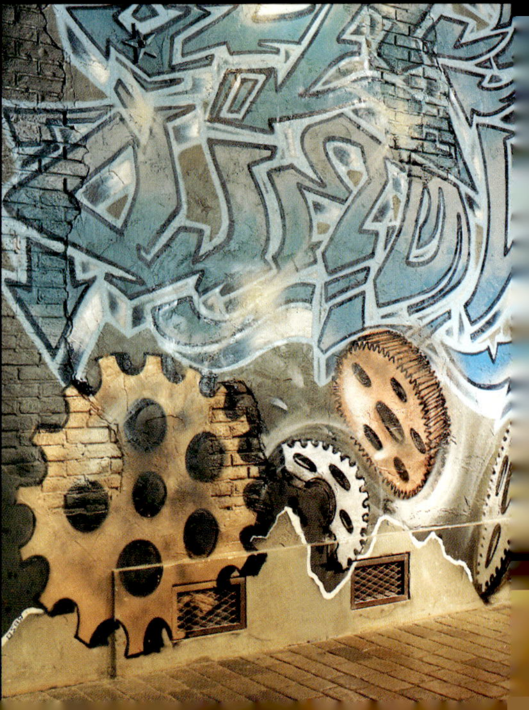

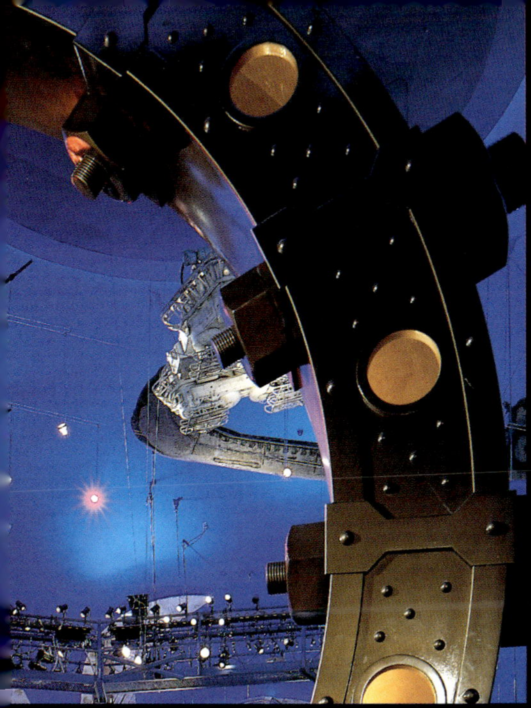
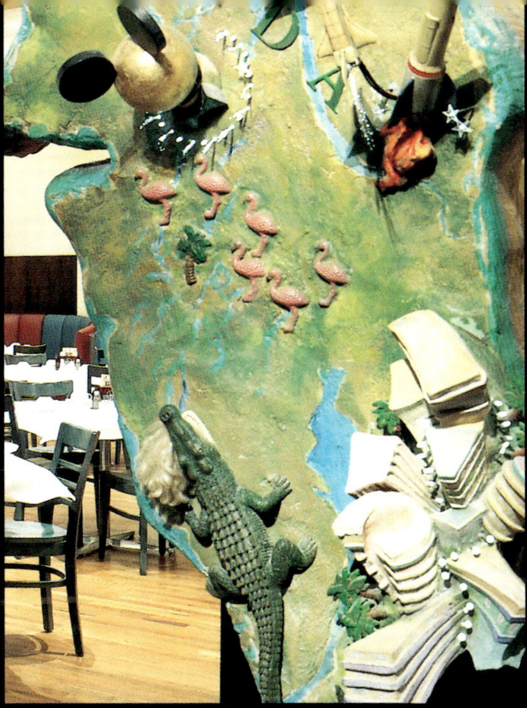
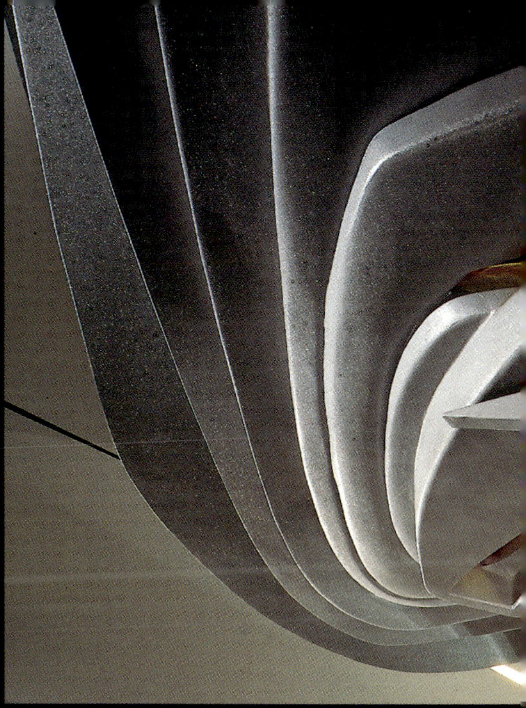
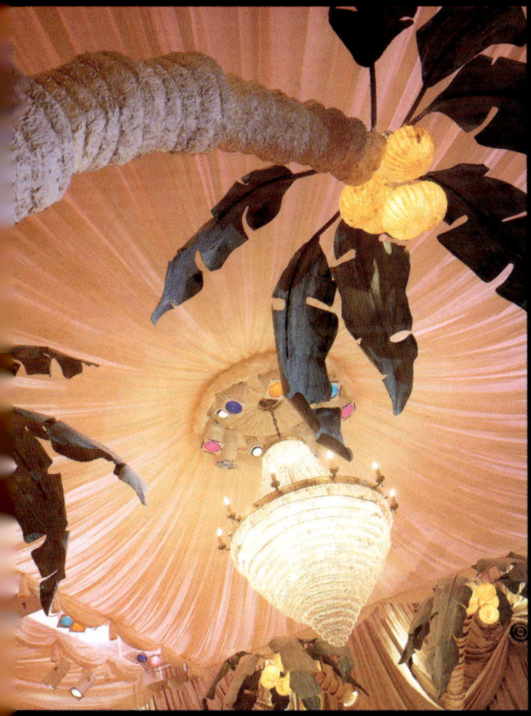
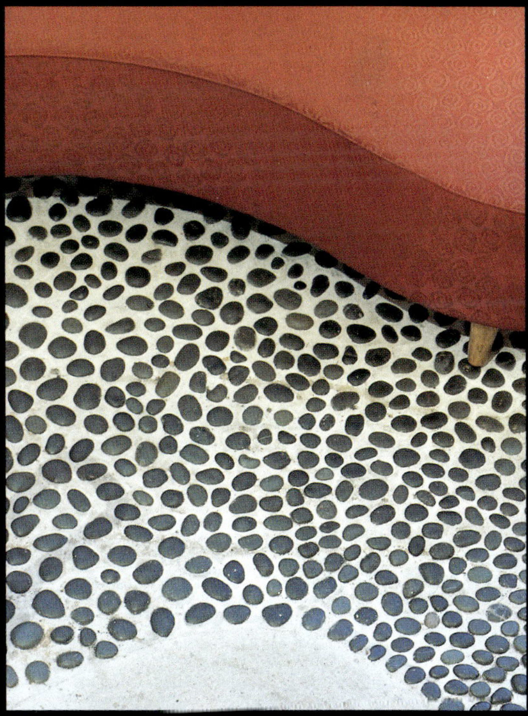
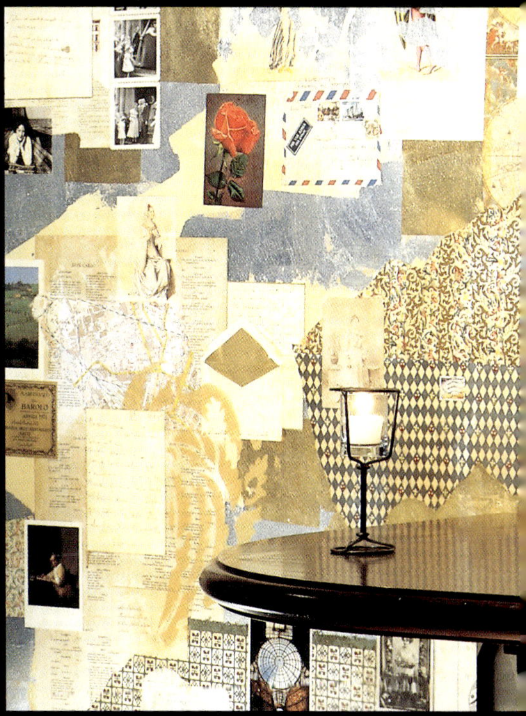
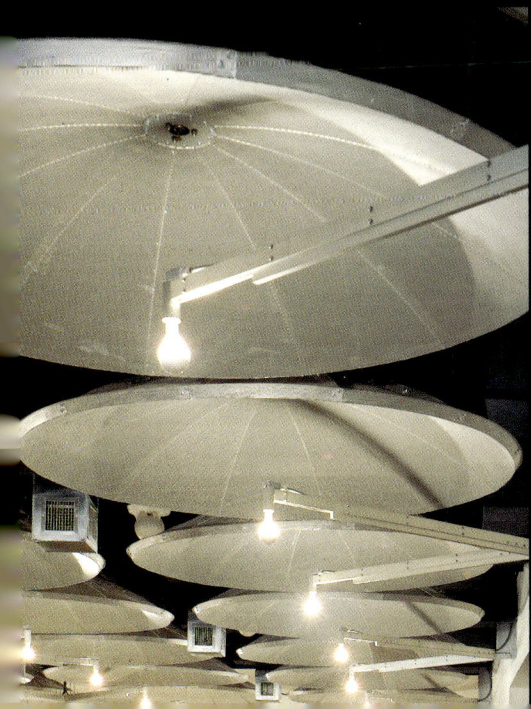
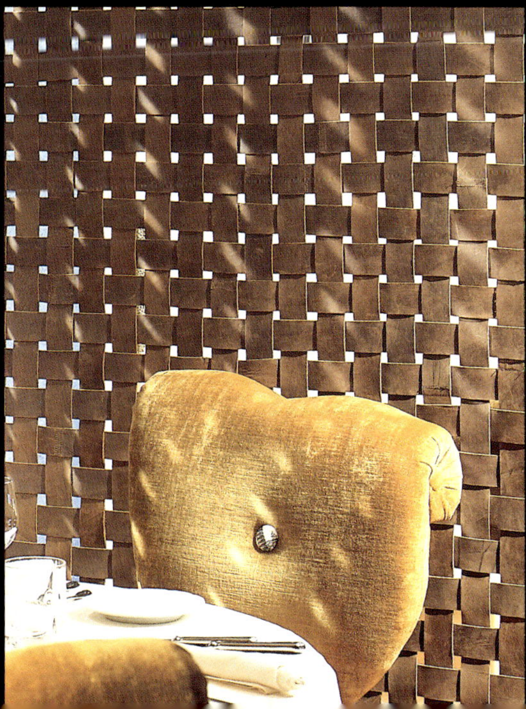
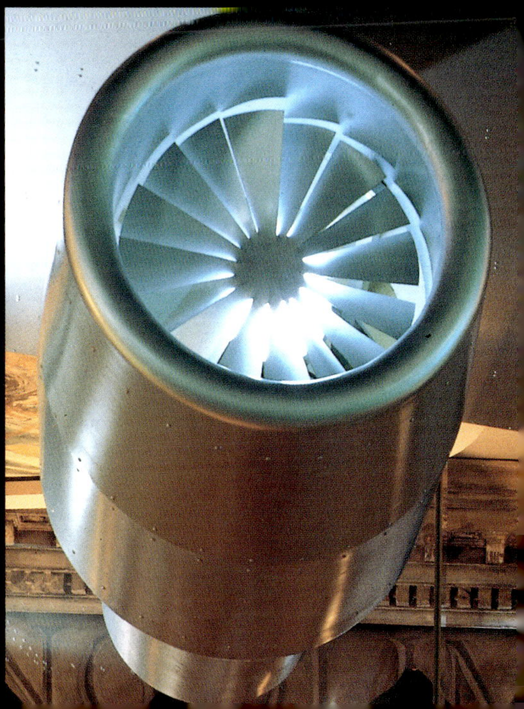

150 WOOSTER RESTAURANT
Diana Agrest e Mario Gandelsonas Architects. New York, NY, USA, 1990

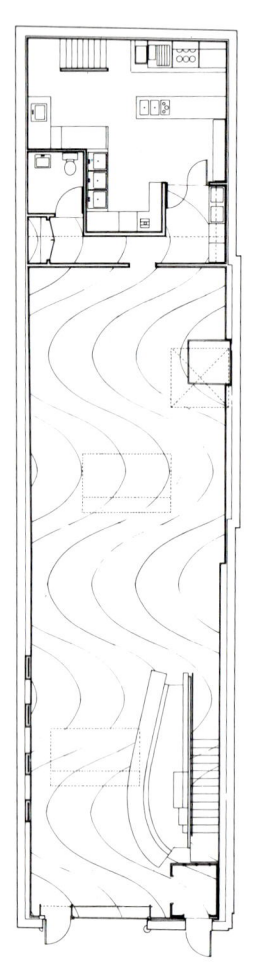

Tucked into a former garage site in Soho, this Brazilian restaurant conjures up a host of ideas and images of that country with deft obliqueness. The new restaurant area, a long and narrow oblong space without windows along the side walls and a single roll-down shutter at the entrance end, is comprised of a small foyer and an entrance bar preceding the restaurant proper, and extends deep into the building where, in the second room the rest rooms and kitchens are neatly hidden behind a new wall built to provide a perspective backdrop with a central doorway and a sloping profile detached from the ceiling. The original garage roller-shutter has been left, complete with graffiti, but a new, well-rusted window forming a rectangular grille aperture has been added for effect. Here an extra side-door has been created, leading to a small vestibule that precedes the wooden bar framed by a pale blue service wall and lowered ceiling. Together with the end wall, the perimeter walls have been equipped with a new architectural "skin" in the form of a clever interplay of abstract surface tricked out with striking colors to give a Brazilian atmosphere. This ethnic conceit is underscored by the palm tree placed just beyond the bar and lit naturally by one of the three skylights overhead, a device that is nicely emphasized by a splash of brilliant blue on the nearby wall. The most resourceful feature, however, is the floor design, consisting of small blue and yellow tiles, which lends this downtown Manhattan food joint a distinctive Brazilian touch. The idea is lifted directly from the Copacabana walkway in Rio de Janeiro designed by Burle Max in 1970 with stylized sea waves, a piece of incomparable design and impact to which this little restaurant pays due homage.

Ricavato all'interno di un piccolo garage a Soho, questo ristorante di cucina brasiliana ricorda nelle soluzioni progettuali temi e figure di quel paese, senza tuttavia ricorrere a rappresentazioni dirette. Lo spazio del locale, un rettangolo regolare di forma stretta e allungata, senza aperture lungo i muri perimetrali e con la sola saracinesca di accesso, è stato suddiviso in due zone: la prima, che comprende l'ingresso e il banco bar, oltre alla sala ristorante, si sviluppa verso il fondo dove, nella seconda, sono ricavati servizi igienici e cucina dietro una nuova parete architettonica pensata come quinta prospettica conclusiva segnata da un passaggio centrale e con profilo superiore inclinato e staccato dal soffitto. La saracinesca del garage è stata mantenuta con i graffiti originali, mentre è stata aggiunta una nuova vetrata con struttura in ferro arrugginito, suddivisa secondo una griglia regolare a moduli rettangolari. Qui è stata ricavata una porta d'ingresso in aggiunta a quella laterale, con piccolo vestibolo, che anticipa il banco bar ligneo incorniciato da una parete attrezzata e da un controsoffitto azzurri. Insieme alla parete di fondo anche i muri perimetrali sono stati rivestiti da una nuova 'pelle architettonica' che forma un suggestivo gioco di superfici astratte da cui emergono forti colori che ricordano l'atmosfera brasiliana. Questa è sottolineata anche dalla palma interna posizionata dopo il banco bar e illuminata in modo naturale da uno dei tre lucernari ricavati nel soffitto, cui corrisponde, quale diretta proiezione parietale, una fascia tinteggiata d'azzurro intenso. Ma è indubbiamente il disegno della pavimentazione, in piastrelline quadrate blu e gialle, che porta nel centro di Manhattan un vero e proprio segno brasiliano. Si tratta della trasposizione figurativa del famoso motivo che caratterizza la passeggiata della spiaggia di Copacabana a Rio de Janeiro, disegnata da Burle Marx nel 1970 a onde marine stilizzate, un progetto di insuperabile eleganza e forza figurativa che questo piccolo ristorante vuole ricordare.

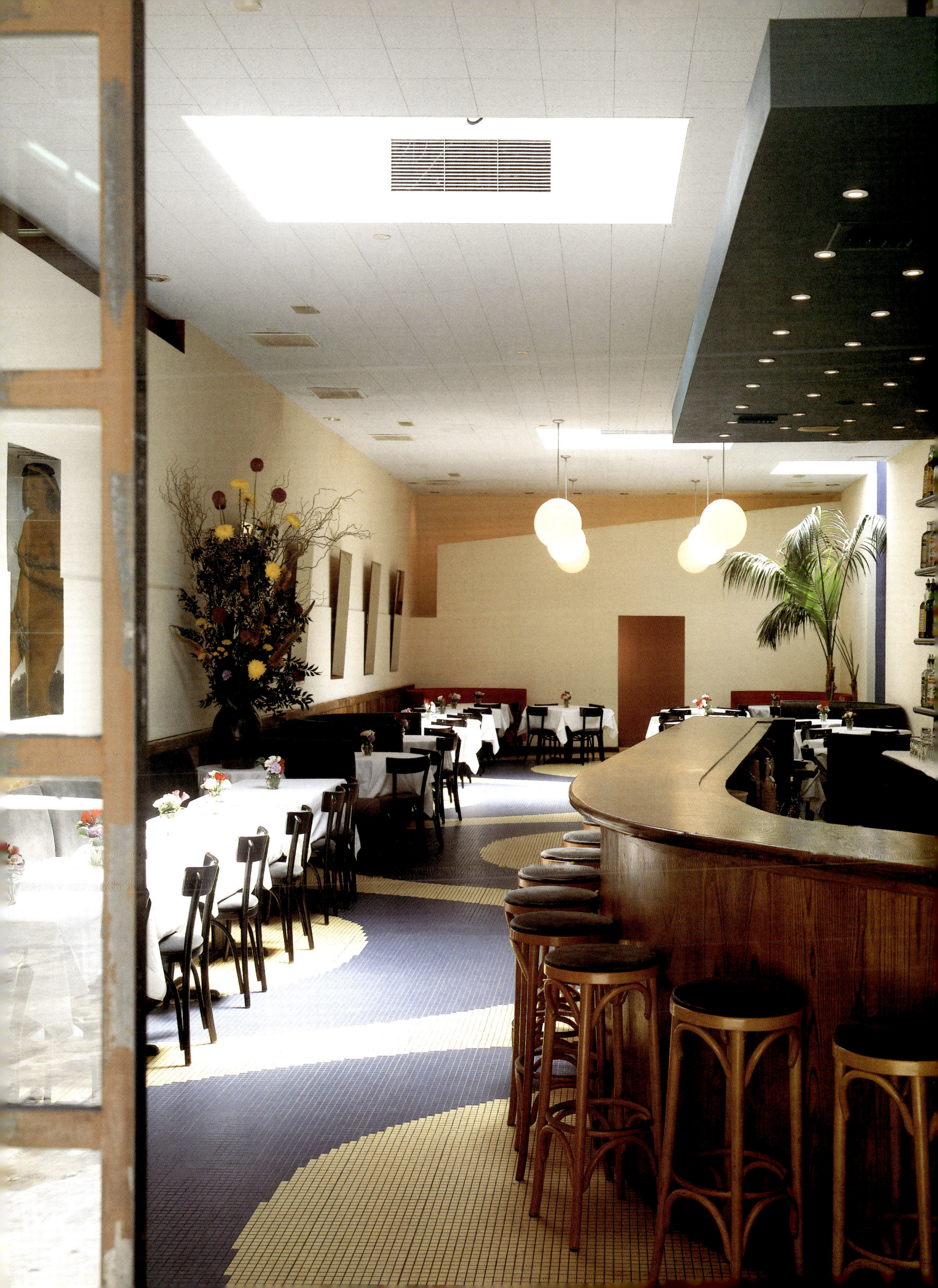

Axonometry / Assonometria

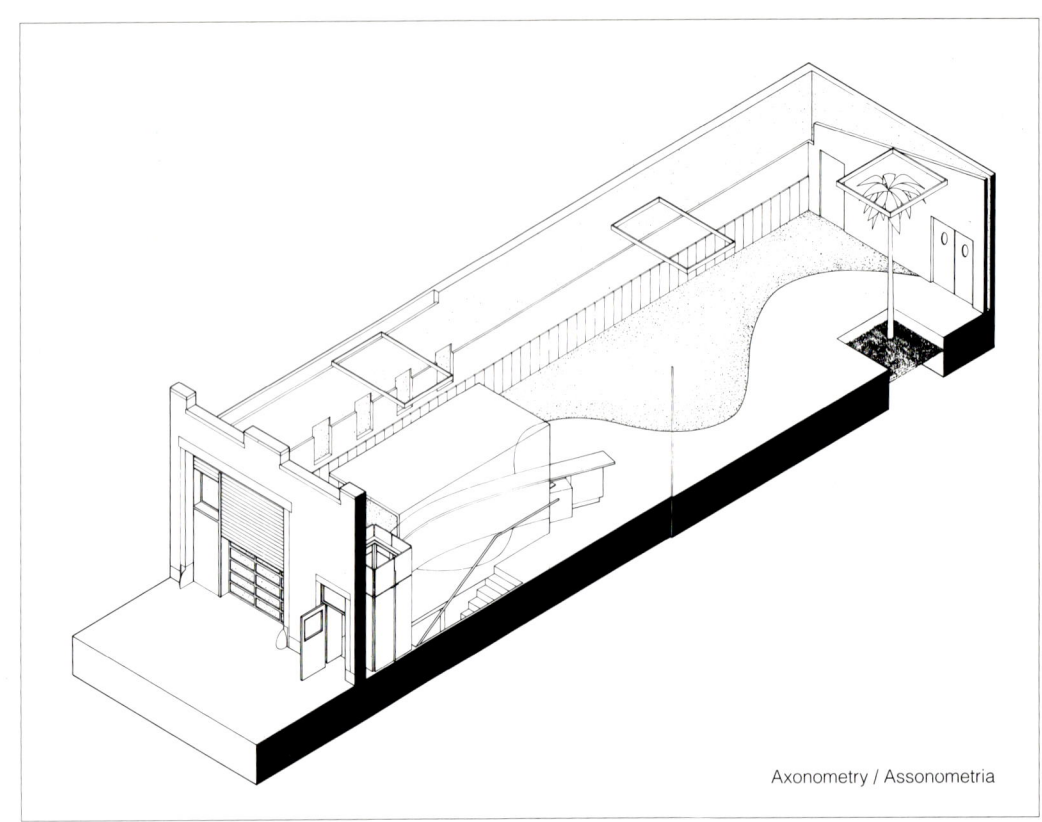

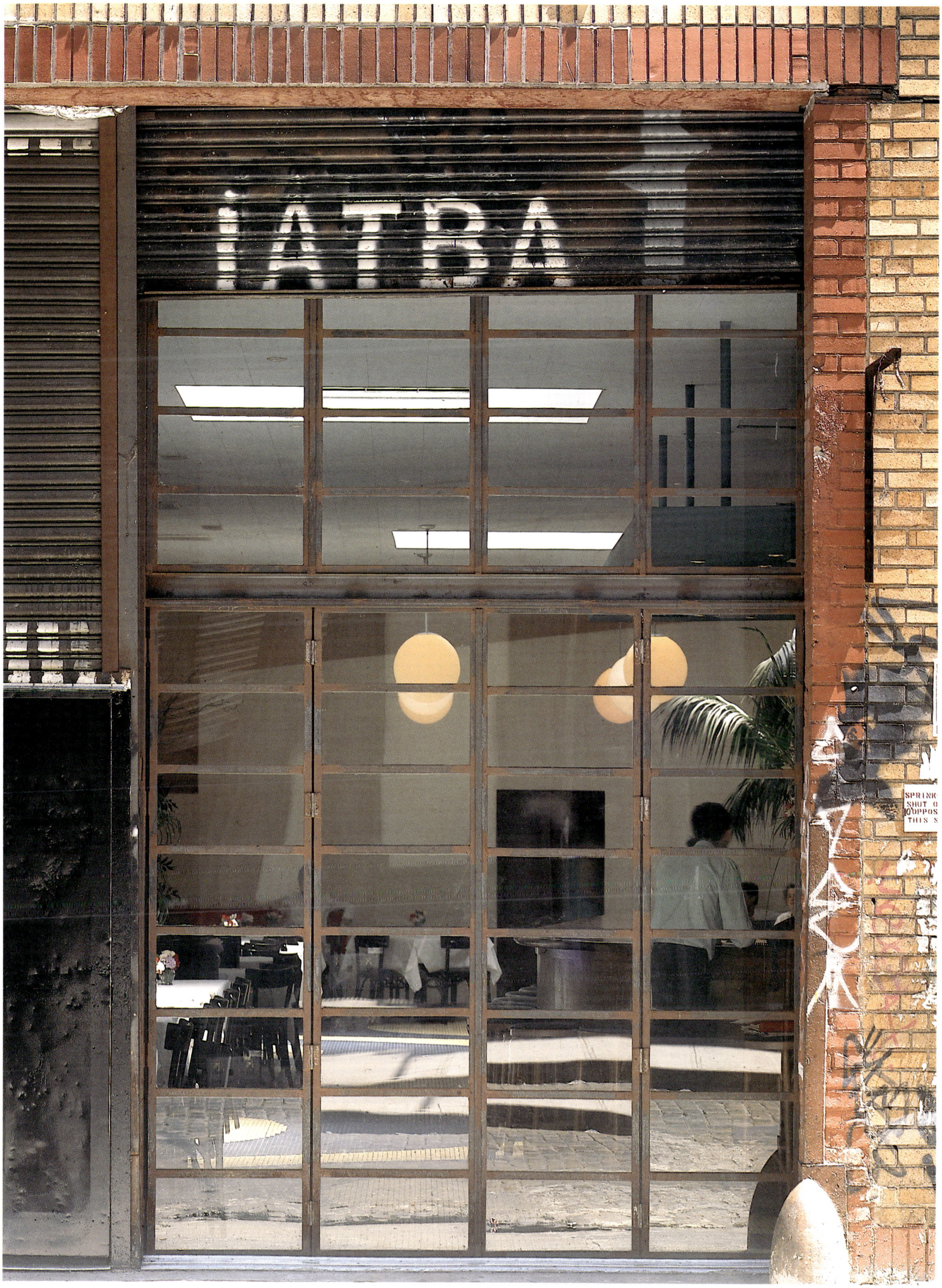

ALL STARS CAFE
David Rockwell Architect. New York, NY, USA, 1995

Situated on the third story of a corner building on Broadway and 45th Street, Manhattan, the All Stars Cafe is a café-cum-restaurant that is wholly given over to the world of sport. A theme-based project, the layout and installation design of this well-sited restaurant pivots on various classic images taken from the universe of sport. First and foremost, the central room is shaped to resemble the arena of a stadium, a solution that dictates the format used for the rest of the place. The entrance lobby, where the elevators are located, leads into the main double-height dining hall built in the form of a miniature stadium with simulated television cameras anchored to balloons suspended overhead from an elliptical track in the ceiling. The sweeping ellipse of the main room, which has several more private dining alcoves off it, is underscored by the ceiling downlighters that simulate the powerful floodlights of a sports ground. The exposed timber structures round the perimeter wall reiterate the stadium theme, and contain a series of giant television screens showing live or recorded broadcasts of televised sports events, with a second bank of smaller screens below. Arranged around the wall of this stadium-restaurant are circular sofas in the form of giant upturned baseball gloves. Together with the museum-style collection of vehicles and sports equipment, sweatshirts and assorted collectors' objects arranged in vitrines, more traditional seating with chairs in yellow wood and fixed upholstered sofa-benches are arranged radially in the intermediate ring between the outer glove-sofas and large bar-island at the room's hub. This feature, raised on a wooden platform, consists of a large counter mimicking a running track, surmounted by a large red volume descending from the ceiling with other television screens set into it. Four high trellises with simulated Olympic torches mark the access to the central area, together with the Pop arrangement on two pillars of a patchwork of balls from different sports.

Ubicato al terzo piano di un edificio all'angolo tra Broadway e la 45esima strada, l'All Stars Cafe è un caffé-ristorante interamente dedicato al mondo dello sport. Ristorante a tema, questo locale trova in numerosi simboli e figure legati al mondo dello sport le proprie ragioni compositive e il proprio risultato formale. Anzitutto la forma della sala centrale ricalca apertamente quella dello stadio e su questo motivo ne organizza l'intera disposizione. Dopo l'ingresso, su cui si affacciano gli ascensori, si apre la grande sala a doppia altezza costruita come uno stadio in miniatura con tanto di dirigibile-cinepresa che 'vola' sospeso su un binario ellittico fissato al plafone. La grande ellisse della sala, cui si affiancano salette private, è sottolineata dalle luci a soffitto che simulano i potenti fari alogeni d'illuminazione dei grandi impianti sportivi. Anche la struttura lignea a vista, che scandisce le pareti perimetrali, simula le soluzioni costruttive degli stadi e contiene nella fascia superiore una serie di maxischermi televisivi che trasmettono senza interruzione immagini delle partite in corso o di eventi sportivi in differita, con l'aggiunta di televisori più piccoli sottostanti. Lungo l'intero perimetro dello stadio-sala ristorante sono posizionati i divanetti circolari, pensati come grandi e stilizzati guanti da baseball rovesciati verso l'alto. Insieme alla musealizzazione spettacolare di veicoli e attrezzature sportivi, maglie da gioco e oggetti vari in vetrina, una serie di sedute più tradizionali, con sedie di legno giallo e divanetti imbottiti fissi, è posizionata a raggiera nella fascia di mezzo tra i guanti-seduta e la grande isola-bar centrale. Questa, rialzata da una pedana in legno, è caratterizzata dal grande bancone a forma di pista d'atletica, sormontato da un volume rosso di metallo che scende dal soffitto per ospitare ulteriori schermi televisivi. Quattro alti tralicci con fiamme olimpioniche artificiali segnano gli accessi alla zona centrale insieme al rivestimento pop di due pilastri secondo un patchwork figurativo di diversi palloni da gioco.

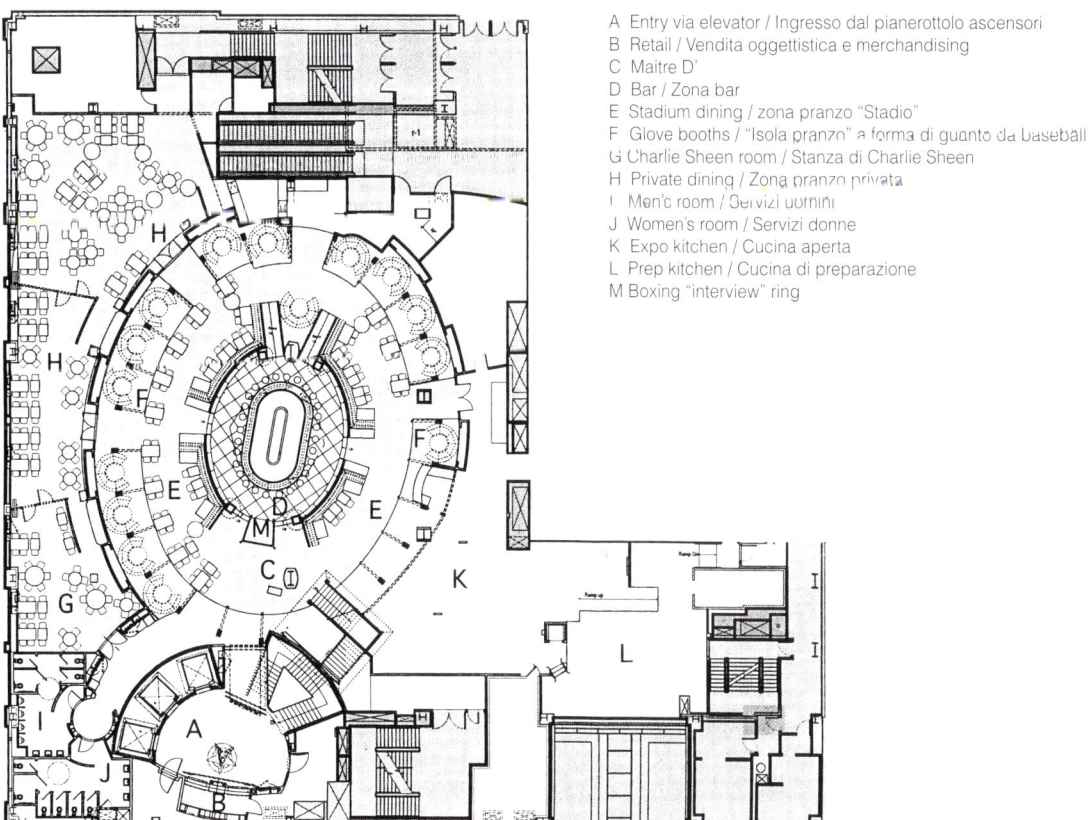

A Entry via elevator / Ingresso dal pianerottolo ascensori
B Retail / Vendita oggettistica e merchandising
C Maitre D'
D Bar / Zona bar
E Stadium dining / zona pranzo "Stadio"
F Glove booths / "Isola pranzo" a forma di guanto da baseball
G Charlie Sheen room / Stanza di Charlie Sheen
H Private dining / Zona pranzo privata
I Men's room / Servizi uomini
J Women's room / Servizi donne
K Expo kitchen / Cucina aperta
L Prep kitchen / Cucina di preparazione
M Boxing "interview" ring

Third floor / Terzo piano

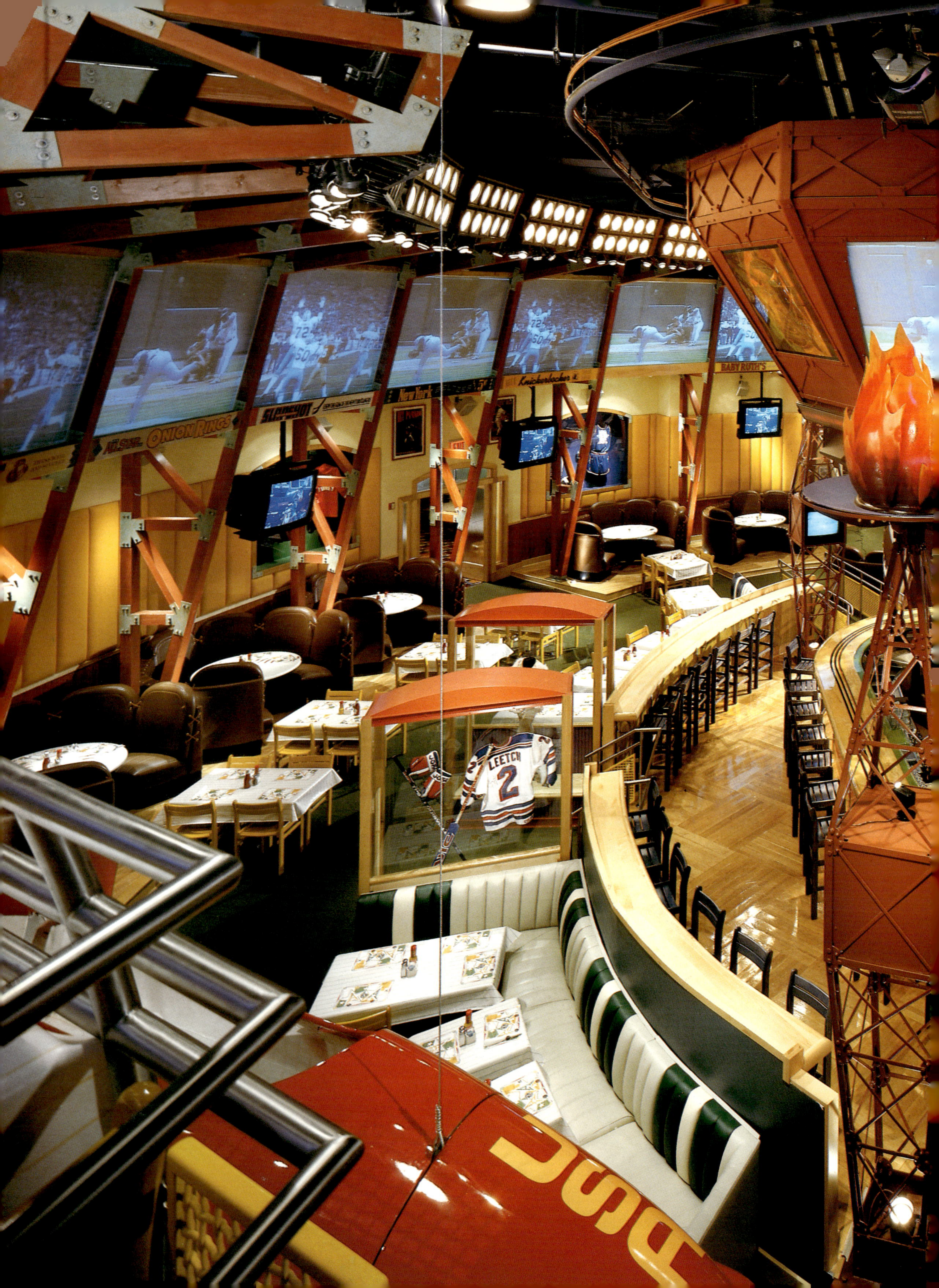
ONION RINGS
New York
Knickerbocker
BABY RUTH'S
LEETCH
2

ALLSTAR
T-SHIRTS
SMART
MODERN
CLOTHES
New York SELTZER 5¢
DOGS
Budweiser

AMBERJACK'S RESTAURANT
Haverson Architecture and design. South Norwalk, CT, USA, 1993

Two large glazed apertures framed by panels of gray granite and surmounted by an art deco frieze announce the entrance of this corner bar-restaurant joint that gives on to the street. The windows boldly bear the yellow-and-red logo of the restaurant: a wind rose design, the quintessential symbol of navigation, which together with the wording "Coastal Grill" openly declaims the stylistic leitmotif of the joint, namely, a yacht on the sea. The yacht also serves as a visual cue for the bar, which is set opposite the entrance and has the form of the prow of a skiff in wooden laths set horizontal to the counter, which is styled to emphasize the boat shape. A timber structure in line with the marble column with its stylized copper capital (a metaphor for the ship's main mast) stands centrally to the prow-bar and holds up bottles of spirits, its slanting design reminiscent of a sail. The perimeter walls of the restaurant are in paneling in two different woods, which continues round the bases of columns, echoing materials and impressions of the large sailboats of the thirties; the wind rose logo is repeated on the floor of the bar area in polychrome grit. The ceiling and walls of the dining lounge are tinted sea blue and carefully lit to point up the large stylized yacht sails lining the walls in an effective decorative feature. Fixed sofas are arranged along the walls as base fixtures anchoring the wall-mounted sail features, and elegant upholstered mahogany seats and stools are arrange respectively at the tables and bar. The perspective backdrop of the room is a sort of submarine-type airlock door set into the metallic end wall, over which hangs a clock. The composition is reminiscent of Captain Nemo's ship, the *Nautilus*, and the door leads into a little separate dining area immersed in deep sea blue, characterized by a large wall-mounted model of a sailboat.

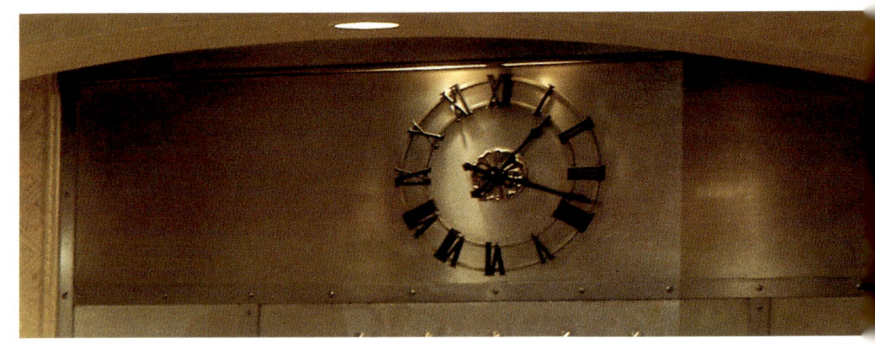

Due grandi vetrate incorniciate da lastre di granito nero e sormontate da un fregio art-déco affiancano l'ingresso di questo bar-ristorante d'angolo aperto verso strada. Sulle vetrate è riportato in giallo e rosso il logo del ristorante: una rosa dei venti, simbolo per antonomasia di ogni navigazione marina, che insieme alla dizione "coastal grill" denuncia apertamente il tema stilistico dell'immagine complessiva; il motivo del mare e della barca a vela. Quest'ultima è assunta come forma di riferimento per il banco-bar, posizionato di fronte all'ingresso e costruito come la prua di uno scafo marino a doghe di legno orizzontali con piano di appoggio che sottolinea la forma della barca. Il banco prosegue lungo la vetrata d'angolo ampliando la zona bar del locale. Una struttura lignea in asse con la colonna di marmo dal capitello stilizzato in rame (assunta qui come metaforico albero maestro), è centrale allo scafo del bar e sostiene le bottiglie dei liquori, ricordando nel disegno inclinato la figura di una vela. Una boiserie di legno in due diverse essenze naturali si estende lungo tutti i muri perimetrali del locale, rivestendo anche i basamenti dei pilastri in marmo e ripercorrendo materie e figure delle grandi barche a vela degli anni '30, mentre il logo della rosa dei venti viene riportato come disegno della pavimentazione della zona bar in graniglie policrome. Soffitto e pareti della sala ristorante sono tinteggiate di blu mare, con una studiata illuminazione che valorizza le grandi vele da gara stilizzate posizionate lungo i muri come efficace decorazione e figura parietale. Divanetti fissi sono disposti lungo le pareti quali funzionali basamenti per le vele, mentre eleganti sedie in mogano dal sedile imbottito come gli sgabelli del bar sono disposte intorno ai tavoli. Conclude la scena prospettica del locale una sorta di grande porta blindata da sommergibile che interrompe la parete metallica di fondo, sormontata da un orologio. Una composizione che ricorda il Nautilus del Capitano Nemo e che conduce in una saletta privata immersa nel blu del mare, da cui emerge un grande modello di veliero appeso alla parete.

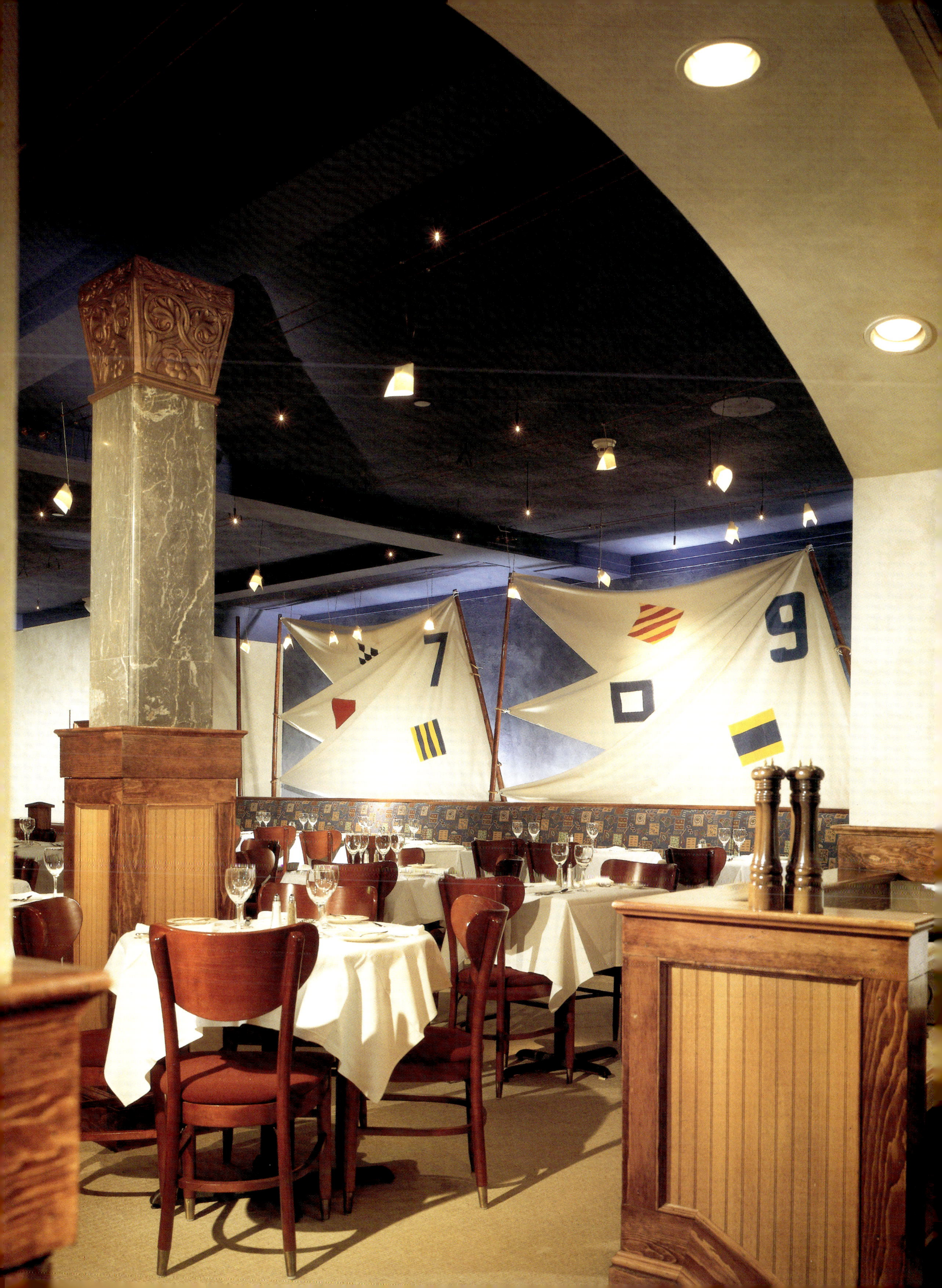
7
9

24

AMERICA RESTAURANT

Ark Restaurant Corp. - Turett Collaborative Architects. Las Vegas, NV, USA, 1997

Slotted into the recently opened New York New York casino, the America Restaurant is spread over a single floor of some two thousand square meters and seats around five hundred dinner guests. As the restaurant's name itself announces, the entire design philosophy of the place pivots on the idea of the United States of America as a nation. In addition to the immediate identification via the Stars & Stripes and the map of the states, the idea is creatively stylized through a range of different compositional and graphic devices. The irregular floor plan of the occupied space has been exploited by creating a central room flanked by three more intimate dining areas, and an entrance foyer where, beyond the neon sign and gadget sales counter, stands a large bar with an irregular-shaped counter in timber. The entrance feature is again the U.S. flag liberally reiterated in the star pattern in the floor and the exhibition console for souvenir tee-shirts and assorted mementos composed of horizontal stripes in two different exposed woods. Serving as a connective feature between the restaurant and the entrance, the bar is in ash with a pale grit counter separated from its wooden support by a striking band of bright blue light. The same color is reused for the wallpaper emblazoned with greetings taken from clients' picture postcards. In the large central room, with its fine maple floor and simple wood chairs stained dark green, the yellow lowered ceiling is scooped in a semicircular shape from which hangs a colorful map-sculpture of the United States (by Jack Doepp), on which the main cities are picked out with their skyline symbols, occasionally with an ironic twist. This same idea is playfully restated in the enlarged fifties-style postcards from all over America, suspended like pictures over the bench-sofas in red and blue stripes, a further a visual reminder of the U.S. flag, together with the downlighters jutting from a dark ceiling like stars in the night sky.

Costruito all'interno del nuovo New York New York Casinò, l'America Restaurant si estende su un unico livello per circa duemila metri quadrati, organizzando circa cinquecento posti a sedere. Come annuncia il nome del locale l'intera filosofia del ristorante assume come tema di riferimento la nazione degli Stati Uniti d'America. Questi, identificati a livello stilistico nella bandiera a stelle e strisce e nella mappa degli stati, vengono creativamente stilizzati attraverso diverse soluzioni compositive, grafiche e figurative. La pianta irregolare della superficie è stata sfruttata creando una sala centrale cui si accostano tre sale più raccolte e la zona ingresso dove, dopo l'insegna al neon con angolo di vendita gadget, è posizionato il grande banco bar di legno a isola rettangolare. L'ingresso assume come riferimento la bandiera americana riprodotta liberamente nel disegno con macrostelle della pavimentazione e nel mobile espositivo di vendita di magliette ricordo e oggettistica varia composto a strisce orizzontali di legno in due diverse essenze di due tonalità naturali. Volume connettivo tra sala ristorante e ingresso, il banco bar è in legno di frassino con piano di graniglia chiaro separato dal suo sostegno ligneo tramite una suggestiva fascia di luce blu intenso. Lo stesso colore è impiegato nel rivestimento della parete laterale da cui emergono le scritte di saluti copiate dalle cartoline dei clienti. Nella grande sala centrale, con pavimento in parquet d'acero e semplici sedie di legno tinteggiate verde scuro, il controsoffitto giallo presenta un semicerchio sfondato da cui discende una mappa-scultura colorata degli Stati Uniti d'America (opera di Jack Doepp) da cui emergono con ironia le maggiori città e i simboli stilizzati, a volte in modo comico, dei diversi stati. Tema ripreso anche nelle riproduzioni a grande scala delle cartoline anni '50 di saluto dai diversi luoghi, posizionate come grandi quadri sopra i divanetti fissi a strisce rosse e blu, che ricordano ancora una volta, insieme ai faretti luminosi che emergono dal soffitto scuro come stelle nella notte, la bandiera della Nazione.

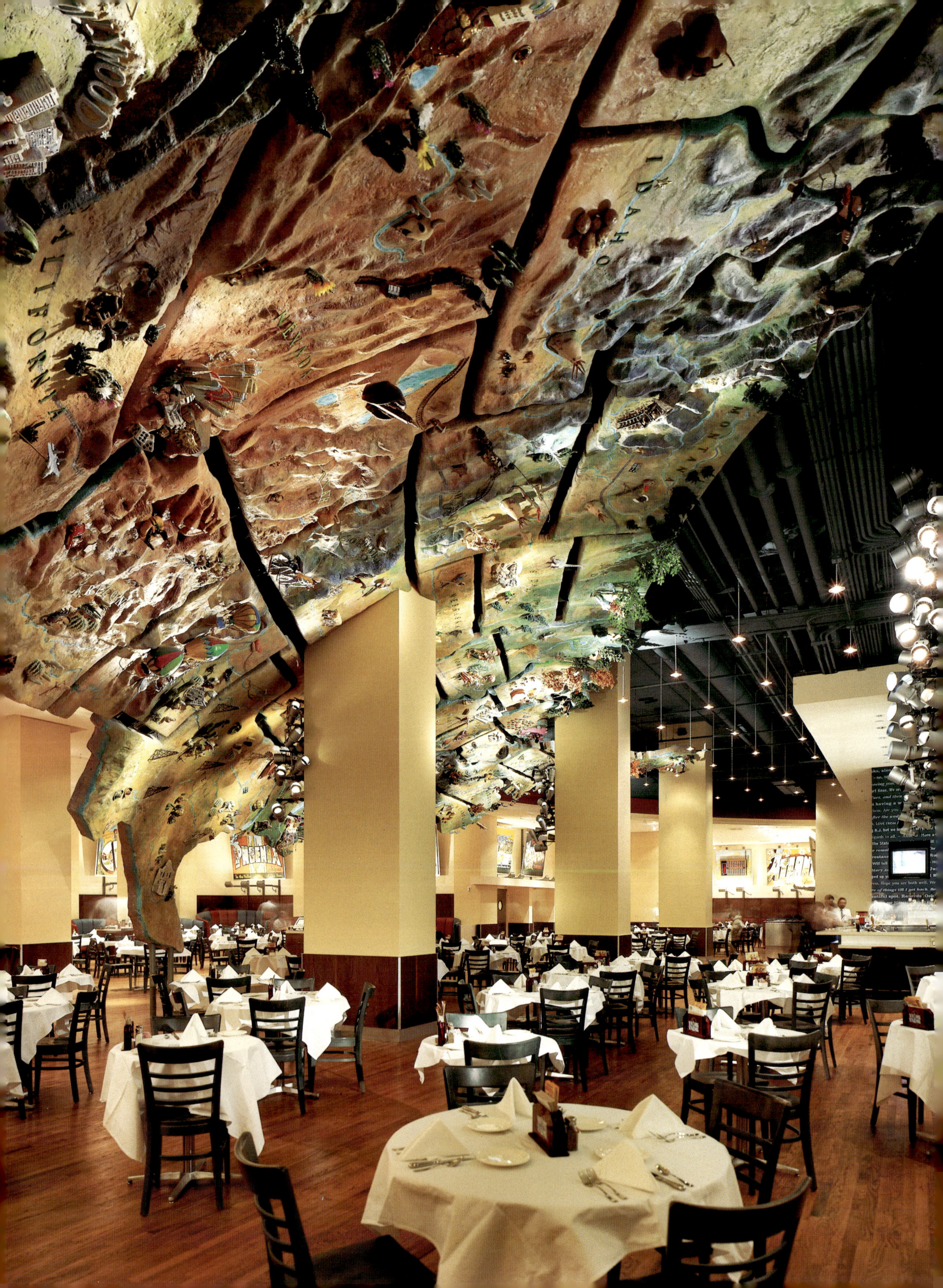
CALIFORNIA
IDAHO

27

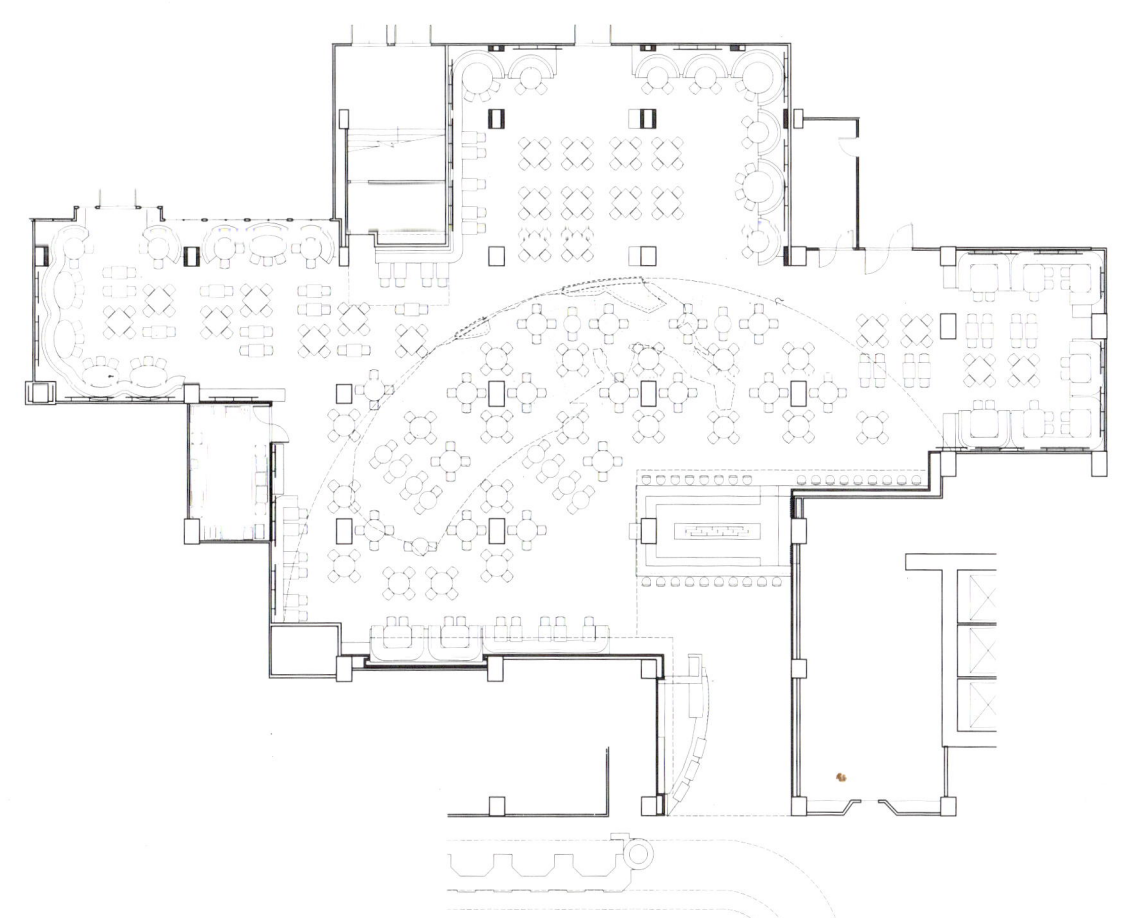

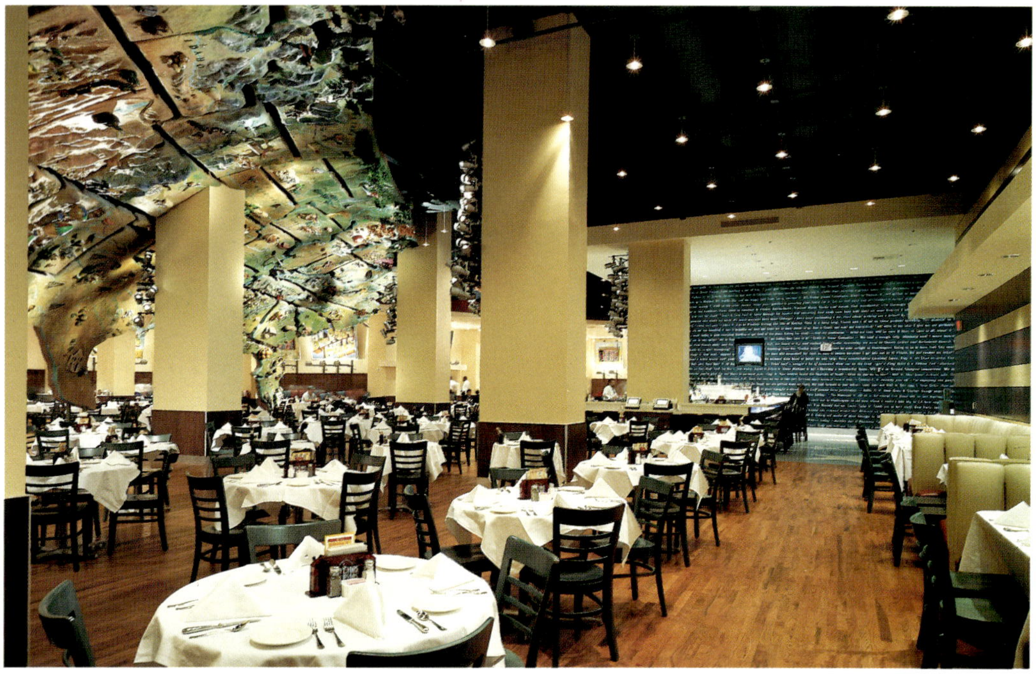

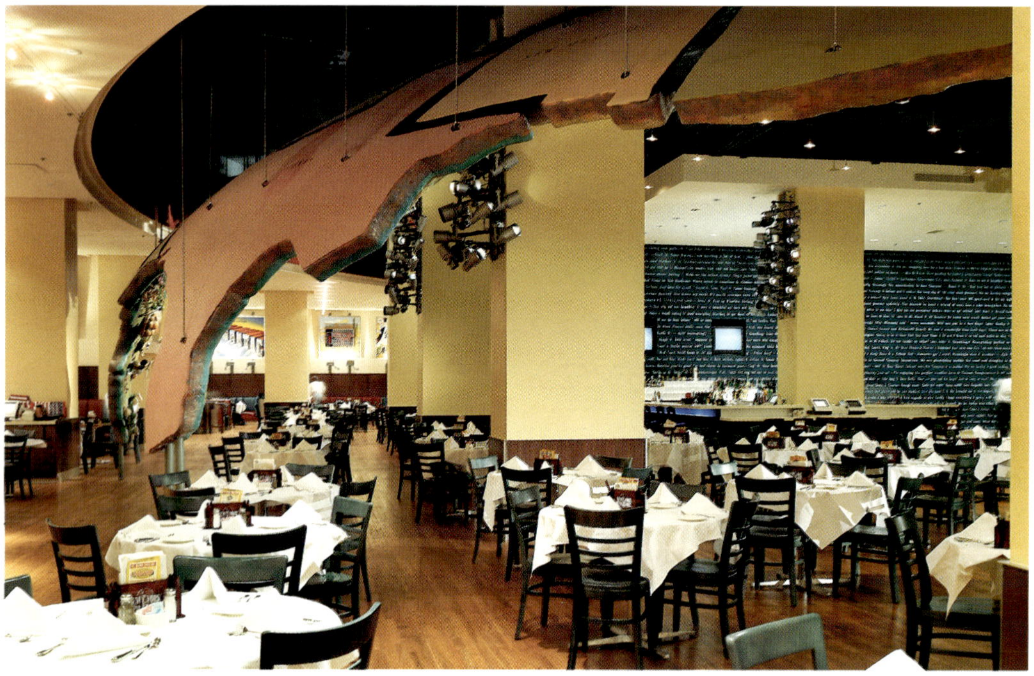

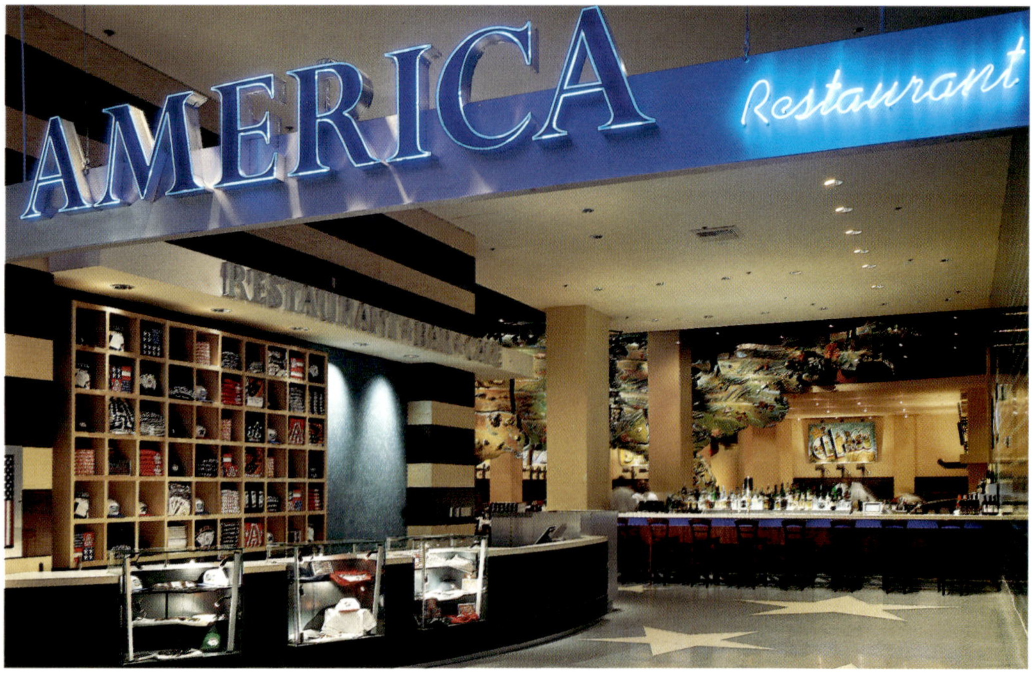
AMERICA
Restaurant

BAANG RESTAURANT
David Rockwell Architect. Greenwich, CT, USA, 1997

The word *baang* in Chinese means to tie or bind two things together. In this case the word's meaning underlines the intriguing admixture of French and Asian cuisine presented on the menu. The restaurant looks onto the street with a large oblong window with an oxidized copper frame, and an entrance door framed in a large zinc portal reminiscent of a hangar. In warmer weather the door is left wide open to enhance connectivity between the outside and inside: a link that is emphasized by the continuous floor design of brick-colored cement squares that act as an extension of the sidewalk. The restaurant lounge, whose décor is a cunning mélange of atmospheric oriental attributes and New York style, is subdivided into a bar area, a space with traditional square tables and an area characterized by a large curved counter in wood separated from the kitchens via a resourceful padded screen wall in a variety of colors. The entire bar-restaurant lies on a wooden plinth raised above street and entrance level. Together with the chromatic interplay, the lowered ceilings, and the cladding of the structural pillars, this device nicely attenuates the somewhat uniform shape of the room, lending a sense of movement while making the restaurant welcoming and comfortable. Mustard yellow, Pompeii red, and acid green are the colors chosen for the otherwise plain walls that are interrupted by illuminated circular wall fixtures and the kitchens, which are completely clad in steel. The same color scheme recurs in the custom-built wood-and-metal seating. The rust-tinted ceiling is partially clad in a series of panels composed of copper tubing and mesh in the style of an ancient pagoda. Copper is also used, albeit this time oxidized, for the cladding of the pillars, turning the four functional supports into conspicuous visual elements, enhanced by interesting light fittings that complement the diffusers hanging from the ceiling, which reflect in the steel bar counter emphasizing its serpentine profile.

Il nome "Baang" nella lingua cinese significa legare o attaccare insieme due elementi. In questo caso il significato del termine vuole sottolineare la curiosa miscela tra cucina francese e asiatica che caratterizza il menù del locale. Il ristorante si affaccia sulla strada, oltre che con una finestra quadrangolare dal serramento di rame ossidato, con una bussola d'ingresso e un grande portale di zinco da hangar. Quest'ultimo nelle stagioni estive viene lasciato aperto per collegare direttamente spazio esterno e interno: un legame sottolineato anche dalla pavimentazione continua in quadrotti di cemento color mattone che si prolungano sul marciapiede. La sala ristorante, che a livello stilistico ricorda con capricciosa creatività atmosfere orientali mescolate a figure newyorkesi, è suddivisa tra zona bar, lo spazio con tavoli quadrati tradizionali e una zona segnata da un grande bancone di legno in curva separato dalla cucina tramite un movimentato schermo imbottito a più colori. Tutta la zona bar-ristorante è rialzata con una pedana in legno rispetto alla quota d'ingresso-esterno. Tale soluzione, insieme allo studio cromatico, al controsoffitto e al rivestimento dei pilastri strutturali, tende a rompere la rigida forma geometrica rettangolare dell'involucro parietale, per movimentare e rendere allo stesso tempo confortevole l'intero locale. Giallo senape, rosso pompeiano e verde acido sono le tinte scelte per le pareti assunte come superfici piene, interrotte da teche circolari illuminate e dal vano della cucina interamente rivestita di acciaio. Colori ripresi anche nelle sedute di legno e metallo su disegno. Il soffitto, tinteggiato colore ruggine, è in parte rivestito con una serie di pannelli composti da tubi e reti di rame pensati per ricordare le coperture delle antiche pagode. Ancora rame, ma questa volta ossidato, riveste i pilastrini strutturali, trasformando i quattro sostegni funzionali in forti presenze figurative e suggestive fonti di luce affiancate a quelle più soffuse a sospensione che scendono dal soffitto riflettendosi nel banco bar di acciaio e sottolineandone la forma sinusoidale.

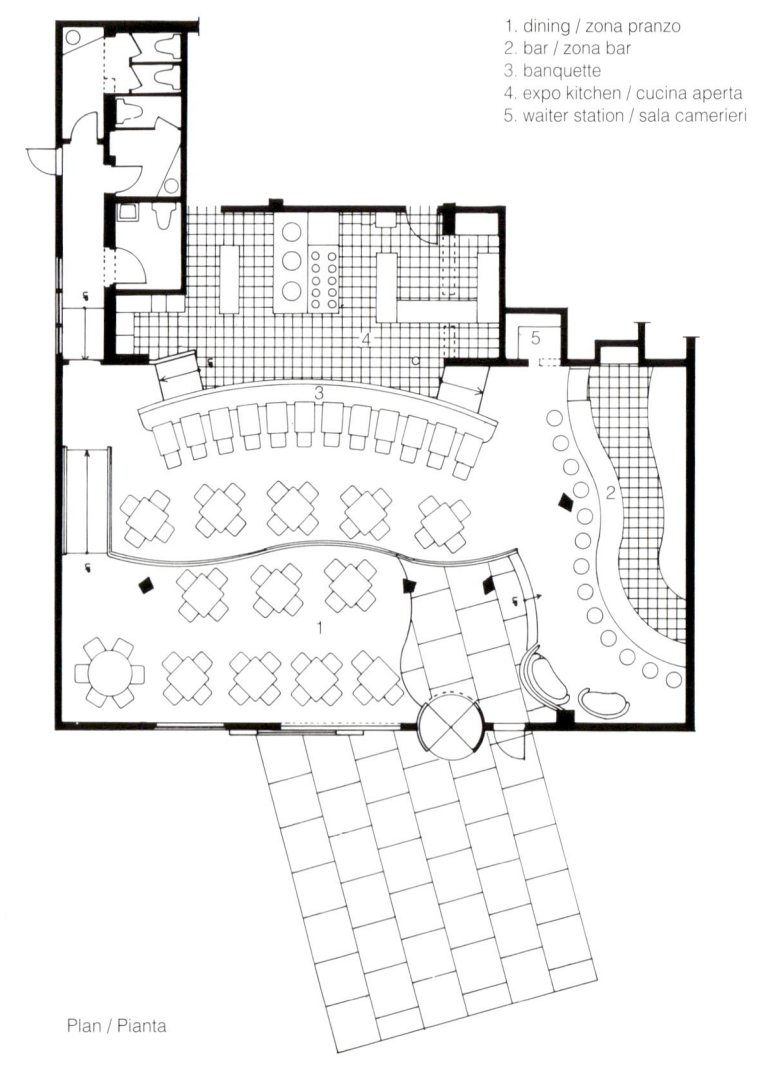

1. dining / zona pranzo
2. bar / zona bar
3. banquette
4. expo kitchen / cucina aperta
5. waiter station / sala camerieri

Plan / Pianta

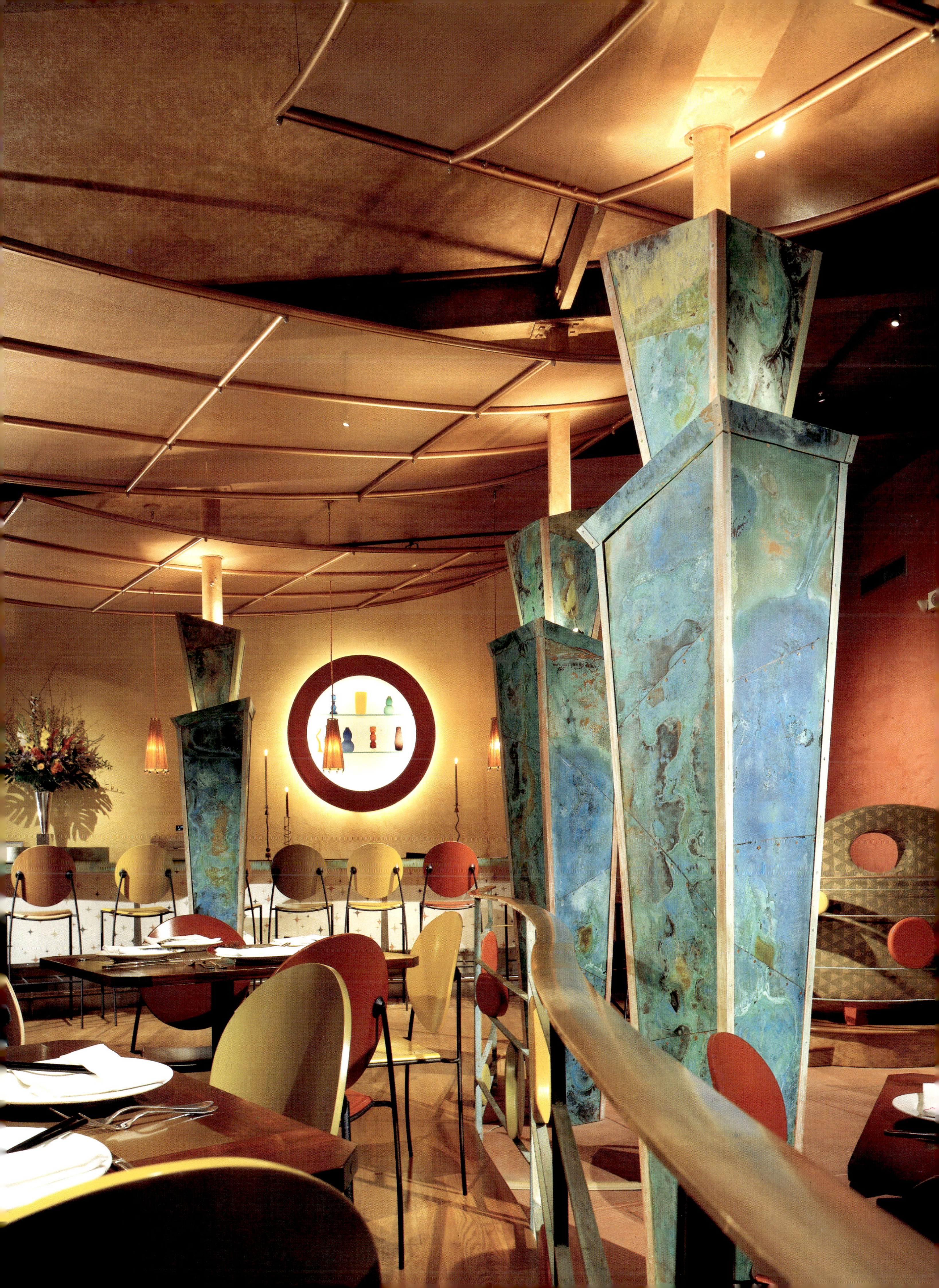

32

BEN'S CUISINE
Haverson Architecture and Design. New York, NY, USA, 1997

A long illuminated marquee and a red combined clock-logo on the street signal the presence of this kosher restaurant. After the entrance lobby, the large open space fans out with an assorted arrangement of seating: fixed sofas with tables and facing chairs, larger bench-sofas with high backs creating partitions, and traditional-style tables are organized in such a way as to make the best use of the space, which can accommodate up to two hundred guests on a busy night. An area with an island counter-bar is stationed to the right of the entrance, directly facing the street; on the left at another long counter diners can purchase take-away meals or grab a quick bite perched on a tall diner-type stool. Further in the depths of the room, and marked off by sliding partitions like decorative screens in wood or glass lie the reserved dining quarters. The curious amalgam of different catering styles (fast food, take away, and traditional dining room) is ingeniously achieved in the overall architectural solutions, which involve a creative revival of art deco motifs and patterns. Two different varieties of plain wood are used for the paneling on the structural pillars, which provide weighty visual dividers for the dining area; dark boards emphasize the profiles and alter the shape of the trunk, which is clad in lighter-toned panels. A jutting fascia composed of panes of white-veined glass and blue corner squares anticipate the concluding stylized metal capitals, while also providing a source of diffuse lighting. This stylistic approach is echoed in the design of the boiseries, alcoves, and fittings, which are partly clad in upholstery that repeats the art deco motifs. The ceiling of the fast-food area involves curious decorative metal panels, whereas the rest of the room is enlivened by a series of bright painted canvases hanging between the exposed beams overhead, creating a brilliant compositional counterpoint to the deco rigor of the whole.

Una lunga pensilina illuminata e il logo rosso con orologio annunciano sulla strada la presenza di questo grande ristorante di cucina kosher. Dopo la bussola d'ingresso, il grande spazio unitario del locale si sviluppa organizzando diversi tipi di sedute: divanetti fissi con tavolini e sedie a fronte, divanetti a isola di dimensioni maggiori con schienale alto tipo séparé, tavoli di tipo tradizionale sono distribuiti ottimizzando lo sfruttamento dello spazio per ospitare più di duecento ospiti. Una zona con banco bar a isola è posizionata a destra dell'ingresso, affacciata direttamente sulla strada, mentre sulla sinistra un lungo bancone caratterizza quella dove si possono acquistare piatti da asporto e gustare in modo veloce delle pietanze al banco, con sgabelli tipo *diner*. Sul fondo della sala, separate da pareti scorrevoli, pensate come schermi decorativi in legno e vetro, sono organizzate le sale riservate. La curiosa commistione tra diverse tipologie di ristorante (fast-food, take-away e sala tradizionale) è brillantemente risolta dalle soluzioni architettoniche complessive che rivisitano con creatività figure e geometrie art déco. Due essenze lignee di diverso colore naturale sono impiegate per rivestire i pilastri che segnano con forza l'intero spazio del locale. Listelli scuri sottolineano i profili e ridisegnano la figura del fusto, avvolto da pannelli più chiari. Una fascia aggettante, composta da lastre di vetro venato bianco e da quadrati angolari blu, anticipa lo stilizzato capitello metallico conclusivo, proponendosi anche come soffusa fonte luminosa. A tale dimensione stilistica si collegano i disegni delle boiseries, dei séparé e degli arredi, in parte rivestiti da tessuti che richiamano ancora motivi art déco. Il soffitto della zona fast-food propone dei curiosi pannelli metallici decorativi, mentre in tutto il resto della sala è caratterizzato da una serie di vivaci teli dipinti, sospesi tra travi di legno a vista, che creano un brillante contrappunto compositivo con il rigore art déco della soluzione complessiva.

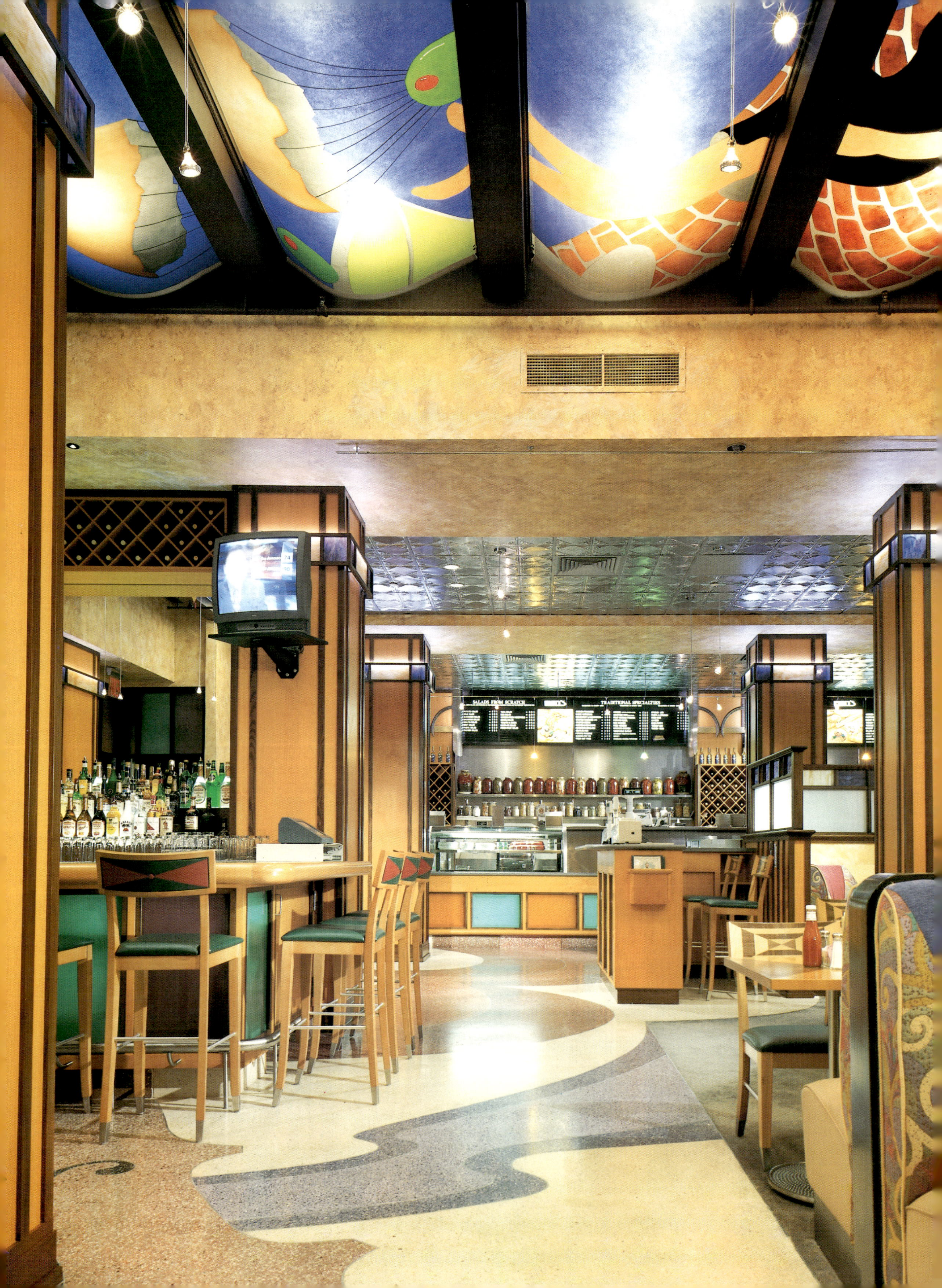
SALADS FROM SCRATCH
TRADITIONAL SPECIALTIES

35

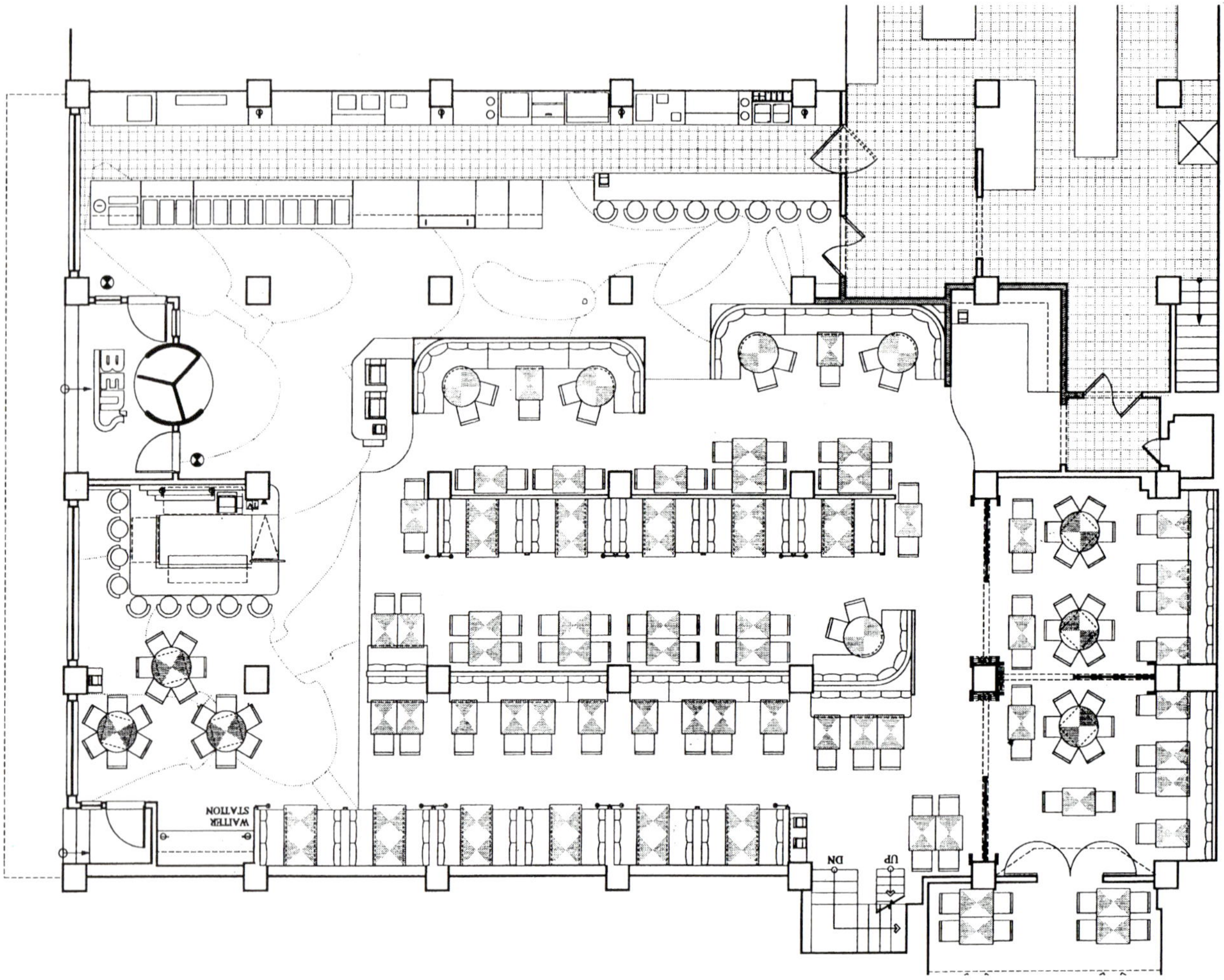
UP
DN

BEN'S
KOSHER CUISINE
BEN'S
RESTAURANT
OUR CHICKEN SOUP CURES EVERYTHING ELSE.
DELICATESSEN
RESTAURANT

BOHEMIA JAZZ CLUB
Branson e Coates Architecture. Tokyo, JP, 1986

Ensconced in the basement of the Takeo Kikuchi building designed by Tadao Ando in the terse minimalist style that is his distinctive hallmark, the Bohemia Jazz Club is somewhat contrasting with the rather austere building above it in terms of its use of materials and composition. The twin-height space available in the basement prompted the designers to create two separate floors, leading the guests in at the upper level, whereby offering them an intriguing overhead view down into the bar below. As in early works, for this project Branson and Coates have once again deftly allied the theatrical element with the architecture, inviting various artists to contribute, intentionally harking back via both materials and imagery to the atmosphere of the London jazz clubs of the fifties. The Bohemia flirts playfully with the aeronautics repertoire that the architects have already used for the Café Bongo, though in this case it has been purged of the classical inferences and retro and futuristic archaeological pointers. The entire composition is markedly characterized by the extensive use of metal surfaces (aluminum and steel), left in their raw state or riveted, as in the mezzanine, to simulate the wing of an airplane, underscored by the bulging engine-housings fixed below the wing, thereby effectively camouflaging the air-conditioning plants. The entrance mezzanine, which is bordered by a lightweight metal banister in various colors, and enlivened by a mural of musical motifs round the walls, houses the orchestra stand, and is linked to the bar level below via a neat spiral staircase. Ranged over the fine wood floor are assorted metal chairs imitating aircraft seats upholstered in brightly colored fabrics. Adorning the perimeter walls beneath the mezzanine-wing device are aircraft seats forming private enclosures, which cleverly conspire to provide a single dynamic figurative assembly. From the ceiling hangs an unusual light fitting composed of toy saxophones in silver plastic, offering a playful reminder of the club's vocation.

Ricavato nel piano interrato del Takeo Kikuchi Building costruito da Tadao Ando secondo il proprio linguaggio minimale, il Boemia Jazz Club si discosta per scelte materiche e compositive dall'immagine rigorosa e muta dell'edificio. Lo spazio a doppia altezza disponibile ha suggerito ai progettisti di organizzare il club su due livelli, prevedendo l'ingresso da quello superiore per offrire la scena del bar sottostante nella sua totalità. Anche in questo progetto Branson e Coates hanno unito la dimensione teatrale e scenografica con quella architettonica, invitando a collaborare vari artisti e designer, nell'intento di evocare l'atmosfera dei jazz club londinesi e americani degli anni '50, rivisitandone figure e materiali. Nel Bohemia si ritrova l'inconsueto vocabolario legato al mondo degli aeroplani impiegato per definire anche il Caffè Bongo, ma in questo caso epurato dall'accostamento con memorie classiche e con archeologie passate e future. L'intera composizione è fortemente caratterizzata dall'impiego di superfici di metallo, alluminio e acciaio, lasciate allo stato grezzo o rivettate come nel soppalco per simulare la figura di un'ala di aeroplano, sottolineata anche dai motori-bongo, scanditi da lesene bombate, fissati sotto l'ala per contenere l'impianto dell'aria condizionata. Il soppalco d'ingresso, segnato da una leggera ringhiera metallica a vari colori e da pitture alle pareti dedicate al tema dell'improvvisazione musicale, ospita la postazione dell'orchestra ed è raccordato al livello del bar con una scala a chiocciola. Sul pavimento di legno sono distribuiti gli arredi che affiancano raffinate sedute metalliche imbottite su disegno a sedili di aeroplano rivestiti con tessuti coloratissimi. Fissati alle pareti perimetrali sotto l'ala-soppalco i sedili, trasposti da una carlinga d'aereo alla dimensione privata e raccolta di un club, formano un unico dinamico assemblaggio figurativo. Dal soffitto scende un curioso lampadario composto da sassofoni-giocattolo in plastica argentata che ricordano ironicamente la vocazione musicale del locale.

38

39

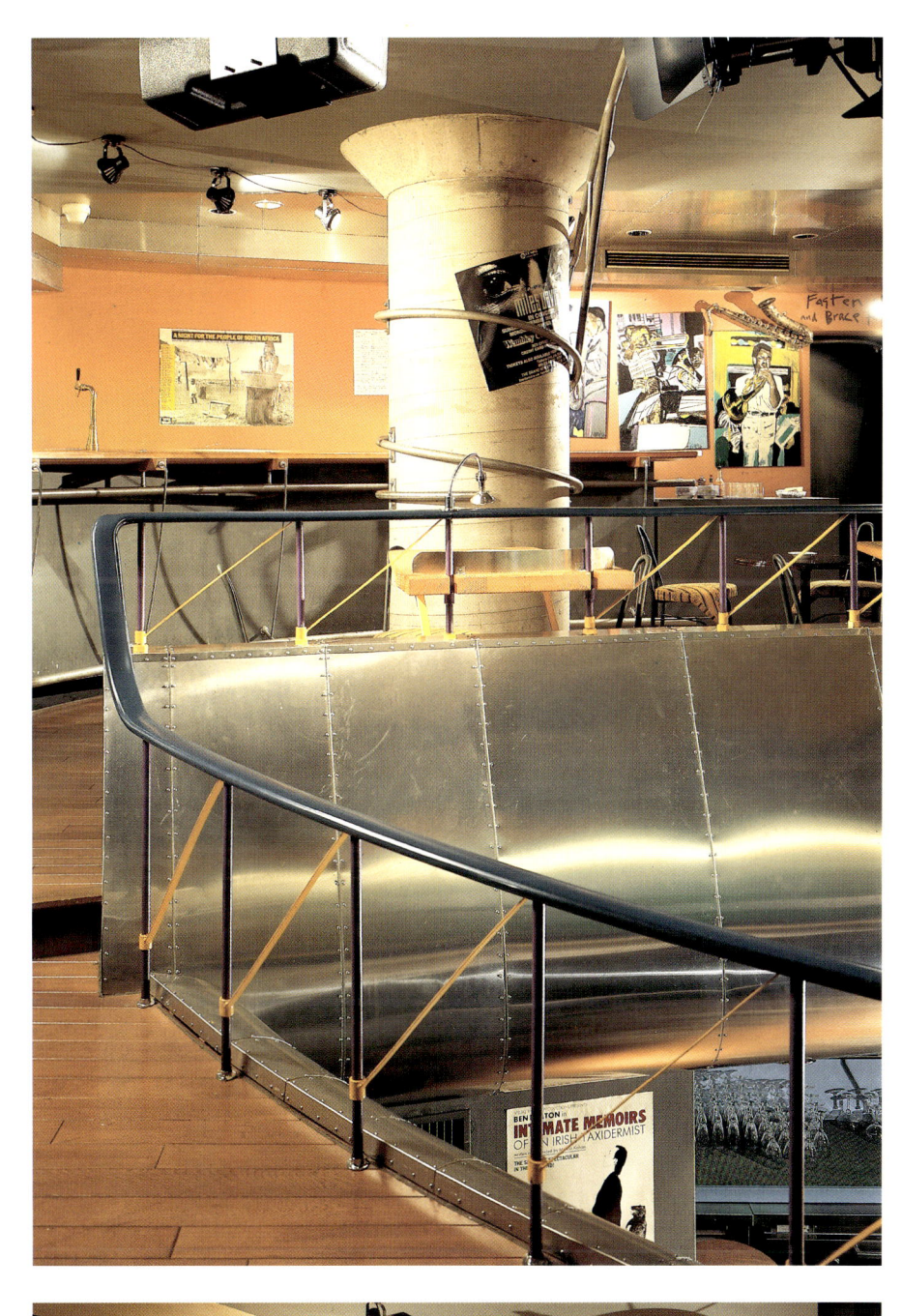

at the Jazz Ear.....

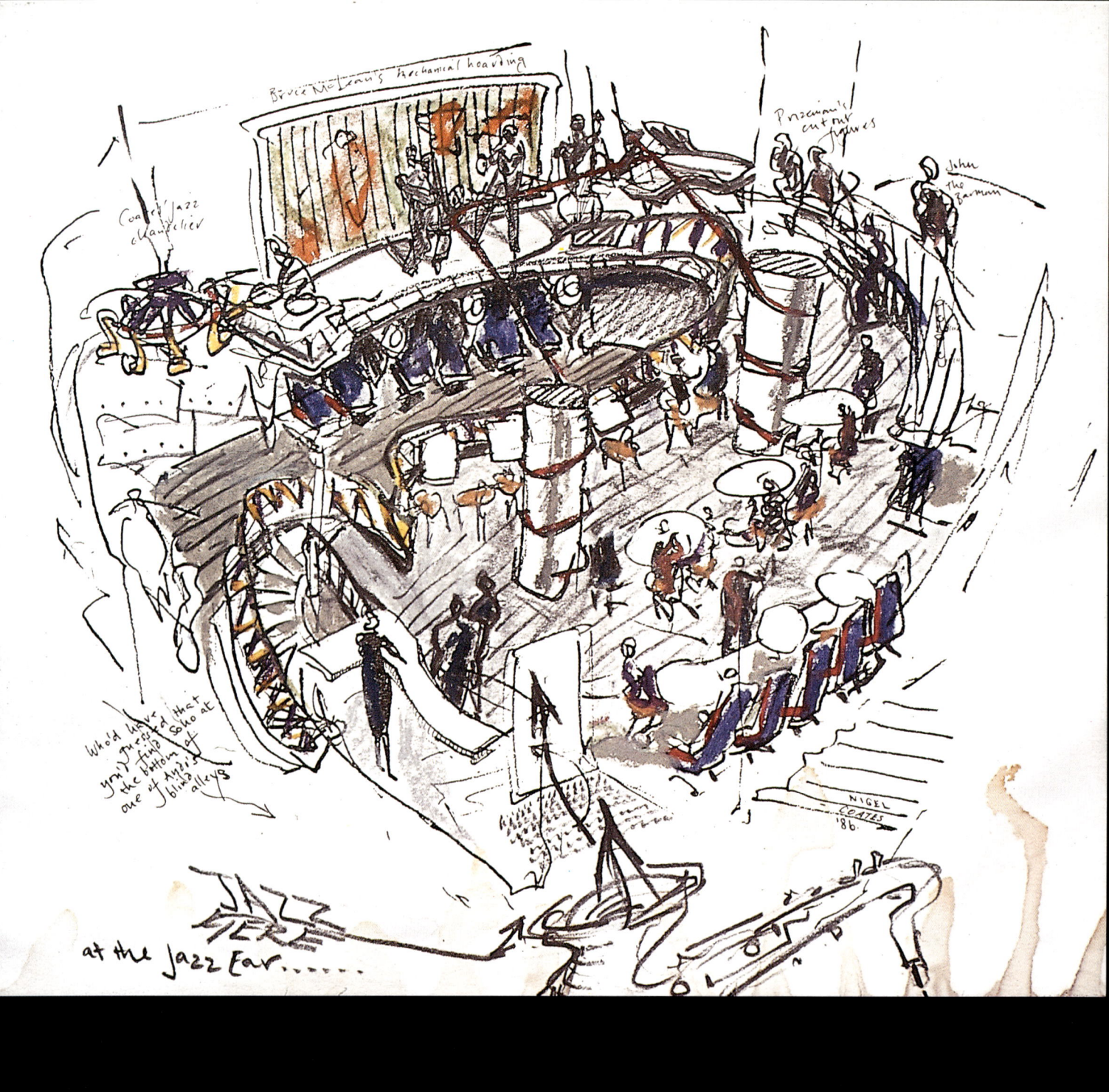

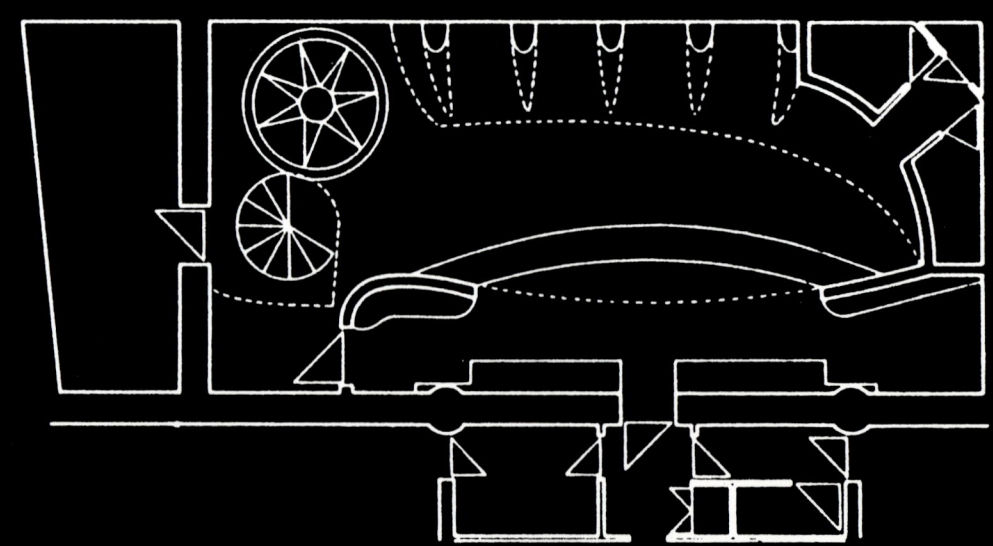

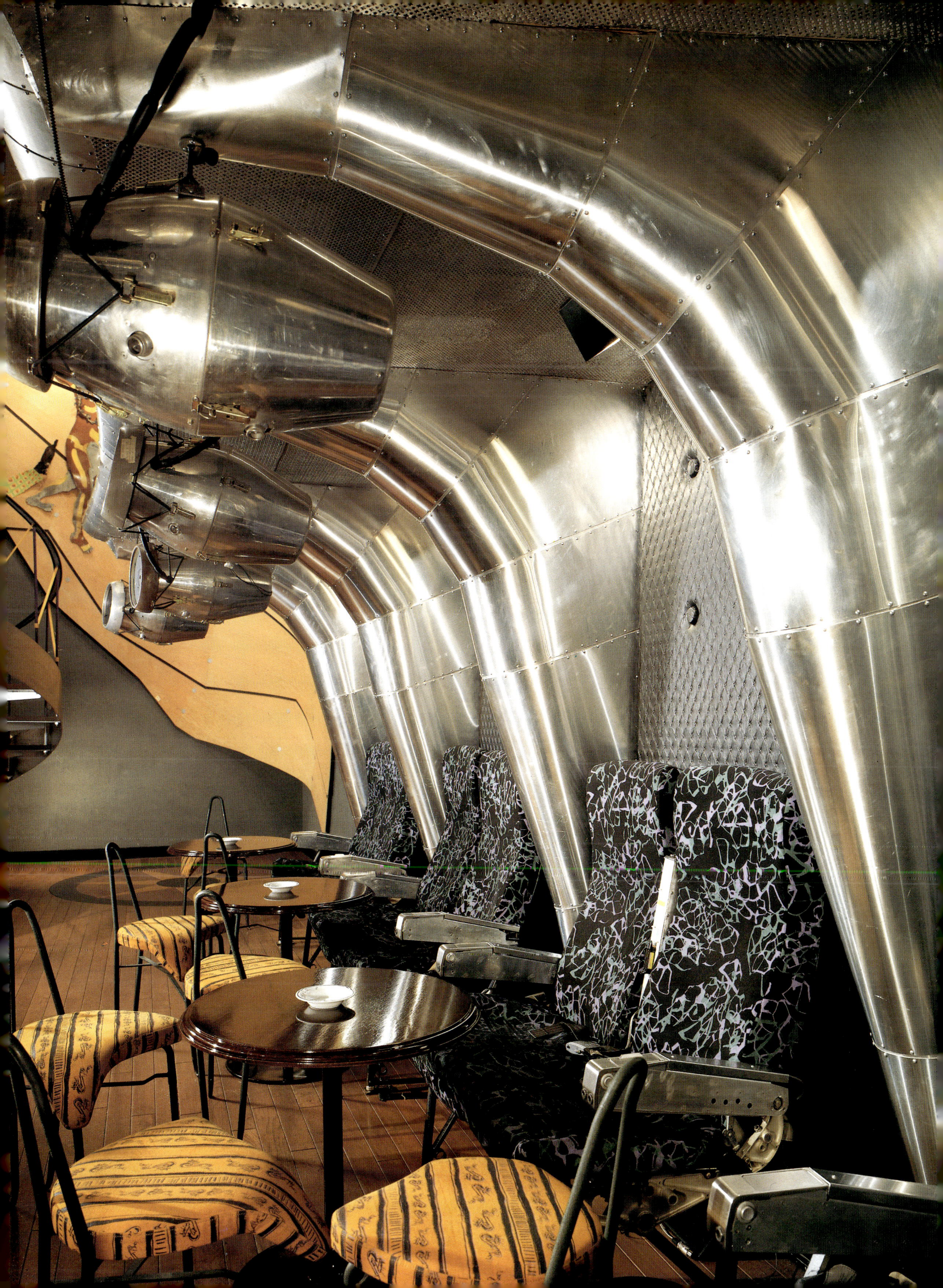

BRYANT PARK GRILL
Hardy Holzman Pfeiffer Associates. New York, NY, USA, 1995

Set in mid-Manhattan just off Times Square on Bryant Park, this new grill restaurant draws on the great tradition of kiosks and pavilions of the kind which adorned public and private parks and gardens in the nineteenth century, elegant sentinels posted amid the greenery, like imaginary dwellings, or eye-catching follies. The small building that hosts the restaurant has been awarded a refined architectural setting at the far end of the park, and links visually with the exemplary Beaux Arts frontage of the New York Public Library, commissioned in 1911 from Carrère & Hastings. In this way, the restaurant qualifies as an authentic example of garden architecture, a sort of greenhouse revisited whose facade offers tall, full-length windows resting on a stone base, ranged with wooden laths designed to support the climbing plants. The roof has been fitted out as a terrace that poses as a splendid urban belvedere. The restaurant interiors cover an overall surface area of around 500 square meters and comprise an elegant bar in the entrance foyer, a large dining room, and a smaller private room off to one side that can also be accessed from outside. The bar proclaims the project's overall design persona: a refined interplay of materials alternating between briar-wood veneer for the main fixtures and the wall paneling, slate for the bar-foyer, and a lush dark parquet for the main dining area. The pillars are dressed in bronze panels, the same material used for the top of the bar counter (whose fine onyx facing is attractively retro-illuminated), and the classical-style lamps of the main room, augmented by overhead "winged lamps" fixed to thin brass tubes, in homage to an installation by Ingo Maurer. The sofa benches set along the walls are complemented by elegant wood chairs with upholstered seats, and these offer appropriate visual linkage with the parquet and the paler wood of the paneling, where here and there wall-mounted fittings sport bunches of freshly cut daisies.

Ubicato nel centro di Manhattan e affacciato sul Parco da cui prende il nome, il Bryant Park Grill si pone nella tradizione delle migliori costruzioni da giardino, chioschi e padiglioni che nell'Ottocento arricchivano il verde pubblico e privato definendosi come architetture tutorie del verde, fantasie abitative o suggestive *folies*. Il piccolo edificio che ospita il ristorante si pone come quinta conclusiva del parco, soluzione architettonica raffinata e leggera raccordata all' imponente edificio Beaux Arts della New York Public Library, costruito nel 1911 da Carrère & Hastings. Il ristorante si configura così come vera e propria 'architettura da giardino', sorta di serra reinventata che propone una facciata con alte finestre verticali, poggianti su uno zoccolo di pietra, ripartite da una serie di lesene lignee, pensate per sostenere il verde rampicante. Il tetto è sfruttato a terrazza, sorta di riuscito belvedere urbano. La distribuzione interna organizza su una superficie complessiva di circa 500 metri quadrati un elegante bar all'ingresso e una grande sala da pranzo cui si affianca una saletta riservata, accessibile anche dall'esterno. Il bar annuncia la filosofia progettuale dell'insieme: una raffinata composizione materica che alterna materiali preziosi, come la radica impiegata per gli arredi fissi e la boiserie, a pavimentazioni in ardesia per il bar-ingresso e in parquet di un'essenza scura e pregiata per la sala da pranzo. I pilastri strutturali sono rivestiti con pannelli di bronzo, lo stesso materiale che caratterizza il piano del banco bar (con fronte in onice retroilluminato) e i lampadari classicheggianti della grande sala, affiancati dalle luci a soffitto del bar composte da 'lampadine alate' fissate a sottili tubi in ottone che rileggono un noto allestimento di Ingo Maurer. Nella sala ai divanetti fissi a muro si affiancano eleganti sedie in legno scuro con seduta imbottita, che fungono da elemento d'arredo connettivo tra il colore del parquet e la superficie chiara della boiserie, a volte pensata come inusitata struttura tutoria per fresche margherite.

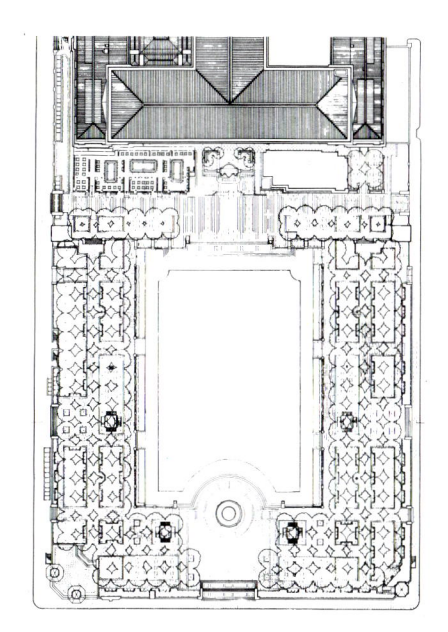

Site plan / Pianta dell'area

43

Elevation / Prospetto

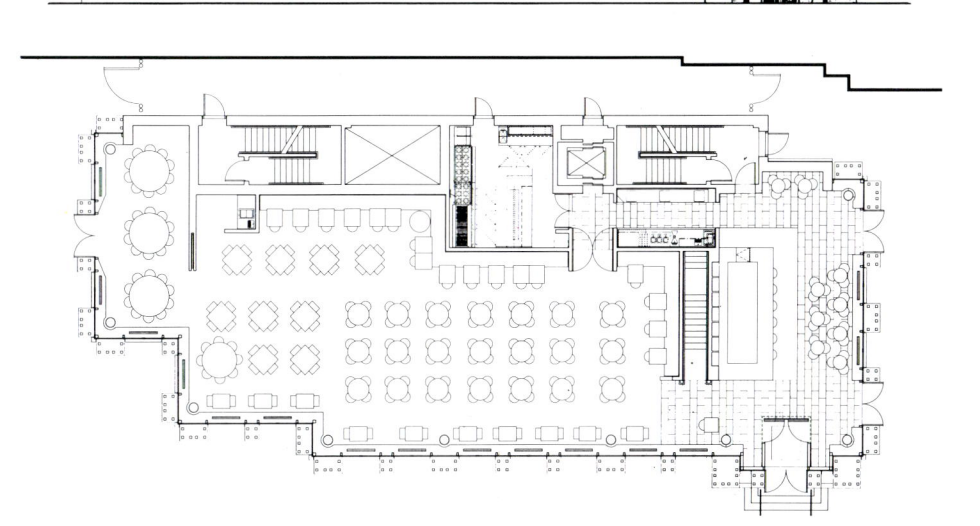

Plan / Pianta

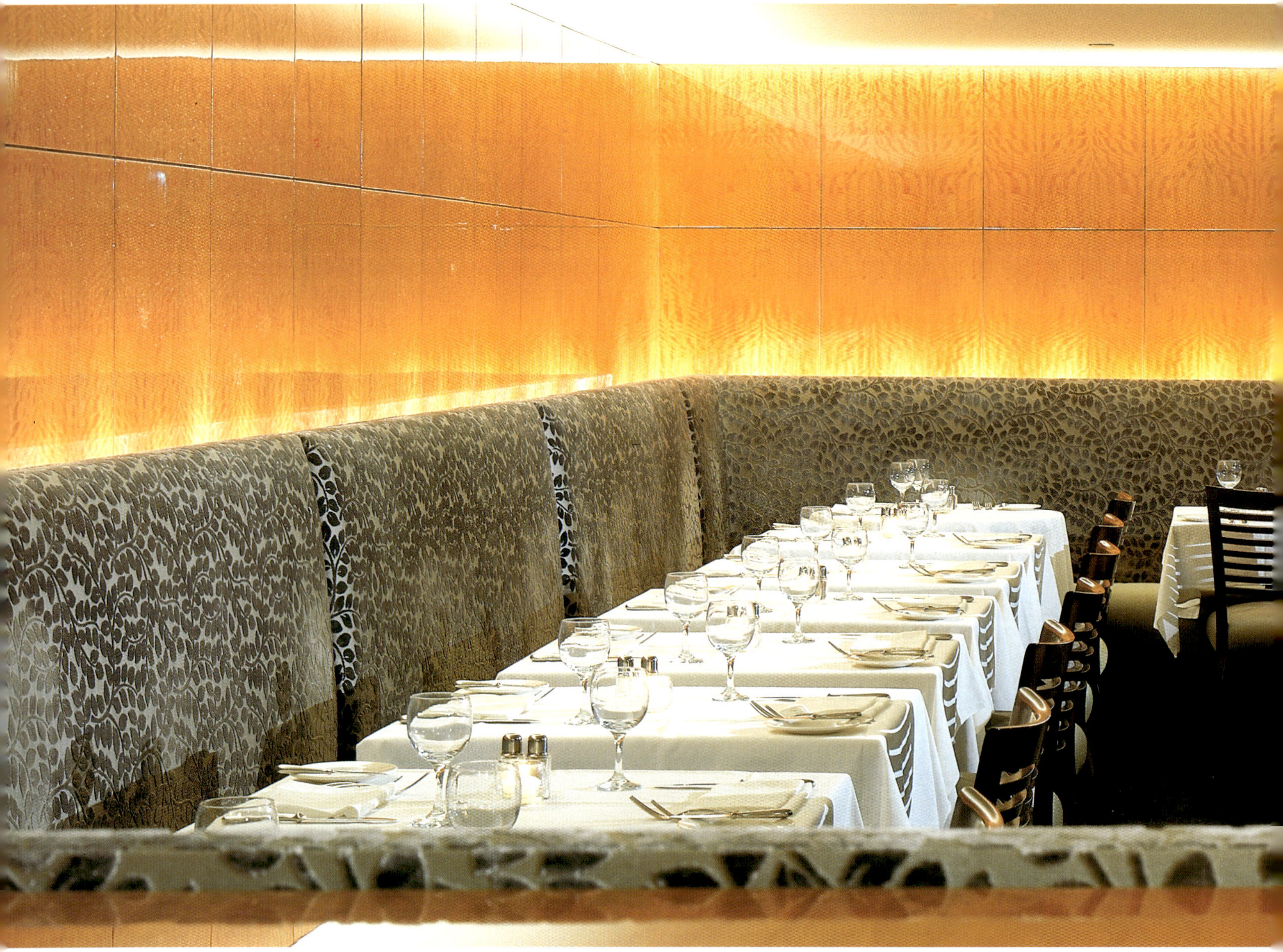

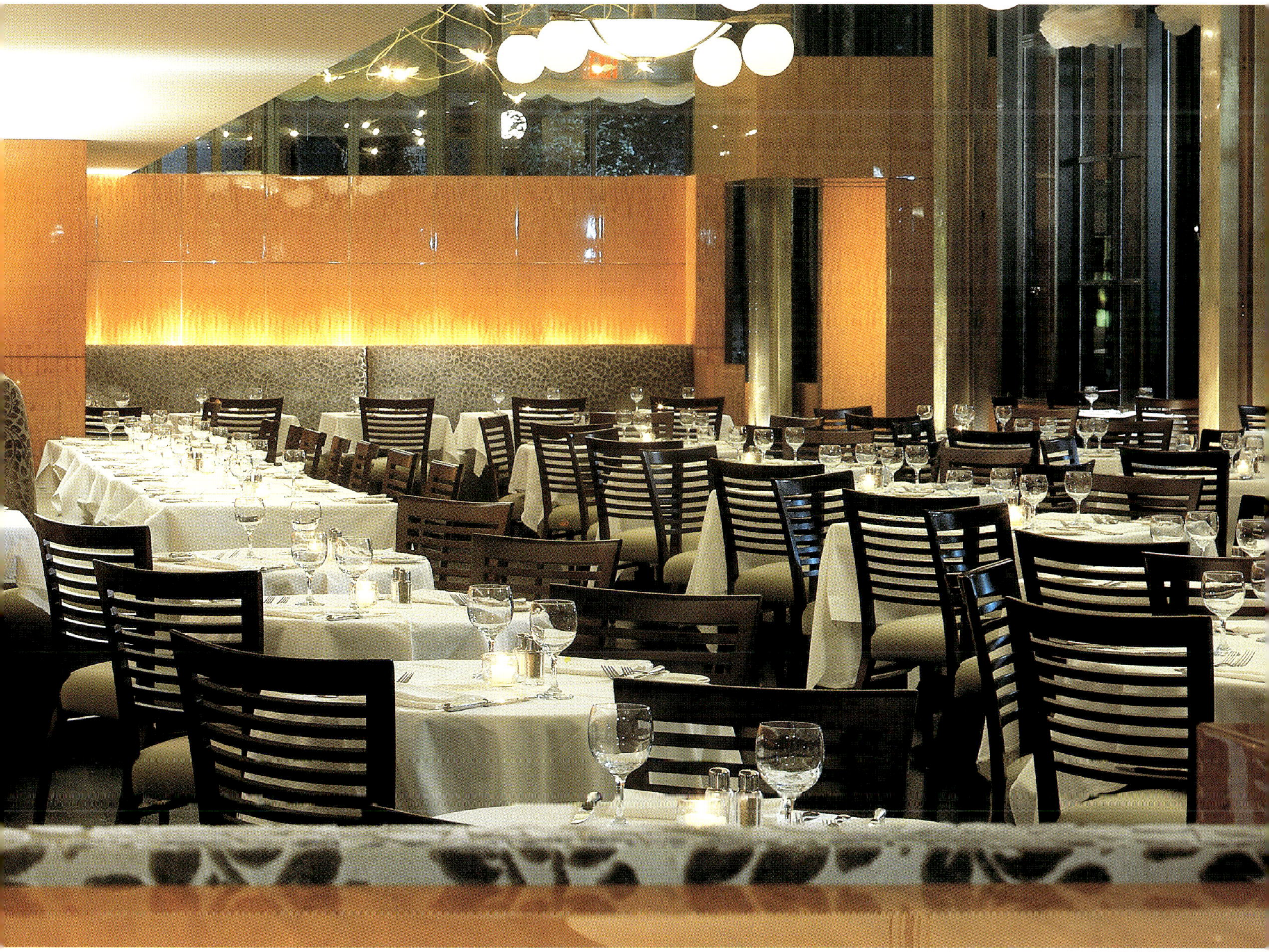

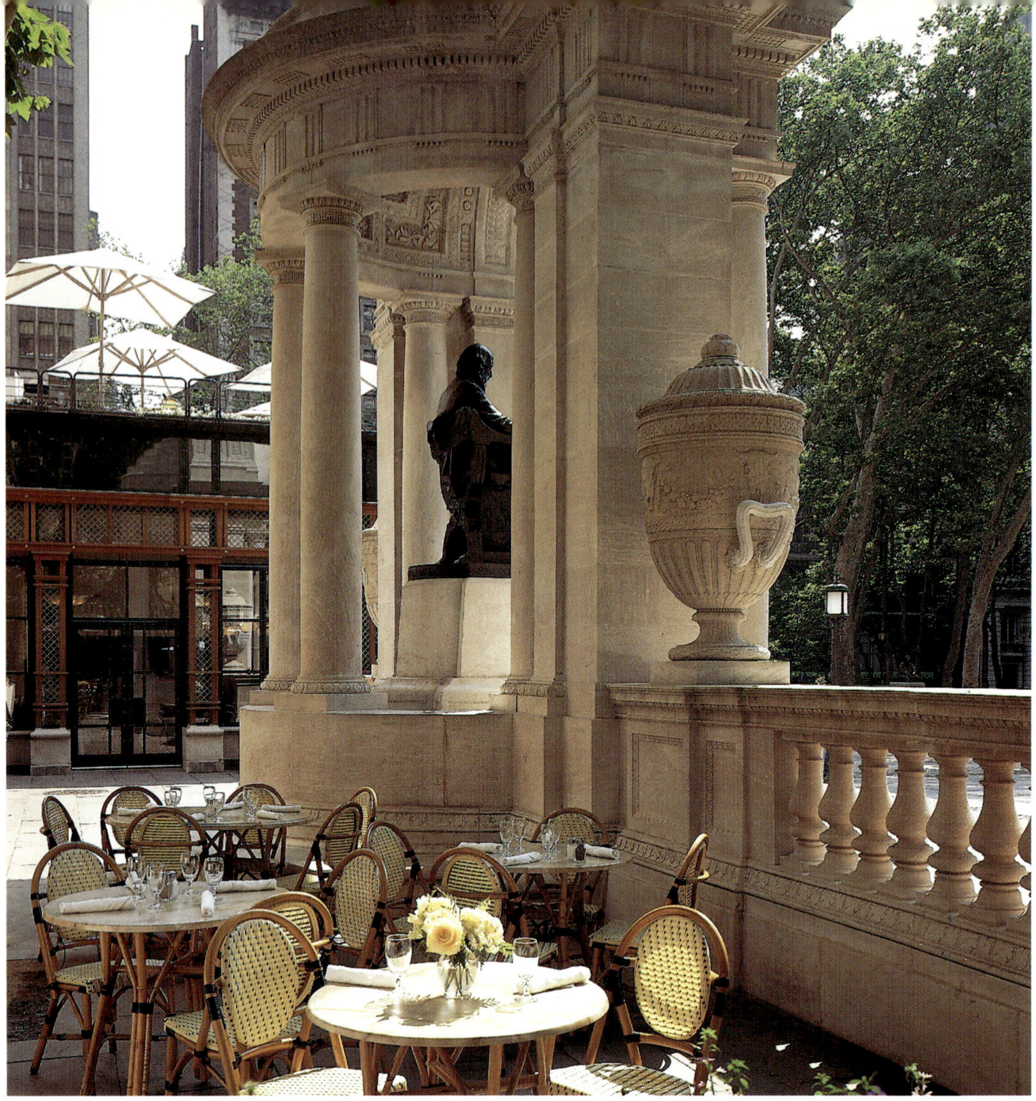

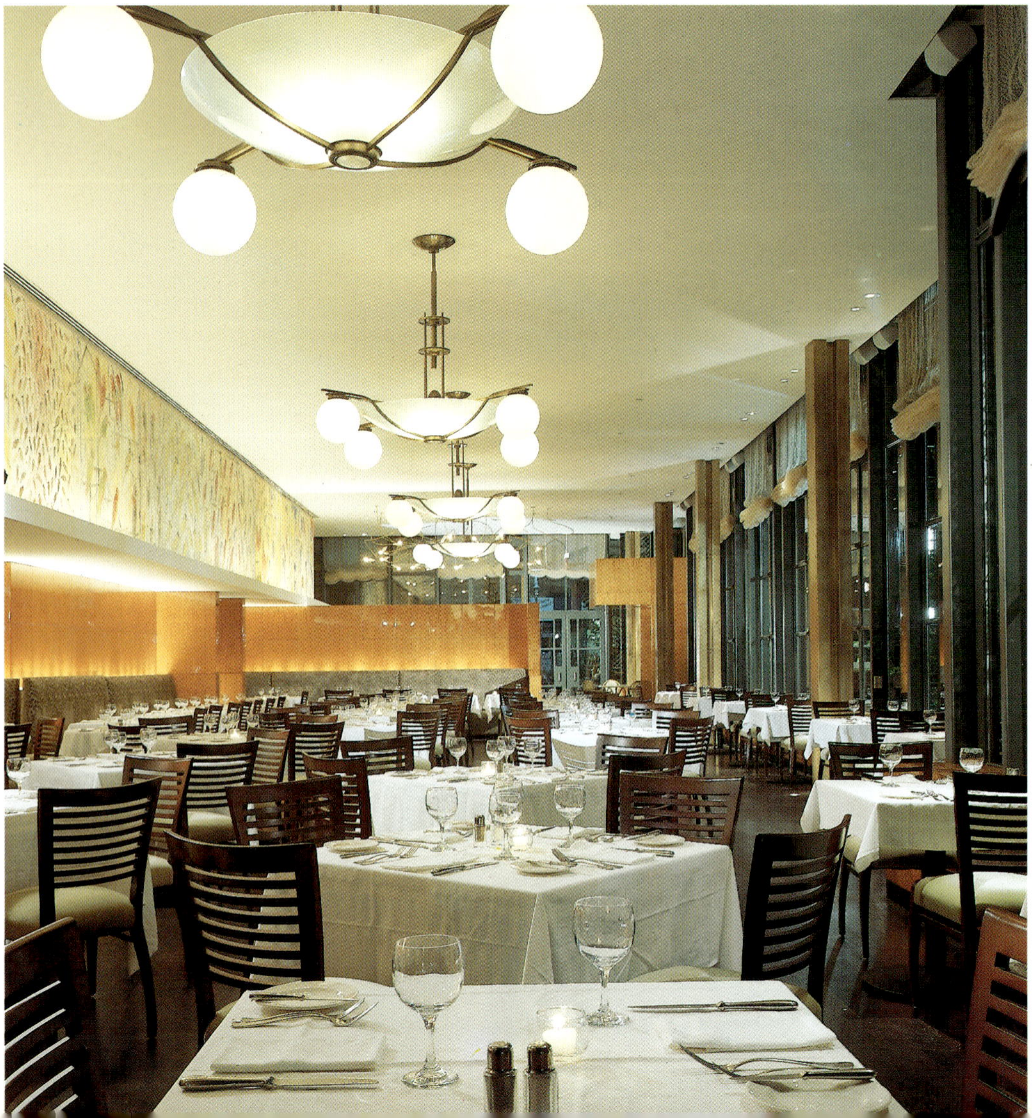

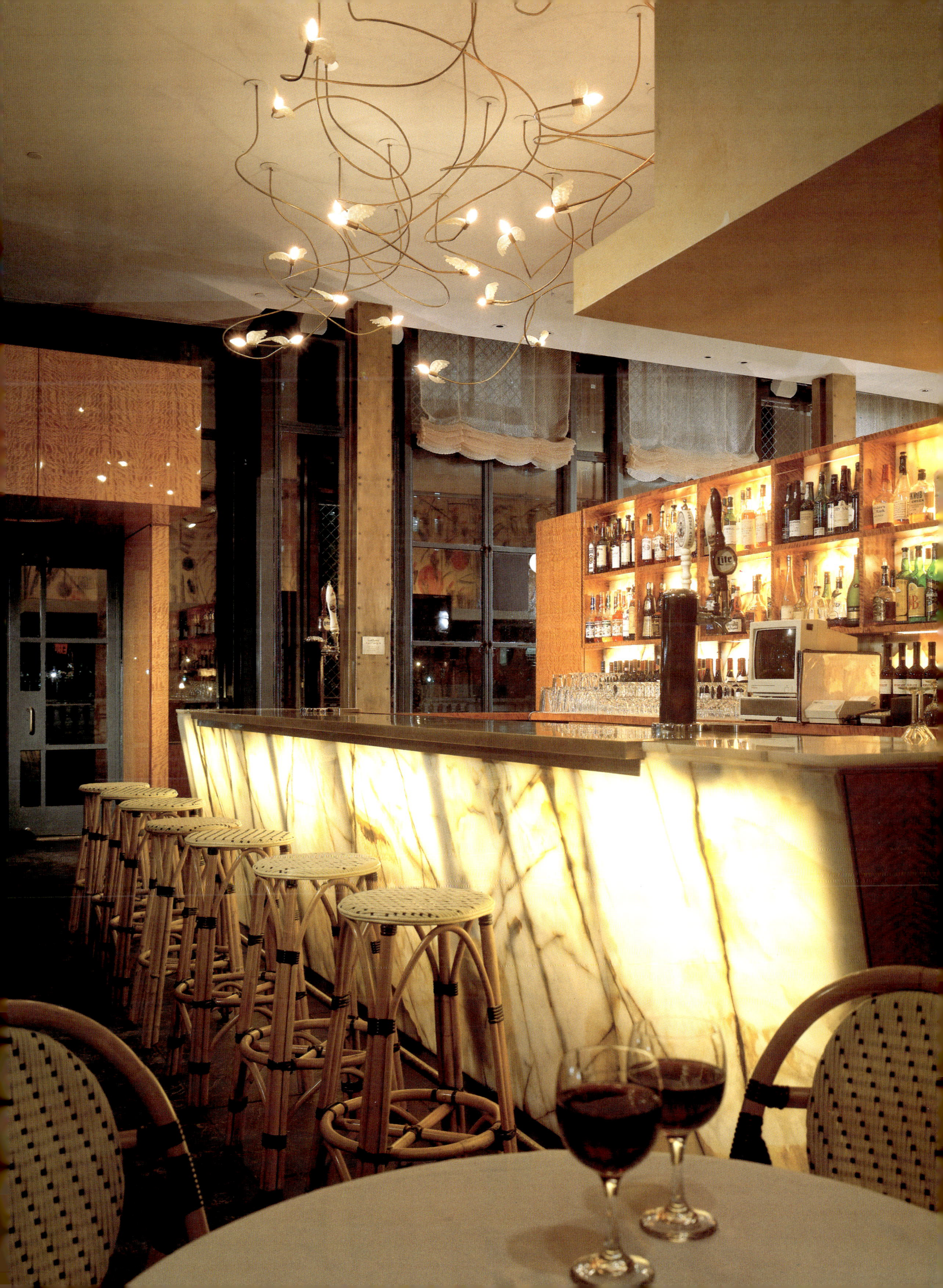
Lite

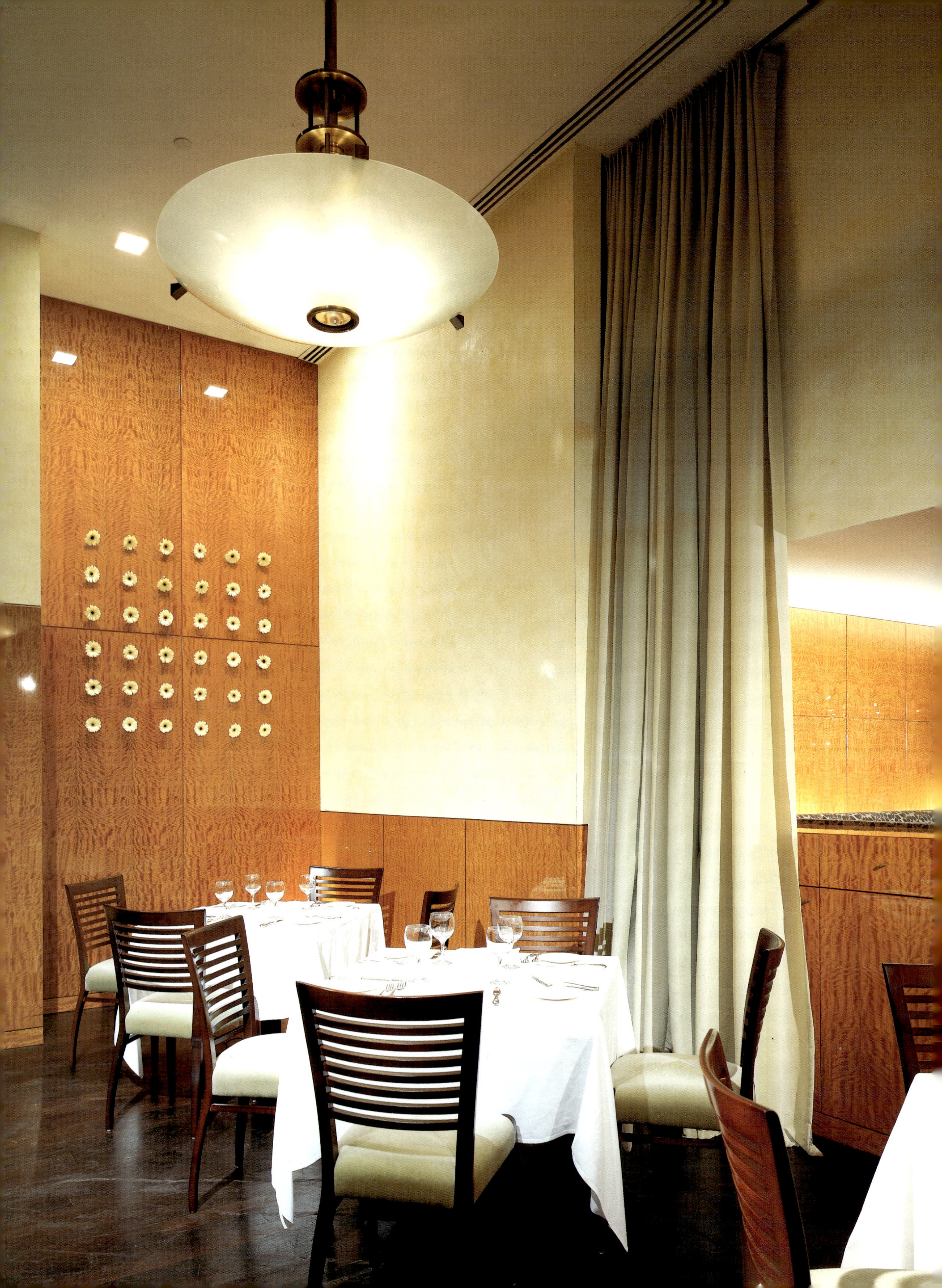

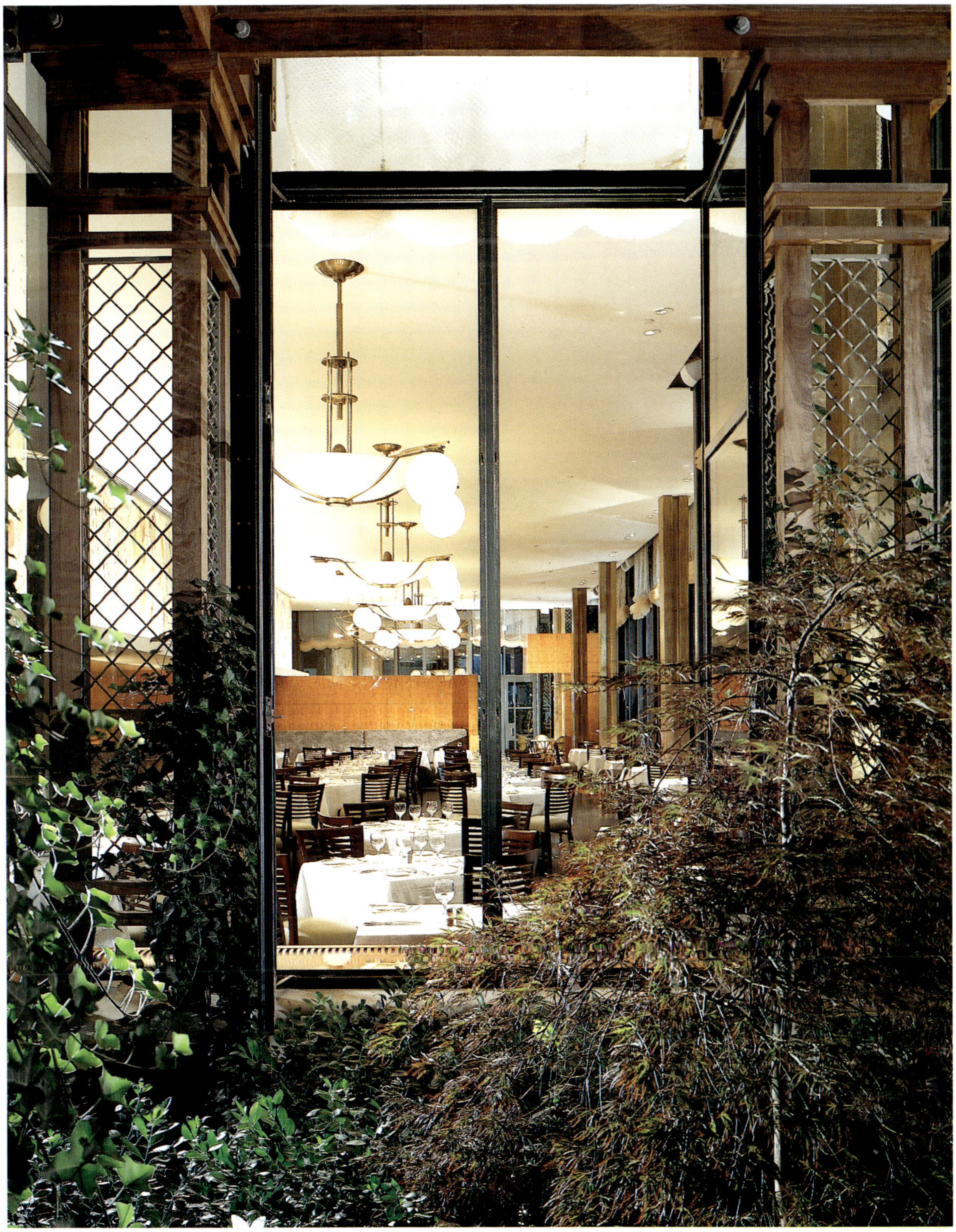

CAFFE' BONGO
Branson e Coates Architecture. Tokyo, JP, 1986

Set in the heart of Tokyo's ever-busy Shibuya-Ku shopping precinct, this new gathering point explodes with unusual figurative verve toward the surrounding landscape, proposing an intriguing mélange of gestures and reminders devised to simulate a sort of "archaeology of the future." The café's facade describes a section of an airplane, a wing balancing on a classicizing pillar complete with Corinthian capitals and chipped surface revealing the brick surface below. Vying with this conspicuous wing device, which inevitably affords the pivotal visual feature of the composition, are the two marquees, one large one small, made of the same material, fixed over the entrance to extend the entranceway inside. The ample windows composing the facade afford an unimpeded vista of the interior to passersby on the street outside. The slender tilted columns in iron and the rusted curved beams sustain a mezzanine, once again designed to resemble the wing of an airplane. This bulges out in a curve marking the perimeter walls inside, and supports a series of classical statues that watch over the guests in silence. The various metallic surfaces and "archaeological" artifacts (such as wrenches and locks) set into the concrete floor, along with fragments of mosaic and illuminated niches, are further enhanced by the theatrical treatment of the walls, which replicate the frontage of an ancient Roman basilica with Corinthian colonnade, entablature, epigraphs, and chipped wall in brick, into which assorted curios and contemporary objects have been inserted, framed by a series of blue drapes. This stark interplay between sections of metal evoking an imaginary post-industrial future, the fake Piranesi-style reconstructions, and the architecture typical of the fifties café, together generate an appealing overall image. To crown the effect, the ceiling is dominated by a grandiose light fitting in glass and metal that depicts the movement of the planets; and the ceiling itself contributes to the spectacle with a sweeping fresco of the cosmos, underscoring the dynamic eclecticism of the whole.

Nel cuore del quartiere commerciale di Shibuya-Ku, il Caffè Bongo esplode con inusitata potenza figurativa verso il paesaggio esterno, proponendo un collage di segni e memorie che sembra definire una seducente 'archeologia del futuro'. La facciata del Caffè propone un frammento di aeroplano, un'ala posta in bilico su un pilastro 'anticato', segnato da capitelli corinzi e con l'intonaco sbrecciato in cui appare il mattone sottostante. La grande ala funge indubbiamente da inequivocabile segno di richiamo, ma anche da grande pensilina che si aggiunge a quella più piccola, dello stesso materiale, fissata sopra l'ingresso per prolungarsi nell'interno. Le grandi vetrate che compongono la facciata permettono così di cogliere in modo immediato l'immagine del locale proiettando verso il marciapiede l'inconsueta scena del Caffè. Delle slanciate colonnine in ghisa inclinate e delle putrelle curvate arrugginite sostengono un soppalco realizzato come un'ulteriore ala di aeroplano. Questa si protende bombata e in curva a segnare i muri perimetrali interni per sostenere una serie di statue classiche che osservano in silenzio i visitatori. Alle varie superfici metalliche e ai 'reperti archeologici' (chiavi inglesi, serrature) incassati nel pavimento di cemento, insieme a frammenti di mosaico e a nicchie luminose, si affianca la soluzione scenografica e architettonica delle pareti interne che compongono il fronte di un'antica basilica romana con colonnato corinzio, cornicioni, epigrafi e muri sbrecciati di mattone pieno, in cui si innestano reperti e oggetti d'uso del presente schermati da una serie di drappeggi azzurri. Questo confronto/scontro tra brani metallici di un futuro post-industriale, false memorie della Roma piranesiana e architettura del caffè anni '50, definisce la complessa e seducente immagine del locale. Infine, un grande lampadario in vetro e metallo che rappresenta il movimento dei pianeti scende dal soffitto caratterizzato da un ulteriore segno scenografico e pittorico: il grande affresco che rappresenta il vortice del cosmo, a sottolineare l'eclettico dinamismo dell'insieme.

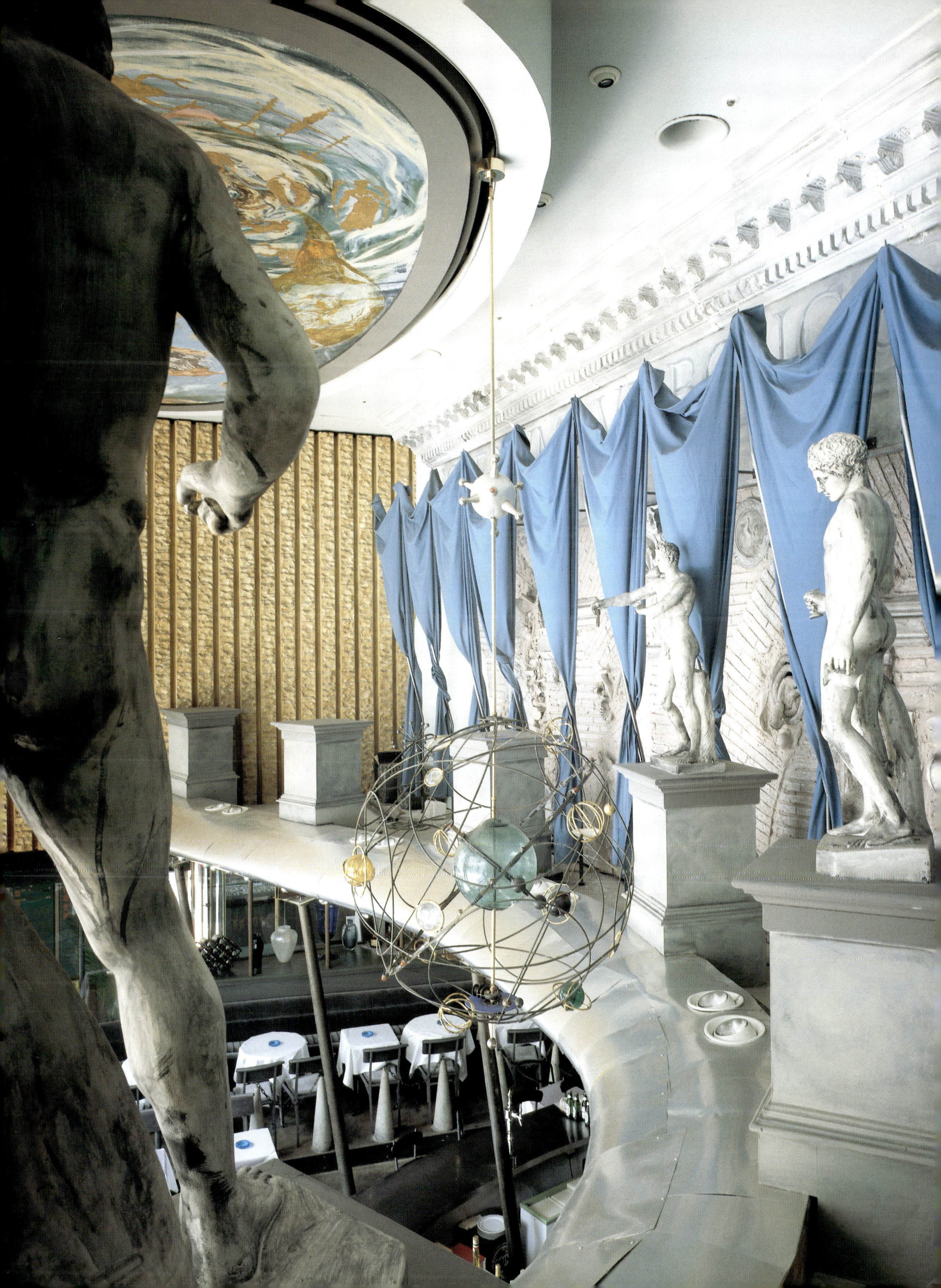

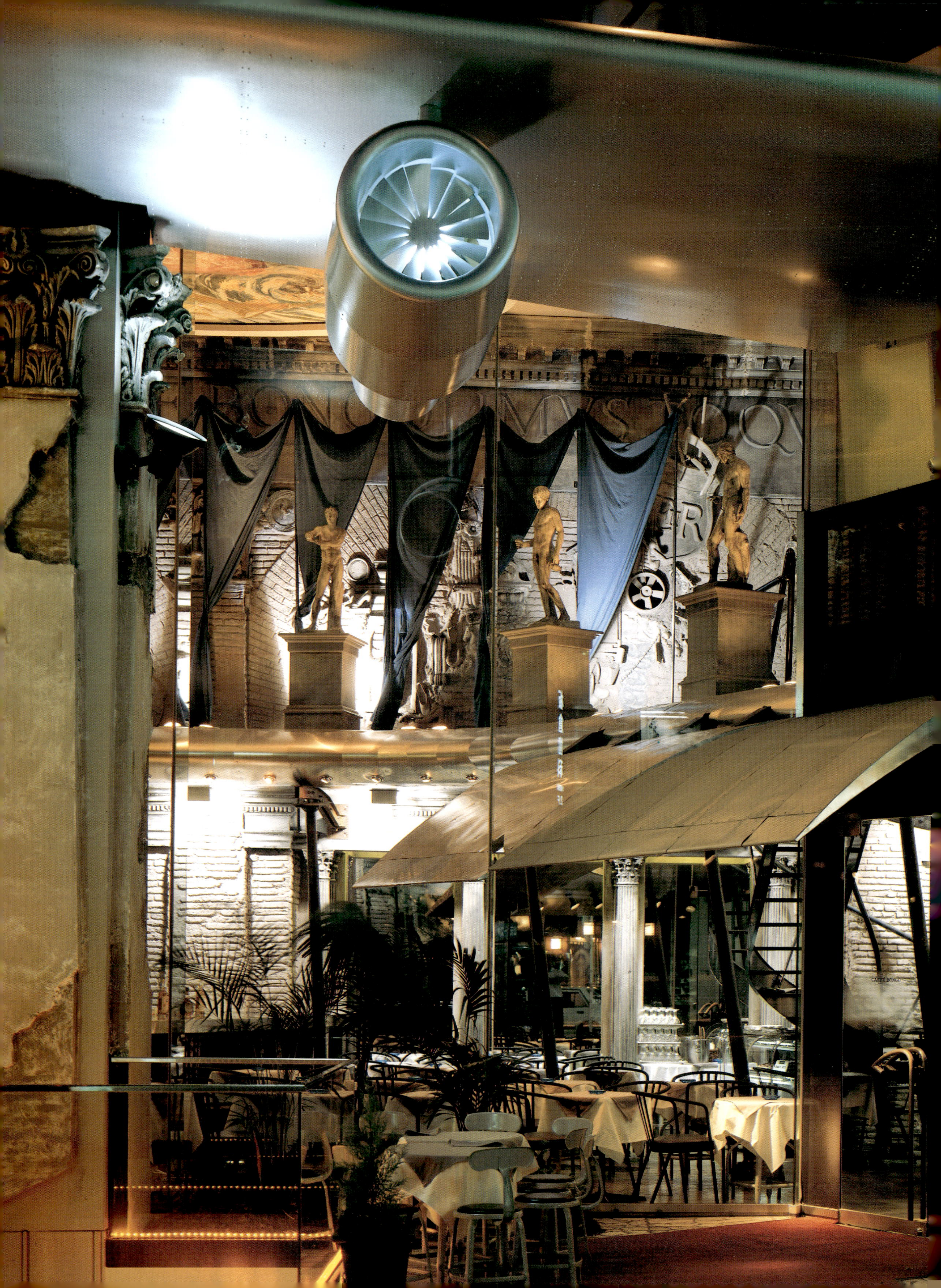

53

Plan / Pianta

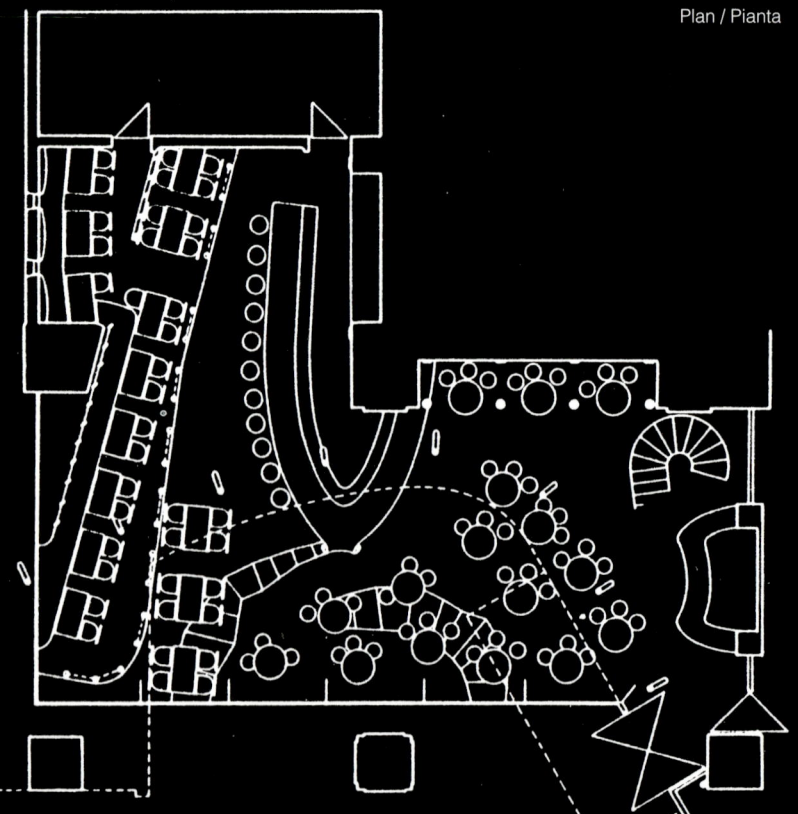

CAN RESTAURANT
Stomu Miyazaki Es Studio Inc., WYS & Partners New York, NY, USA, 1990

Berthed in a corner lot in an unassuming building on West Broadway and Houston Street in Soho, surrounded by art galleries and painter's studios, this restaurant eschews an architectural solution in favor of a more distinctly art-oriented design and style. The entire scheme pivots on a metaphor for the elements of nature, in which each landscape is translated at both compositional and material level: mountain, plain, river, underground stream, rocks, and minerals. The facade of the building occupied by the entrance and the main window of the restaurant has been refaced to provide a new, neutral surface to be explored. Besides the restaurant's logo, composed of brass letters in relief, the entrance corner is dressed in earth-colored stucco in an uneven pattern that simulates the jagged outline of a mountain. This compositional feature is repeated in the base of the corner windows, continuing inward past the built-in planter that travels along the stair down to the bar. Set alongside the entrance, the bar offers a two-height space starting with the basement floor, and is illuminated by ample glazing overhead. In the basement itself, where the service areas and kitchens are lodged, the floor is in green marble, while a large slab of onyx creates a backdrop for the bar – materials respectively evoking underground water and minerals. At the entrance a band of floor in concrete set with pebbles and stones extends along the corridor along the original exposed-brick wall in a wavy pattern that suggests a river, and the timber floor in oak represents the earth. An archway of brick in ziggurat form leads into the restaurant proper, which is partly fitted out with brick set in irregular patterns to suggest the ruins of a previous building.

In uno spazio d'angolo di un anonimo edificio tra West Broadway e Houston Street, nel quartiere di Soho, caratterizzato dalla presenza di numerose gallerie d'arte e da studi di pittori, è stato ricavato questo ristorante che per filosofia progettuale e scelte stilistiche sembra avvicinarsi più alla dimensione artistica che a quella architettonica. L'intero progetto si basa su una riflessione metaforica degli elementi naturali che formano ogni paesaggio tradotti in soluzioni compositive e materiche: la montagna, il terreno, il fiume, l'acqua sotterranea, le rocce e i minerali. La facciata dell'edificio occupata dall'ingresso e dalle vetrate del ristorante è stata rintonacata e proposta come nuova superficie neutra su cui intervenire. Oltre al logo del locale, composto da lettere d'ottone in rilievo, l'angolo d'ingresso è stato decorato con stucco colore terra secondo un disegno irregolare che simula uno stilizzato profilo di montagna. Questo primo elemento compositivo segna anche la base delle vetrate angolari, per proseguire nell'interno affiancato da una fioriera incassata che si sviluppa lungo la scala di discesa al bar. Posizionato di fianco all'ingresso, il bar caratterizza come spazio a doppia altezza parte del piano interrato, illuminato dalle ampie vetrate soprastanti. Nell' interrato, dove sono anche organizzati i servizi e la cucina, la pavimentazione è di marmo verde, mentre una grande lastra di onice fa da sfondo al banco-bar; materiali chiamati a rappresentare rispettivamente l'acqua sotterranea e i minerali. Dall'ingresso una superficie calpestabile di cemento con sassi e pietre incassate si sviluppa per tutto il corridoio lungo il muro originale di mattoni faccia a vista seguendo un disegno ondulato che vuole ricordare il corso di un fiume, mentre il parquet di rovere che le si affianca assume il valore simbolico della terra. Un arco di mattoni posti a ziqqurat introduce alla sala ristorante, in parte rivestita con lo stesso materiale secondo motivi irregolari proposti come rovine preesistenze dell'edificio.

Ground floor / Piano terra

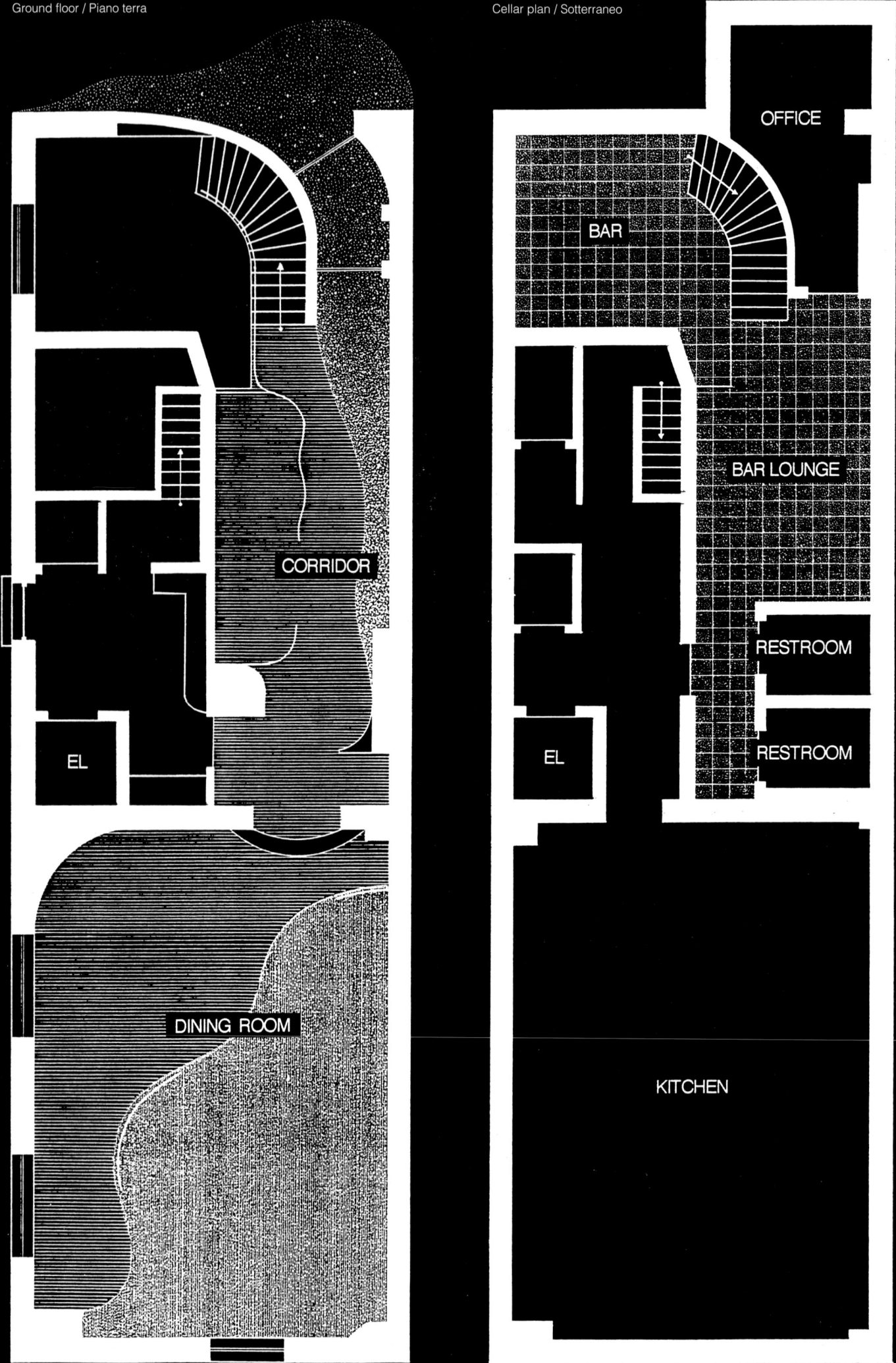

Cellar plan / Sotterraneo

CORRIDOR

EL

DINING ROOM

OFFICE

BAR

BAR LOUNGE

RESTROOM

RESTROOM

EL

KITCHEN

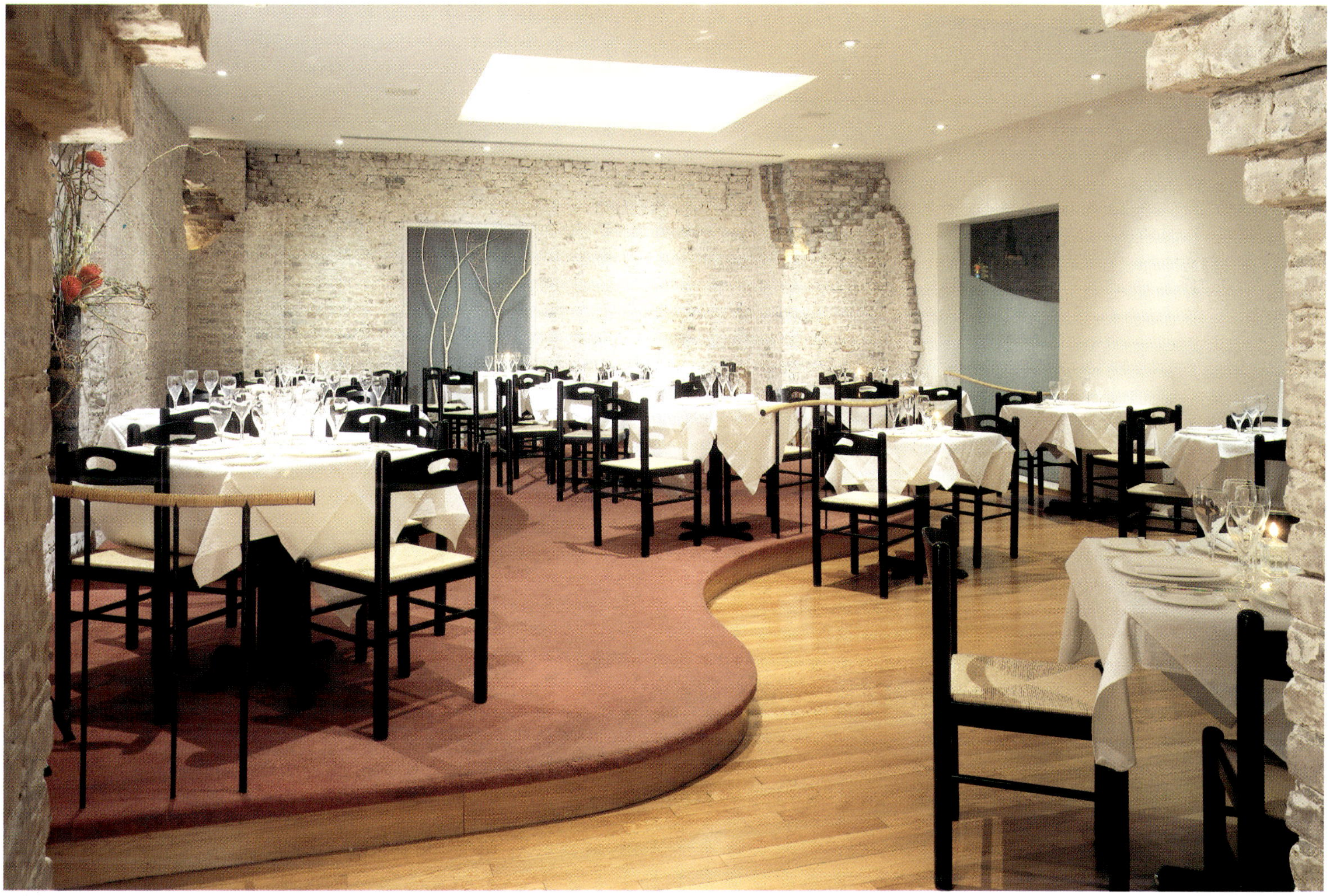

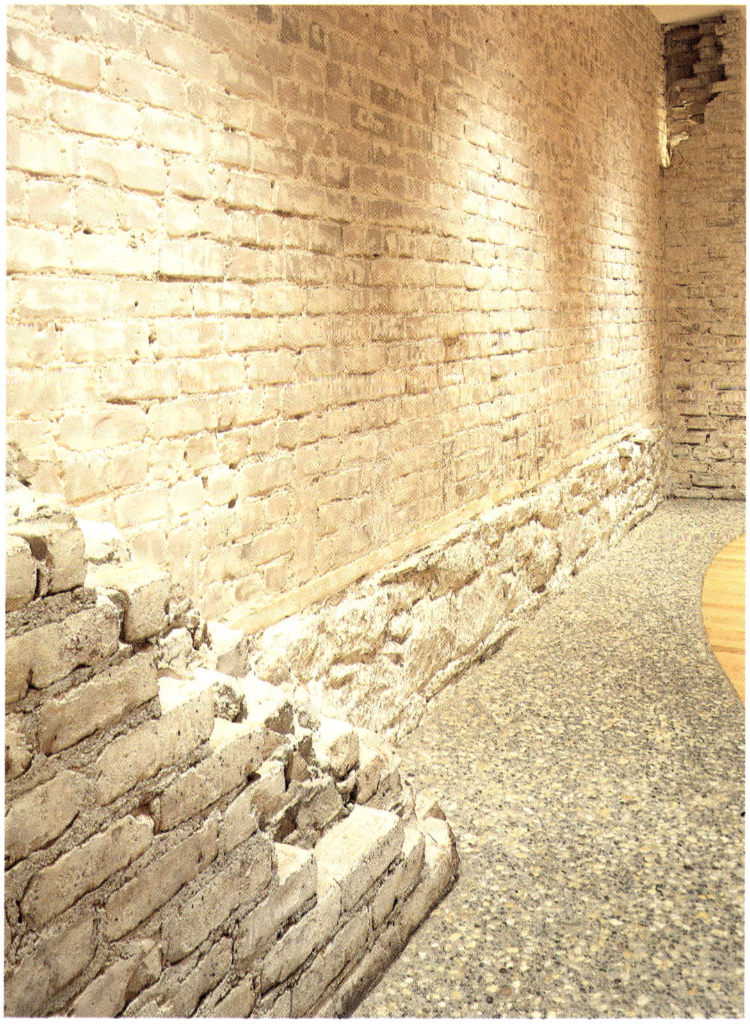

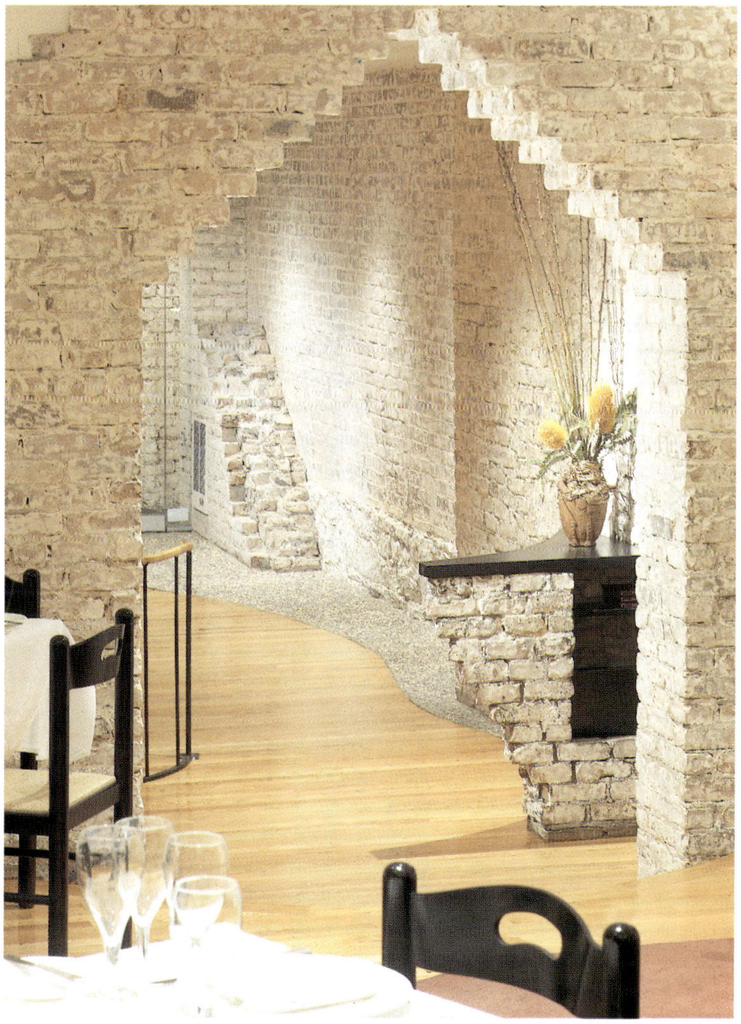

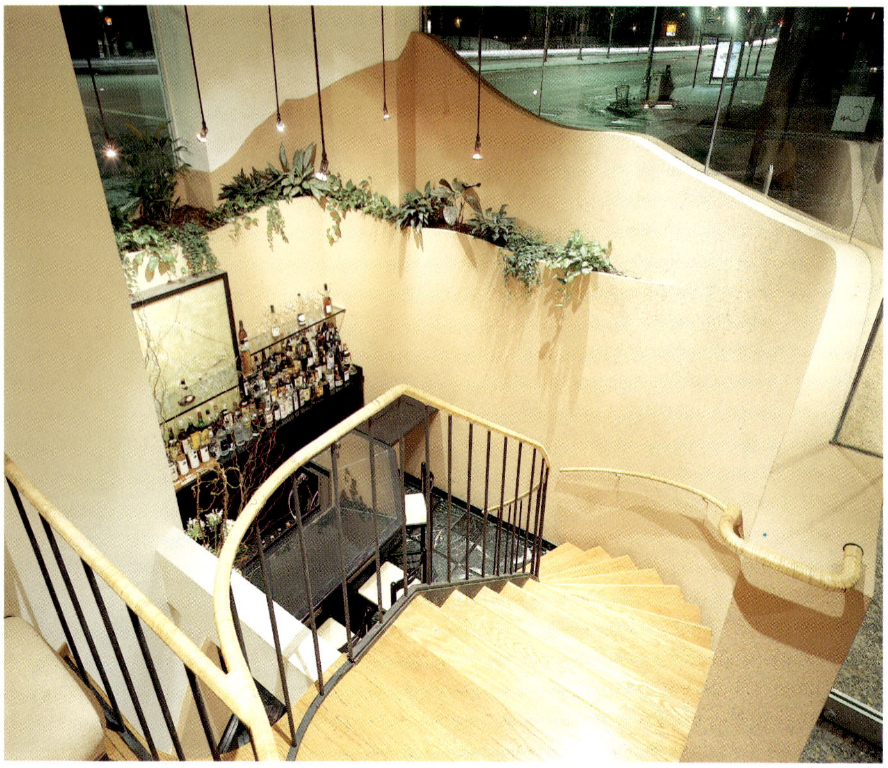

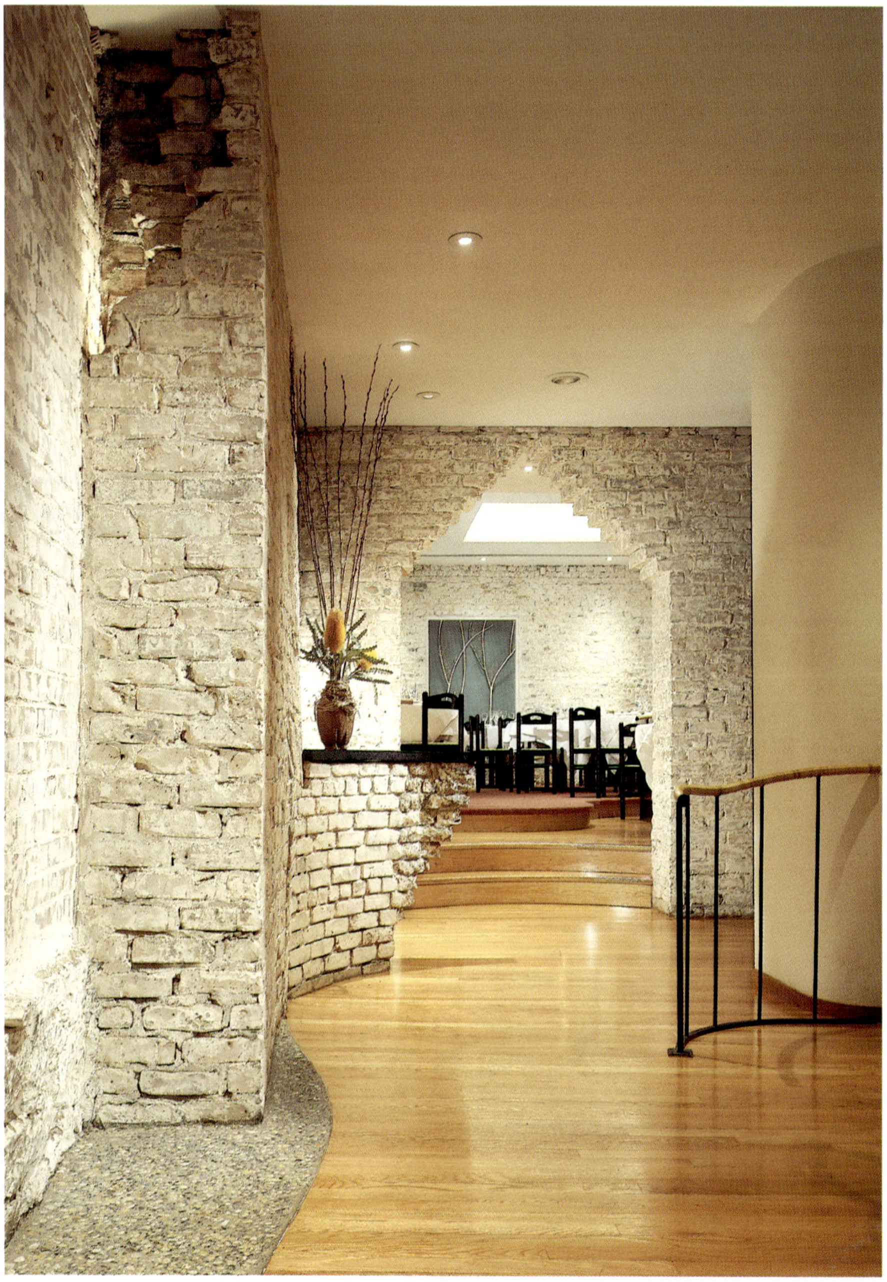

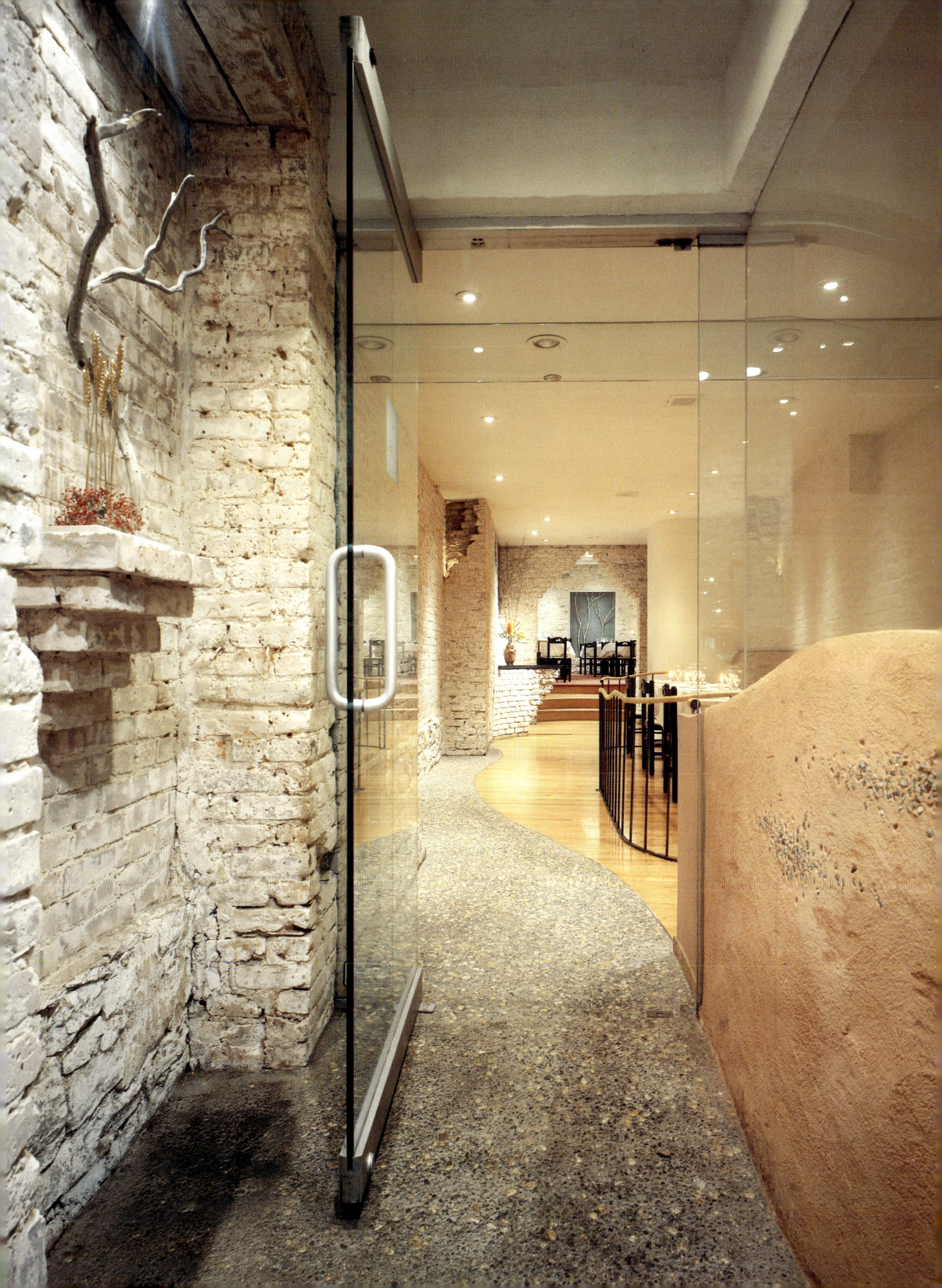

CHINA GRILL
Jeffrey Beers Architects. Miami South Beach, FL, USA, 1996

The theme explored by Jeffrey Beers in defining the complex architectural image of the China Grill – an extensive, one-story restaurant boasting a floorspace of some 900 square meters – is the clever espousal of European and Chinese cuisine. The two kitchens are open onto the dining room, allowing dinner guests an unabashed view of the chefs and their assistants at work; thus exposed, the kitchens themselves offer the visual framework around which the other spaces of the restaurant complex are judiciously arranged. Three self-sufficient bars, each with its own distinct design characteristics, a room devoted to the display of an eminent selection of wines, and a series of offices, are distributed through a large space divided into three dining areas marked off by a dais, each one with a wooden floor of a different design. These platforms cleverly dissemble the single-space effect by means of different room heights, with lowered ceilings that lend a strong sense of rhythm to the whole. The two main bars form a kind of central pivot around which the other spaces rotate in a medley of interior schemes: traditional circular bench-sofas in oriental fabrics arranged around a table; upholstered stools alongside cane chairs; cane barstools lining the cherry and onyx counter, with concealed lighting to bring out the natural patterns of the materials. The variety of furnishings and their solicitous arrangement, the wealth and juxtaposition of materials, the drapes, and the striking ceiling lamps in translucent material, all conspire to create a pleasing, well-balanced whole. The stone floor is inlaid with black and gold mosaics depicting scenes from the travels of Marco Polo, the fourteenth-century Venetian journeyman who first brought East and West together with his treks to China. Two curved partitions housing the telephone cabins screen off the entrance to the washrooms, contributing stylistically to the room's composition with their geometrical wooden frame set with parchment panels.

Un grande ristorante esteso su un unico livello per più di novecento metri quadrati dedicato all'incontro tra cucina europea e orientale; è questo il tema affrontato da Jeffrey Beers nel definire la complessa immagine architettonica del China Grill. Le due cucine sono aperte sulla sala in connessione con le zone operative retrostanti; le cucine 'in mostra' si configurano come elementi di riferimento principali attorno cui si dispongono gli altri calibrati spazi del ristorante. Tre bar indipendenti e dalle diverse soluzioni compositive, una sala dedicata all'esposizione dell'accurata selezione dei vini e una serie di uffici amministrativi sono distribuiti nel grande spazio suddiviso in tre zone pranzo disposte su ampie pedane costruite in differenti essenze lignee. Le pedane-balconate cancellano la dimensione uniforme originaria proponendo varie altezze che movimentano così l'intero locale anche grazie al gioco dei controsoffitti. I due bar principali disposti centralmente organizzano un percorso rotatorio che offre diverse soluzioni di arredo; dai tradizionali alti divanetti circolari con tavolo centrale rivestiti con diverse stoffe a motivi orientali, a sedute imbottite affiancate a poltroncine in rattan, lo stesso materiale impiegato per gli sgabelli del bar con bancone di ciliegio e onice, illuminato dal retro per valorizzarne le caratteristiche naturali. La varietà degli arredi e la loro studiata disposizione, la ricchezza e il confronto dei diversi materiali, le tende a drappeggio e le scenografiche lampade a guscio in tessuto traslucido appese al soffitto danno alla dimensione del locale una calibrata varietà compositiva. Nel pavimento in pietra sono riportati, in mosaico nero e oro, alcuni episodi del viaggio di Marco Polo, simbolo del ristorante in quanto unione tra Oriente e Occidente. Due alti paraventi in curva, in cui sono collocate le cabine telefoniche, schermano l'ingresso ai bagni proponendosi come forti riferimenti compositivi, scanditi da una struttura geometrica in legno e pergamena.

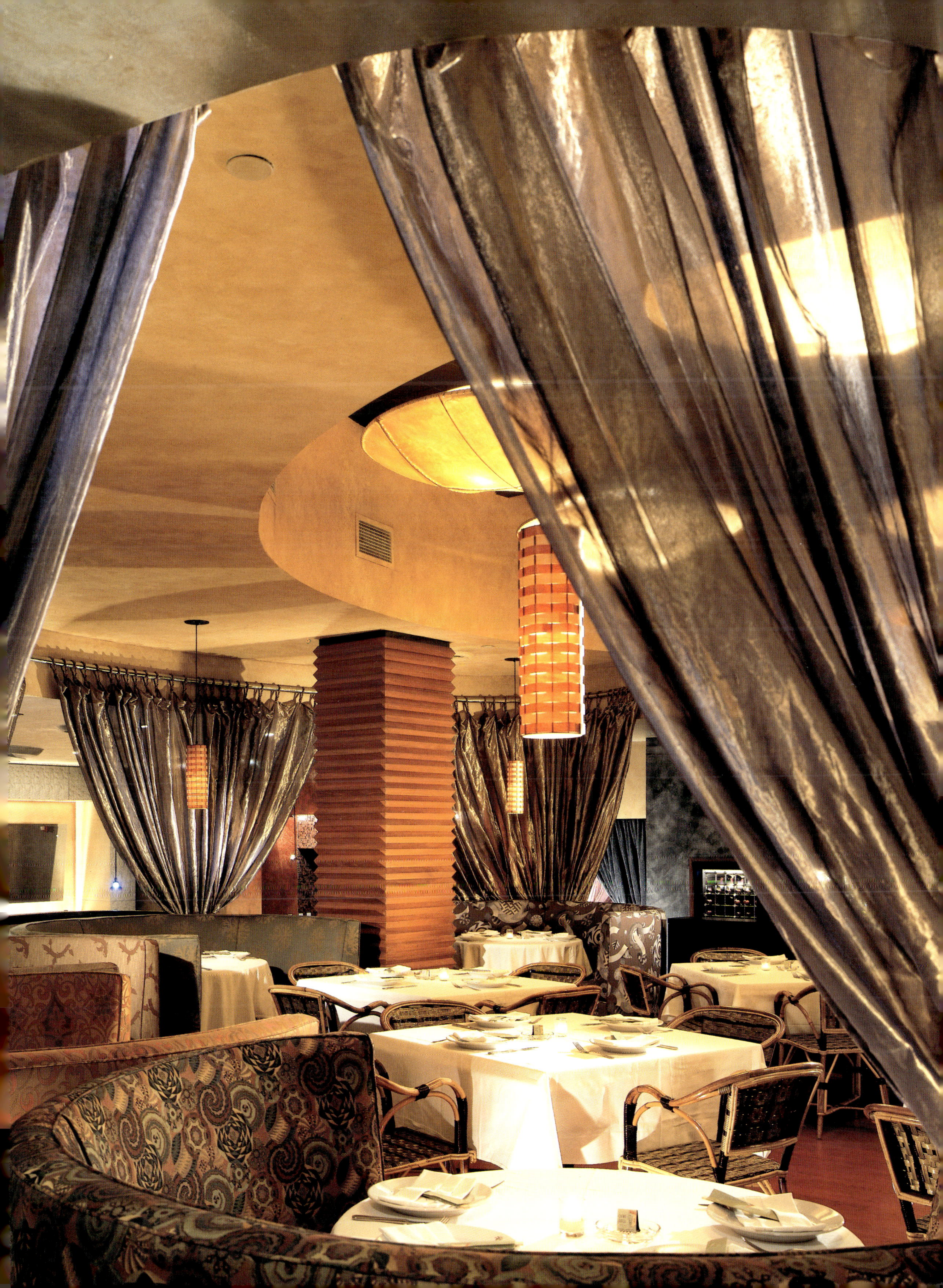

Ground floor / Piano terra

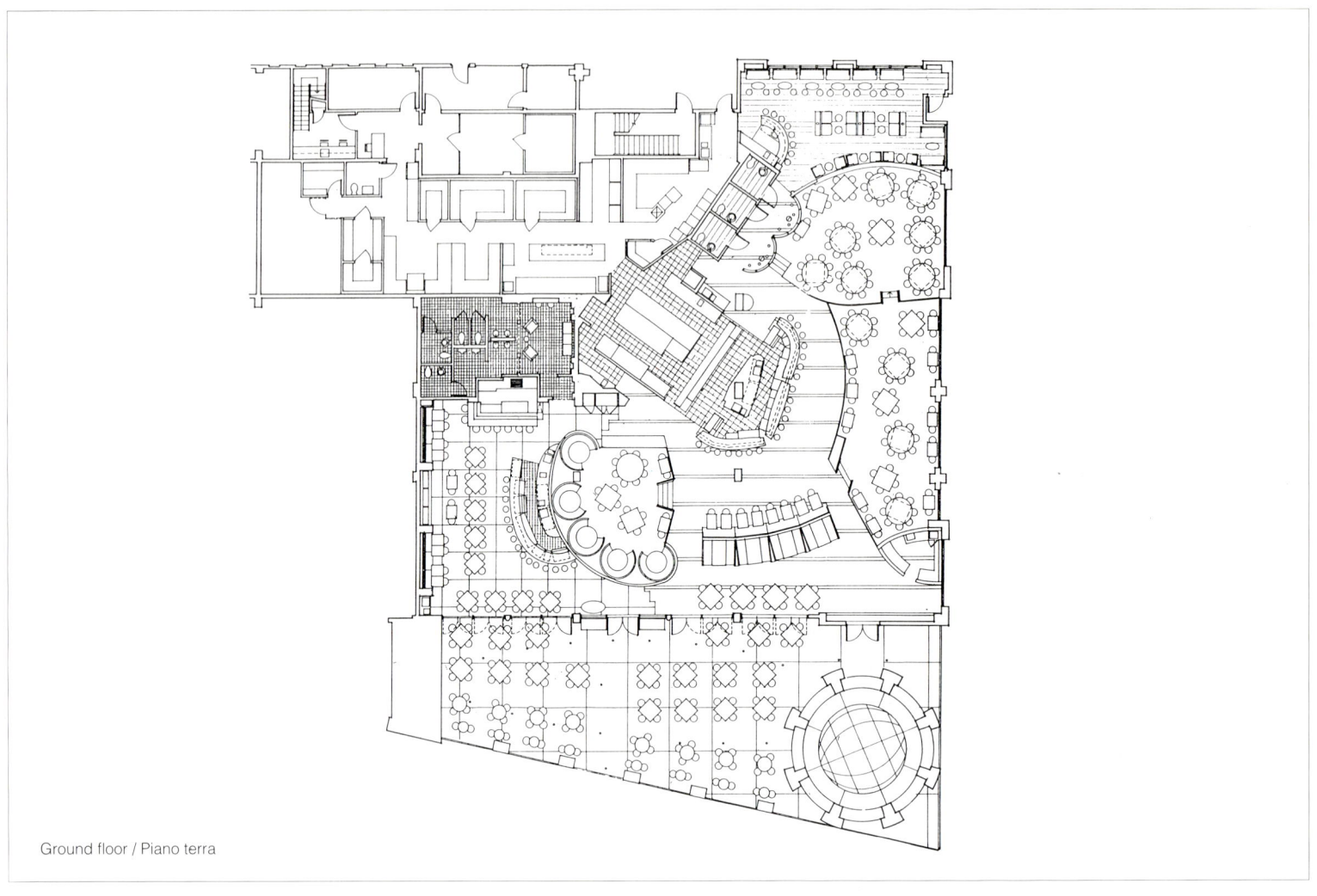

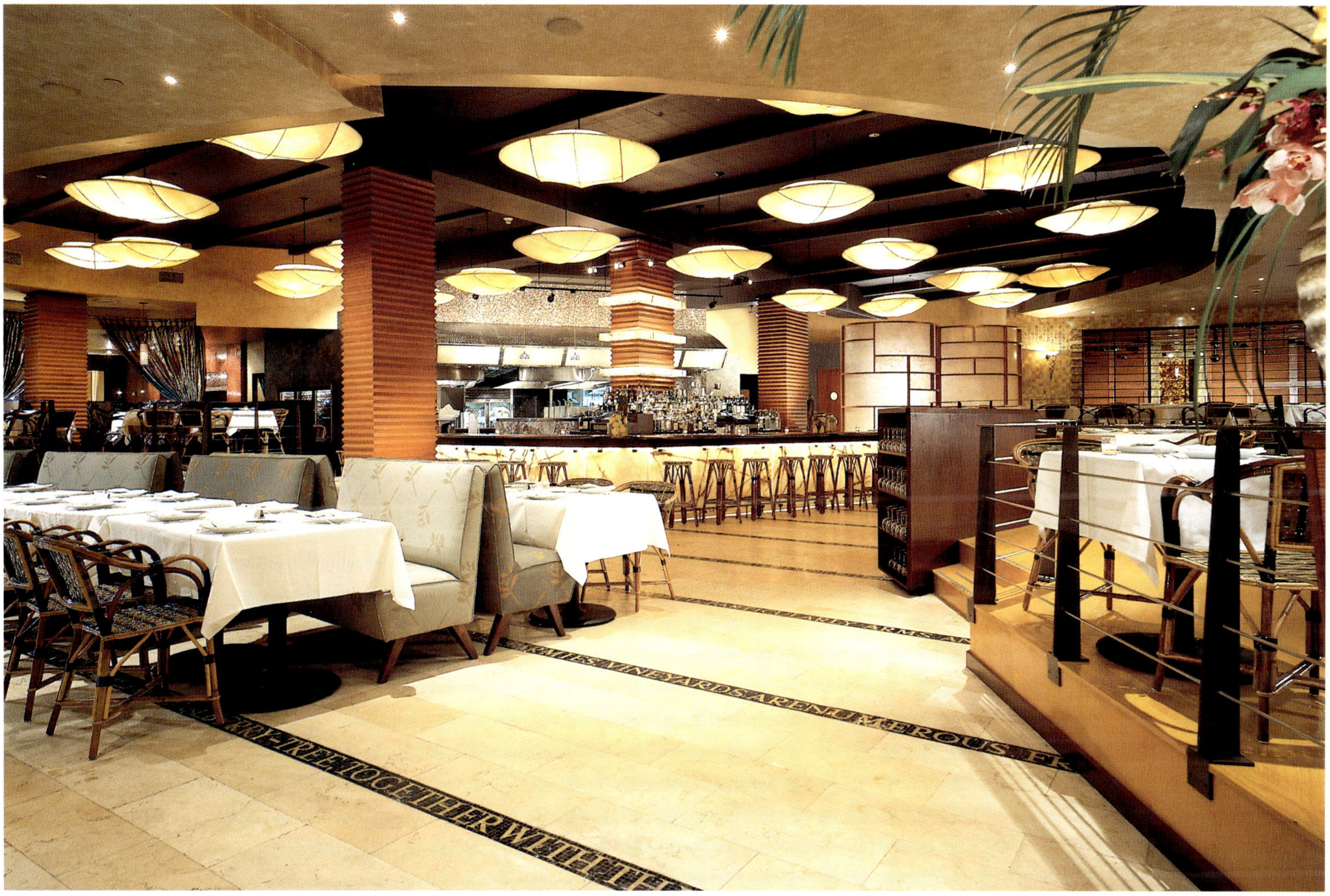

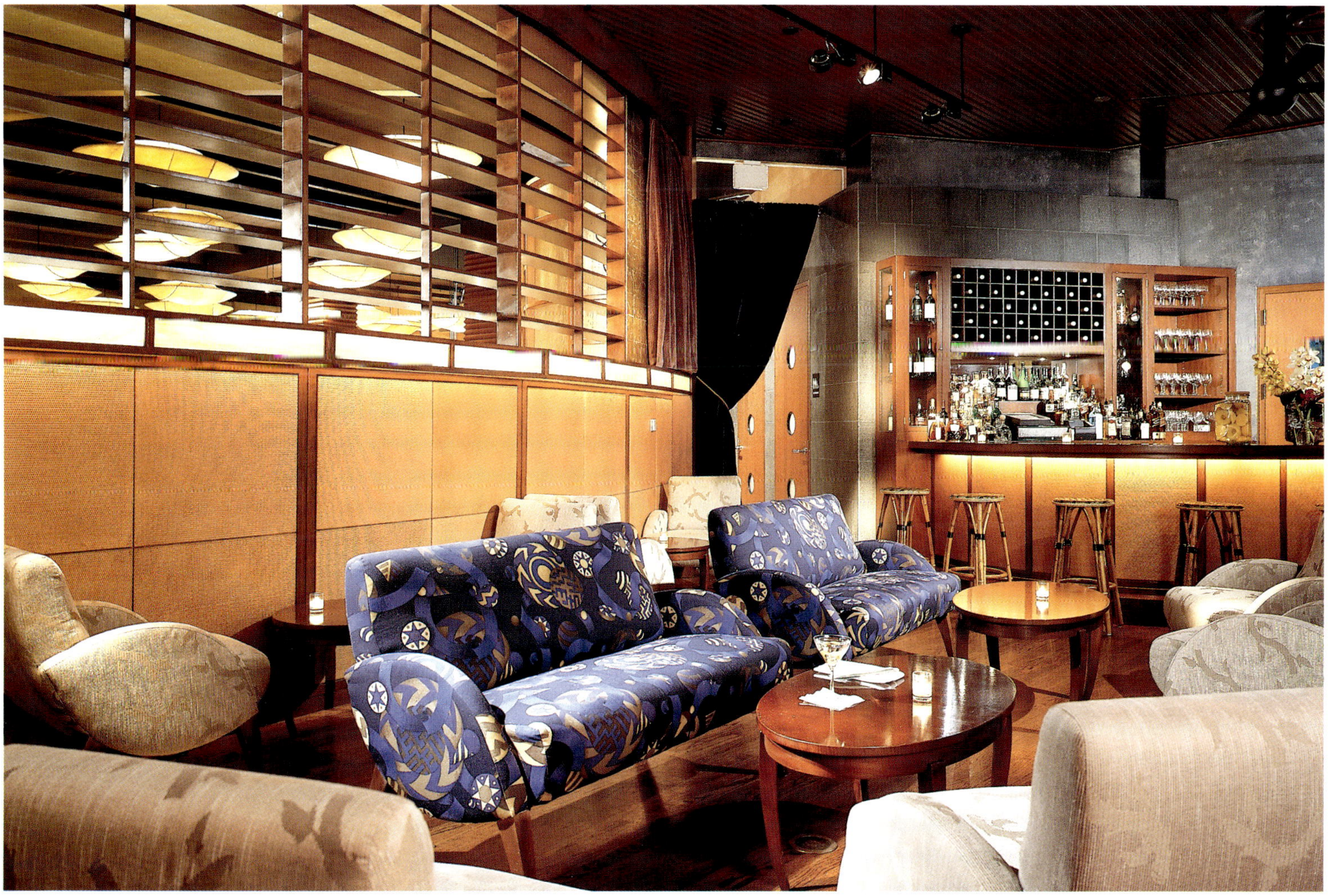

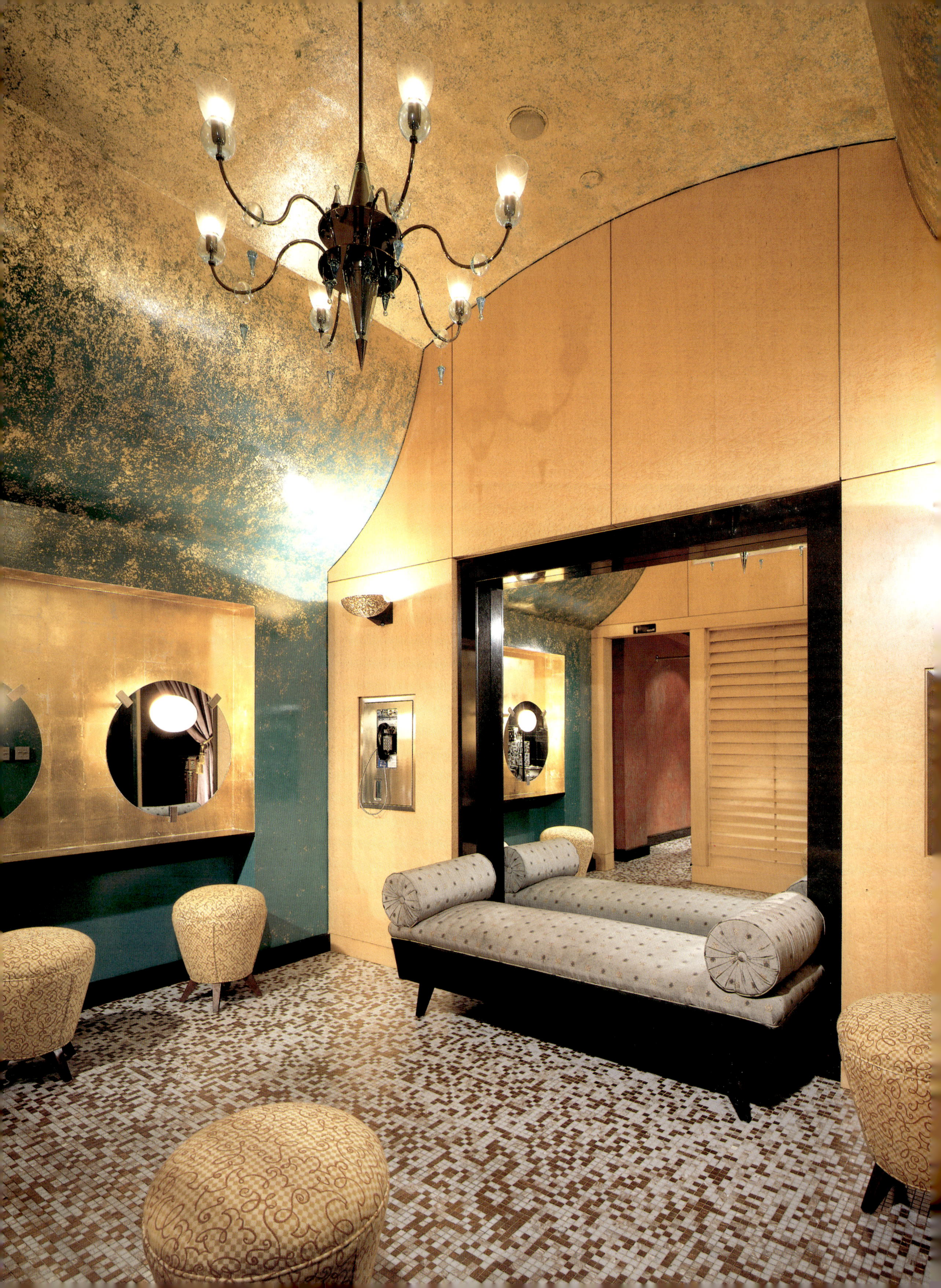

CHRISTER'S RESTAURANT
David Rockwell Architect. New York, NY, USA, 1993

The culinary specialty of this restaurant is its unusual cross between the Scandinavian and American cuisines, a peculiarity that David Rockwell took as his narrative point of reference for this set of rooms designed with a revival look that evokes the stunning fjord landscapes of northern Europe. The restaurant boasts a floors place of some 270 square meters, and is divided into two separate areas linked by a narrow corridor. The first room, accessed directly from the entrance foyer, contains the bar, several dining tables, and a corner adorned with a fixed sofa bench, which in both cases provide little alcove ideal for more private dinner engagements, devised to function independently from the main rooms. The Nordic accent that characterizes the décor entire restaurant is immediately noticed in the treatment of the walls of the first room, which comprises log cross-sections set in a close pattern. Wood is in evidence everywhere: in the weathered timber beams that split up the ceilings and house the recessed downlighters, in the bar counter, and in the access to the connecting corridor, which has been devised as a scaled-down covered bridge that leads to the restrooms and the two dining rooms. Wood is also used throughout for the plank flooring, and for the assorted seating – some slightly rustic in plain wood, others more lightweight and stained lively colors. The ceiling is clad in large scales of copper and studiously lit to give the effect of fish swimming near the water's surface in the gilded light of sundown. Further marine imagery is employed, this time three-dimensionally, be means of fish wall-lamps in glass and in the pattern on the blue parquet, which creates a sort of shimmering sea inhabited by multicolored fish in the second room. The central dining room is dominated by a large stone fireplace with wood fittings, overshadowed by a ceiling of rough trunk beams interlaced with a veil of pink fabric; this central space looks onto the second room, whose ceiling is configured with white sails among plain timber beams, and traditional Nordic wall-paneling composed of vertical laths stained a creamy color that contain a series of typical objects from northern Europe.

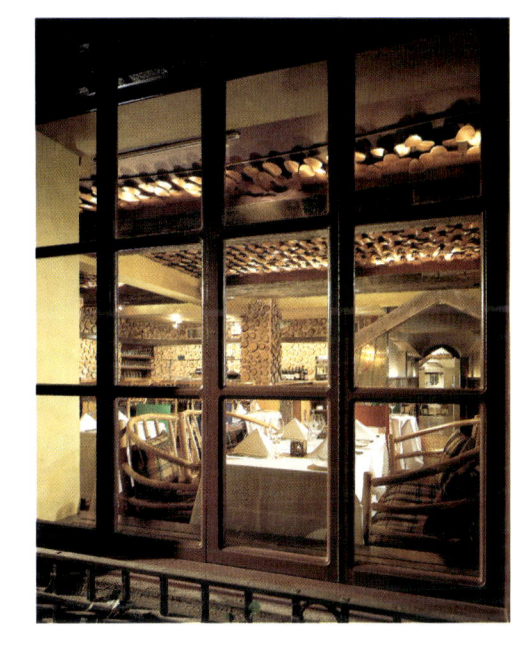

Il particolare carattere culinario del locale, un inconsueto incrocio tra cucina Scandinava e Americana, è stato assunto come tema narrativo di riferimento per ricostruire una serie di stanze e figure creativamente rivisitate che si potrebbero trovare nella regione dei fiordi nordici europei. Il ristorante, di circa 270 metri quadrati, è diviso in due locali uniti da uno stretto corridoio. Nella prima sala su cui si affaccia il vestibolo d'ingresso sono organizzati il bar, alcuni tavoli da pranzo e un angolo con divanetto fisso a muro che possono funzionare in modo indipendente dalle altre due sale da pranzo successive. L'atmosfera di 'fantasia nordica' che caratterizza tutti gli spazi si legge subito nel rivestimento parietale della prima sala composto da dischi di tronco d'albero incollati in stretta successione. Il legno appare come protagonista anche nelle travi invecchiate che spezzano il soffitto e nel banco bar e nell'accesso al corridoio, pensato come ponte coperto in scala ridotta, che conduce ai bagni e alle due sale da pranzo. Il legno è impiegato anche per il pavimento a doghe e per le sedie dall'aspetto rustico o di forma più essenziale e tinte a colori vivaci. Infine il soffitto è interamente ricoperto da una serie di grosse scaglie di rame che, illuminate con studiata regia, vogliono richiamare l'immagine di un branco di pesci che nuota a fior d'acqua nell'ora del tramonto. Altre figure marine sono proposte in chiave tridimensionale, come lampade-pesce in vetro a parete e come decorazione sul parquet blu, sorta di mare fisso nella sala da pranzo conclusiva, in cui nuotano dei pesci multicolore. La sala centrale si caratterizza per il grande camino in pietra con decorazione lignea e per la struttura che segna il soffitto, composta da massicci tronchi grezzi fra cui è collocato un leggero tessuto rosa. La sala da pranzo centrale è rivolta con ampie aperture verso quella conclusiva in cui troviamo, sotto un soffitto coperto da vele bianche sospese a travi in legno naturale, una tradizionale *boiserie* nordica, composta da listelli verticali tinteggiati color crema, che sostengono una serie di oggetti tipici dei paesi del Nord Europa.

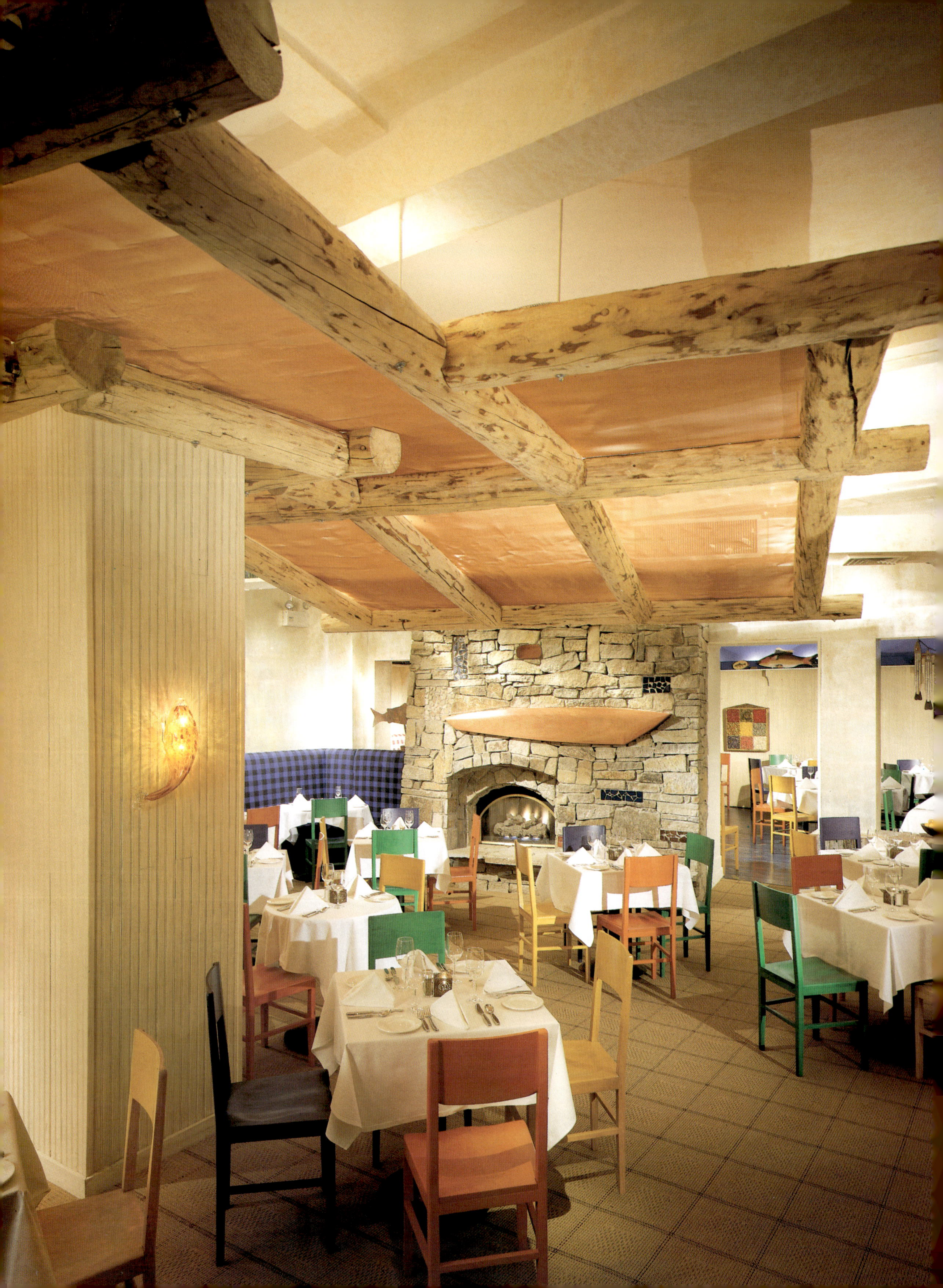

67

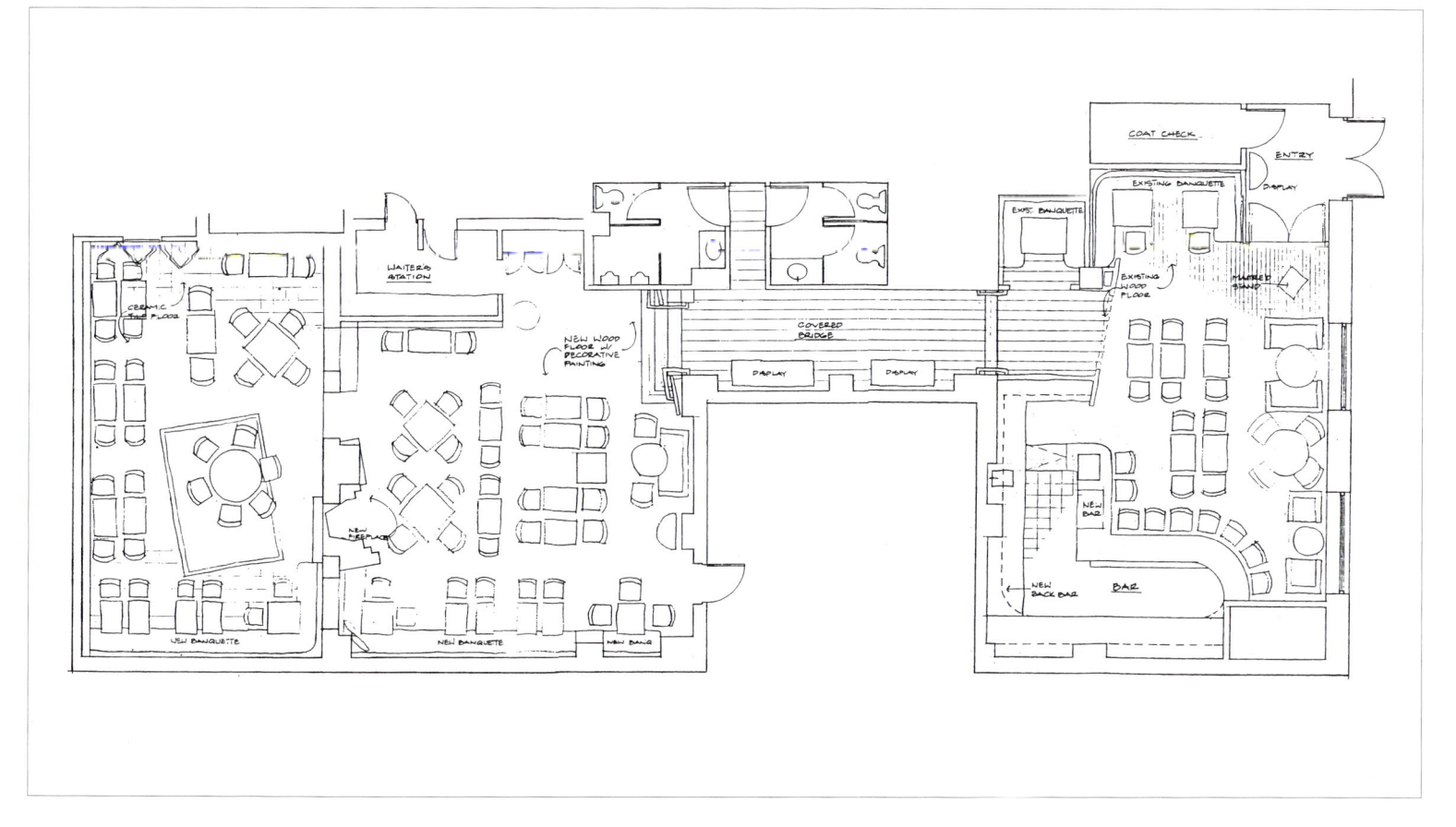

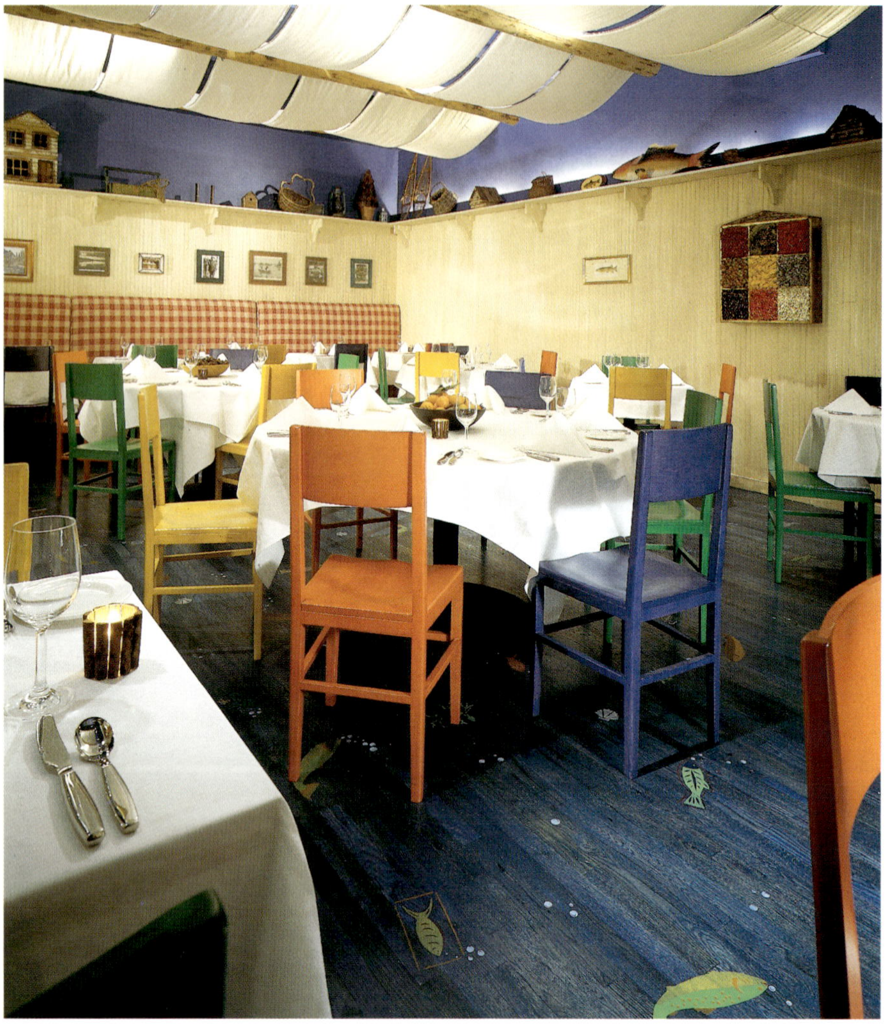

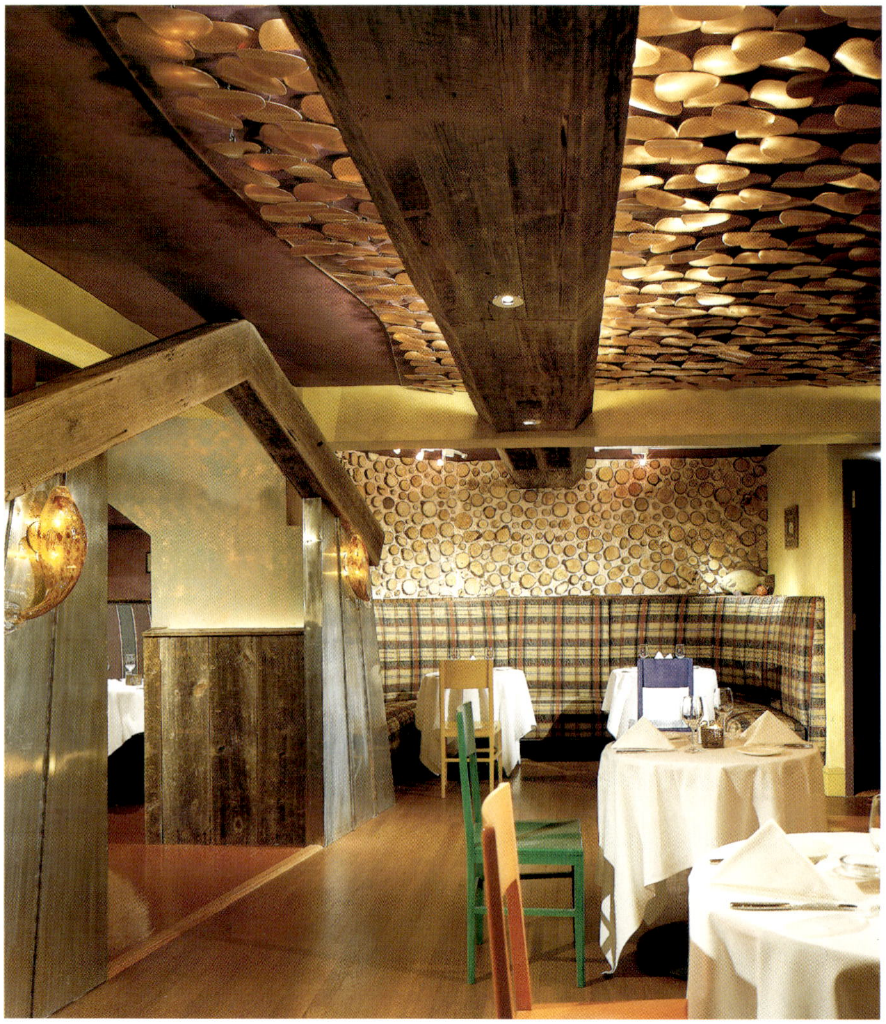

FISH DANCE RESTAURANT
Frank Gehry Architect. Kobe, JP, 1984

Boldly enthroned amid the chaotic port landscape of Kobe, Japan, in which industrial buildings jostle fitfully with shipyards, cranes, and traffic streaming over a busy urban flyover, the Fish Dance restaurant provides a kind of landing-stage preluding the Inland Sea Public Park, and an unmistakable visual landmark visible from all over. The building is a sculpture composed of three distinct bodies that have been linked with the Los Angeles architect's hallmark stringency: a giant carp in metal mesh stands on its tail offering a striking symbol for the Japanese cuisine tradition and boldly marking the restaurant's site amid the urban fabric (much as the American burger houses advertise their presence along the freeways). The fish-shaped building is flanked by a construction in blue corrugated metal on a trapezoid plan that is reminiscent of a suburban factory shed but cleverly snubs this functional banality by means of large irregular windows that allow light into the interior, and by the glazed tower with a metal framework that breaks the even profile of the roof and gives extension to the building's perimeter. The tower preludes the upward thrust of the large copper-clad spiral that houses the bar, providing a further sculptural mass alongside the huge fish-symbol. The logo in neon is held up by a wooden trellis that poses as a stylized tree of sorts. Inside, the plants and structures are left exposed to view, thereby disclosing the structural features and unveiling the application of simple materials of the kind normally employed for industrial buildings. The full-height open space comprises a mezzanine with kitchens and a suspended room for the Japanese-style grill (*teppan-yaki*), while at the base of the copper spiral lies the bar space. The polished concrete floor gives an extra factory-type feel to the place, a theme that is endorsed by the fixtures and fittings.

Calato con decisione nel caotico paesaggio portuale di Kobe, dove si affiancano in un casuale e affascinante gioco di sovrapposizione edifici industriali, cantieri navali, gru e un'autostrada urbana a doppio livello sovrapposto, il Fish Dance Restaurant si pone come avamposto dell'Inland Sea Public Park e come forte e inequivocabile segno urbano. L'edificio-scultura si compone di tre oggetti distinti e collegati tra loro secondo la stridente sintesi architettonica del noto architetto angeleno. Una grande carpa in rete metallica, posta con la testa all'insù, rivisita una figura simbolo della tradizione giapponese segnalando nel contesto urbano la presenza del ristorante (secondo la tradizione americana delle costruzioni a forma di hamburger, di ciambella e di caffettiera che venivano costruite lungo le *freeways* come sorta di efficaci e immediate architetture pubblicitarie). Al grande pesce si affianca una costruzione in lamiera ondulata azzurra di pianta trapezoidale che ricorda nel materiale gli edifici industriali limitrofi, ma che allo stesso tempo ne nega la banalità funzionale con il disegno delle grandi aperture irregolari che illuminano lo spazio interno e con la torre in vetro dalla struttura metallica che spezza il profilo regolare della copertura e amplifica il profilo perimetrale. La torre anticipa la verticalità della grande spirale rivestita in rame che contiene il bar, proponendosi come ulteriore segno scultoreo a fianco del pesce-simbolo. Il logo al neon è sostenuto da un traliccio ligneo che si propone come stilizzato albero artificiale. Nell'interno impianti e strutture sono lasciati a vista, denunciando il carattere della costruzione senza nascondere il corretto impiego di materiali semplici, in genere usati per edifici industriali. Lo spazio unitario a tutt'altezza ospita un soppalco con la cucina e una sala sospesa per il grill giapponese (teppan-yaki), mentre nella base della spirale in rame è organizzato lo spazio bar. Il pavimento di cemento lisciato sottolinea il carattere 'industriale' della costruzione in sintonia con la semplicità degli arredi.

Sketch

First floor / Primo piano

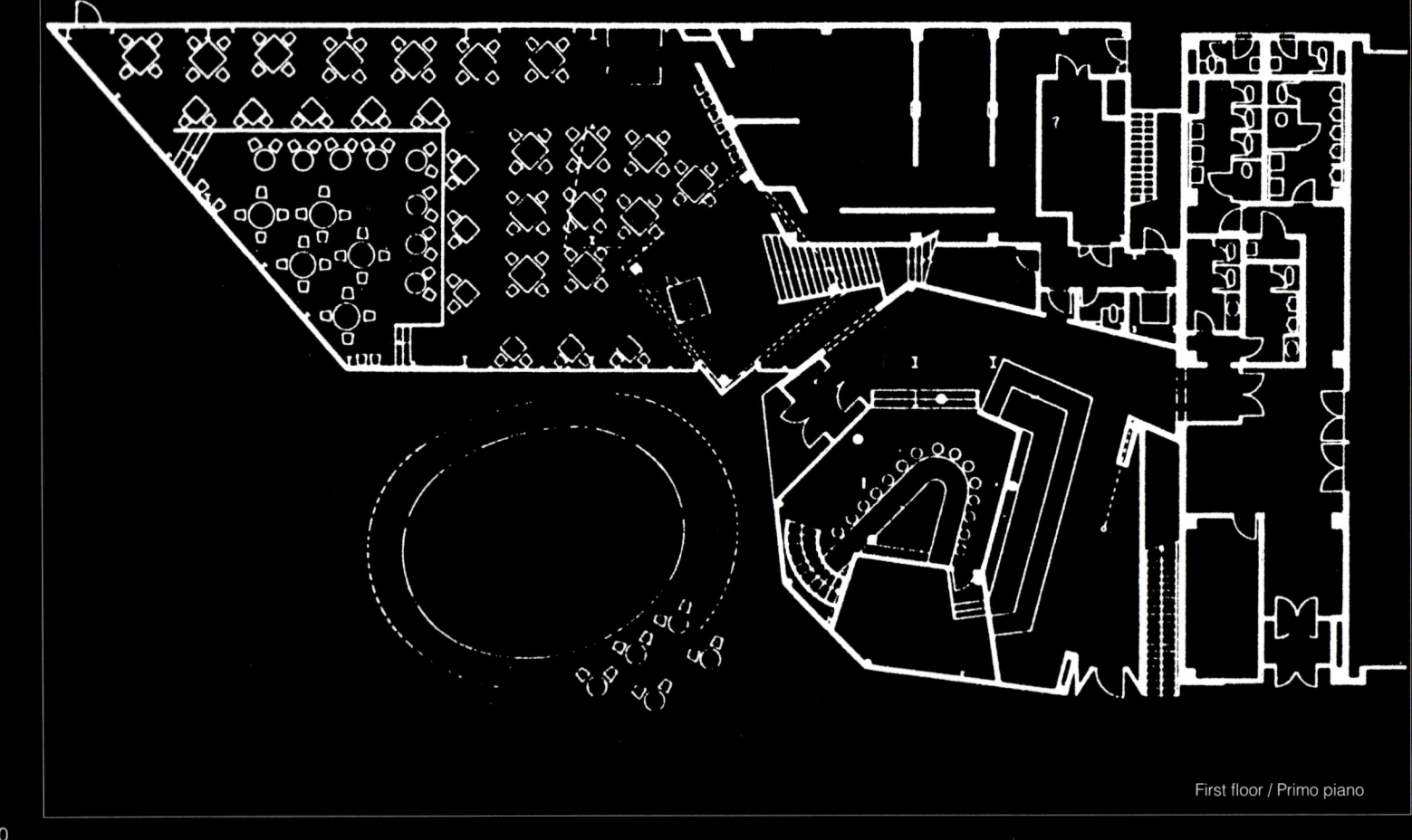

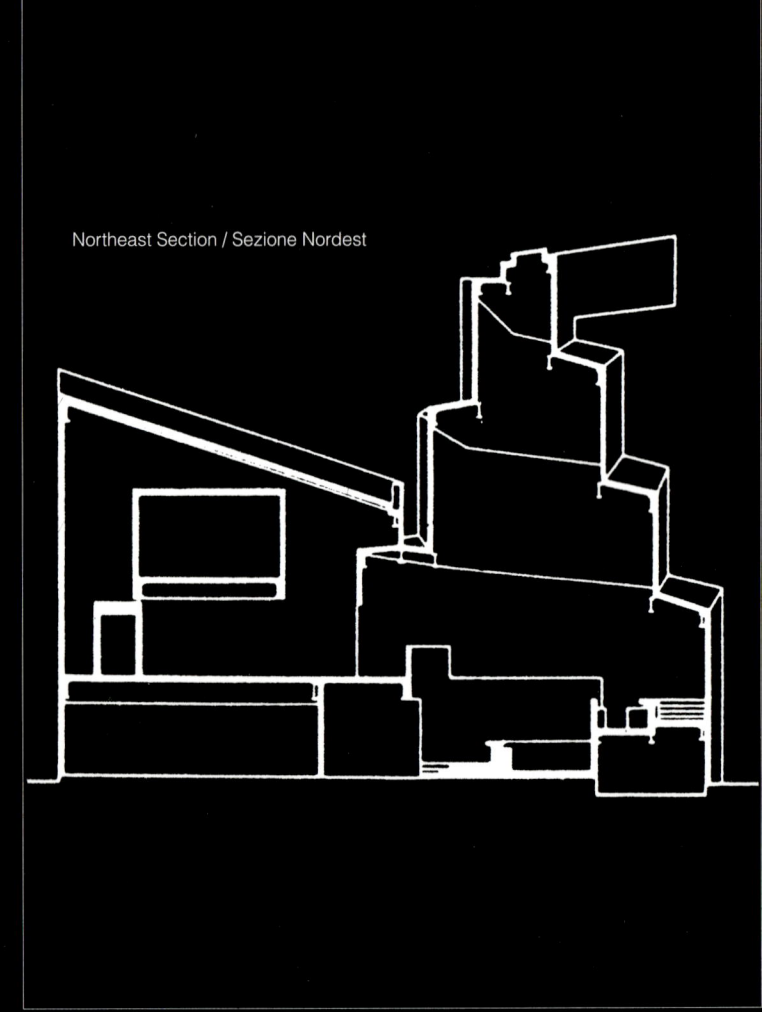

Northeast Section / Sezione Nordest

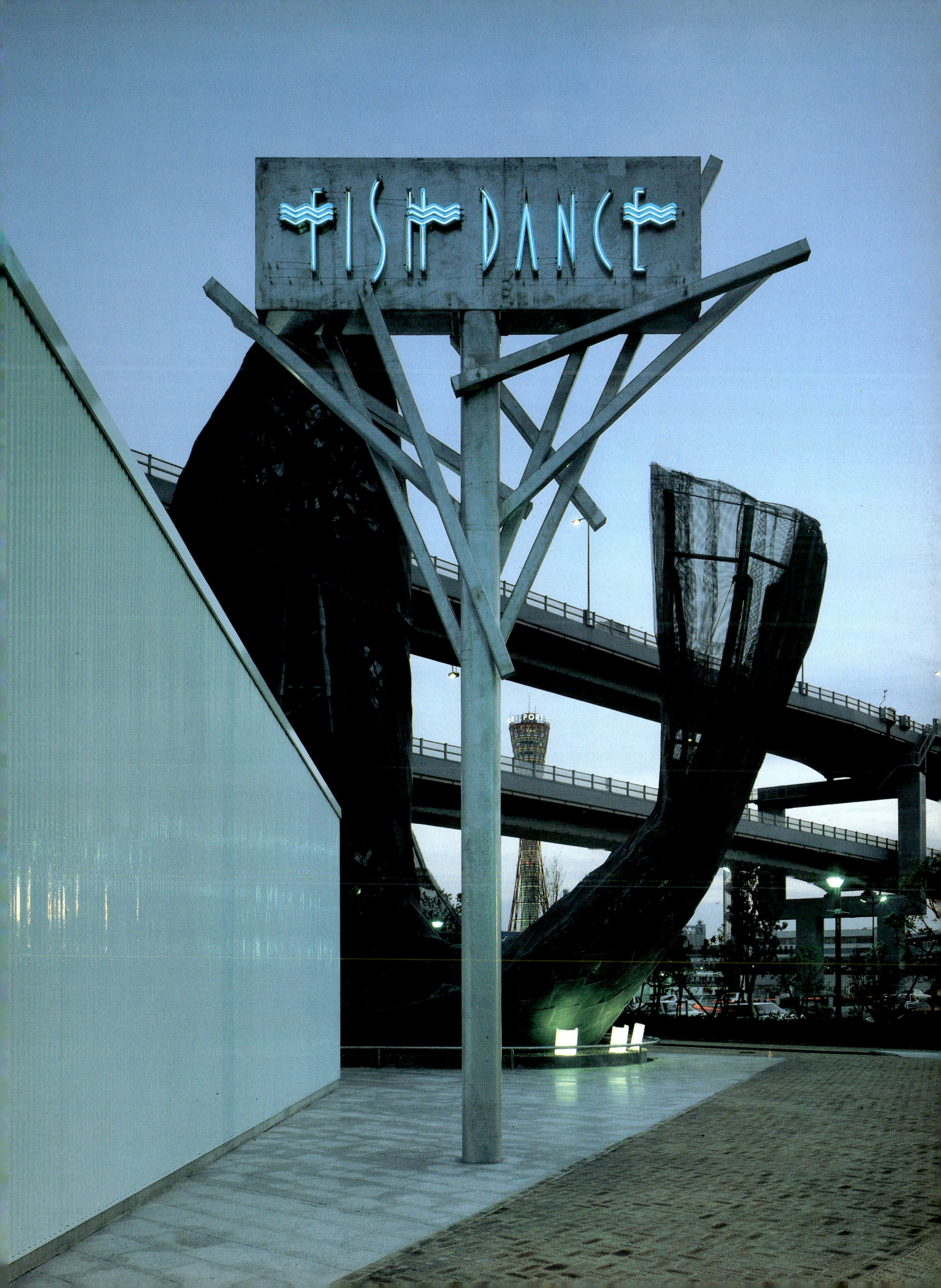
FISH DANCE

72

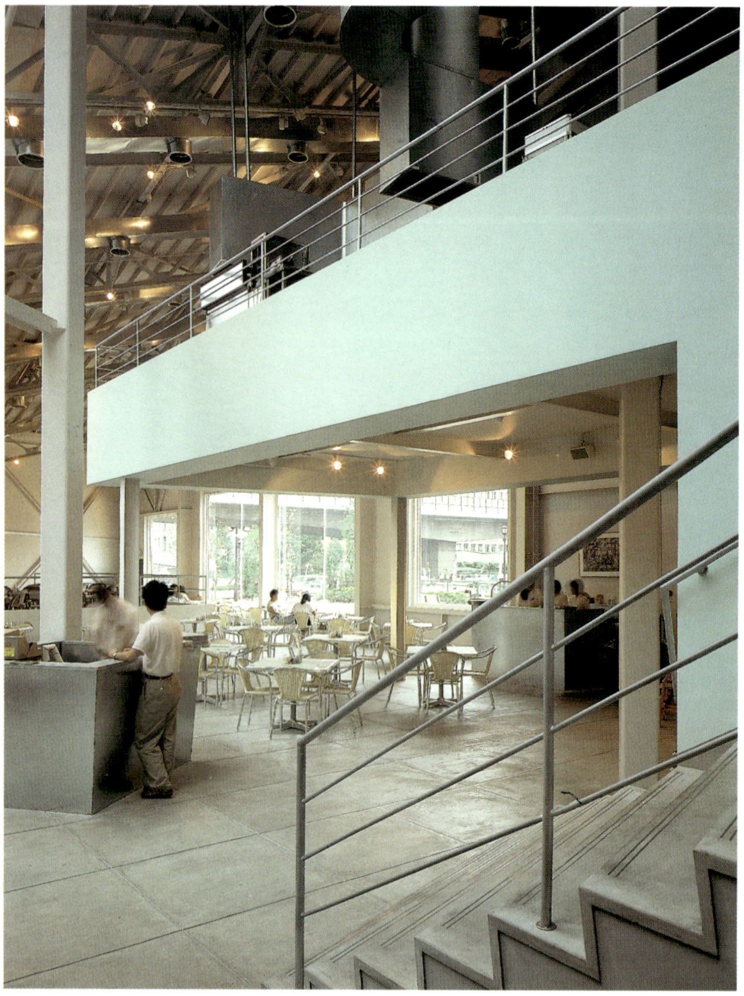

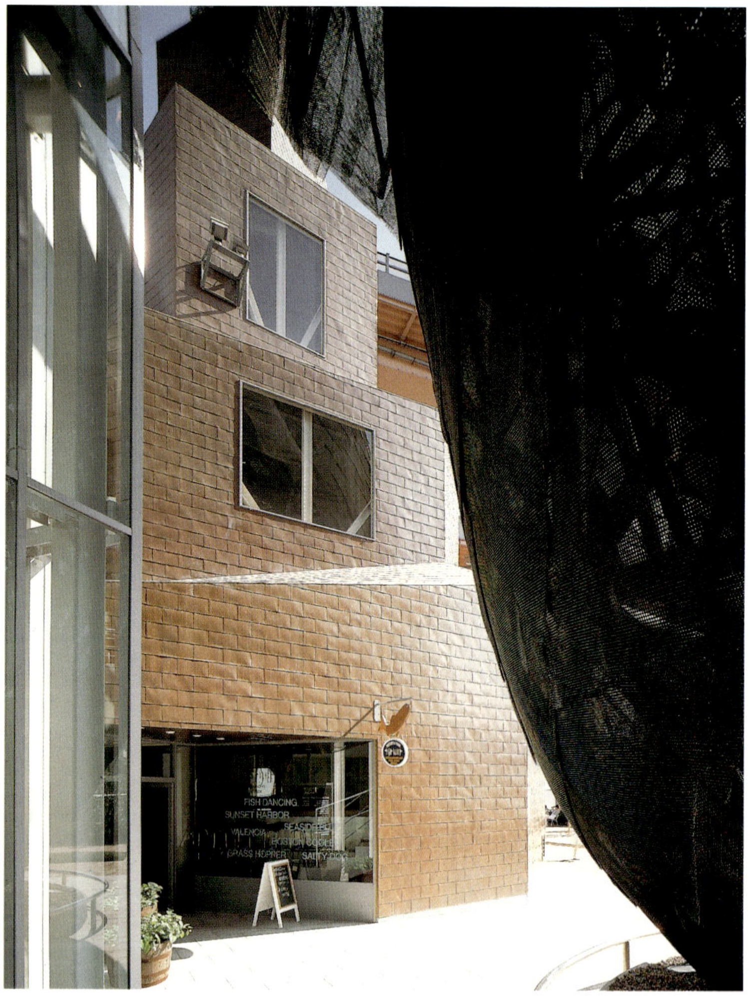

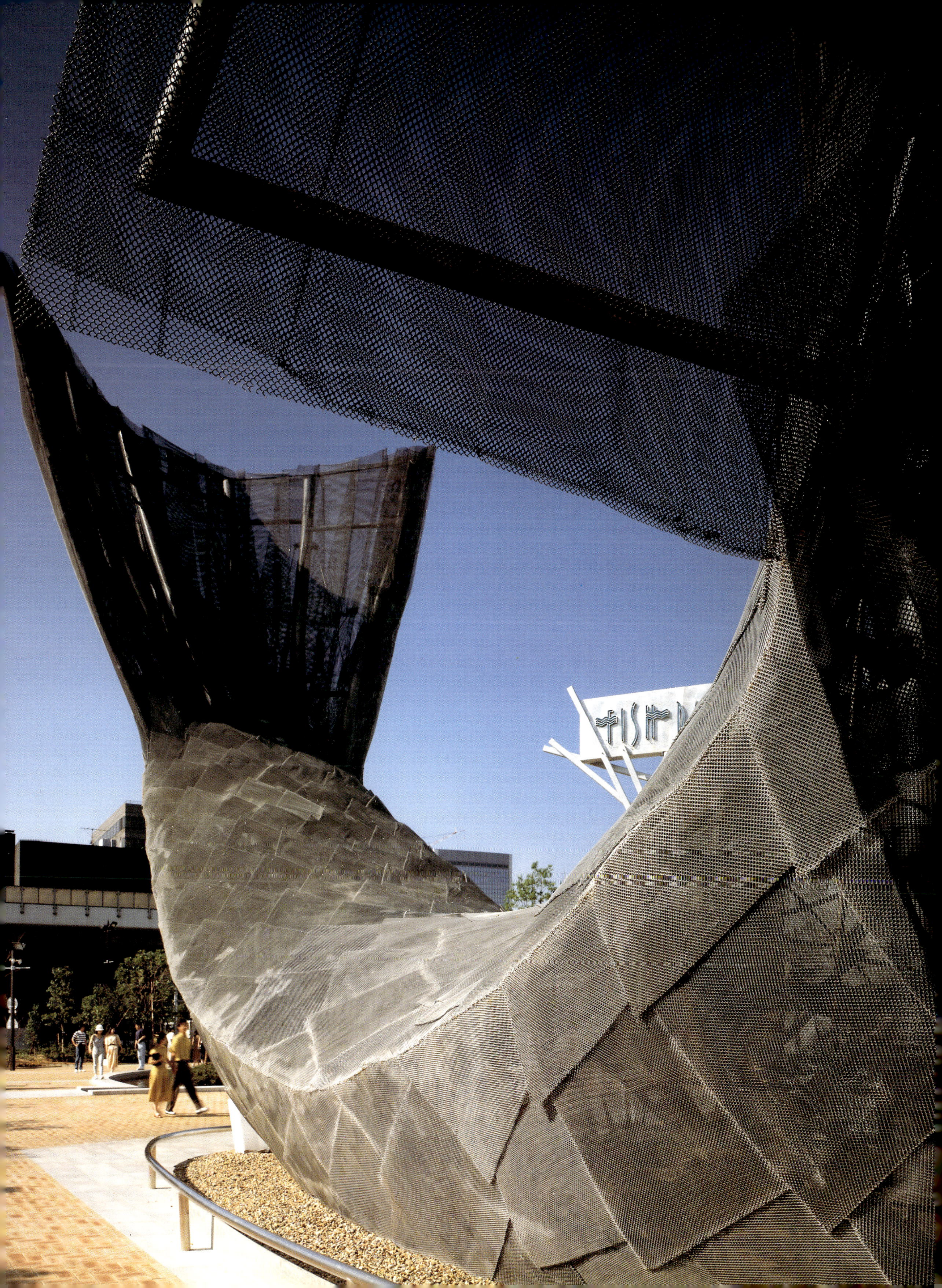
FISH

74

75

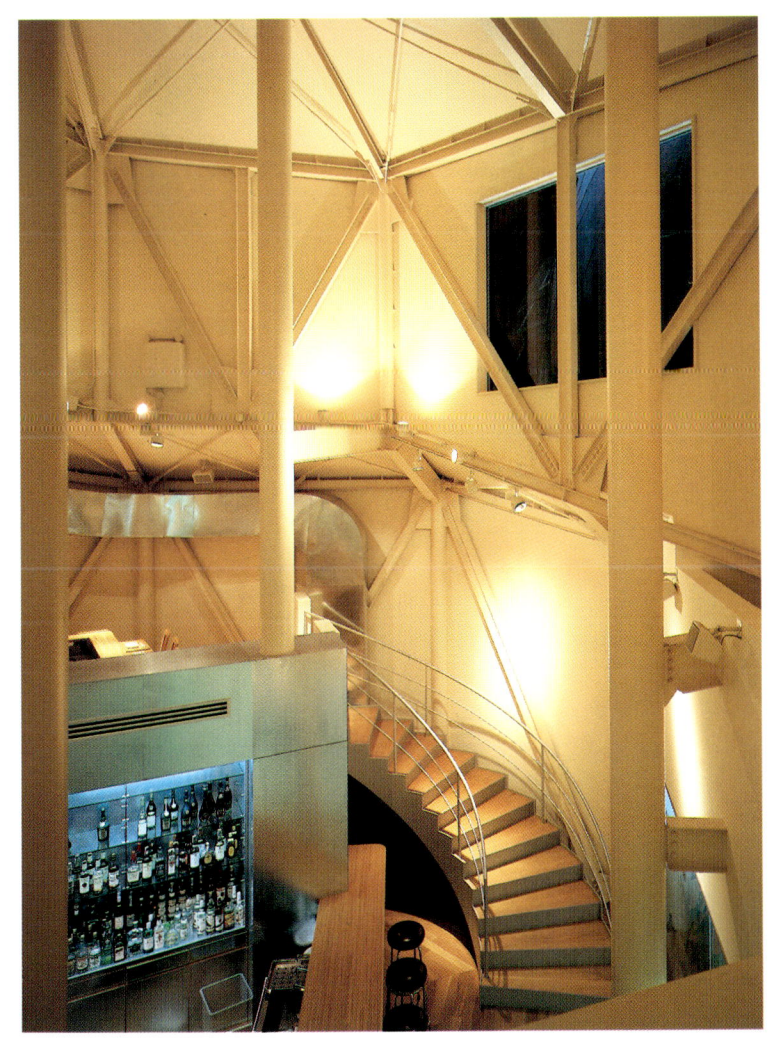

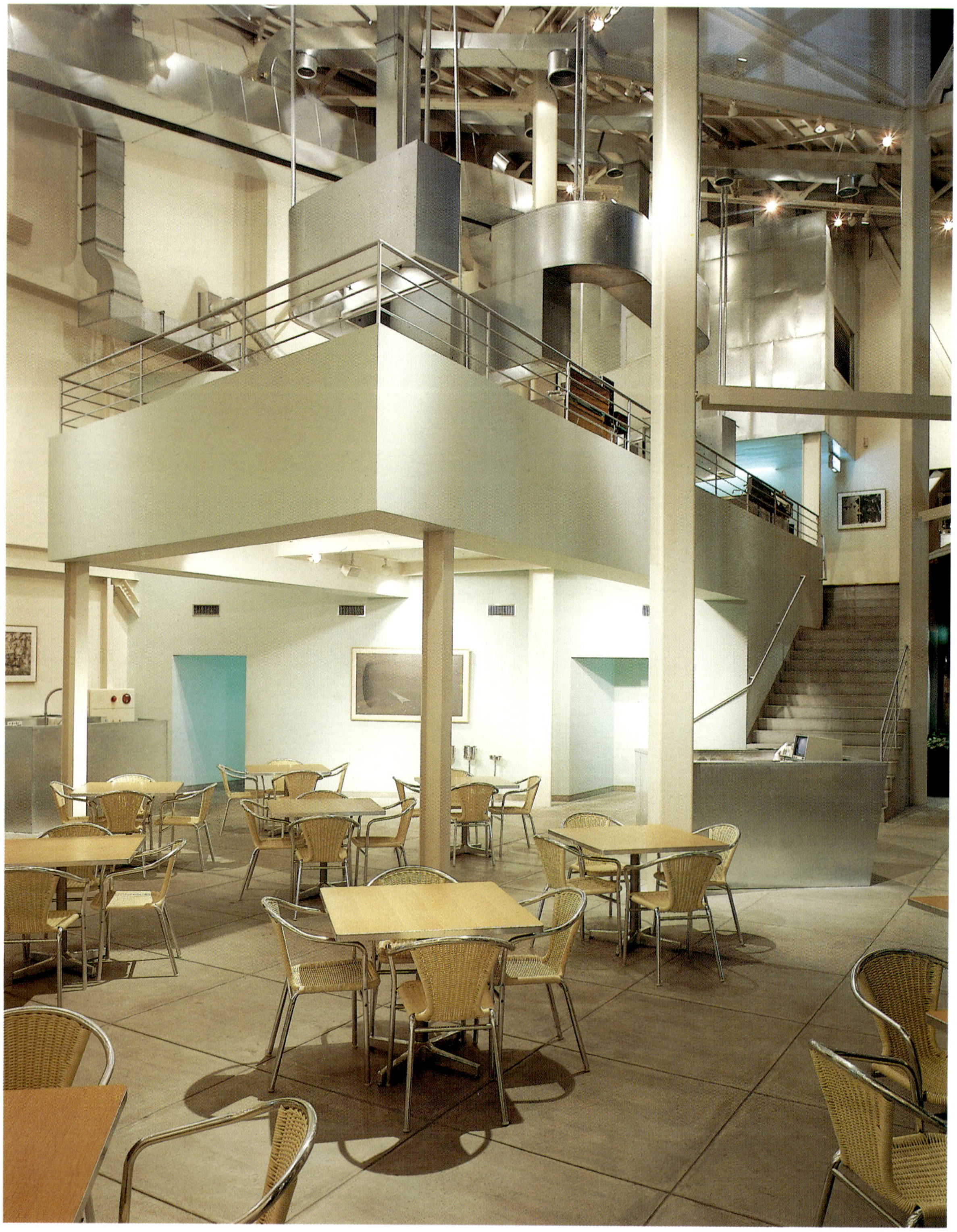

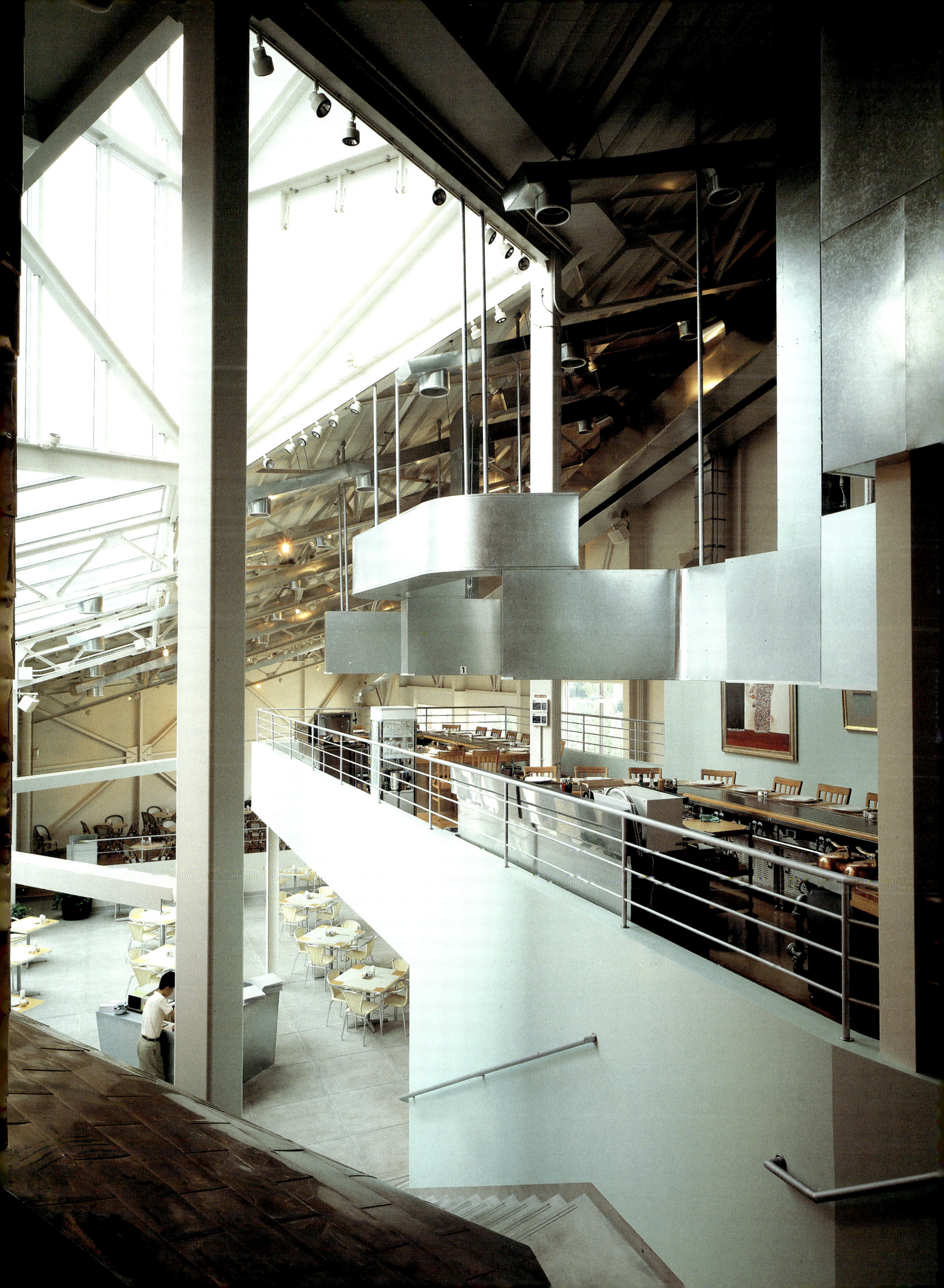

MARKET AT NEWPORT RESTAURANT
Turett Collaborative Architects. New York, NY, USA, 1995

An elegant and studiously modern self-service eatery distributed over a floorspace of some two thousand square meters, the Market at Newport is one of those rare examples of interior design in which composition and use of materials are employed to define what would normally be resolved at functional level alone. The lot into which the restaurant has been slotted is a rectangular space has three blind walls and a frontage with a strip window that extends beyond the perimeter in a sweeping semicircle that affords a double-height view right down onto the ground-floor lobby. Arranged along the glazed frontage is an entrance saloon which looks onto the large dining room, though remains independent from it. One bar counter faces inward toward the dining hall; another two command the entrance lobby, one of which follows the curve of the semicircle of the aperture giving onto the lobby, rather like a functional balcony. The entrance to the self-service area of the diner is fitted with revolving subway-style barriers, as is the exit. The space is shared out between the kitchens, the food counter, and the actually eating area. A zigzag wall decorated with rough plaster in a lively shade of blue separates the self-service counter from the seating area; the pillars are clad in panels of wood stained bright yellow or left plain, set in a haphazard pattern thereby transforming the simple structural pillars into sculptural visual devices. A stone floor and bright red counters, together with the steel mesh ceiling, characterize the self-service area, with video screens announcing the specialty of the day. The dining area is furnished with blue wooden chairs, steel-topped tables, and sofas fixed along the wall, which is decorated with a mural. The lowered ceiling comprises four projecting discs of aluminum from which simple lamps hang, illuminating the entire room, thereby giving a coherent visual framework for the whole, enlivened by a bold color scheme.

Raffinato e moderno self-service, distribuito su una superficie di circa duemila metri quadrati, il Market at Newport appare come raro esempio di riferimento in cui attenzioni compositive e materiche sono chiamate a definire un locale che rientra in questa tipologia, in genere affrontata e risolta solamente a livello funzionale. Lo spazio disponibile, di forma rettangolare regolare, è caratterizzato da tre lati senza aperture e dalla parete frontale segnata da una vetrata continua che si estende oltre il perimetro, disegnando una semicirconferenza in aggetto che propone uno spazio a doppia altezza affacciato sulla lobby del piano terreno. Lungo la facciata vetrata è stata organizzata la zona bar-ingresso rivolta verso la grande sala da pranzo, ma nello stesso tempo da essa indipendente. Un banco bar è affacciato verso l'interno della sala mentre la fascia d'ingresso ne accoglie altri due, uno dei quali segue il perimetro semicircolare del foro aperto sulla lobby, configurandosi come riuscita balconata attrezzata. L'ingresso al self-service avviene attraversando i girelli meccanizzati tipo metropolitana, che sono posizionati anche all'uscita. Lo spazio è suddiviso tra cucina, zona dove poter scegliere le pietanze e sala da pranzo. Una parete a zig-zag, decorata a stucco spatolato di un vivace colore azzurro, separa la zona dei cibi dalla sala dove consumarli, mentre i pilastri sono rivestiti con pannelli di legno tinto giallo acceso e di essenza naturale scura, posati in modo irregolare per trasformare in presenze plastiche dei semplici sostegni strutturali. Una pavimentazione di pietra caratterizza, insieme ai banconi rosso acceso e al controsoffitto di rete di acciaio, la zona self-service, con video che annunciano le pietanze del giorno. La sala da pranzo è arredata con sedie in legno blu, tavolini dal piano di acciaio e divanetti fissati lungo la parete decorata con un murale. Un controsoffitto formato da grandi dischi bombati di alluminio da cui discendono semplici lampadine copre tutta la sala, caratterizzandone fortemente la figura complessiva, vivacizzata dai forti colori scelti nel progetto.

NEWPORT THE MARKE

Floor plan / Pianta piano terra

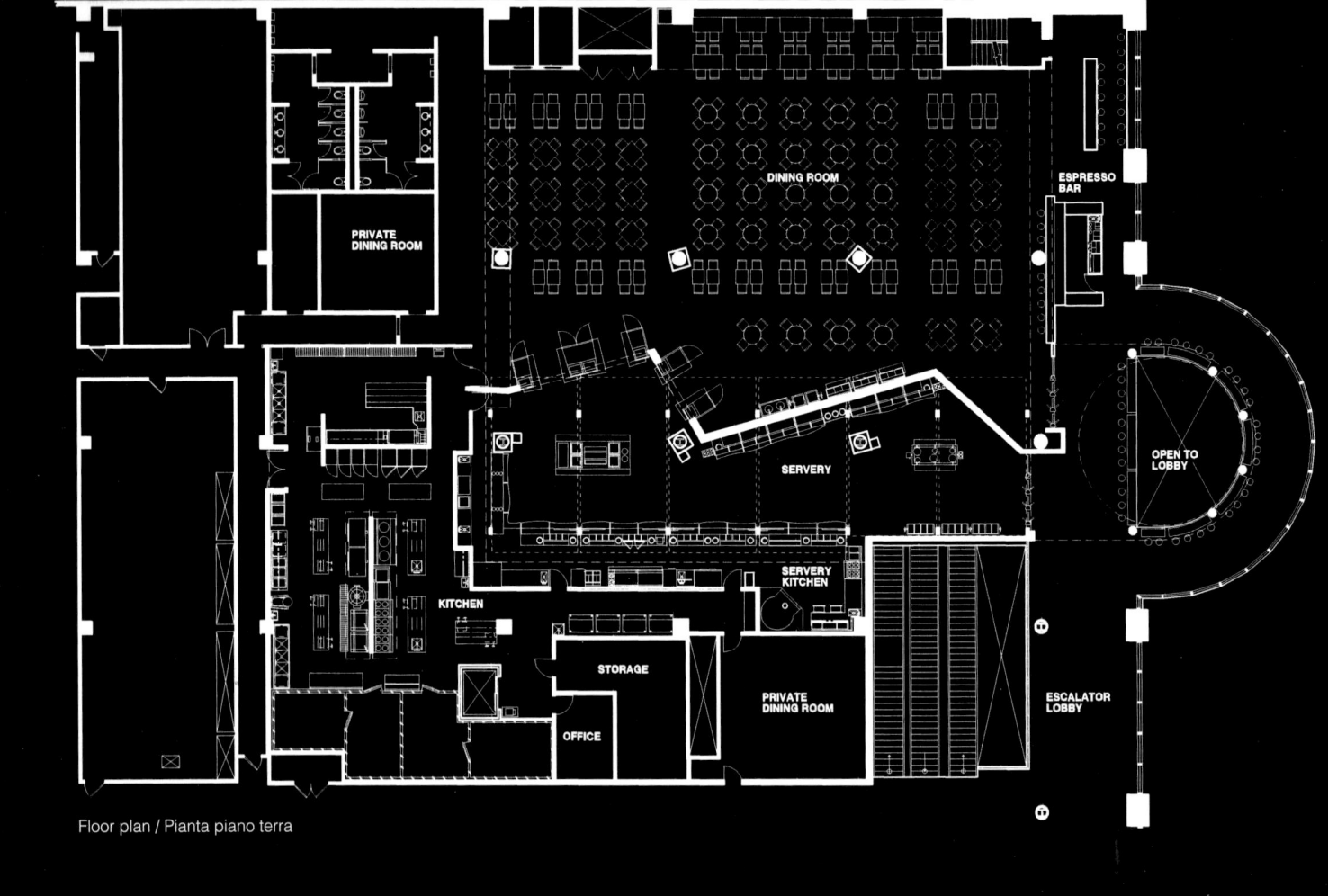

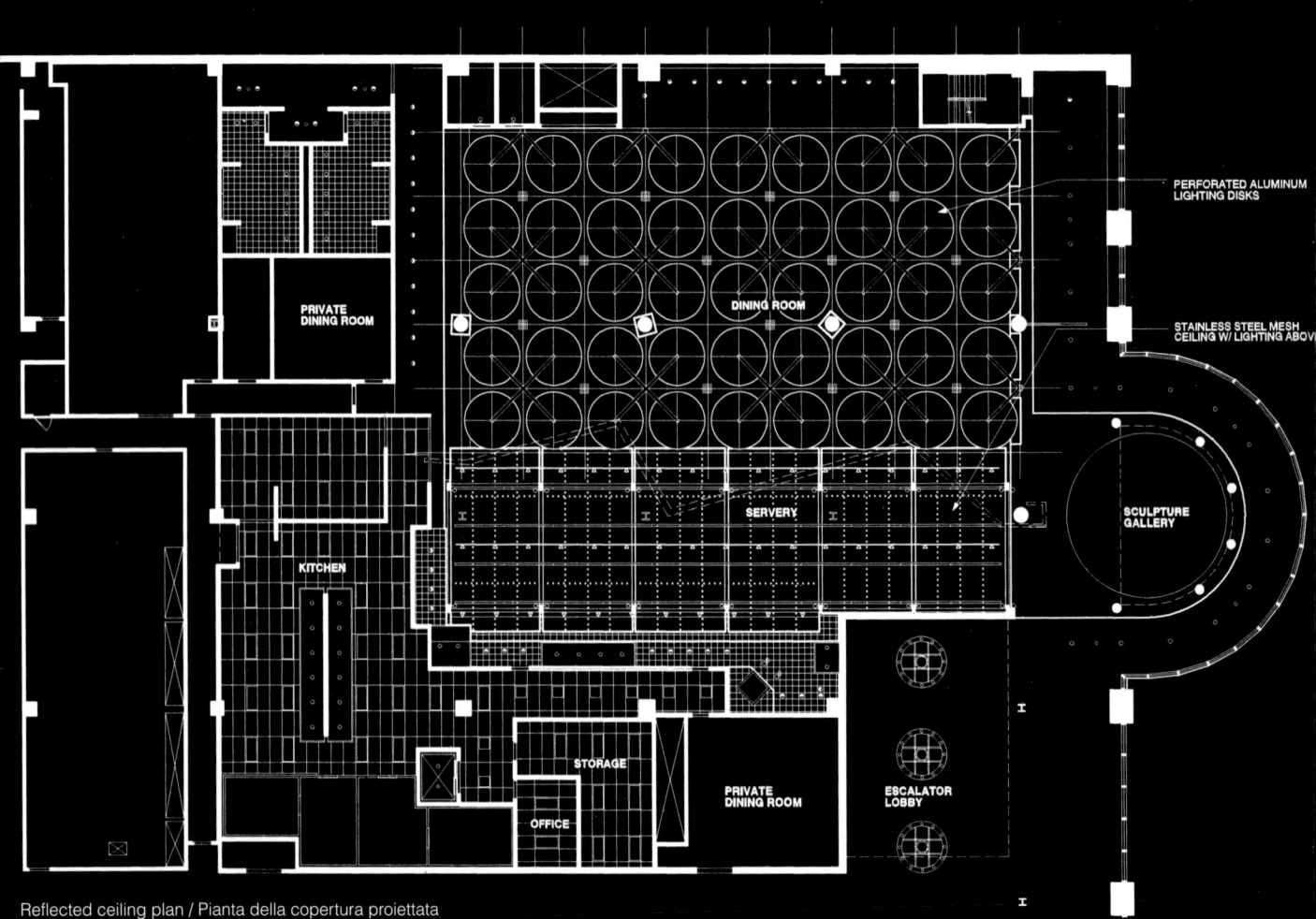

Reflected ceiling plan / Pianta della copertura proiettata

81

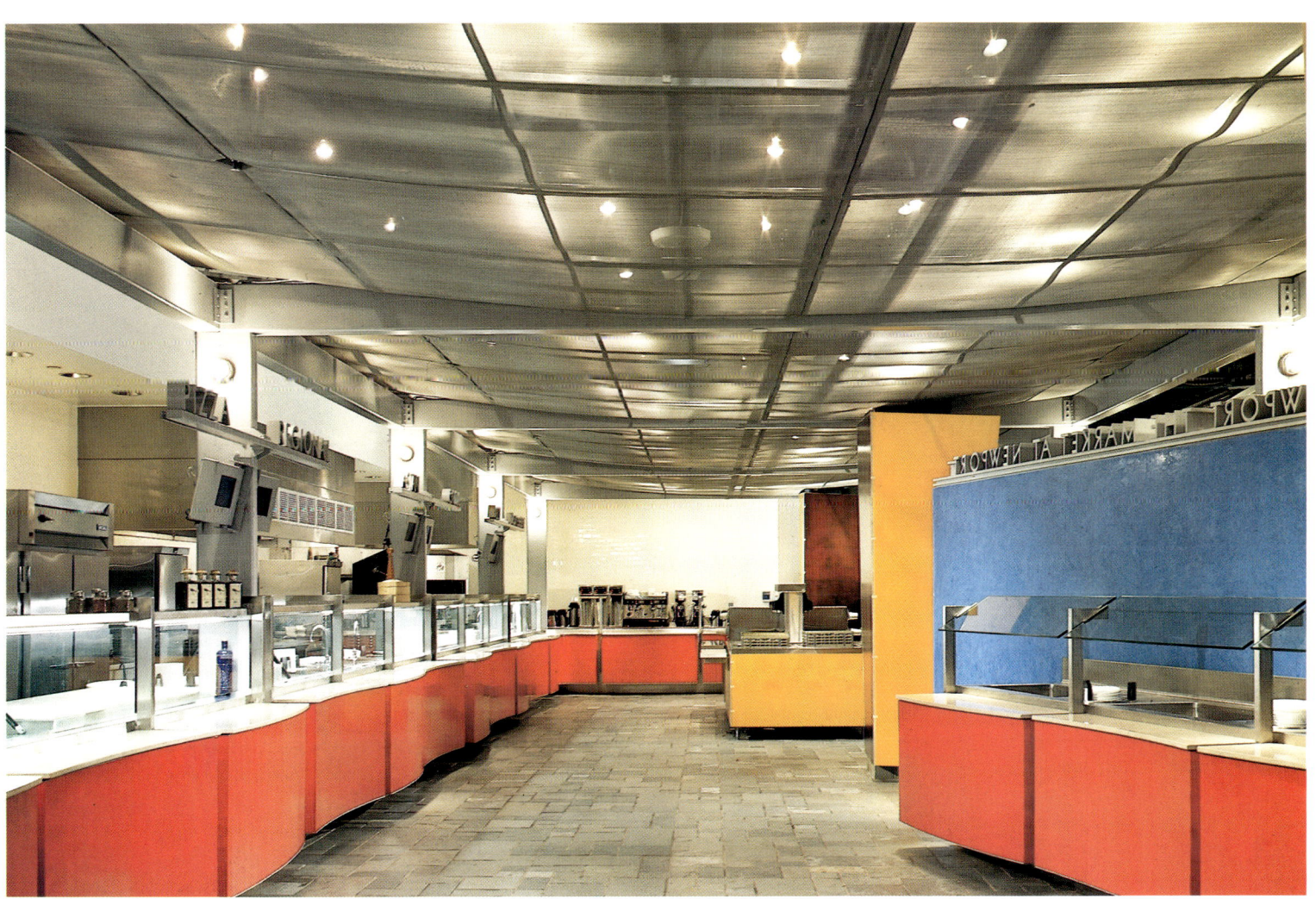

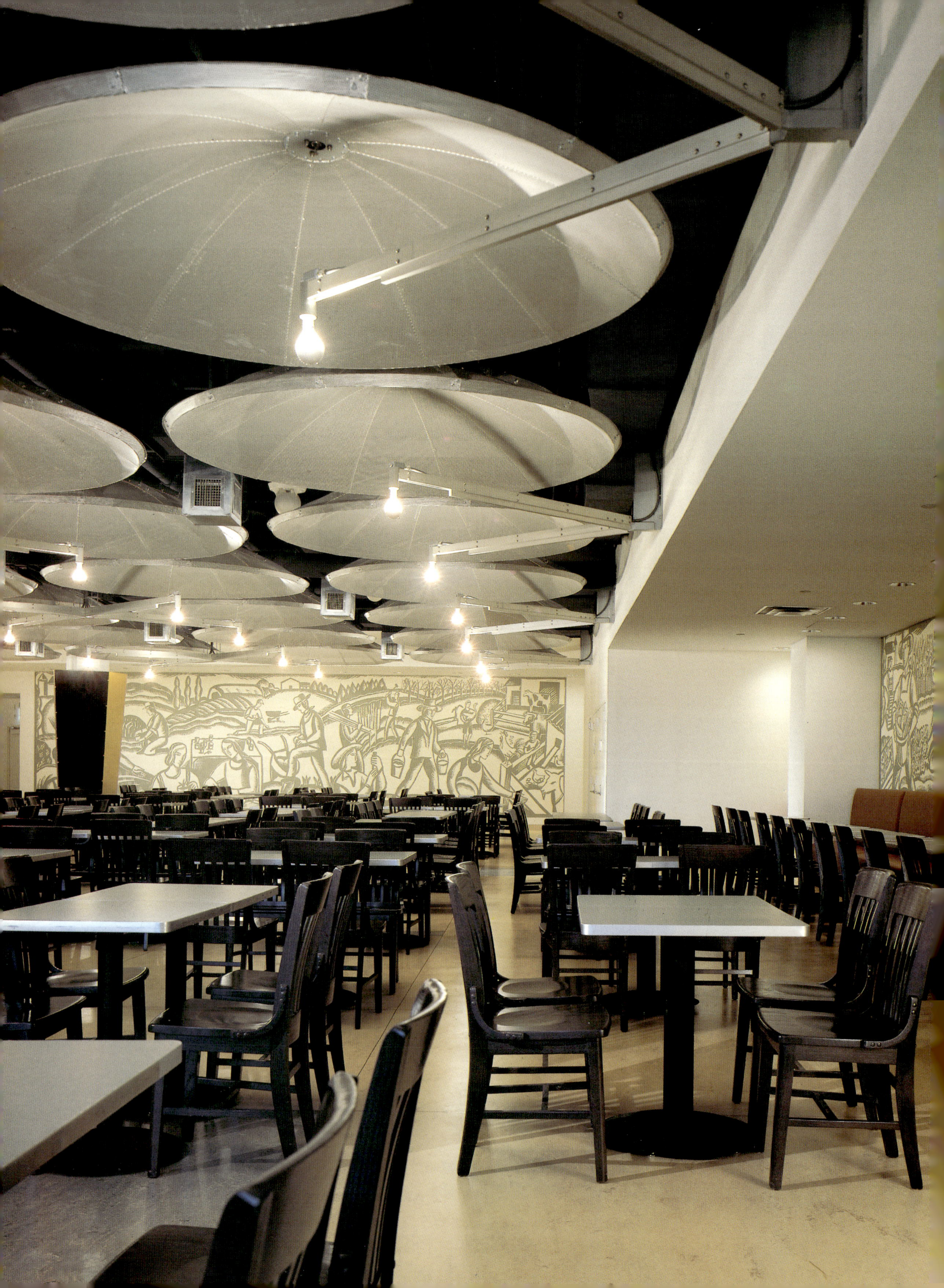

83

METROPOLE

Branson e Coates Architecture. Tokyo, JP, 1985

The first commission in Japan for the young British designer-architects Branson and Coates, the Metropole is slotted into around 200 square meters of converted garage space in the Roppongi district, an are particularly well-stocked with fashionable gathering places frequented by foreign visitors. The new interiors draw on the English-style club atmosphere for their conceptual framework, figurative ideas, and design features. As shown by the preliminary sketches, the facade of the building has been brilliantly transformed by grafting a Corinthian colonnade with small recessed portico leading to the restaurant. The basic theme is the London "gentleman's club" coupled with a classical ruins effect. The spaces inside are characterized by a narrative-style layout in which the first room, complete with bar counter and bookshelves above (loaded with old leather-bound volumes purchased from antiques dealers in England), is screened off from the dining area by a heavy stage curtain in maroon velvet; a smaller separate room offers a more secluded atmosphere for private dinner parties. The architectural attributes consist of original English objects and furnishings picked up here and there, interspersed with customized items designed by Branson and Coates (such as the seating, which harks respectively back to classical types of chair) and other designs by Tom Dixon, who was responsible for some of the wall light fittings. The bar-room in the entrance and the main dining room, with its blue ceiling, are separated by a plush stage-type curtain whose theatrical origin is echoed in the scenes painted on the ceiling. The little private room gives vent to a more classical expression, with a floor in white and black mosaic bordered with classic Greek fret patterns, and a wall decoration of painted curtains that conceals the door, and is interrupted only by a central niche housing an appealing classicizing statue. The impact of this visual vocabulary of the Metropole, with its mêlée of archaeological, classicizing references, is one of a highly personal, dynamic arrangement of ideas.

Primo progetto giapponese ad opera dei giovani designer e architetti inglesi Branson e Coates, il Metropole, ricavato in un garage di circa 200 metri quadrati nel quartiere di Roppongi, ricco di locali alla moda e di visitatori stranieri, ha ricercato nella ricca tradizione dei 'club' inglesi i suoi presupposti concettuali, le analogie figurative e gli spunti progettuali. Come dimostrano gli schizzi di studio, la facciata dell'edificio è stata brillantemente trasformata con l'innesto di un colonnato corinzio da cui, tramite un piccolo porticato rientrante, si accede al ristorante. Il tema di riferimento del locale è quello del *gentleman's club* londinese affiancato dal senso di 'rovina classica' in una studiata regia progettuale. Lo spazio è caratterizzato da una sorta di percorso compositivo di tipo 'narrativo', dove una prima sala, con bancone bar e soppalco libreria (con antichi libri recuperati da antiquari inglesi), è separata con un drappo teatrale in velluto bordeau dalla grande sala da pranzo, affiancata da una sala più piccola per pranzi riservati. La scena architettonica dell'interno è composta da oggetti e arredi sia inglesi originali rintracciati in vari luoghi, sia disegnati appositamente da Branson e Coates (la serie di sedute che rileggono con creatività la tipologia delle sedie classiche) e da altri progettisti come Tom Dixon, cui si devono alcune lampade a parete. La sala-bar d'ingresso e quella da pranzo coperta da un soffitto blu sono separate tra loro mediante il sipario-cornice teatrale cui si aggiunge una scena dipinta che scende dal soffitto. La saletta privata si propone invece come spazio di memoria antica, con pavimento a mosaico bianco e nero ripartito dalle classiche greche perimetrali e con una decorazione parietale a tende dipinte che nasconde anche la porta di accesso e si interrompe solo per ospitare nella nicchia centrale conclusiva una candida statua classica. Il vocabolario visuale del Metropole, ricco di referenze archeologiche e classicheggianti, annuncia la personale formula progettuale di un assemblaggio dinamico, calibrato e suggestivo.

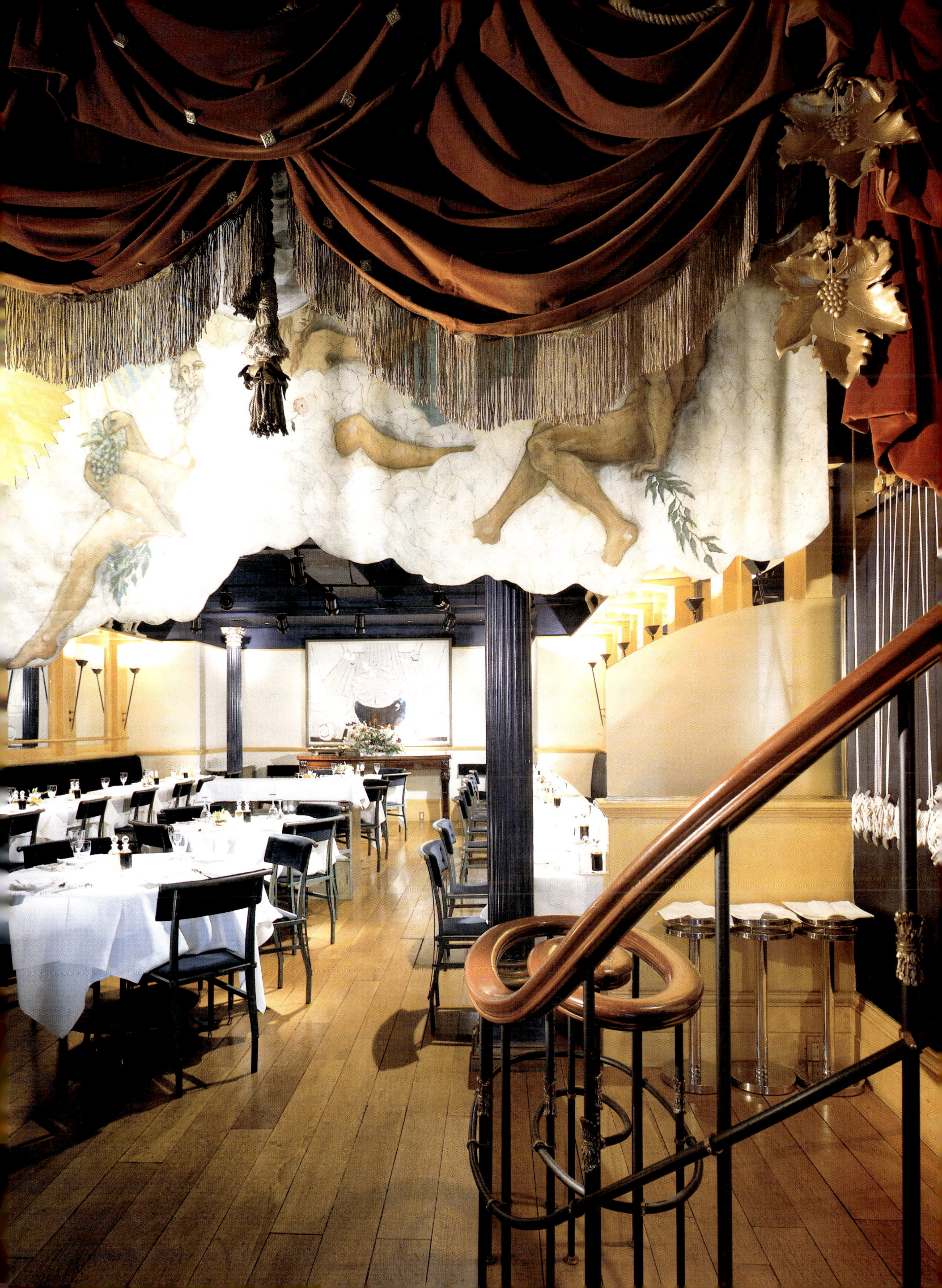

86

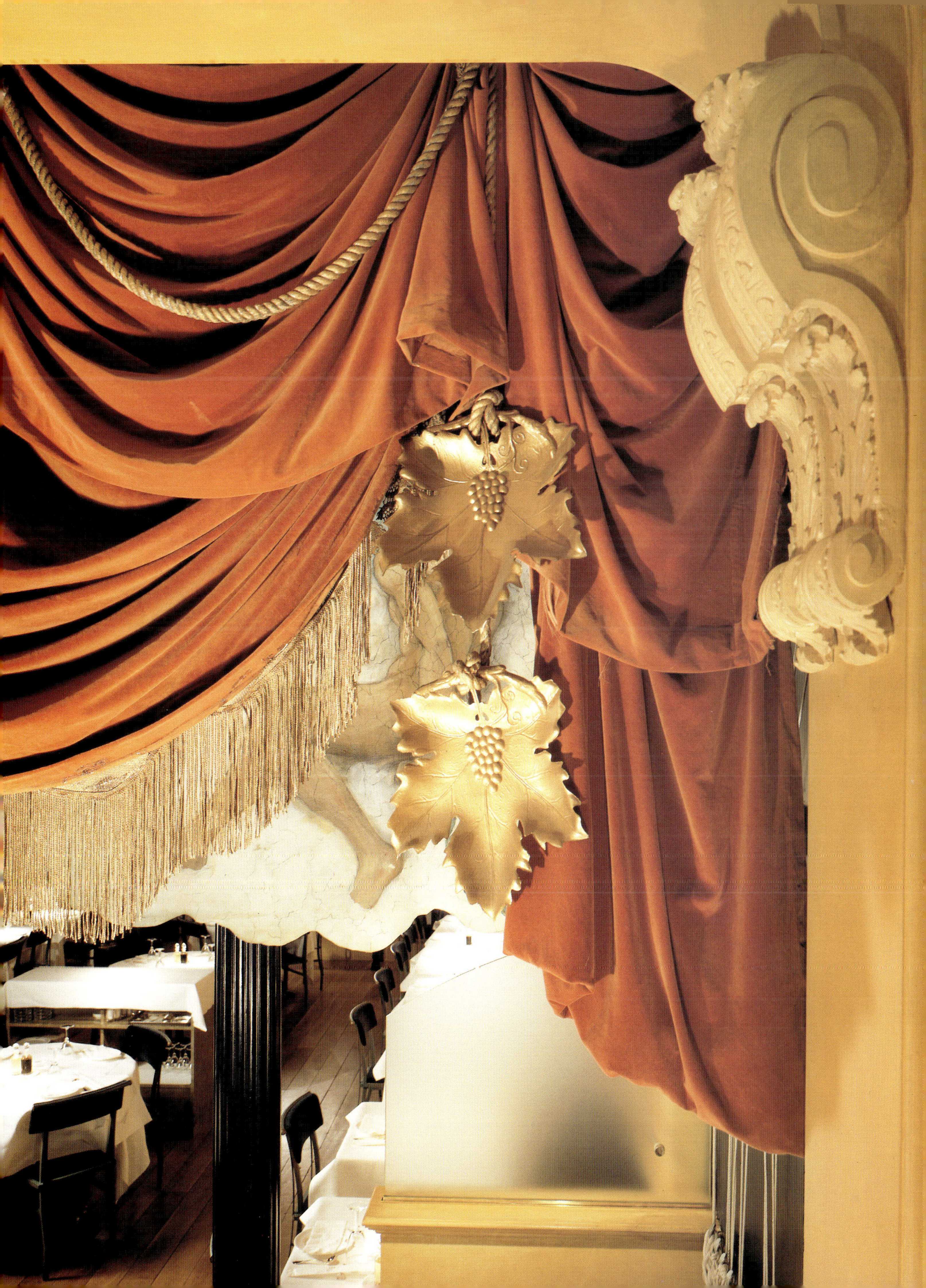

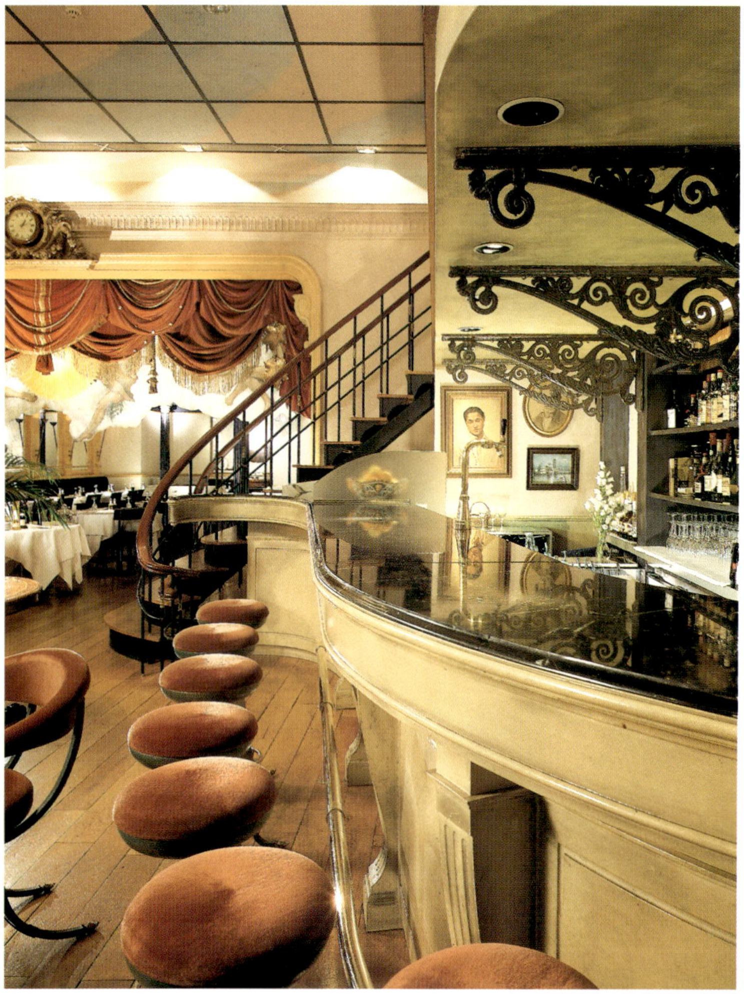

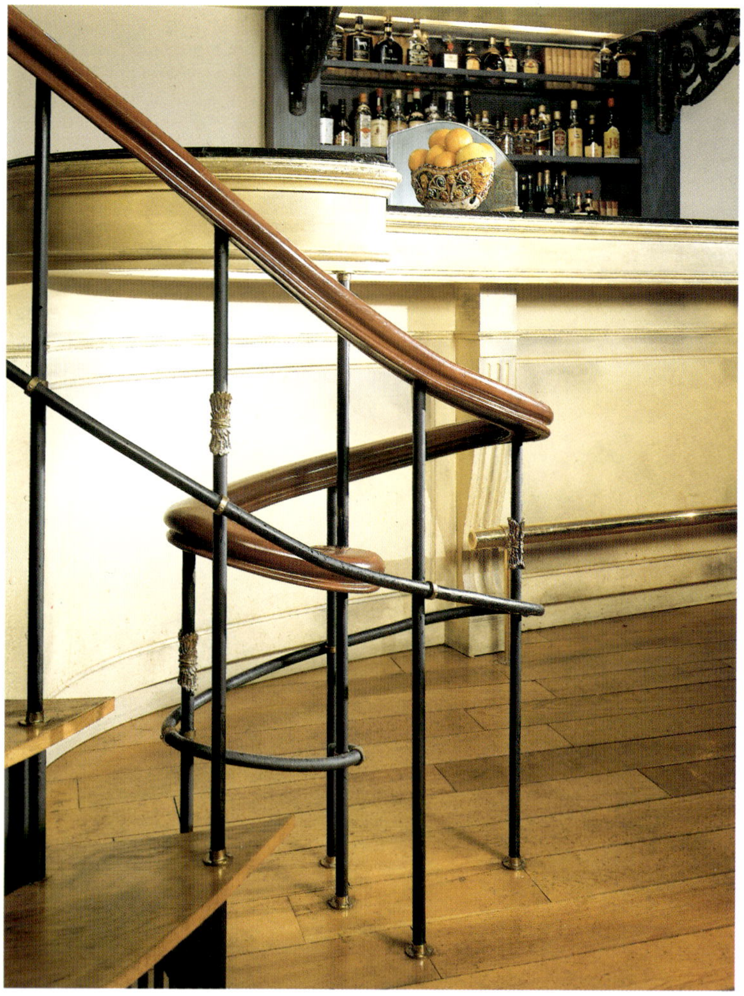

MIREZI RESTAURANT
Gene S. Park, Min Yang Architects. New York, NY, USA, 1996

The Korean word *mirezi* means "space of the future," in a mystical rather than technological sense, however. The architectural scheme of the overall design pivots on this concept, and on the Asian accent of the cuisine, which is perceivable from the outside. On the street front the part of the facade affected by the two stories of the restaurant has been completely redesigned in the form of an elegant double portal with two long vertical openings interrupted by a sort of horizontal entablature that provides an essential marquee over the doorway. In the foyer the first-story floor has been set back from the wall line to create a double-height space that neatly unites the two otherwise separate stories. A rather oriental-looking pebble floor leads to the elliptical staircase in red travertine, under which nestles a small reception-type floor at street level. The stairway leads up to the first level of the restaurant and down to the one below, which is slightly lower than the entrance floor. Both levels have a bar located near the stairs, and dining rooms furnished with creative elegance. Walls in rough earth-colored plaster provide a lively set of backdrops alternating with sections of wall in softer hues and the lowered ceiling of gesso caissons of the first floor. The stucco partitions host ranks of small television screens that show films about Asia. This wistful contrast between imagery of oriental origins, the pre-existing New York structures, and the high-tech gadgetry is deftly continued in the design of the geometrical lights and the back-lit rice-paper and wood screens, but also in the bamboo place-mats and chopsticks arranged on the dining tables with their unusual copper-sheathed tops. The delicate counterpoint of material and styles creates an unusual and engaging atmosphere, a refined and exclusive ambiance, enhanced by an alcove that forms a cozy private enclosure where diners can withdraw to eat and enjoy each other's company in an architectural niche accessed via a tall bowed doorway.

Mirezi in Coreano significa "spazio del futuro" in un'accezione mistica e non tecnologica. A questo significato e al carattere asiatico della cucina si è rapportato il progetto architettonico dell'immagine complessiva che già dallo spazio esterno caratterizza il locale. Sulla strada la parte di facciata interessata dai due livelli del ristorante è stata completamente ridisegnata, proponendo un doppio elegante portale segnato da due aperture verticali, interrotte da una lastra in pietra aggettante che funge da essenziale pensilina. Nell'ingresso la soletta del primo piano è stata arretrata per creare uno spazio a doppia altezza che unisce in un unico ambiente i due livelli prima nettamente separati. Una pavimentazione in ciottoli di fiume dal sapore orientale connette la scala ellittica di travertino rosso in cui è stato ricavato un piccolo pianerottolo-reception a quota stradale. La scala distribuisce al primo livello e a quello sottostante, leggermente ribassato rispetto alla quota d'ingresso. Entrambi i livelli ospitano un banco bar nella prossimità della scala e sale da pranzo arredate con creatività ed eleganza. Pareti in stucco spatolato dalle tonalità terra si alternano come efficaci quinte ai muri tinteggiati con colori più morbidi e al controsoffitto in gesso a cassettoni del primo piano. Le quinte a stucco ospitano all'interno piccoli schermi televisivi che trasmettono filmati sull'Asia. Il confronto tra figure che vogliono ricordare motivi orientali, preesistenze newyorkesi e spunti tecnologici prosegue con il disegno dei lampadari geometrici e degli schermi in carta di riso e legno retroilluminati, ma anche nell'allestimento della tavola con tovagliette di bambù e bacchette di legno poste sugli insoliti piani rivestiti in rame dei tavoli da pranzo. La serie di raffinati contrappunti materici e stilistici riesce a creare un'atmosfera insolita e accogliente, ricercata ed esclusiva, dove non manca lo spazio dell'"alcova", qui tradotta in un piccolo spazio raccolto e riservato dove poter pranzare in una nicchia architettonica segnata da un alto portale bombato.

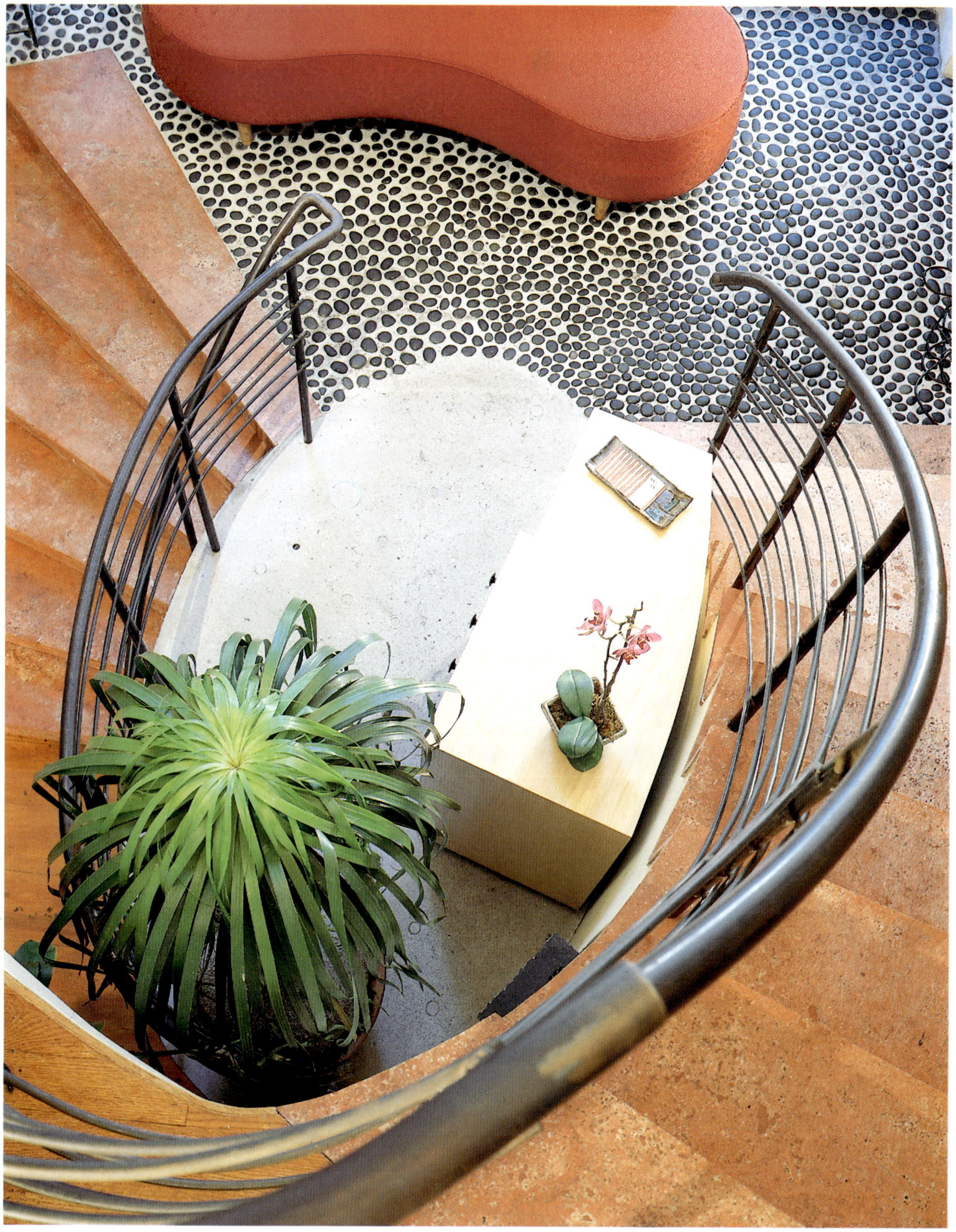

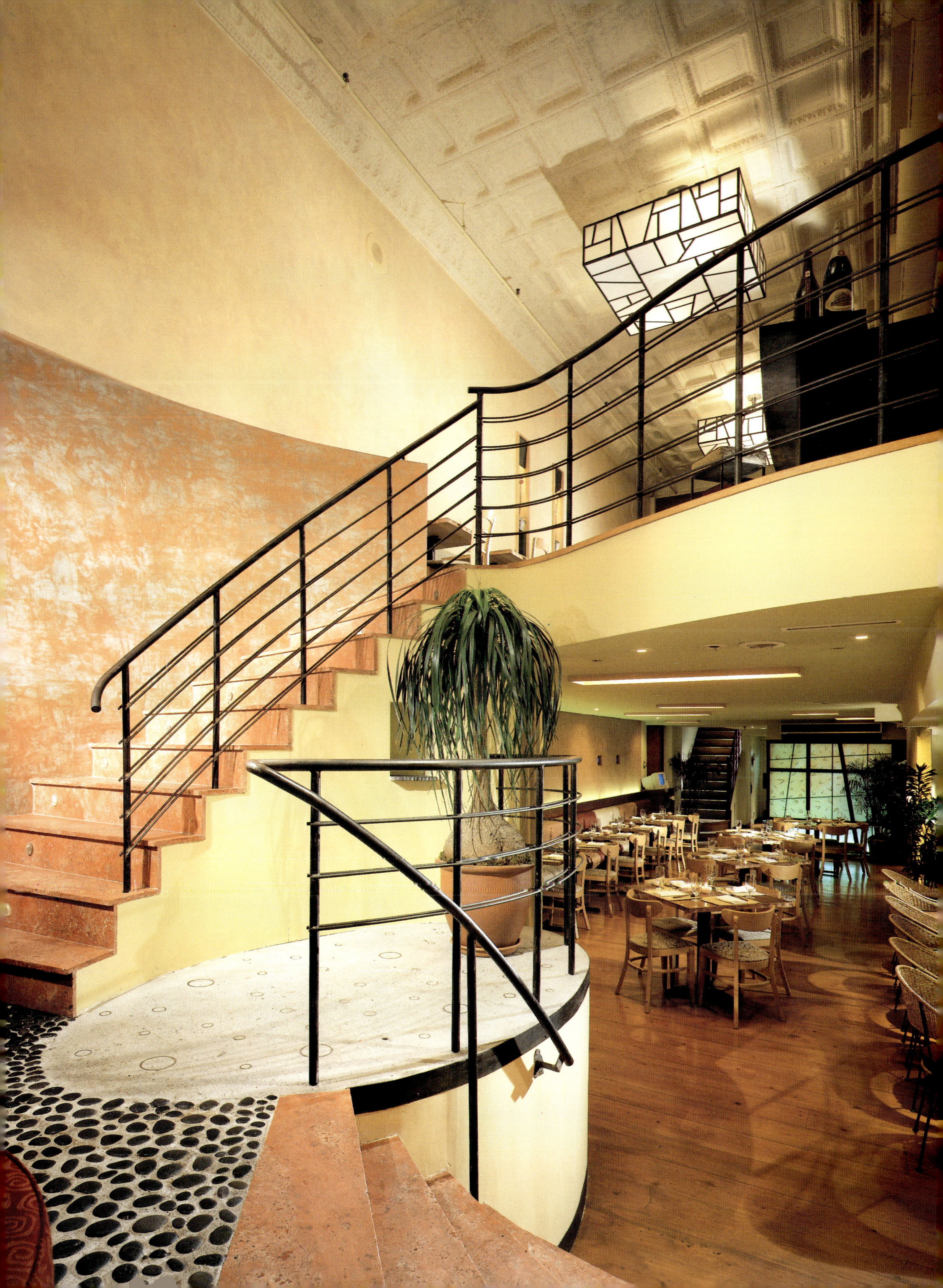

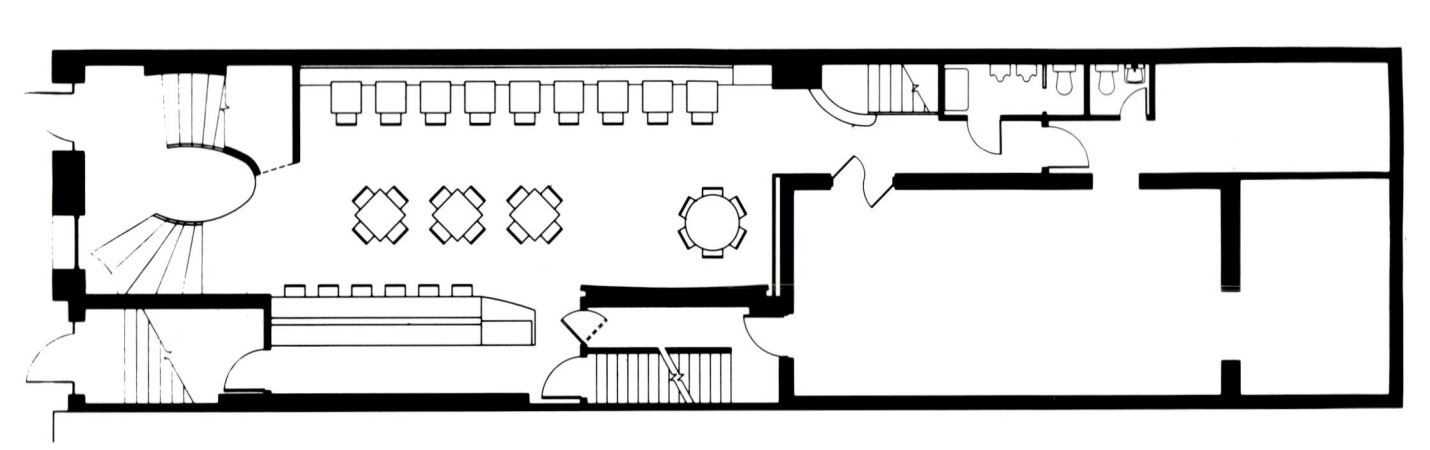

Lower level dining / Pranzo livello inferiore

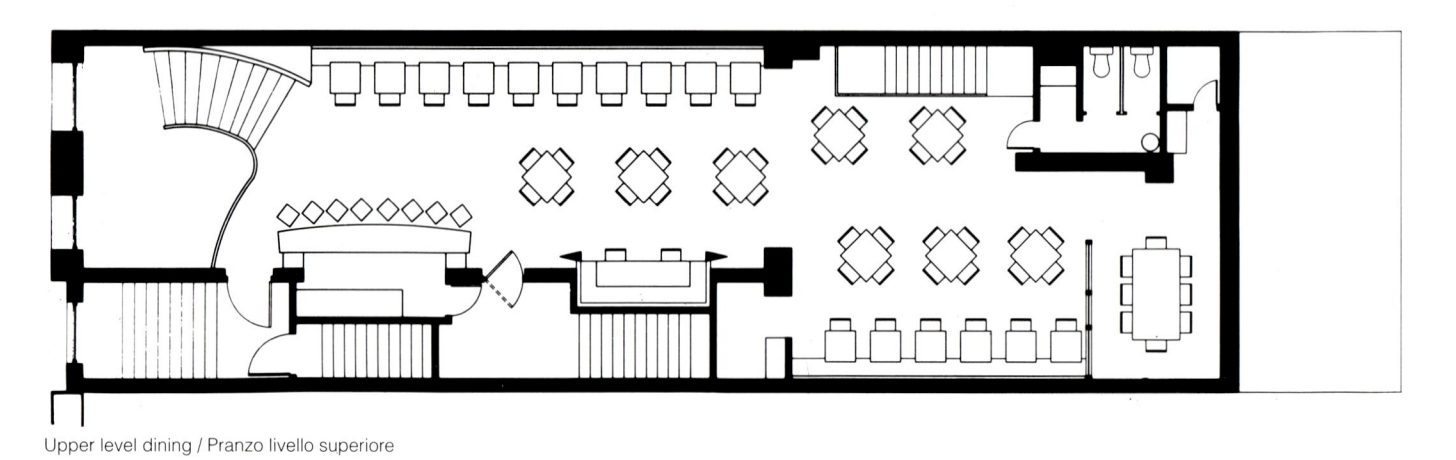

Upper level dining / Pranzo livello superiore

MONKEY BAR
David Rockwell Architect. New York, Ny, USA 1994

Housed in the Hotel Élysée, in the thirties and forties the Monkey Bar was one of Manhattan's most lively and fashionable dinner joints whose regulars included sports personalities, stage actors, film stars, and other figures of fame such as Marlon Brando, Ava Gardner, Joe DiMaggio, and Tennessee Williams. The new Monkey Bar has undergone a face-lift that shows keen sensibility for the place's original look and feel, with the addition of a new dining room. The bar performs the function of gateway to the rest of the venue, offering a foyer-saloon that precedes the new restaurant area. The saloon design follows the irregular contours of the building, drawing on a classic arrangement with a grand piano alongside the zigzagging drinks bar styled in mahogany with a paneled front upholstered in maroon-colored leather. The bar, the murals, and most of the fixtures and fittings were carefully restored to conserve and reinstate the original atmosphere, with the clowning monkeys repeated in the large cartoon murals and the animal-shaped light fittings on the walls. The original large wall mirror framed in stylized bamboo, the banana-leaf pattern on the blue linoleum floor, and the watermelon-shaped stools are all there to create a lively tropical atmosphere. Two tall screens in quilted blue velvet mask the door to the elevator and the emergency exit, meanwhile underlining the linkage to the restaurant. The dining room proper, at a slightly lower level than the bar area, is ranged with a series of solid-looking pillars accoutered in maroon-colored fabric and wooden bases that reiterate the motifs that line the perimeter paneling. A balcony at a higher level to the central area lends a dynamic and comfortable accent to the overall look of the furnishings, in tune with the bar atmosphere of the past. Elegant upholstered chairs complement the fixed sofas lined along the walls, the corner ones of which are curved. Here, the illuminated screens in sanded glass are engraved with Manhattan skylines, while a large blue panel at the center of the end wall provides a kind of notice board on which photographs of the Monkey Bar's heyday are nostalgically pinned up for the diners' perusal.

Ubicato all'interno dell'Hotel Elysée, il Monkey Bar è stato negli anni '30 e '40 uno dei locali più alla moda di Manhattan, frequentato da star del cinema, dello sport e del teatro, da protagonisti della vita pubblica e mondana come Marlon Brando, Ava Gardner, Joe DiMaggio, Tennessee Williams. Il nuovo Monkey Bar si basa su un'operazione di creativo restauro che ha saputo recuperare con attenzione e sensibilità l'immagine originaria, aggiungendovi una nuova sala ristorante. Il bar costituisce l'ingresso dell'intero locale, anticipando la nuova sala da pranzo. Di forma irregolare, il bar segue le pareti dell'edificio secondo la disposizione di un tempo, con pianoforte a coda di fianco al bancone a zig-zag in mogano con bordo imbottito rivestito in pelle bordeaux. Il banco bar, i murales e la maggior parte degli arredi sono stati restaurati recuperando pienamente le atmosfere del passato, con il motivo delle allegre scimmiette ripetuto nelle grandi vignette sui muri e come applique zoomorfe alle pareti. L'originale grande specchio incorniciato da uno stilizzato bambù, le foglie di banana giganti disegnate nel pavimento di linoleum blu e gli sgabelli-anguria vogliono invece ricordare l'atmosfera tropicale. Due alti paraventi di velluto blu capitonné nascondono la porta dell'ascensore e l'uscita di sicurezza, sottolineando il percorso di connessione al ristorante. La sala da pranzo, a una quota inferiore rispetto al bar, presenta una serie di forti pilastri rivestiti in fasce imbottite di tessuto bordeaux, con basamenti lignei che riprendono il motivo della boiserie perimetrale. Una balconata rialzata rispetto alla zona centrale rende dinamica e confortevole la soluzione d'arredo complessiva, in sintonia con le atmosfere di un tempo. Eleganti sedute imbottite si affiancano a divanetti fissi allineati al muro o di forma ellittica per segnare gli angoli. Qui, dei paraventi-lampada in vetro sabbiato riportano motivi architettonici che disegnano lo skyline di New York, mentre un grande pannello blu, centrale al muro di fondo, si propone come bacheca per esporre foto d'epoca del periodo d'oro del Monkey Bar.

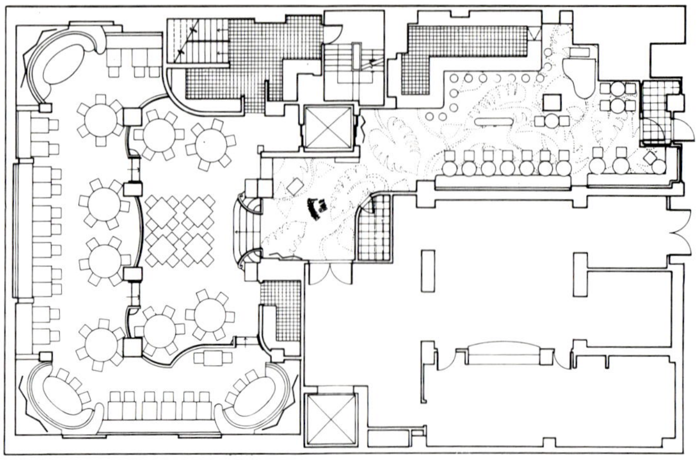

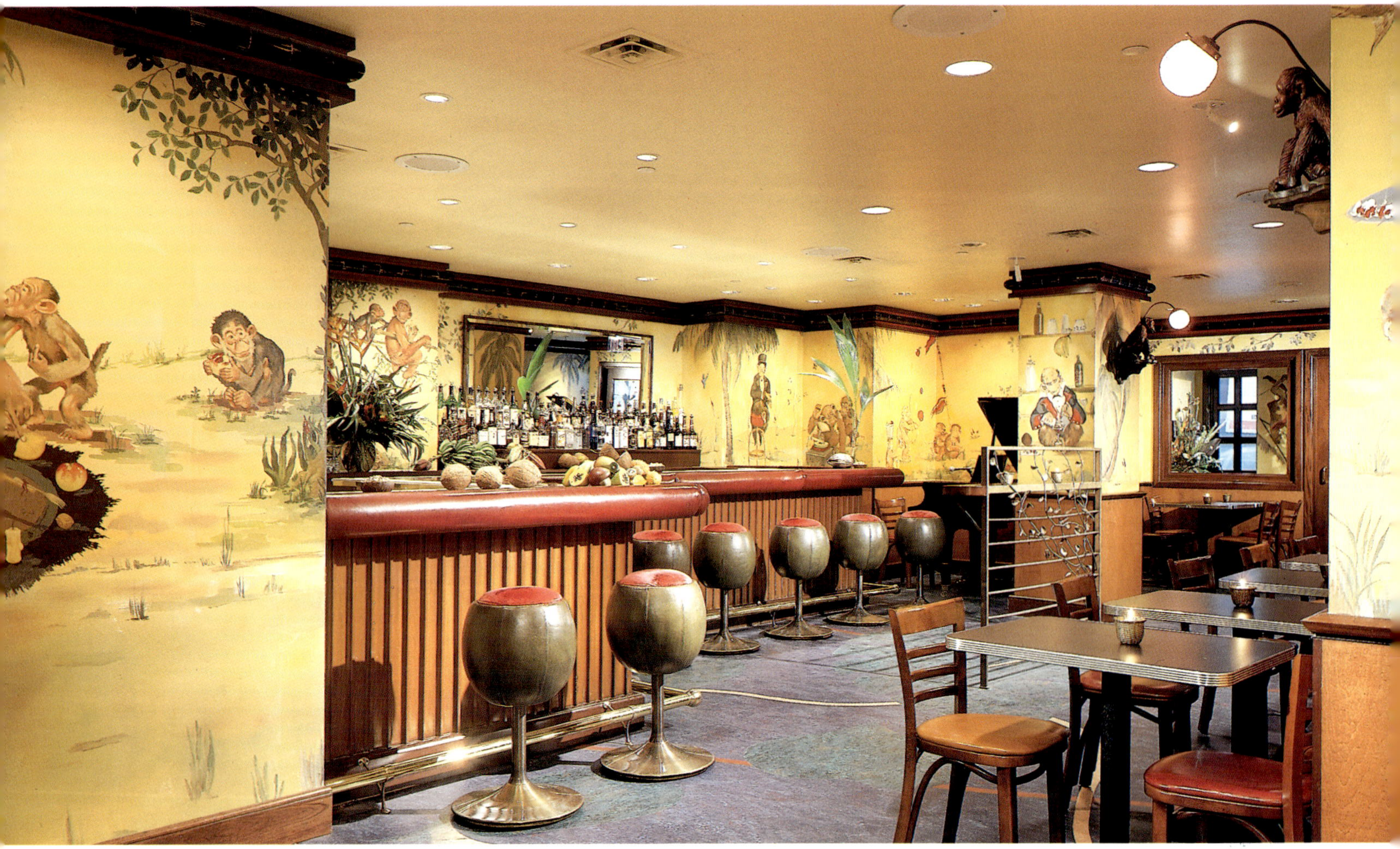

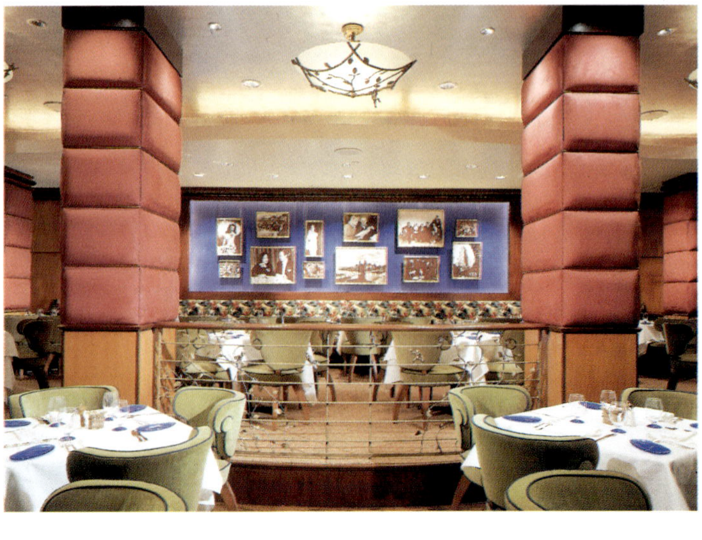

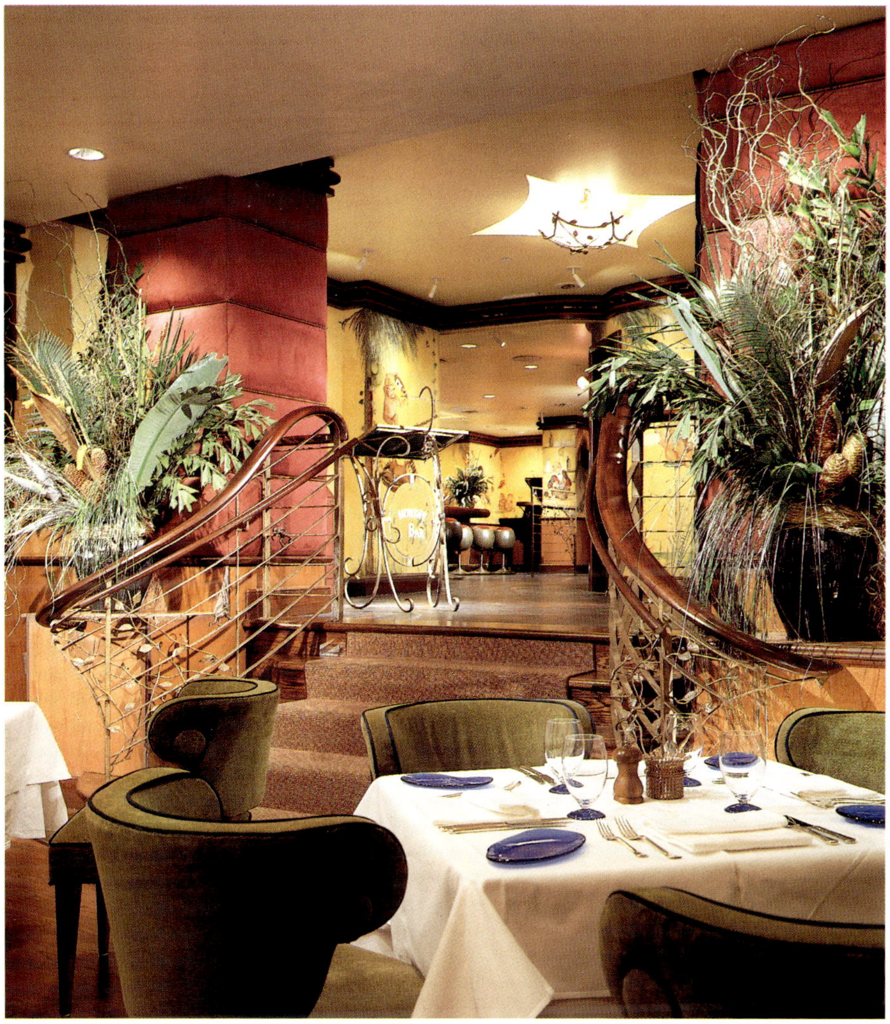

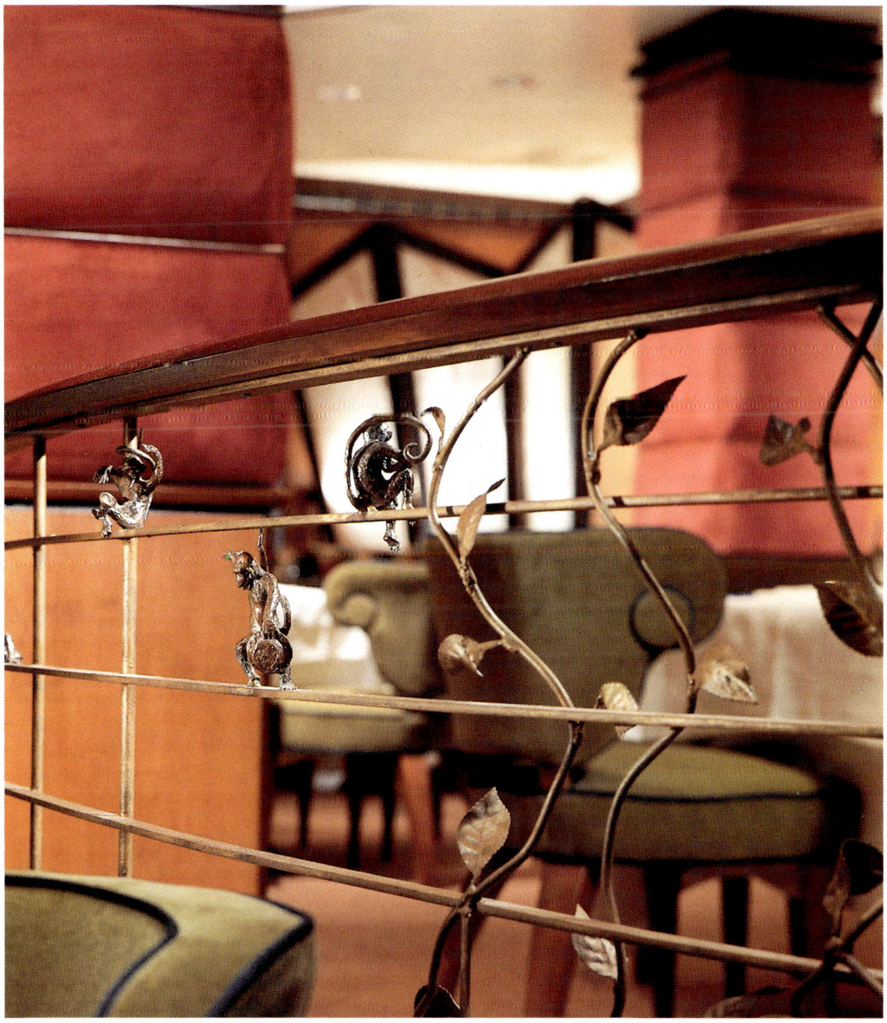

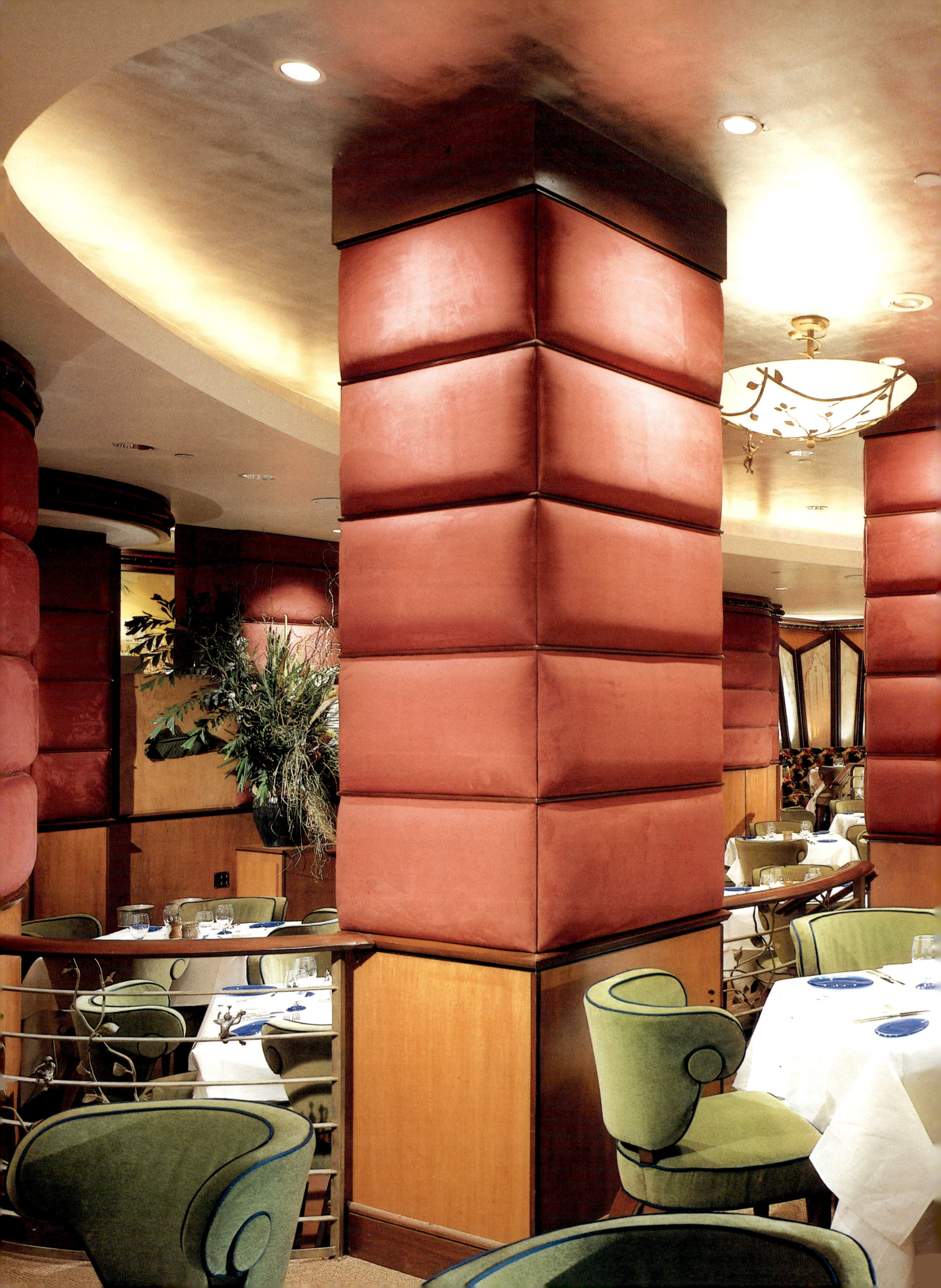

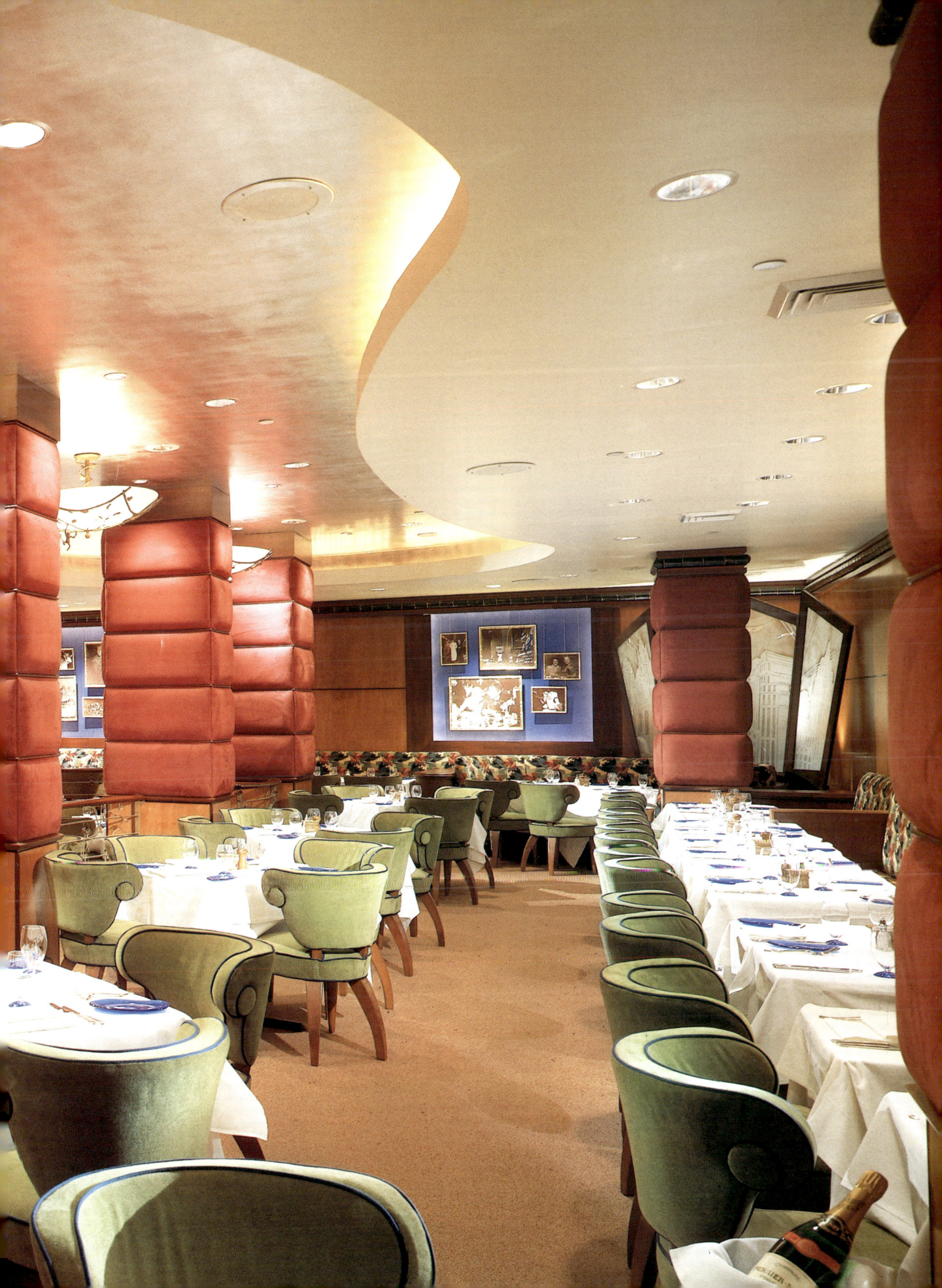

98

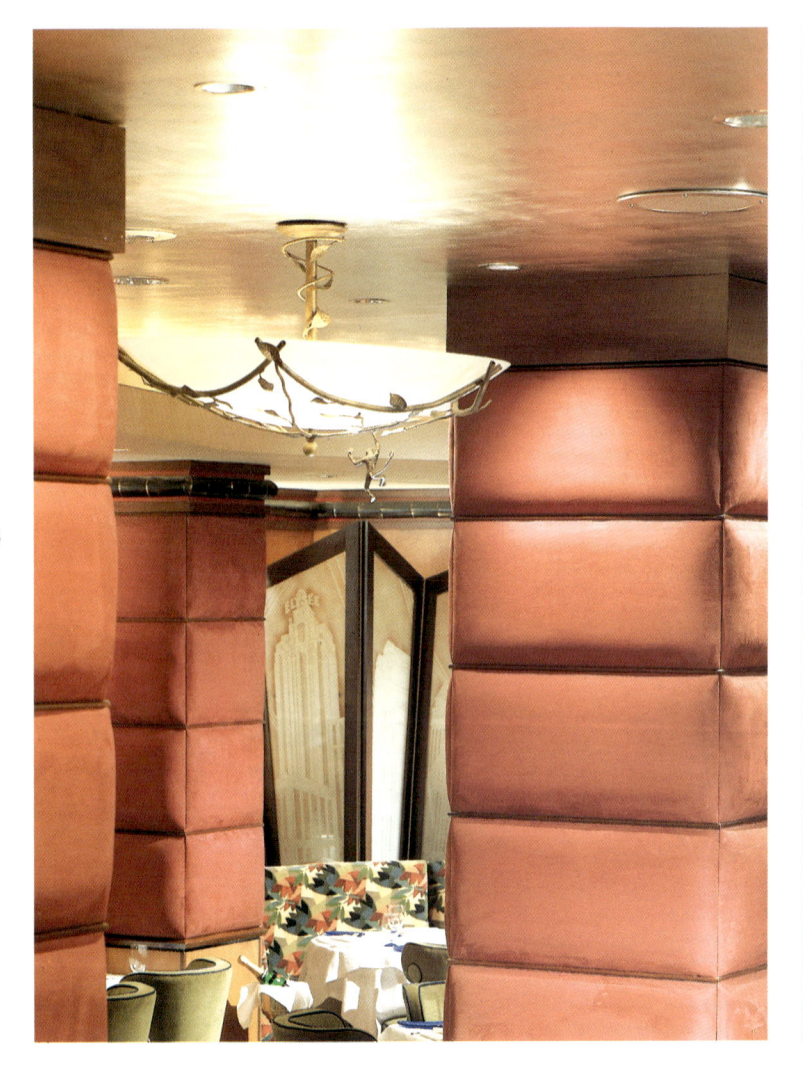

MOONSOON RESTAURANT
Zaha M. Hadid Architect. Sapporo, JP, 1990

This restaurant split on two levels represents a sort of programmatic manifesto of the new architectural poetics of the coming millennium. With this commission Zaha Hadid has expressed the potential of an architectural grammar phrased in a highly plastic dynamism taken to extremes of expressive potential, a scheme that is employed to create strikingly unusual and innovative spaces that convey a kind of dissonant formal and material elegance. The Moonson is installed in a rigorously designed building in reinforced concrete of recent construction. Hadid's handiwork vies with the building's stark motionlessness with a scheme of completely opposite spirit, a design that seems to burst out beyond the restaurant's walls. The tone of the new interiors are foretold even before you enter, by means of the door handle shaped like a thunderbolt and the small marquee over the doorway, which fearlessly scatters the obstinate linearity of the building's facade. On two floors, the ground level of the new restaurant interiors are a metaphor for a decaying world after an imaginary ice age. The basic color used throughout its gray, which determines the glass surfaces used here and there as facing for the back-lit walls and for the long glazed table tops, resembling irregularly shaped slabs of ice borne up by curious geometrical steel supports. The same visual device crops up again in the vertical props along the front of the counter lining the wall and the stairway up into the restaurant. Ingeniously concealed lighting in carefully placed crevices overhead transform the ceiling into an uncanny illuminated surface of light and shadow. An upturned metal spiral winds its way down from the ceiling as if sucking up the space below and projecting it with imaginative flair to the bar level above, whose high-temperature imagery is the utter opposite to the iciness of the restaurant floor: a series of amebic black sofas with highly colorful backrests are arranged in an eye-catching composition of fiery tongues in brilliant red, yellow, and orange that rise from the floor, licking upward like flames toward the transparent dome of the ceiling and into the sunlight.

Un ristorante su due livelli assunto come 'manifesto programmatico' di una nuova poetica progettuale per l'architettura del prossimo millennio. Con questo interno Zaha Hadid ha espresso le potenzialità di una grammatica architettonica scandita da un dinamismo plastico portato al massimo delle potenzialità espressive, in grado di configurare degli spazi architettonici inusitati e innovativi, caratterizzati da una dissonante eleganza formale e materica. Il Moonsoon si trova all'interno di un rigoroso edificio in cemento armato di recente costruzione: alla staticità di questa composizione Hadid risponde con un progetto in netta antitesi, che sembra volere esplodere con studiata regia al di là dei muri perimetrali. L'intervento, annunciato in facciata con la maniglia di acciaio a forma di fulmine e con la pensilina che rompe volutamente il filo di facciata, si divide in due sale distribuite sui diversi livelli. Al piano terreno è stato organizzato il ristorante: metafora di un decomposto universo frutto di un'improbabile glaciazione. Il grigio è la tonalità di riferimento cui si rapportano le superfici di cristallo impiegate in alcuni punti come rivestimento parietale retroilluminato o come piani dei lunghi tavoli, sorta di lastre di ghiaccio irregolari sostenute da affascinanti geometrie di acciaio. Figure ripetute nei montanti verticali che scandiscono il bancone lungo il muro e nella scala di salita. Studiati tagli nel soffitto nascondono fonti luminose trasformando il plafone in efficace presenza figurativa. Una spirale capovolta di metallo scende dall'alto risucchiando lo spazio sottostante per proiettarlo, con un forte salto progettuale e creativo, al piano superiore dove è posizionato il bar. Questo appare come l'opposto del piano inferiore, con una serie di divani-ameba neri con schienali-scultura coloratissimi disposti intorno a una mirabolante composizione di lingue infuocate colorate di accesi rossi, gialli e arancioni, che dal pavimento si sviluppano in modo ascensionale sino alla cupola trasparente del soffitto, da cui catturano i raggi del sole.

100

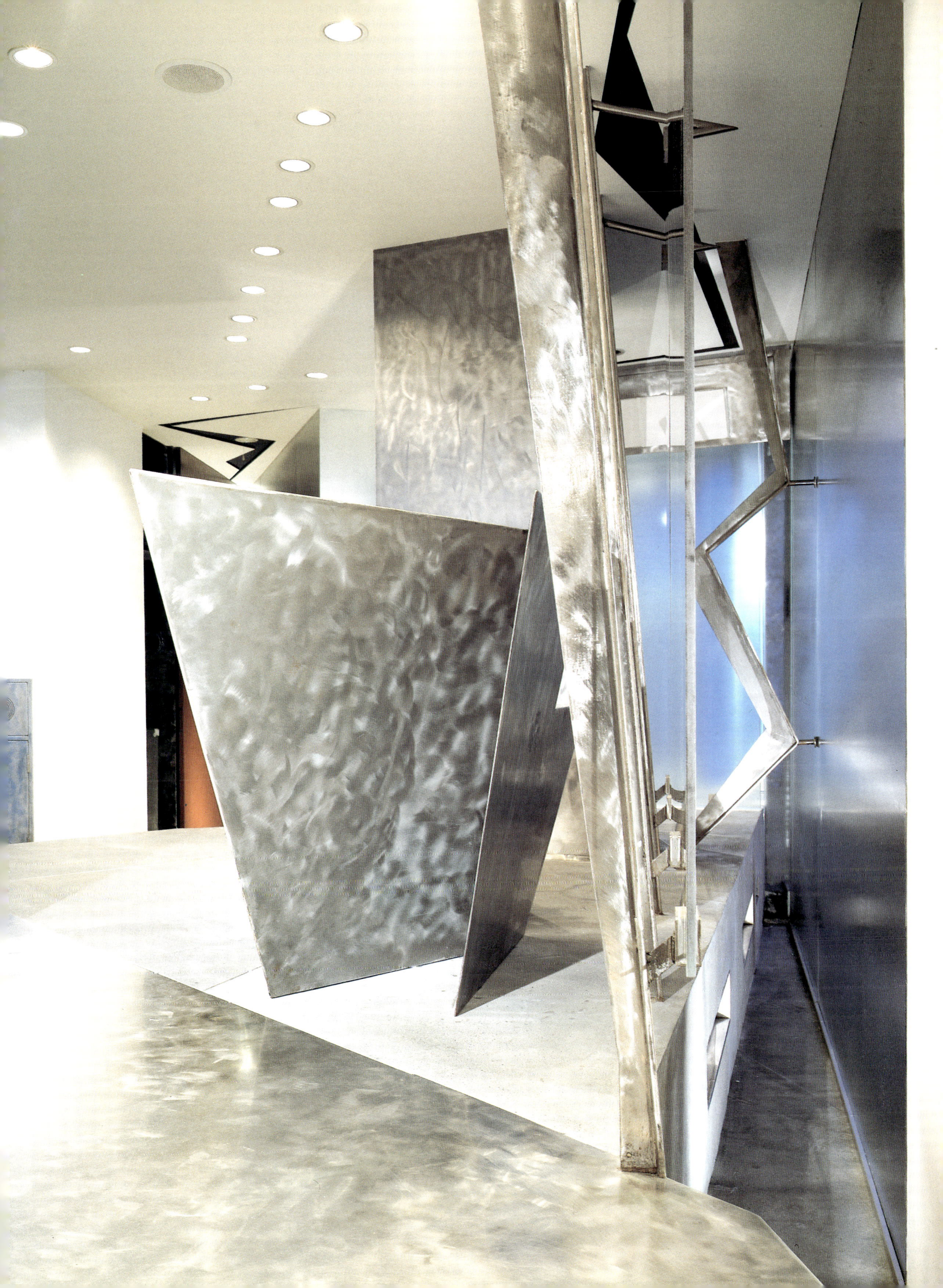

Ground floor plan / Pianta piano terra

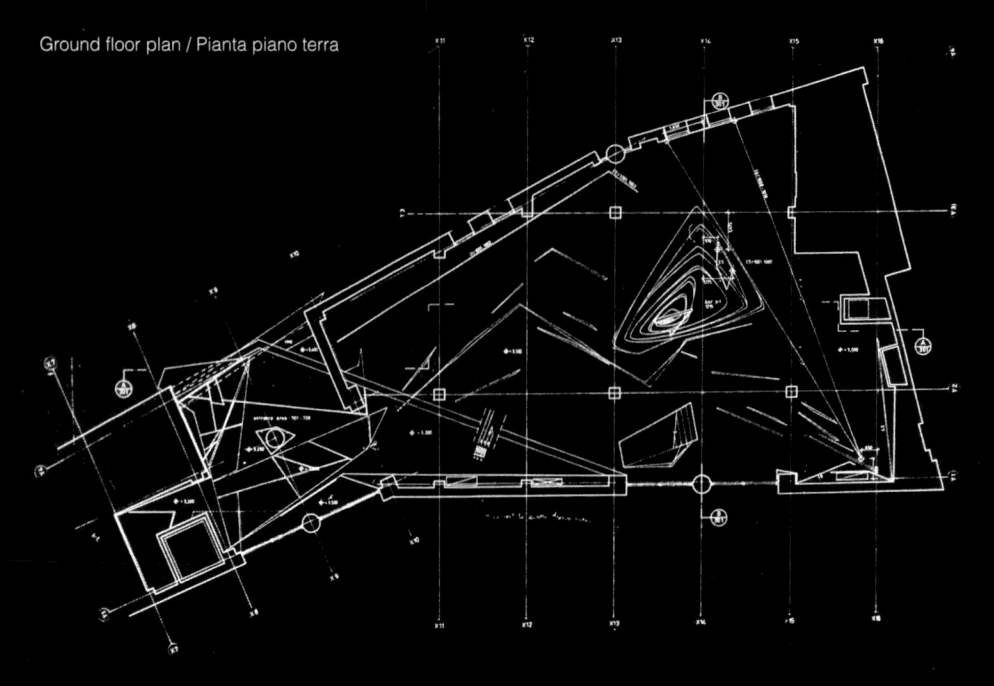

Longitudinal and transversal section / Sezione longitudinale e trasversale

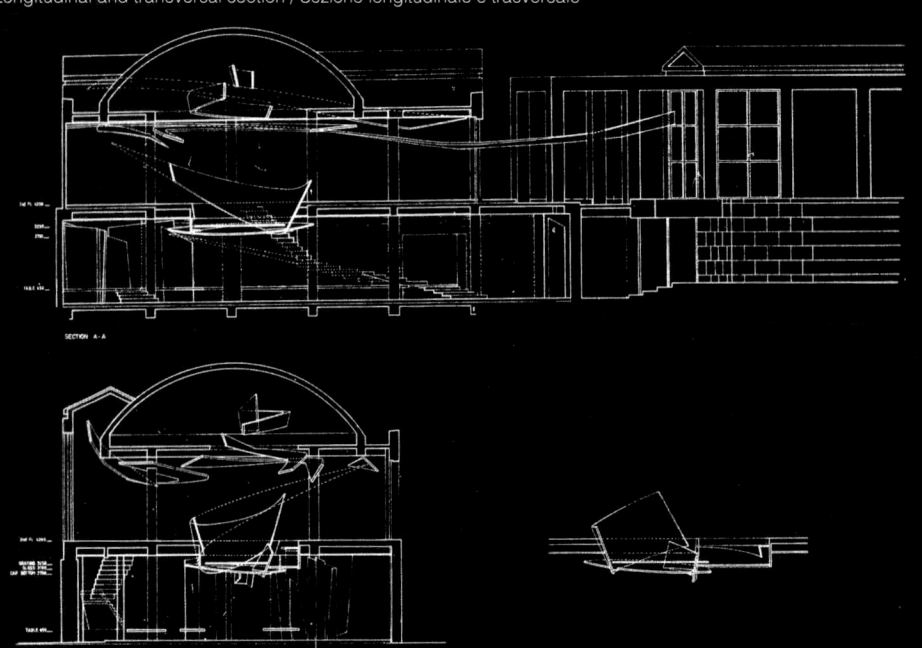

102

Ground floor axonometry / Assonometria piano terra

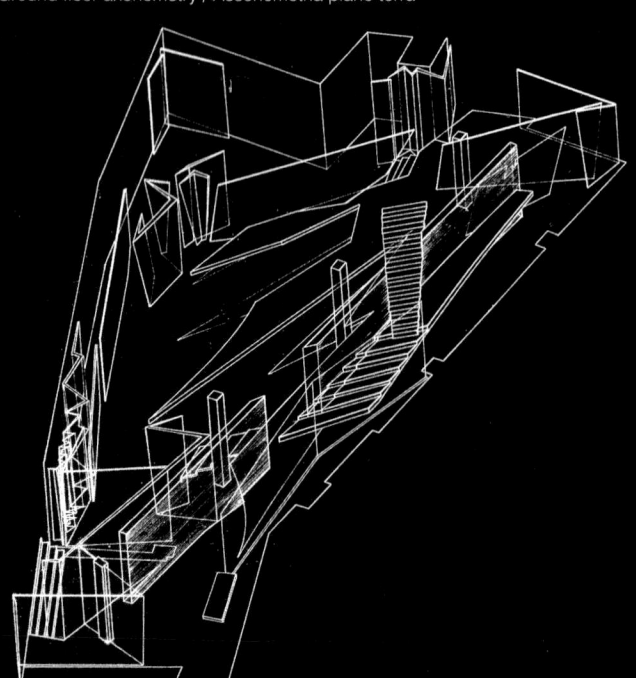

First floor axonometry / Assonometria primo piano

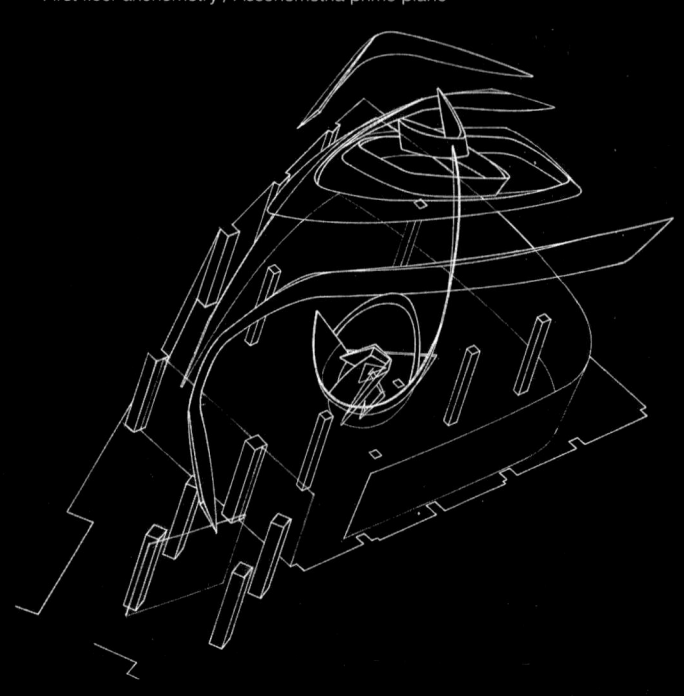

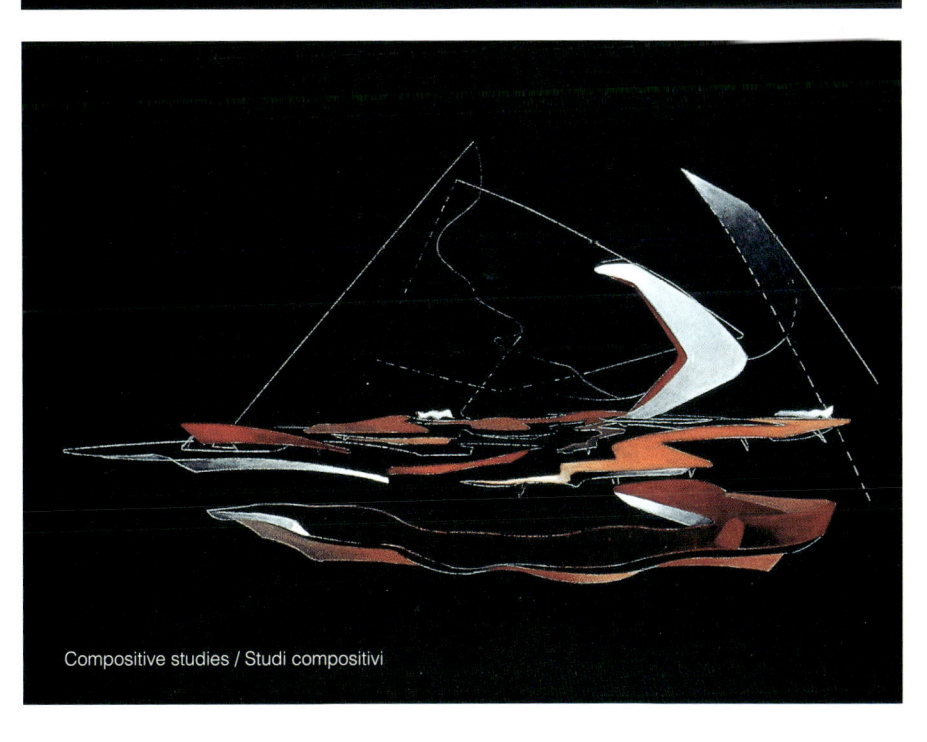

Compositive studies / Studi compositivi

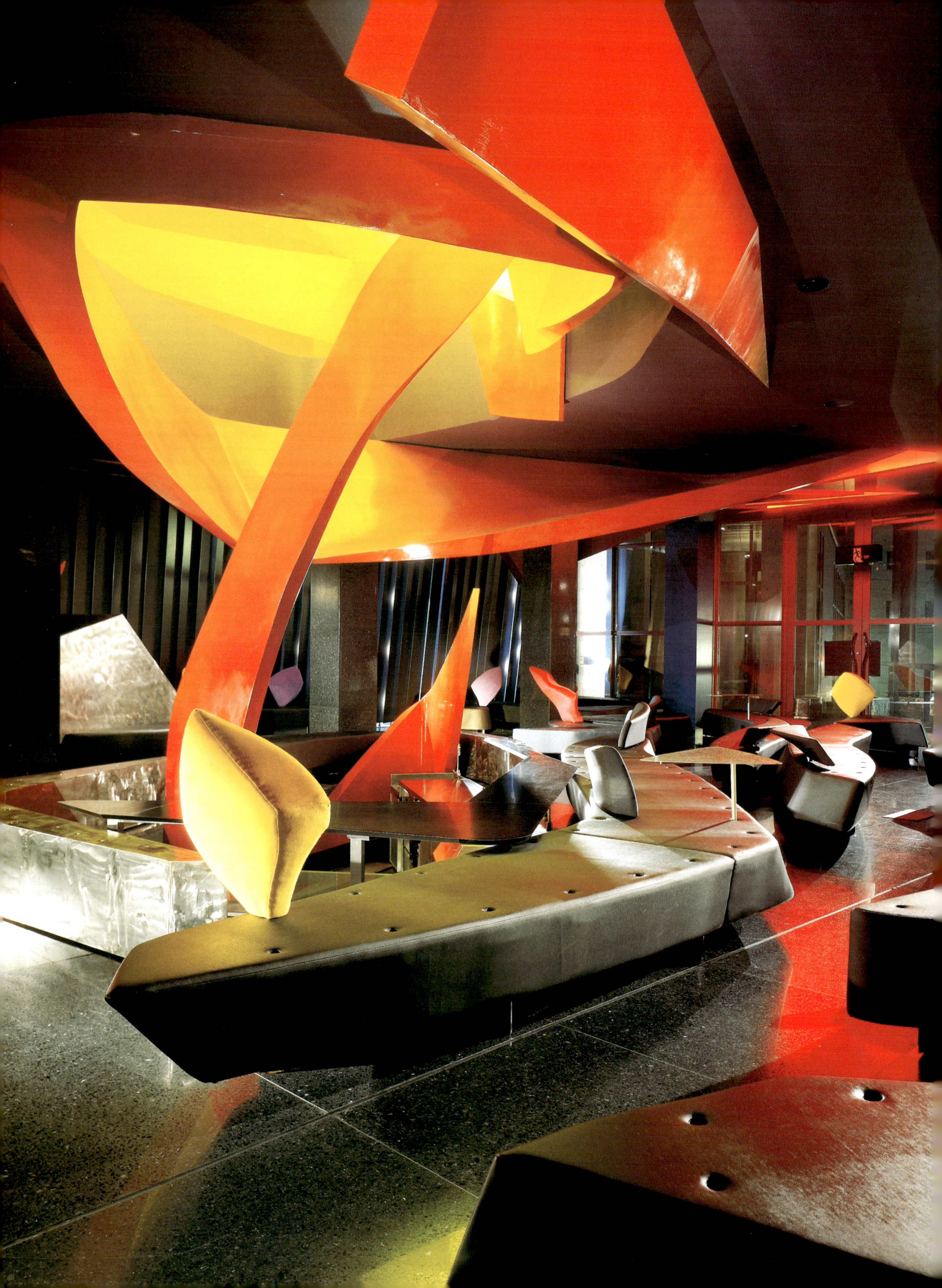

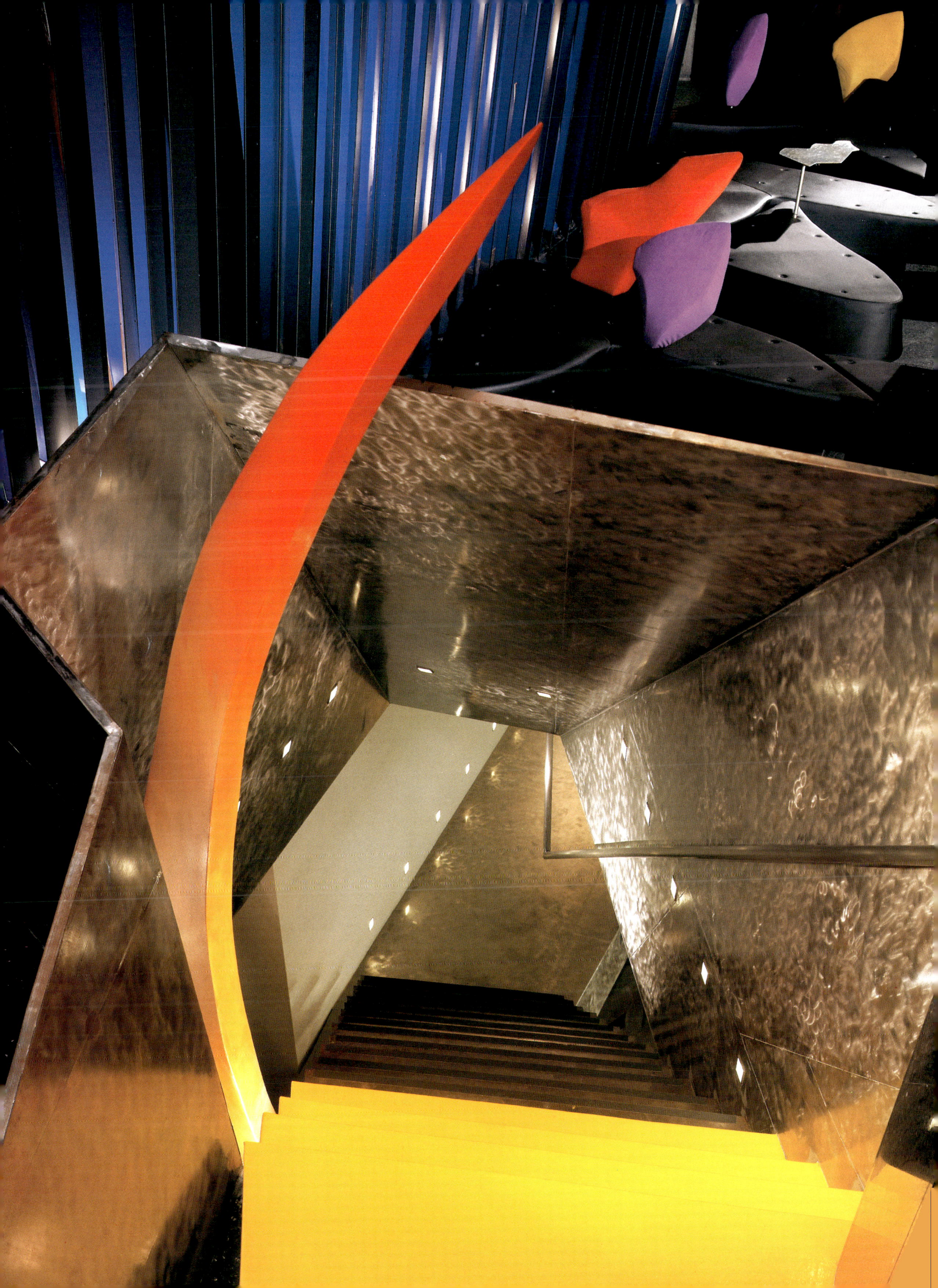

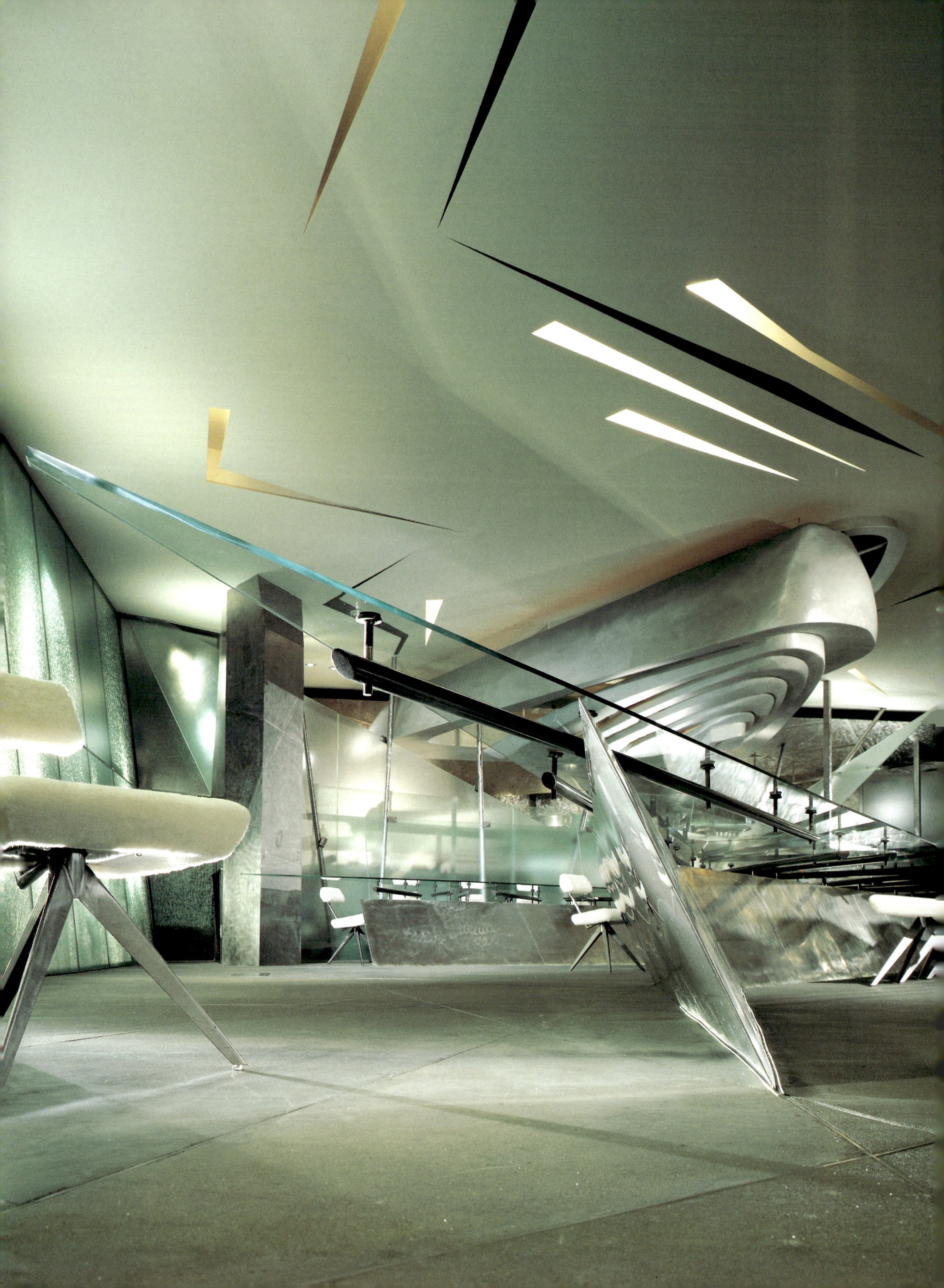

107

108

MOTOWN CAFE
Haverson Architecture and Design. Las Vegas, NV, USA, 1997

An integral part of the architectural composition of the New York New York Casino, the Motown Cafe commands a corner site that is reminiscent of Manhattan's famous Radio City Music Hall. The vertical neon sign offers a sneak preview of the café's focus on all things Motown, the recording company that spawned a whole new generation of black musicians, many of whom are featured here in the restaurant's museum-like interiors, along with memorabilia of the heyday of soul music. The restaurant's entrance is surmounted by an illuminated sign with black letters styled to resemble a 1950s movie theater marquee, beneath which stands a white Continental ridden by gilded effigies of Motown stars. Statues of other singers are dotted about the interiors, keeping the diners company. In the lobby a merchandising corner flanks a "celebrity staircase" the leads up to the first level. The stairs are used to underscore the theme of the restaurant: the risers are studded with copies of the most famous Motown hits, and two stylized brass mikes prop up the banisters, which are made of outsize records printed with vintage labels, continuing along the upstairs balcony and again on the roof of the large dining room that follows. At this point the restaurant opens out dramatically into a lofty musical hall, complete with a "dress circle" looking onto the dining area, which can be turned into a dance floor. Large screens transmit videos non-stop alongside giant blow-ups of Motown artists, who are also represented by carefully arranged life-size statues. The colors and materials are all tuned to re-evoke the feel of the period. Alongside the disc jockey's booth is a special room tricked out in honor of the "supreme" Diana Ross, queen of soul.

Parte integrante della composizione architettonica del New York New York Casinò, il Motown Cafe si propone come volume d'angolo conclusivo che ricorda nella figura il famoso New York City Music Hall. L'insegna verticale al neon che segna la facciata annuncia il carattere 'a tema' di questo locale dedicato al fenomeno della "Motown Music", che verso la fine degli anni '50 lanciava sul mercato americano il nuovo genere 'soul' di grande successo. Tutto il progetto è incentrato sul ricordo di quei motivi e sulla musealizzazione spettacolare di figure, materiali e atmosfere di quel periodo. L'ingresso al ristorante è annunciato da un'insegna luminosa con lettere nere riportate come nei cinema e nei teatri degli anni '50, sotto cui è parcheggiata una Continental bianca abitata dalle statue dorate di alcuni protagonisti del movimento musicale; altre sono collocate all'interno, distribuite nelle sale da pranzo. Nell'ingresso uno spazio dedicato al merchandising del ristorante si affianca alla "scala delle celebrità" che conduce al soppalco del primo livello. La scala è assunta come occasione per sottolineare il tema di riferimento del locale; nei gradini sono incastonati i dischi d'oro più famosi, mentre due microfoni in ottone stilizzati fungono da sostegni alla base della balaustra, formata da grandi dischi che simulano gli originali per caratterizzare anche tutto il parapetto della balconata e in dimensione minore il controsoffitto della grande sala da pranzo successiva. Qui il ristorante si trasforma in una sorta di esplosivo 'teatro musicale' a doppia altezza, con balconata affacciata sulla zona pranzo trasformabile in pista da ballo. Grandi schermi trasmettono videoclip affiancati da macrofotografie dei protagonisti immortalati anche nelle statue dorate disposte con attenta regia. I colori e i materiali impiegati rileggono con creatività lo stile dell'epoca. Di fianco alla postazione del DJ è stata ricavata l'esclusiva saletta dedicata a Diana Ross, regina indiscussa del genere.

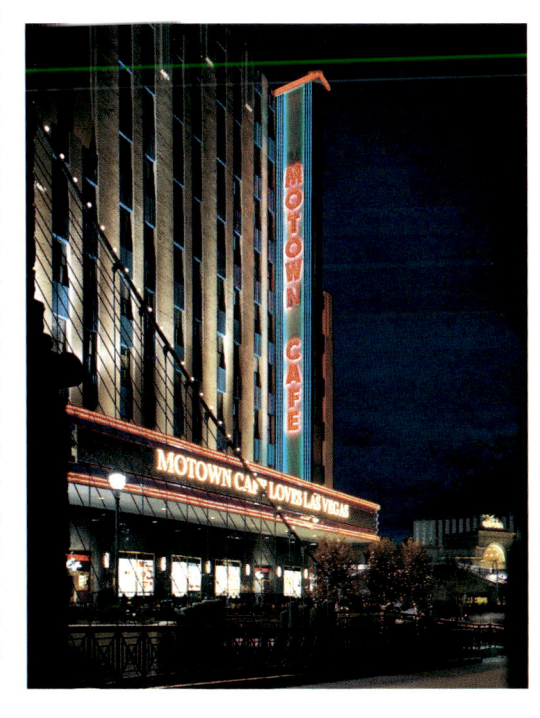

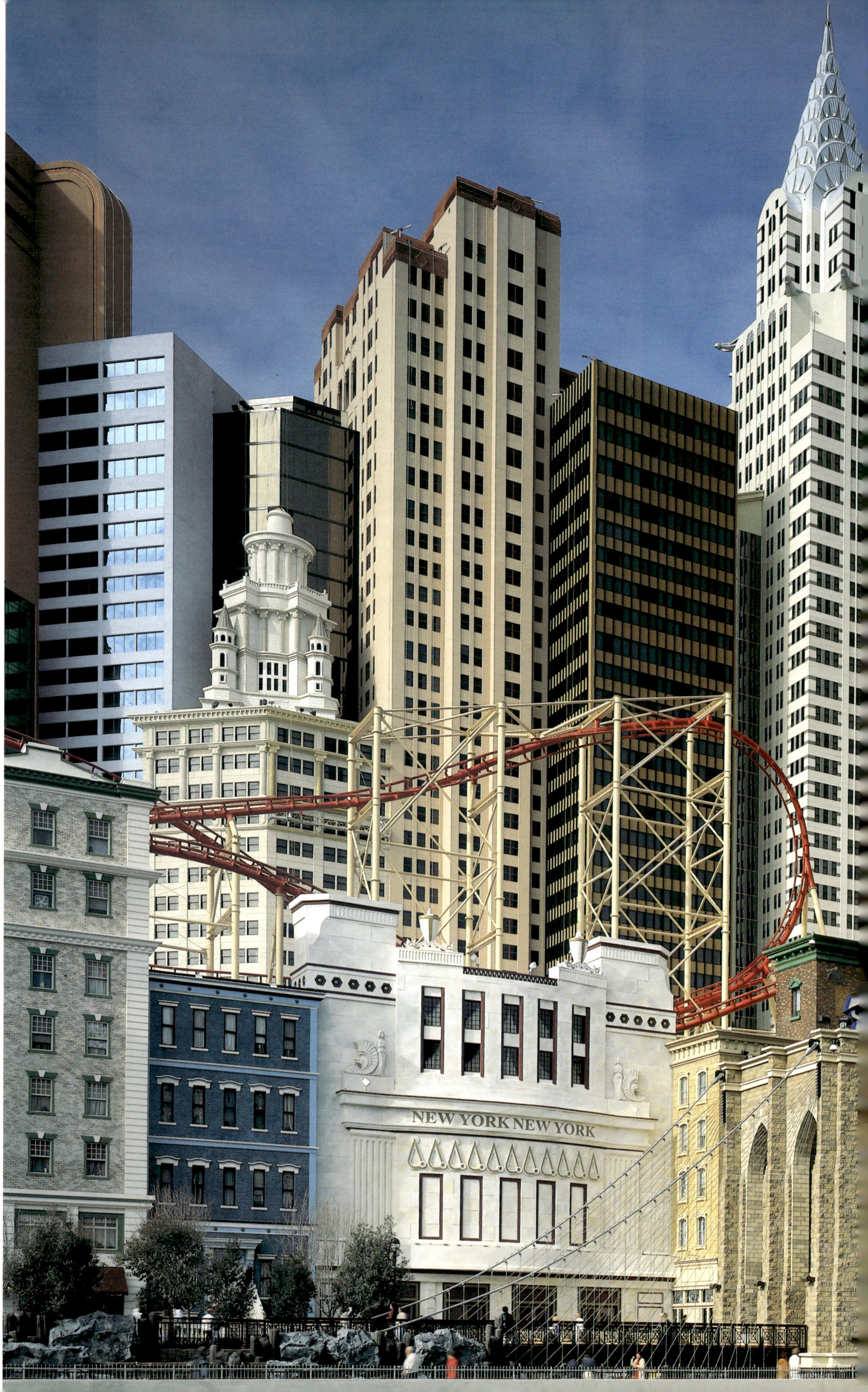
NEW YORK NEW YORK

111

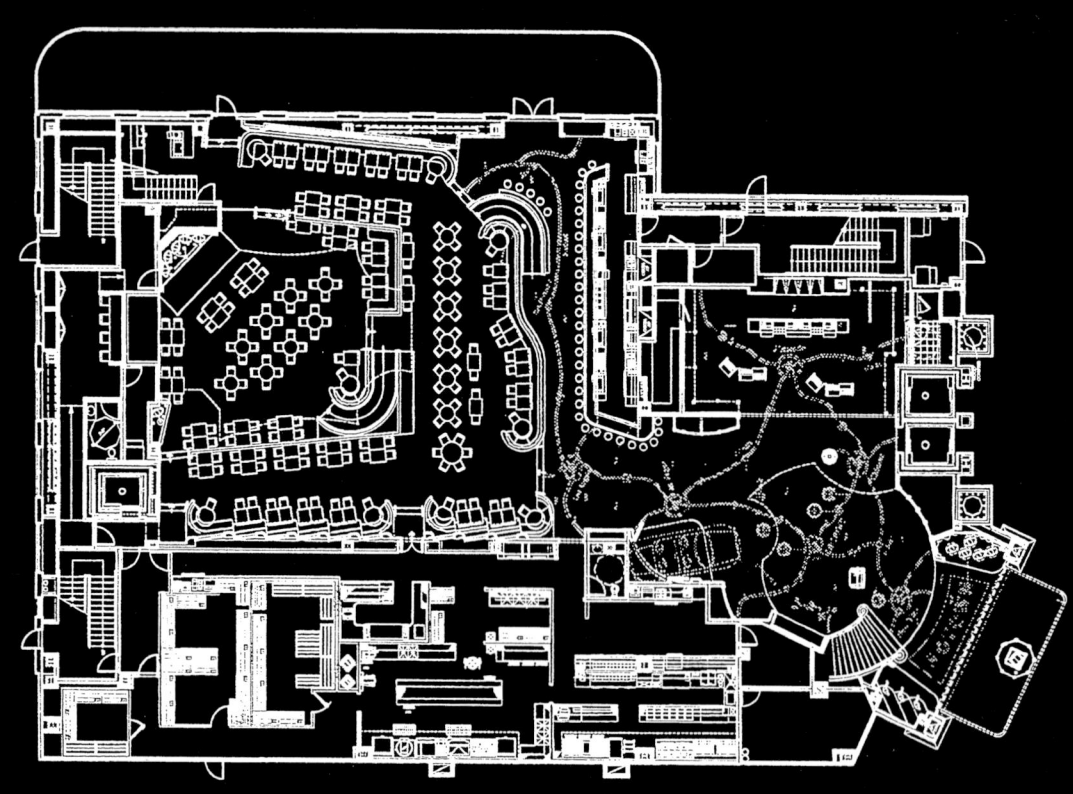

Ground floor / Piano terra

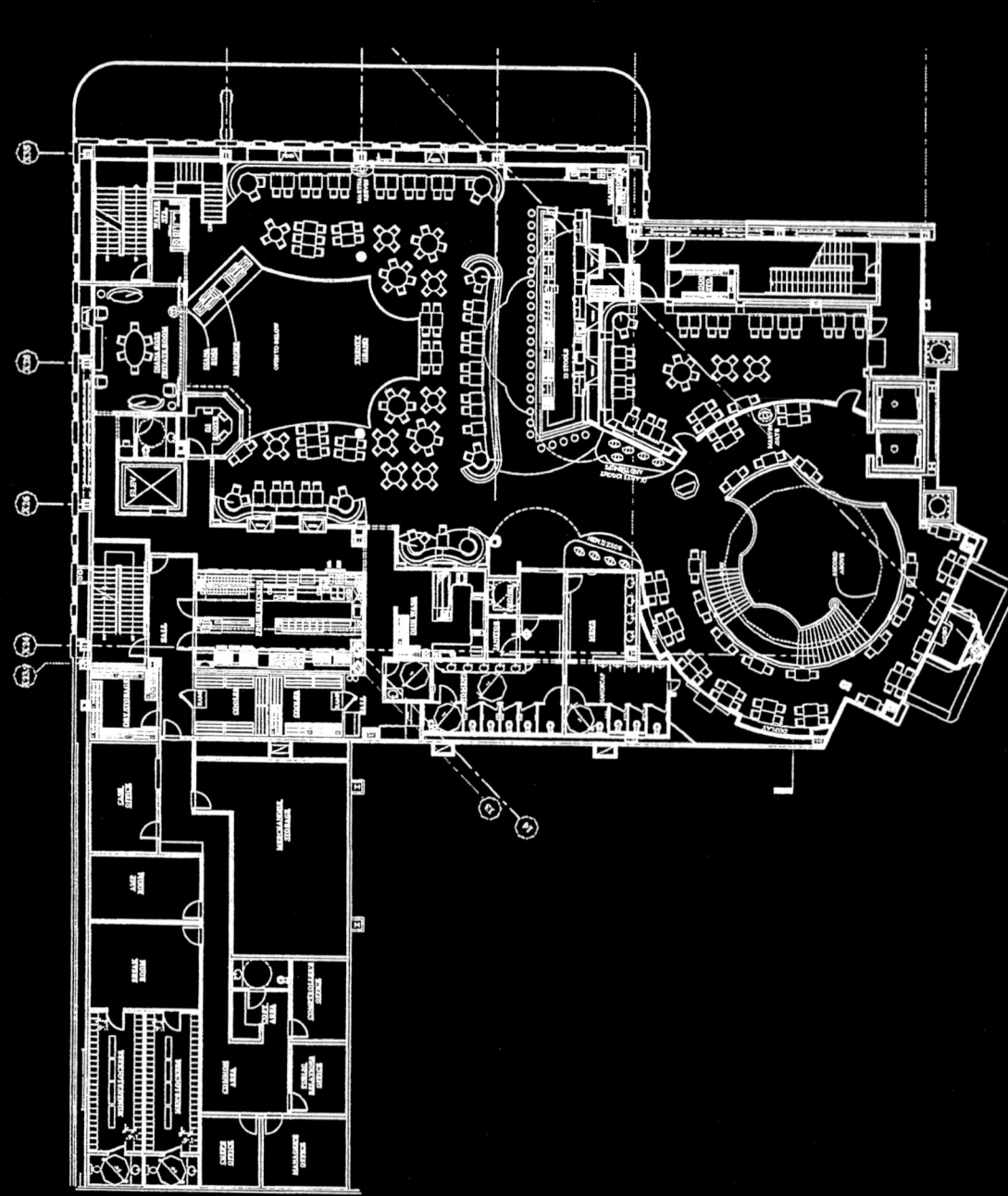

First floor / Primo piano

113

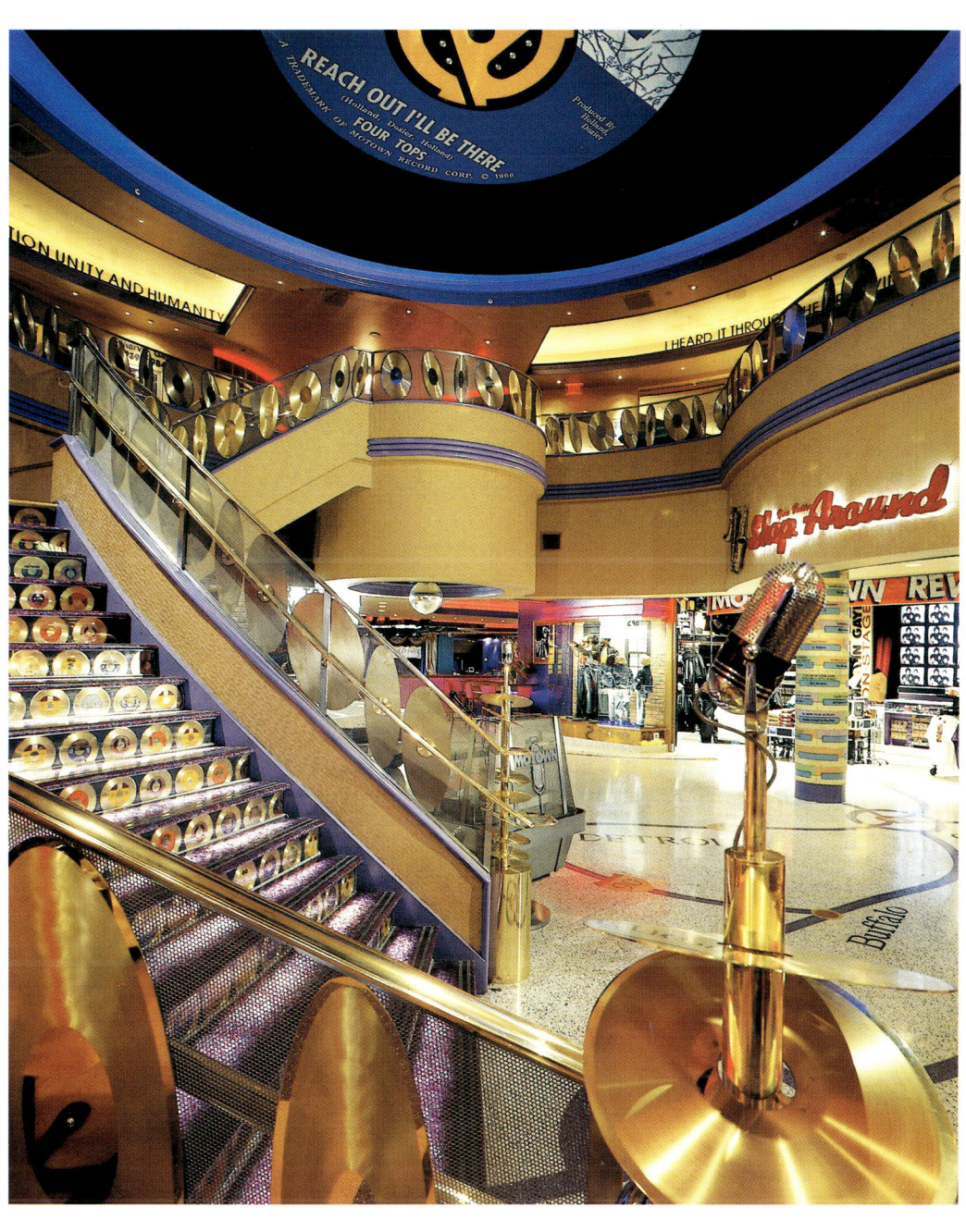

FOUR TOPS
LIVE !
FOUR TOPS
LIVE
MOTOWN
LAS VEGAS
CASINO
SOLD OUT
4 TOPS
Las Vegas

114

MOTORTOWN
MARVIN GAYE
ON STAGE
ELETTES

115

116

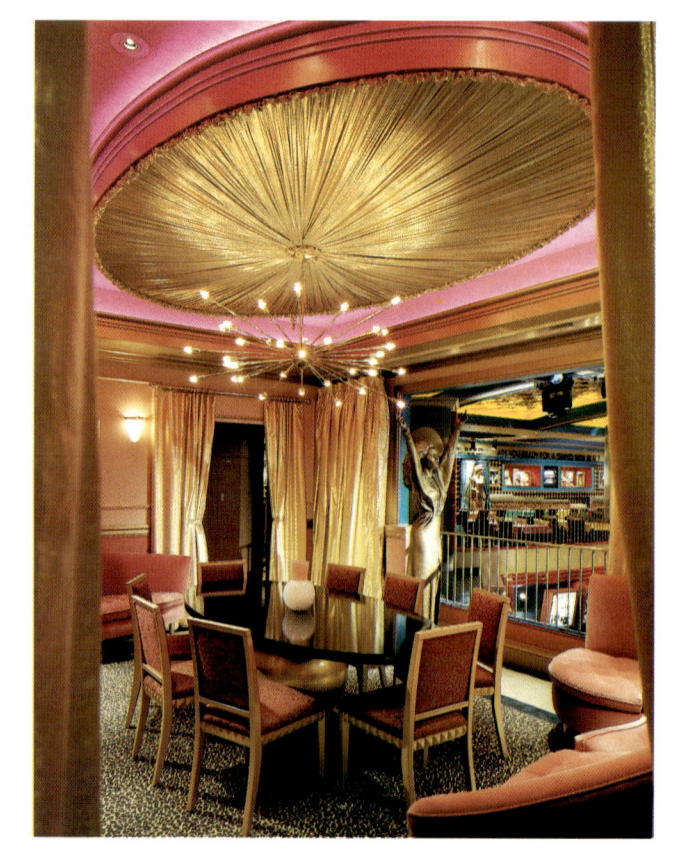

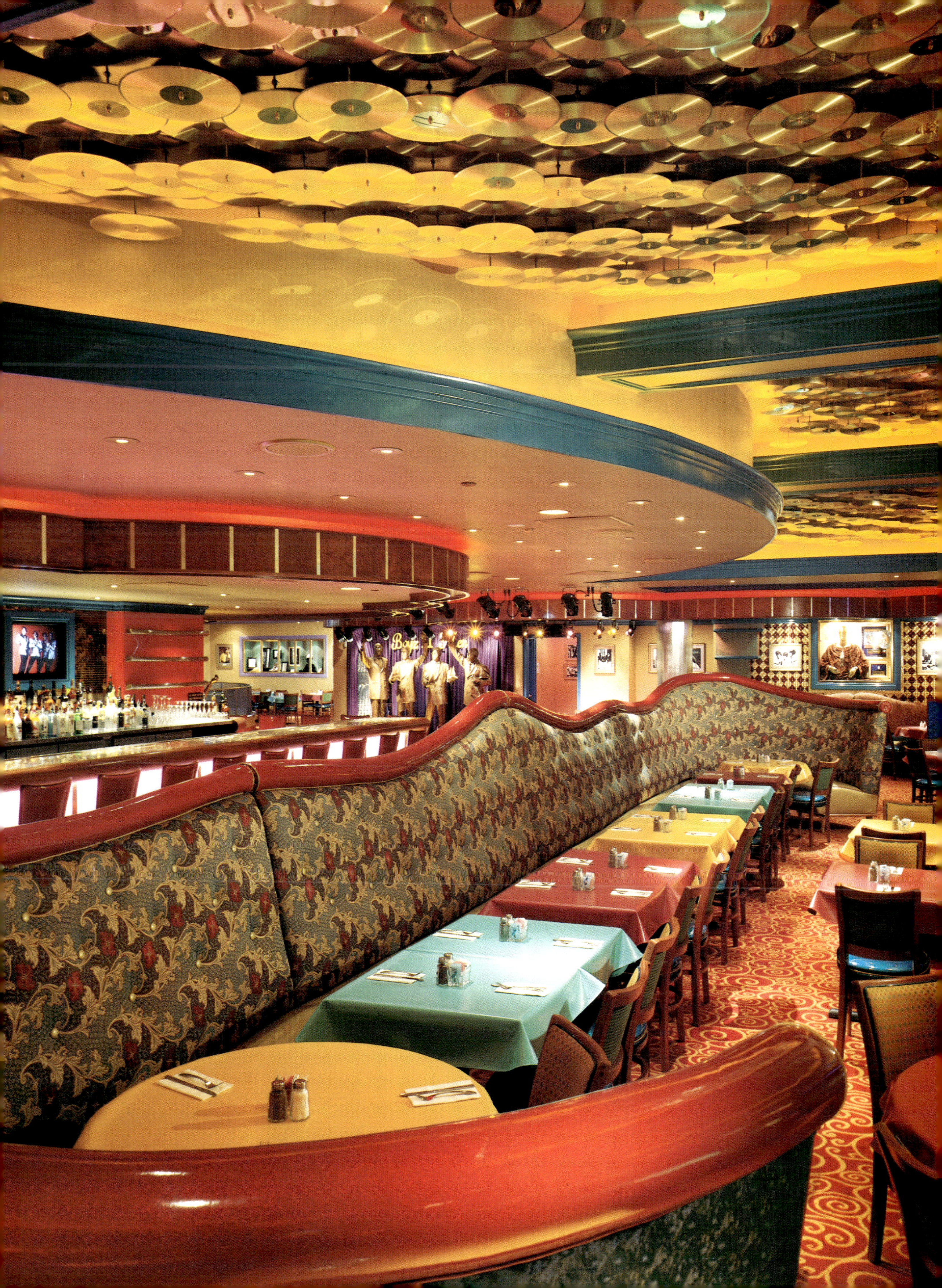

MOTOWN CAFE
Haverson Achitecture and Design. New York, NY, USA, 1995

Slotted into a Deco building erected in 1930, the Motown Cafe in Manhattan was inaugurated a couple of years prior to its counterpart in Las Vegas. In both cases, the décor and image pivots on the inimitable Motown sound. The New York venue established the style and mood of the interiors that were used for the ensuing outlets all over the world: a large split-level central space is overlooked by a theater-style balcony, all preceded by a carefully studied entrance foyer. Here several functional and stylistic elements are repeated, including the floor in multicolored floor set with the restaurant logo, the "celebrity staircase" with its risers studded with golden hits, the merchandising corner for the sale of posters, photos, and records, and not least the life-size replicants of the stars of the Motown sound. A long bar counter extends to the left leading to the tall central dining room, with its characteristic décor of statues, motifs and materials all in tune with the carefully recreated atmosphere of the Motown era. The fixed sofas with their tall, curved backrests define the layout of the dining room, marking out the circulation routes and seating areas, together with the colorful upholstered chairs. The second dining room on the mezzanine floor is accessed via a staircase with terracotta walls – a feature that was already there. This follows a private room decorated to simulate part of the Roostertail Club in Detroit, the home of Motown. The ceiling is decorated with a giant reproduction of a Motown 45 rpm, a kind of outsize icon that decides the tone of this double-height space with its theater-style balcony that does the full circuit of the room, interrupted only by the disc jockey's booth. The walls are spangled with gold records, period photographs, Motown mementos and paraphernalia, screens showing video clips, statues and life-size pictures of the Motown stars, accompanied by their hits transmitted through a sophisticated sound system, turn the whole venue into a dynamic little museum.

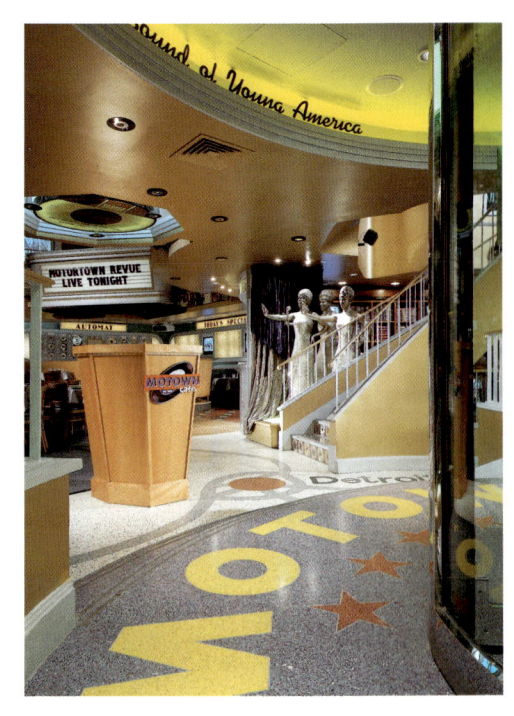

Ubicato all'interno di un edificio Art Déco del 1930, Il Motown Cafe newyorkese precede di due anni il locale omonimo di Las Vegas. In entrambi i casi il tema, non solo stilistico, di riferimento è la celebrazione della Motown Music. Il locale newyorkese ha definito per primo la tipologia interna da ripetere nel mondo: un grande spazio a doppio livello centrale circondato da balconata e anticipato da uno studiato ingresso. Qui sono ripetuti diversi elementi funzionali e stilistici, tra cui il pavimento in seminato a più colori con il logo del ristorante, la 'scala delle celebrità' con i 'dischi d'oro' incastonati nell'alzata dei gradini, l'angolo merchandising per la vendita di oggettistica e dischi, le statue a grandezza naturale dei protagonisti di questo famoso genere musicale. Un lungo banco bar si sviluppa sulla sinistra per introdurre alla sala da pranzo centrale a doppia altezza, caratterizzata per la ricerca di figure, motivi e materiali in sintonia con il riuscito sforzo di ricostruzione di atmosfere e sapori del periodo. Dei divanetti fissi, dallo schienale curvilineo, alto e pronunciato, segnano la disposizione della sala definendo percorsi e zone di seduta insieme alle colorate sedie di legno imbottite. Prima della saletta riservata che riproduce parte del Roostertail Club di Detroit, una scala preesistente, con pareti rivestite in terracotta, è stata conservata e restaurata per condurre al mezzanino dove è organizzata un'altra sala da pranzo. Un immenso disco in vinile a 45 giri è posizionato sul soffitto, come icona di riferimento, caratterizzando fortemente lo spazio a doppia altezza circondato dalla balconata interrotta dalla postazione radio del DJ. Dischi d'oro, fotografie d'epoca, oggetti e cimeli, grandi schermi per filmati e videoclip, statue e fotografie a scala reale dei cantanti, accompagnati dalle loro canzoni diffuse da un sofisticato impianto sonoro, sono disposti lungo le pareti configurando il locale come un piccolo e spettacolare museo.

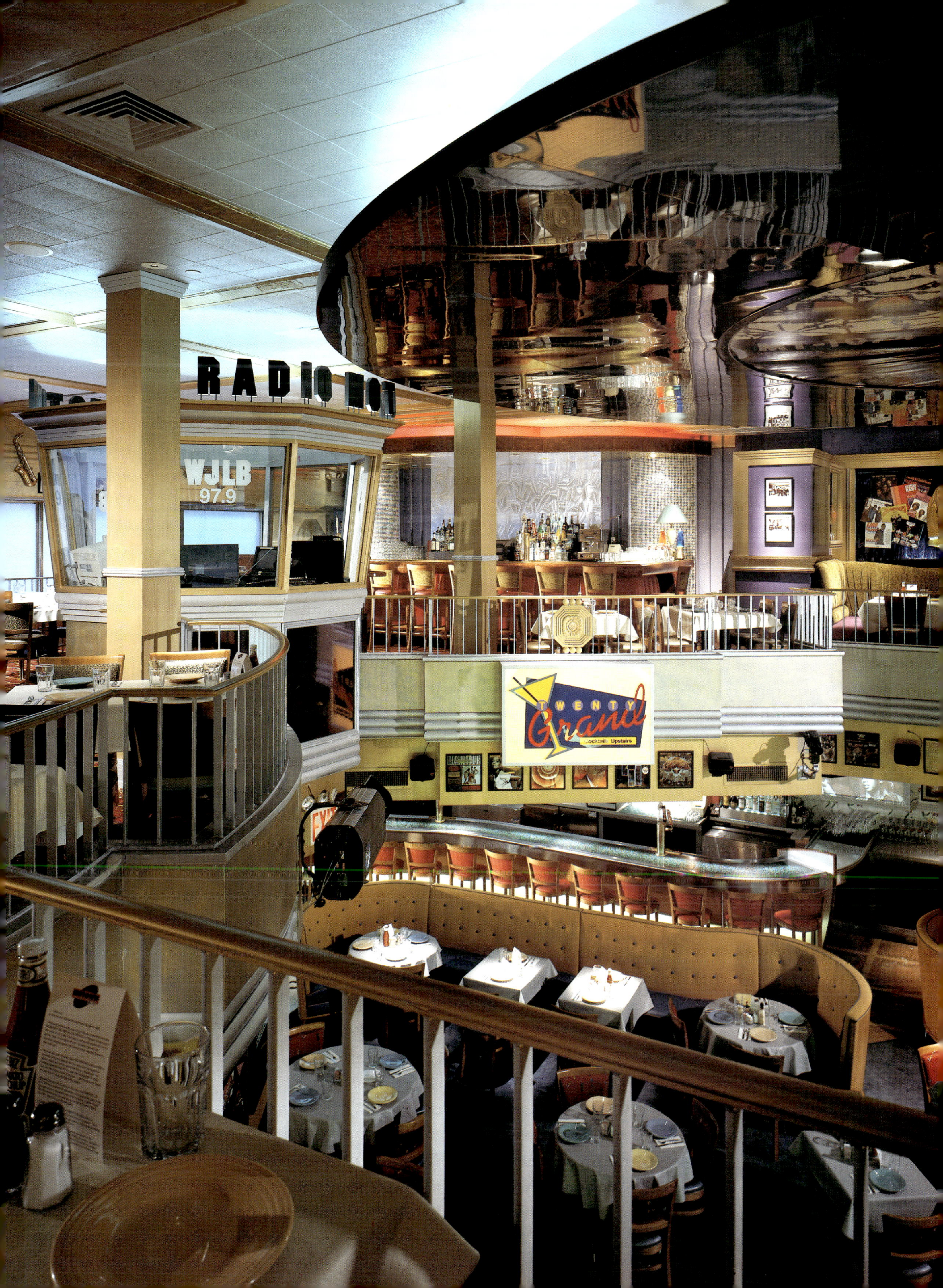

RADIO HOT
WJLB
97.9
TWENTY
Grand
Cocktails Upstairs

TOWN REVUE
BIG CHILL
HEINZ
TOMATO KETCHUP
GREY POUPON
DIJON MUSTARD

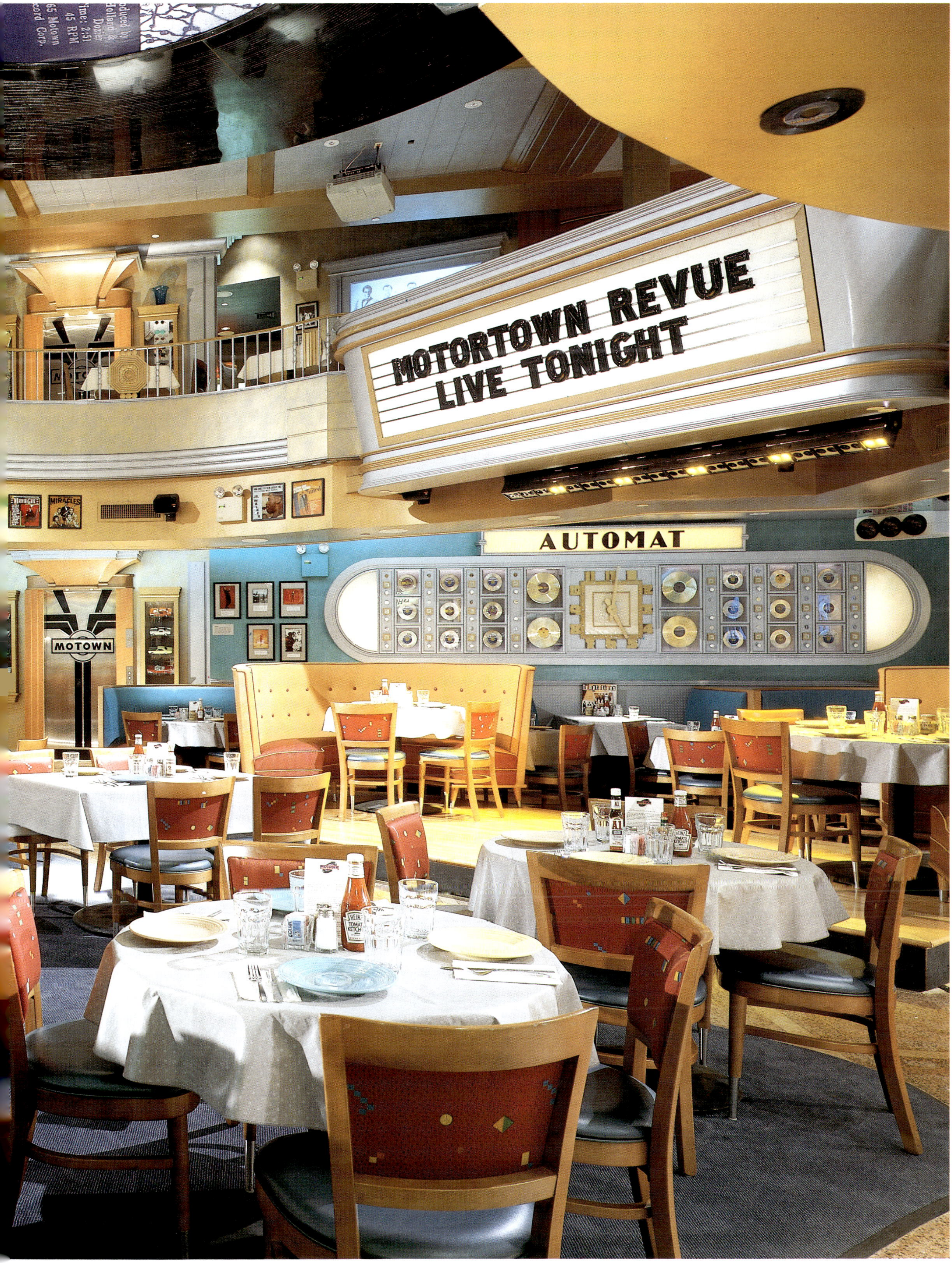
MOTORTOWN REVUE
LIVE TONIGHT
AUTOMAT
MOTOWN

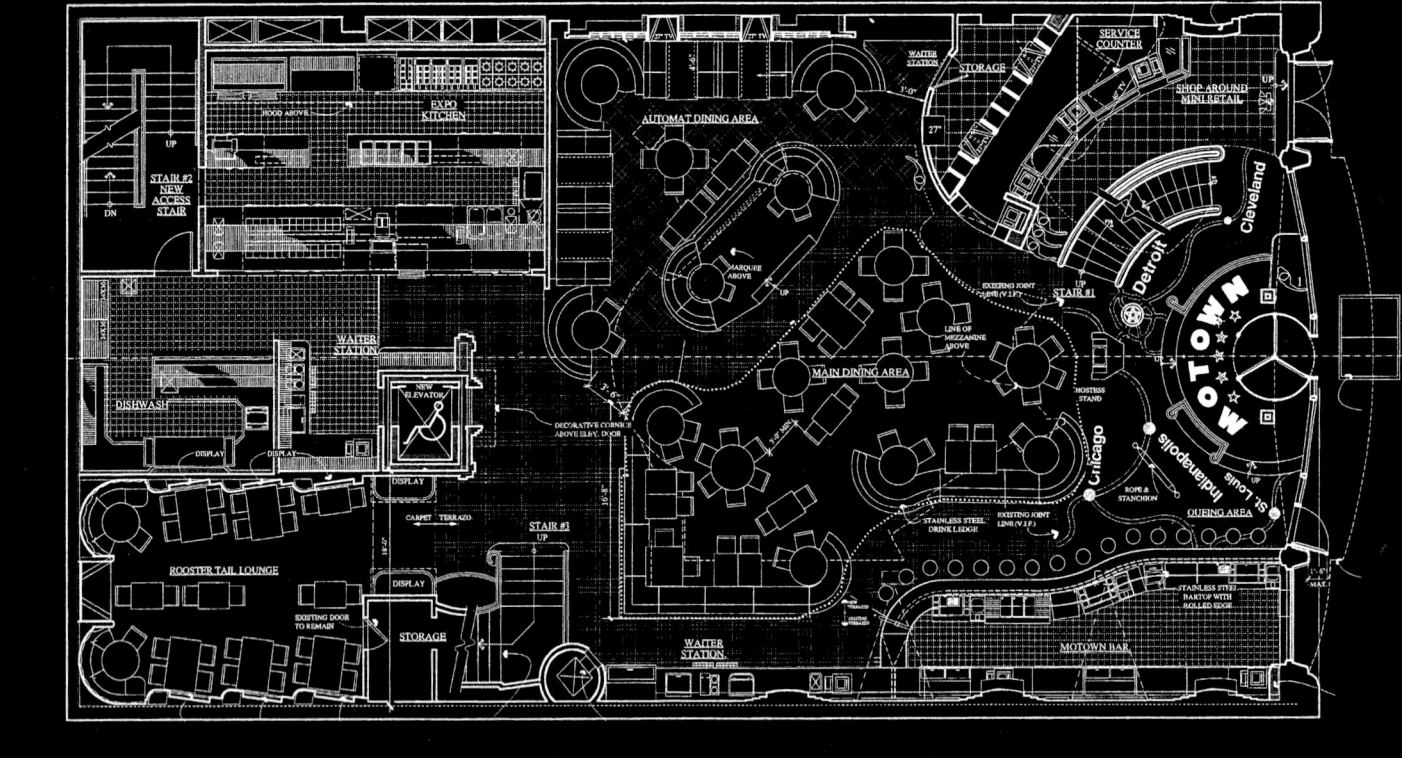

Ground floor / Piano terra

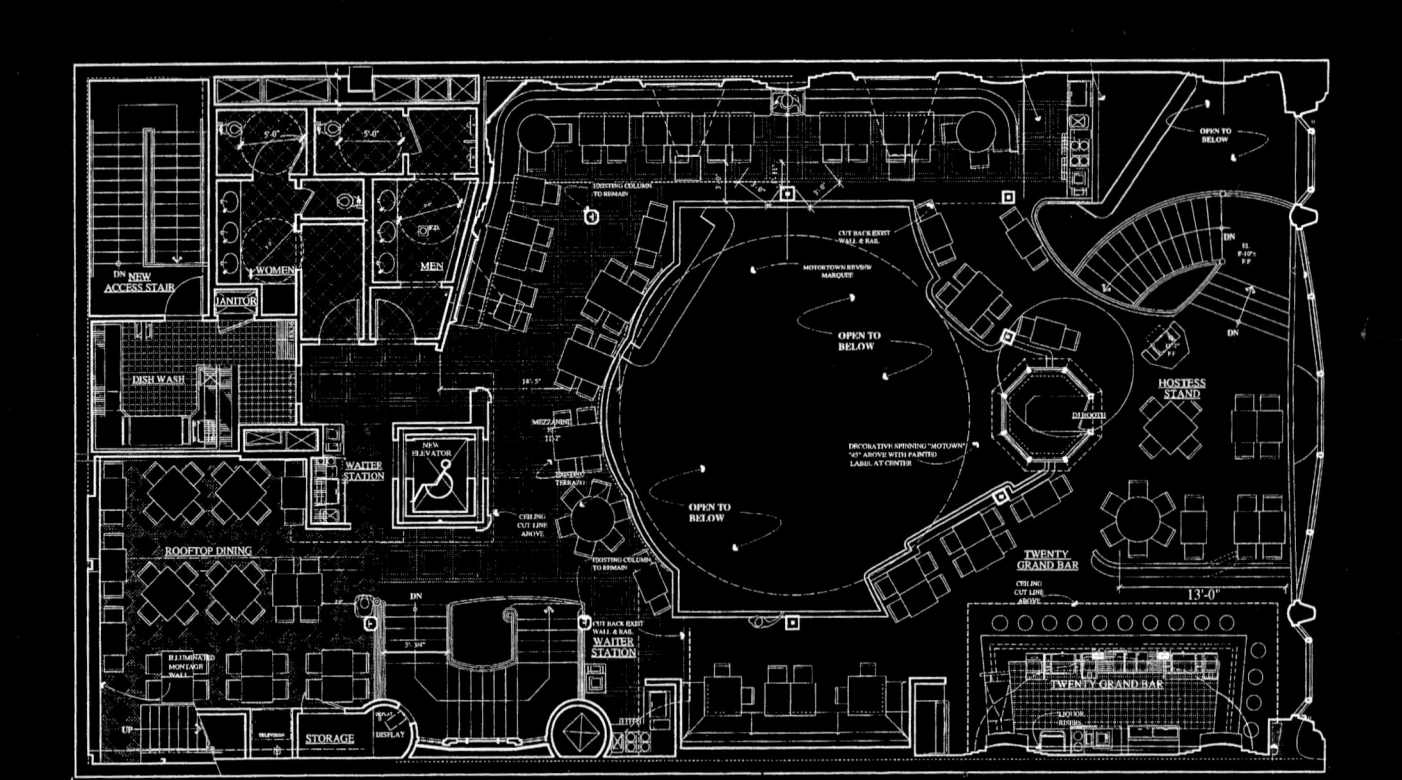

123

NOBU RESTAURANT
David Rockwell Architect. New York, NY, USA, 1994

The sources of inspiration for the design of this restaurant were the rural landscape of Japan and Kabuki theater. What intrigued the architect was the strong contrast between the horizontal and vertical plains of the kabuki stage sets, prompting a series of slender abstract elements that stretch from floor to ceiling, arranged throughout the interiors in homage to the Japanese countryside. The resulting space is indeed like a theater set, inward-looking and informed with an attentive and creative use of the materials aimed at defining a functional but poised atmosphere. The presence of four structural pillars suggested organizing the space to create a visual perspective that draws the eye from the entrance into the depths of the restaurant. The pillars are clad in wood frames enclosing portions of smooth gray plaster. These are flanked by tree-like sculptures that double up as light sources; these stylized presences, composed of trunks of birch, plates of rusted metal, and geometrical branches of ash, project a series of theatrical shadows on the pink stucco ceiling, while their trailing pink flowers made of colored wood are encased in the parquet. At the center stands the sushi bar, the heart of the restaurant. The seating, whose backrests are in the form of giant lacquered chopsticks, are arranged along the counter, with its illuminated onyx front, burnished wood top, and assorted bronze and brass detailing. Behind the sushi bar a sophisticated wall composed of rice-paper panels in soft pink and green hues offers a visual reminder of Japanese style. Alongside this stands the second visual landmark, a monolithic curved partition spangled with polished black pebbles, screening off the passage to the kitchens. A private room, obscured by a series of large wooden frames enclosing delicate compositions of dried branches concludes the vista with a further stylistic reminder of the Japanese landscape.

I motivi d'ispirazione di questo ristorante sono stati il paesaggio rurale del Sol levante e il teatro Kabuki: "è stato proprio lo studio del palcoscenico di un teatro Kabuki, il forte contrasto tra piani orizzontali e verticali espresso dalle sue scenografie, che mi ha suggerito il disegno di slanciati elementi astratti, che vanno da pavimento a soffitto, collocandosi negli ambienti come un omaggio alla dimensione rurale giapponese" (D.R.). Lo spazio si propone così come ambiente scenografico e introverso, caratterizzato da un attento e creativo uso dei materiali tesi verso la definizione di atmosfere ricercate e funzionali. La pianta segnata da quattro pilastri ha suggerito di organizzare una prospettiva interna che dall'ingresso si sviluppa verso il fondo. Ai pilastri, rivestiti da cornici di legno che riquadrano porzioni di intonaco grezzo lisciato, si affiancano degli alberi-scultura impiegati anche come sorgenti di luce. Queste scenografiche presenze arboree stilizzate, composte da tronchi di betulla, piatti di ferro arrugginito e rami geometrici di frassino, proiettano sul controsoffitto in stucco rosa le loro ombre teatrali lasciando cadere sul pavimento i fiori rosa (in legno colorato, incastonati nel parquet). In posizione centrale il sushi-bar è il cuore del locale: delle sedute con schienale composto da due grandi bacchette laccate sono posizionate di fronte al bancone con base in onice retroilluminata, piano di legno brunito e decorazioni in bronzo e ottone. Dietro al banco sushi, una raffinata parete composta da quadrati di carta di riso, a colori sfumati dal rosa al verde ricorda toni e materiali del Giappone, affiancandosi alla seconda forte presenza materica costituita dal monolitico schermo in curva ribassato, rivestito con sassi di fiume neri lucidati che protegge l'ingresso della cucina. Una saletta riservata, separata con una serie di grandi cornici in legno che contengono sottili rami secchi, conclude la prospettiva con un ulteriore richiamo stilistico al paesaggio naturale giapponese.

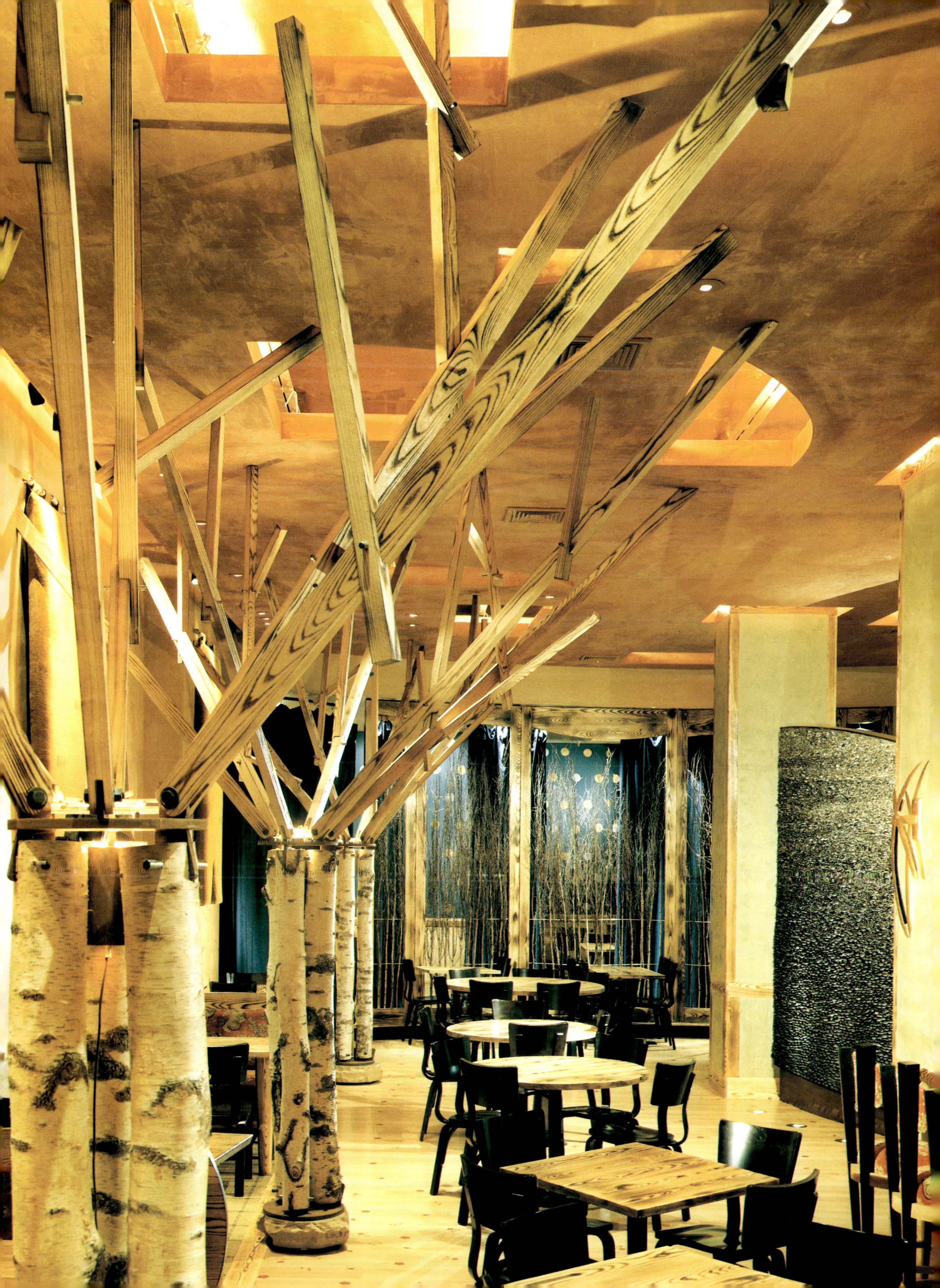

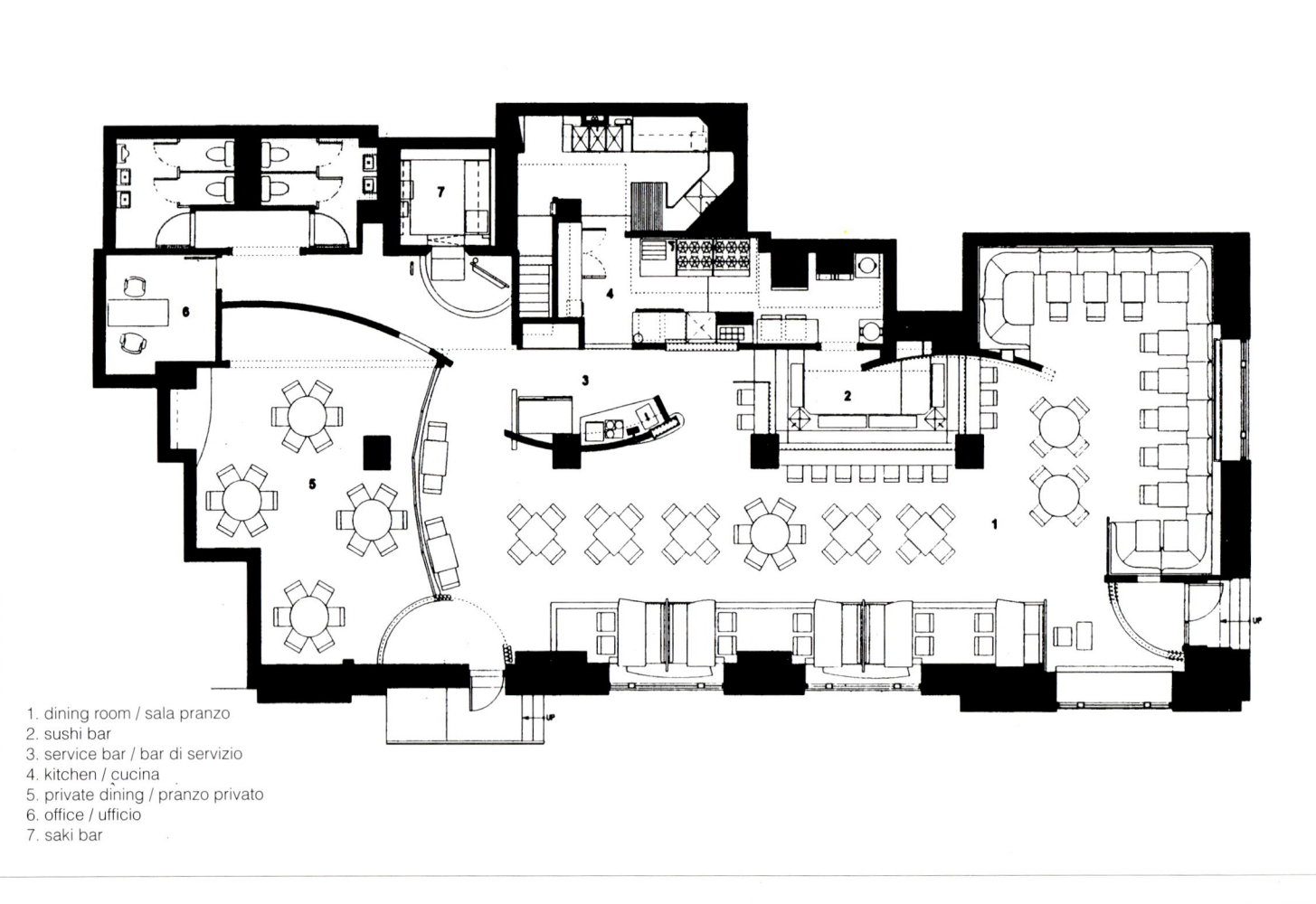

1. dining room / sala pranzo
2. sushi bar
3. service bar / bar di servizio
4. kitchen / cucina
5. private dining / pranzo privato
6. office / ufficio
7. saki bar

127

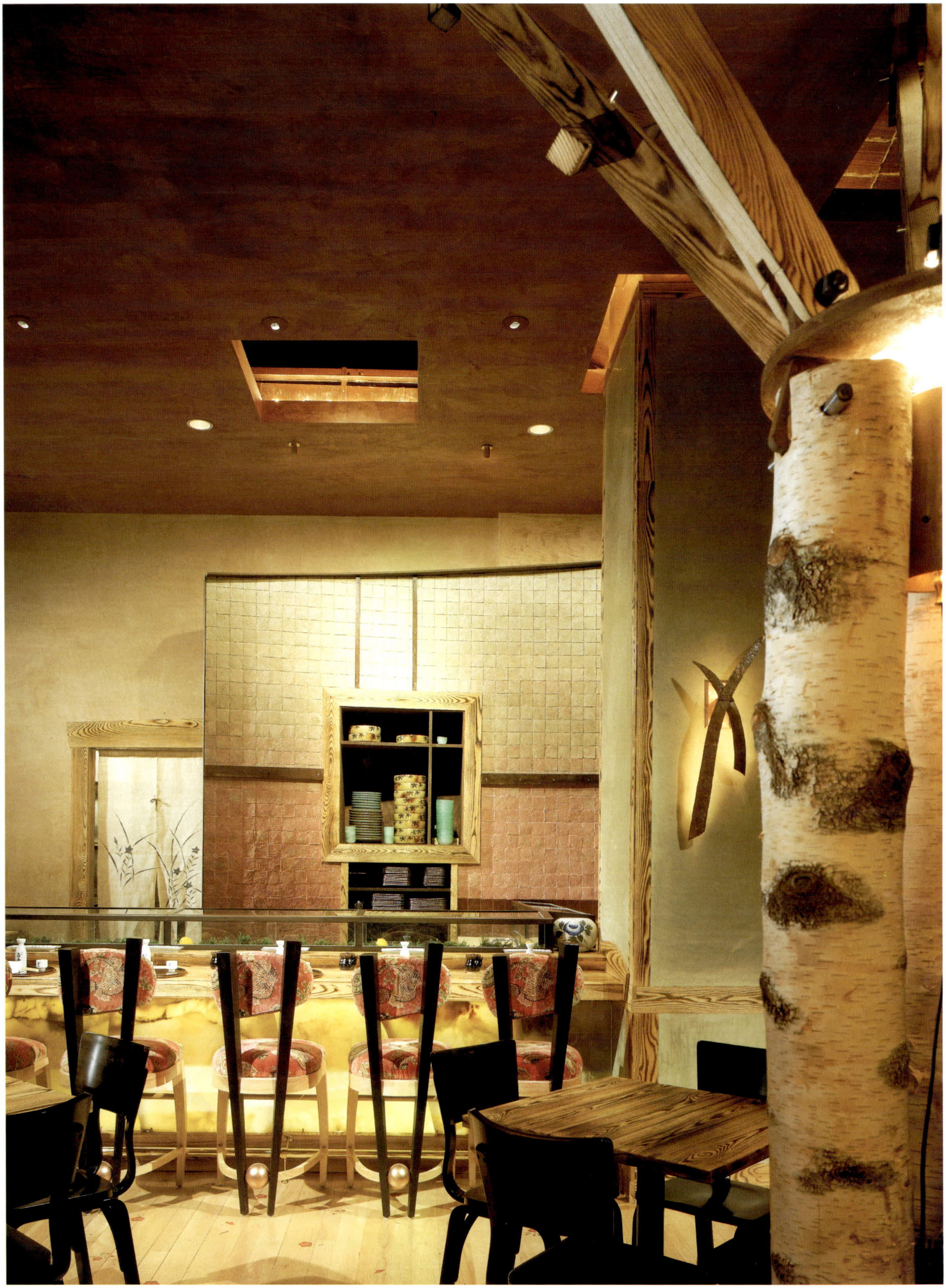

PLANET HOLLYWOOD
David Rockwell Architect. Orlando, FL, USA, 1994

The Planet Hollywood outlet slotted into the heart of the Walt Disney World in Orlando, Florida, represents something a departure from the usual format of the restaurant chain. Apart from the fact that it was built from scratch, its décor borrows from the image of rides and roller coasters of the past. A large blue sphere, sustained by a metal framework that reiterates the overall spherical form, is suspended over an artificial lake, like a spaceship that has come to land in the magical world of Disney. Crowning another vertical trellis is a smaller sphere bearing the illuminated logo of the eatery, which is repeated on a larger scale on the building's facade. The stairway has been inserted into a tilted cylinder linked to a large overhanging walkway composed of a luminous metal disk. Three separate levels look down onto the large open-space interior via ample galleries with walls pink walls and zebra- and leopard-patterned carpets, also used as a wall covering. The philosophy behind this chain of theme restaurants is to create a playful "museum" of the Hollywood universe, using ideas from movies for the interior design, the customized fittings, the wooden seating, the curios and costumes, memorabilia and original models featured in many box-office successes. The movie exhibits in the display cases, hanging on the walls and ceiling, together with stills and studio portraits of stars, and compositions of actors' silhouettes, and a huge screen on which film clips and advertising is shown non-stop. For the Orlando outlet, this barrage of cinemania has been pushed to its utmost expression: beneath the spherical roof are countless extraordinary items from film sets, such as bits of ship, aircraft, buses, automobiles, spaceships, bicycles, monsters, super-heroes, all dangling in space in an exciting jumble of impressions.

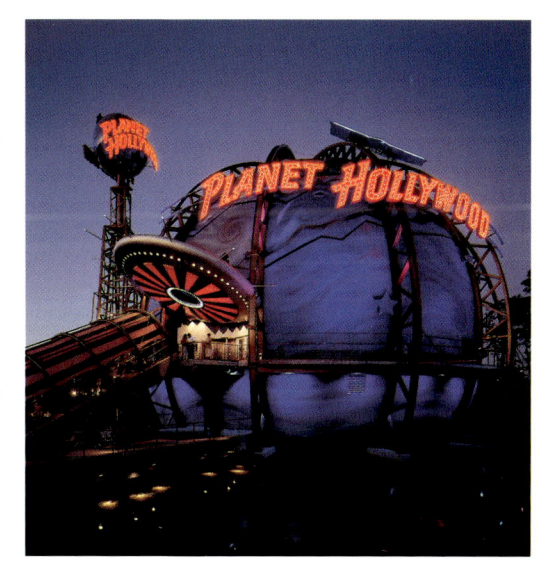

Costruito nel cuore di Walt Disney World, il Planet Hollywood di Orlando, se da un lato ripropone la filosofia degli omonimi ristoranti distribuiti nelle maggiori città del mondo, dall'altro si caratterizza per essere una costruzione ex-novo, che rivisita le figure delle giostre dei luna park del passato. Una grande sfera blu, sostenuta da tralicci metallici esterni che seguono la superficie sottolineando la figura complessiva, è sospesa sul lago artificiale come una sorta di simpatica astronave atterrata nel magico mondo Disney. Sopra un traliccio metallico verticale, una sfera più piccola si affianca a quella del locale per scandire il logo luminoso, ripetuto anche sulla copertura-facciata in scala maggiore,. La scala di accesso è posizionata all'interno di un cilindro inclinato raccordato con la grande pensilina aggettante, costituita da un disco metallico luminoso. L'interno si propone come grande spazio unitario dove tre livelli si affacciano uno sull'altro con ampie balconate caratterizzate da muri rosa e pavimenti in moquette zebrata e leopardata impiegate anche come rivestimento parietale. La filosofia della catena di questi ristoranti 'a tema' è quella di musealizzare in modo divertente il mondo del cinema americano, chiamando ad arredare gli spazi interni, oltre agli arredi su disegno e alle sedie di legno naturale, cimeli e costumi, oggetti e modelli originali impiegati nei maggiori film di successo. A questa serie di oggetti posti in bacheca, appesi ai muri o sospesi al soffitto e alle fotografie originali d'epoca, si affiancano i diorami con le silhouette degli attori famosi, il megaschermo dove proiettare film e spot. Per il Planet Hollywood di Orlando la spettacolarizzazione museale è stata portata al massimo livello espressivo e sotto la copertura sferica troviamo una fantastica rassegna di oggetti d'eccezione come navi, aeroplani, autobus e automobili, navi stellari, biciclette, mostri alieni e super-eroi, sospesi nel vuoto in un dinamico e strepitoso confronto.

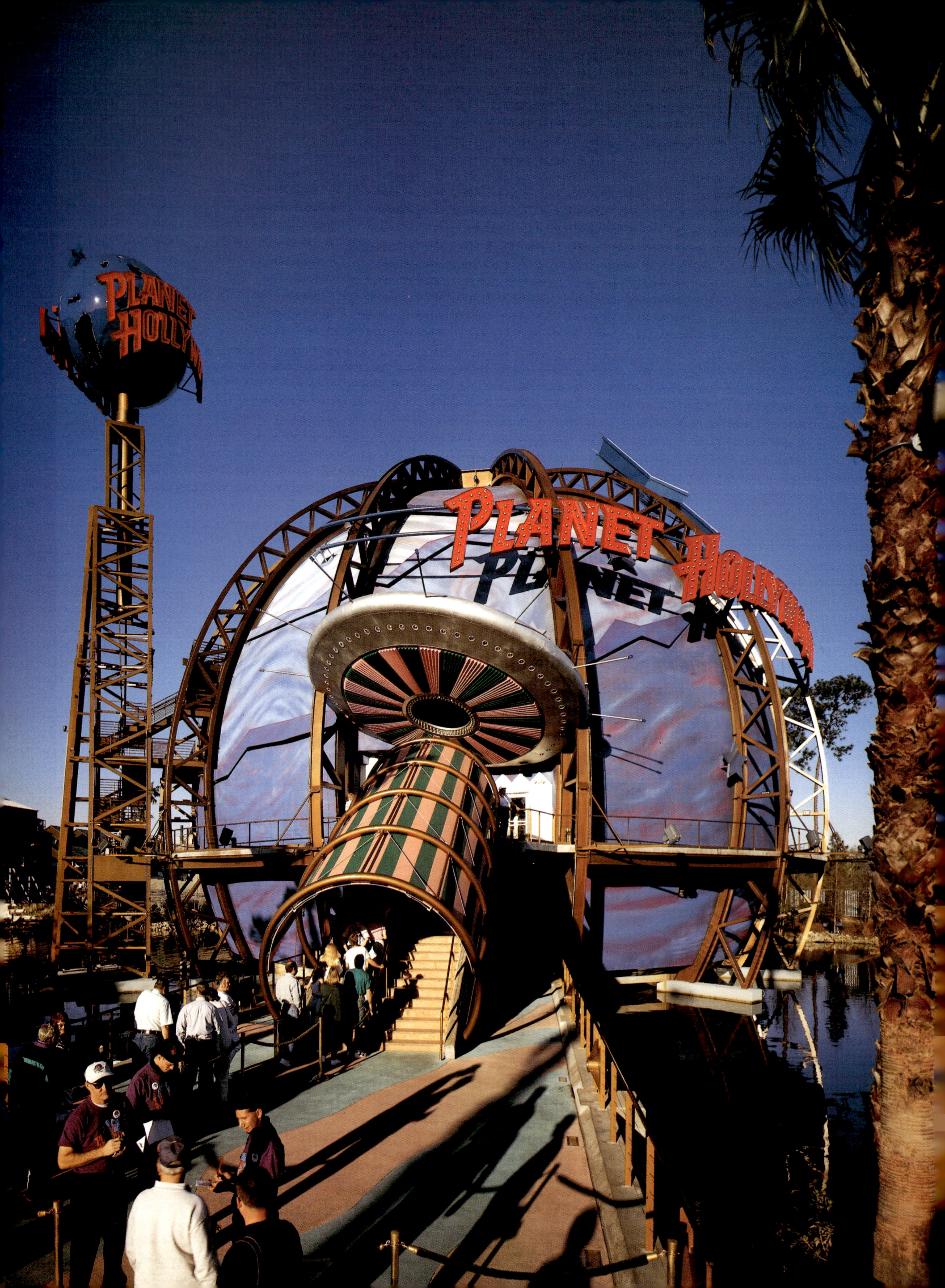
PLANET HOLLYWOOD
PLANET HOLLYWOOD

Lower level / Piano inferiore

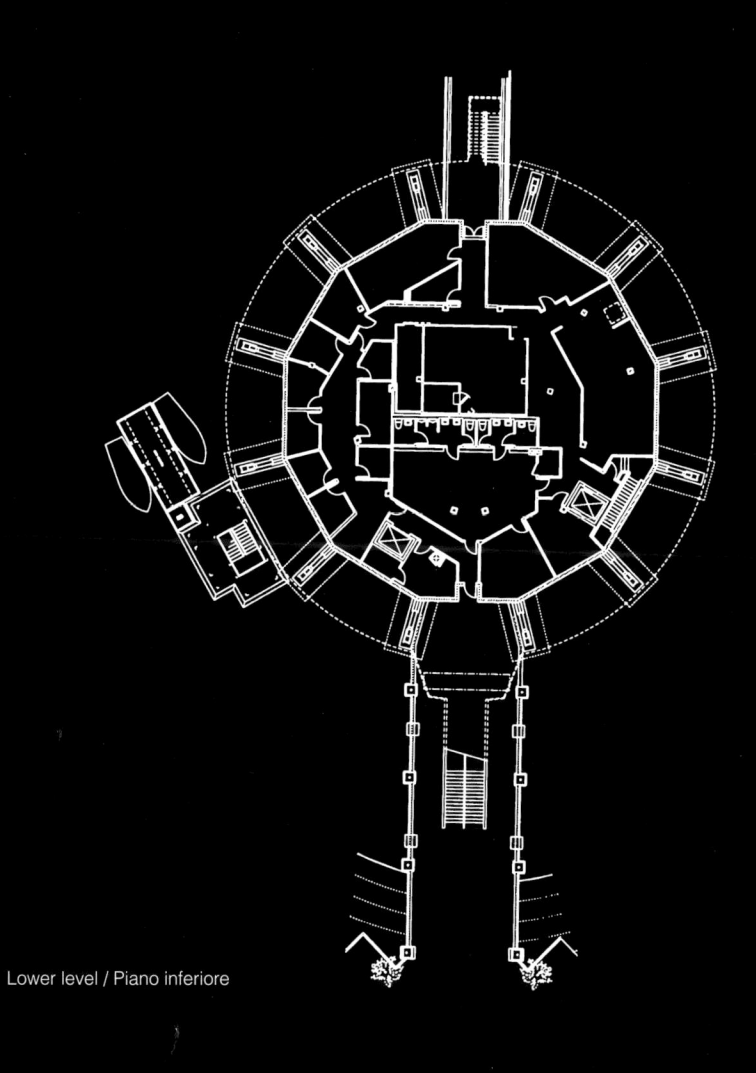

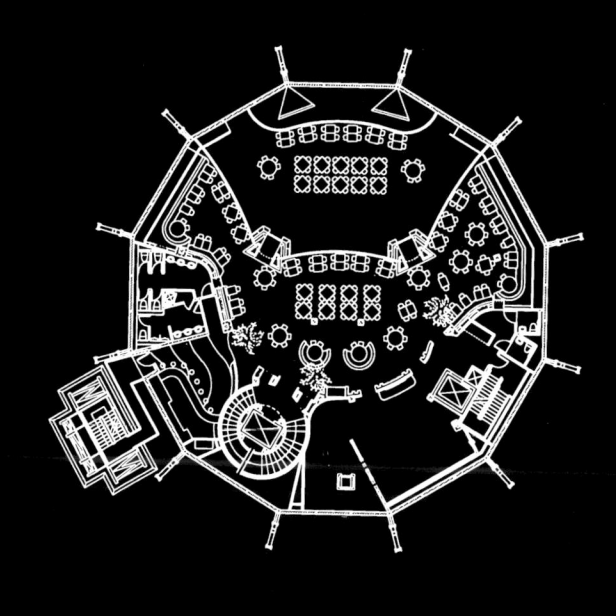

Main dining level / Piano zona pranzo principale

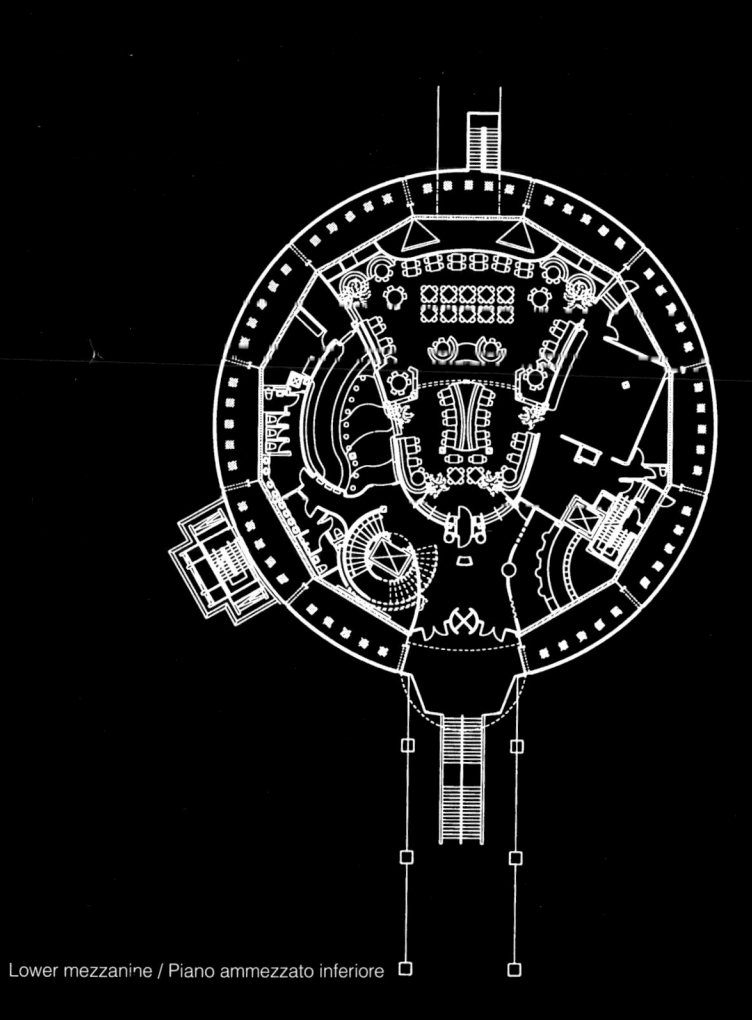

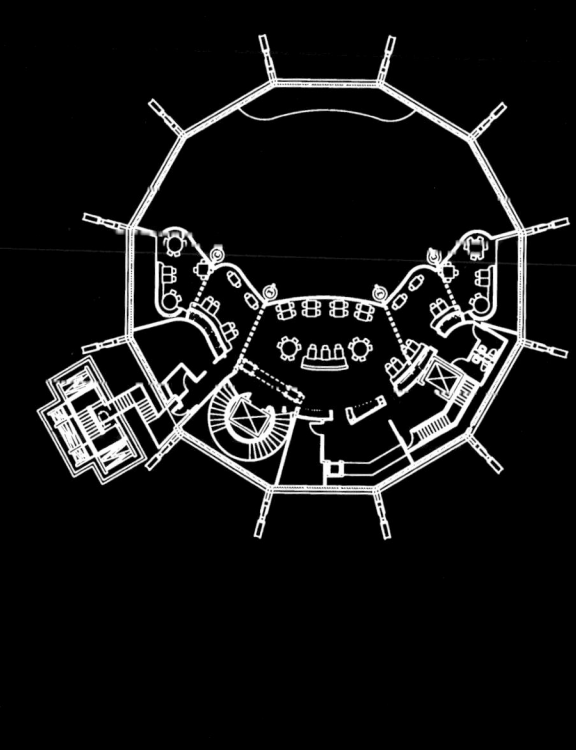

Lower mezzanine / Piano ammezzato inferiore

Upper mezzanine / Piano ammezzato superiore

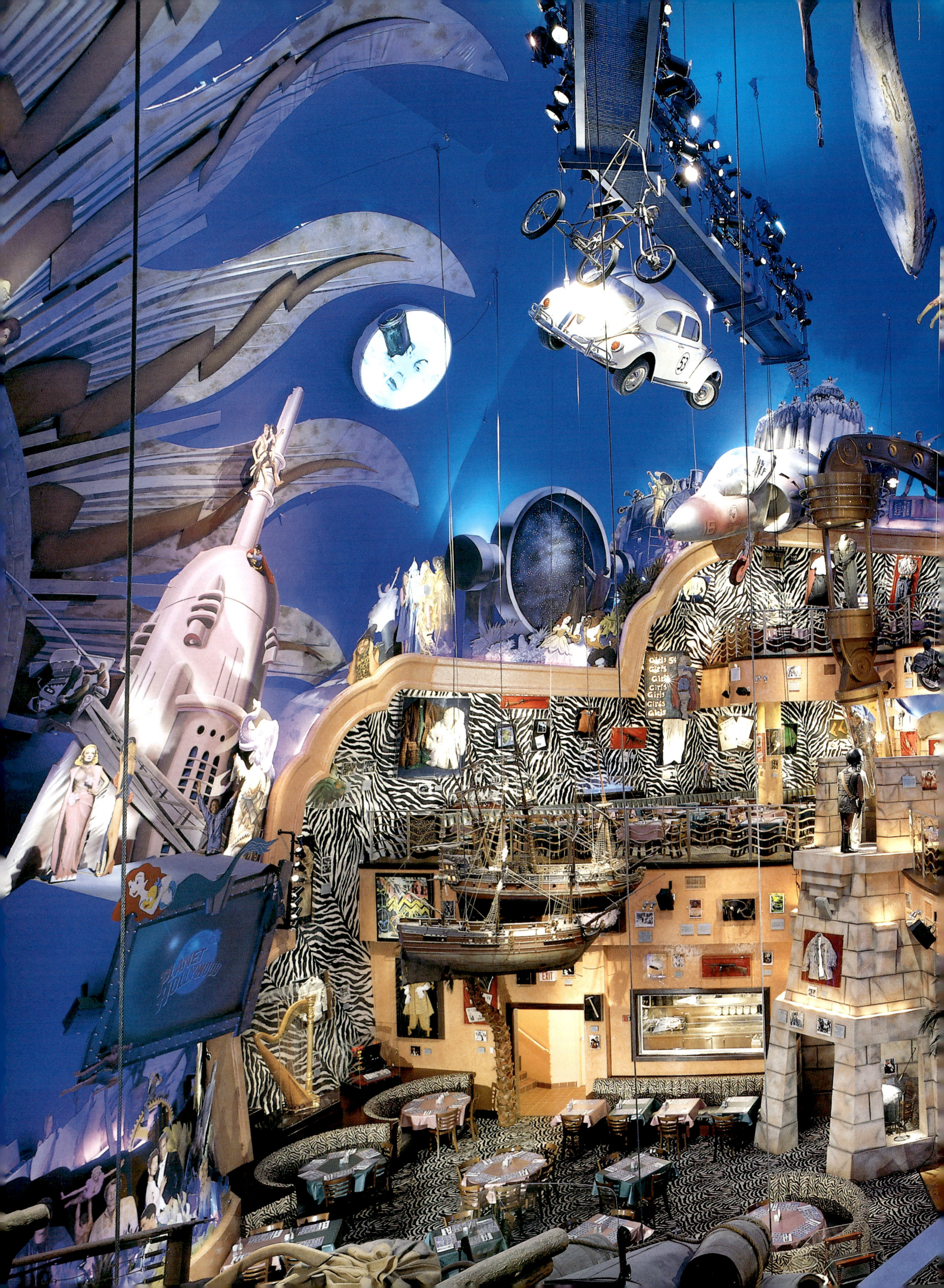

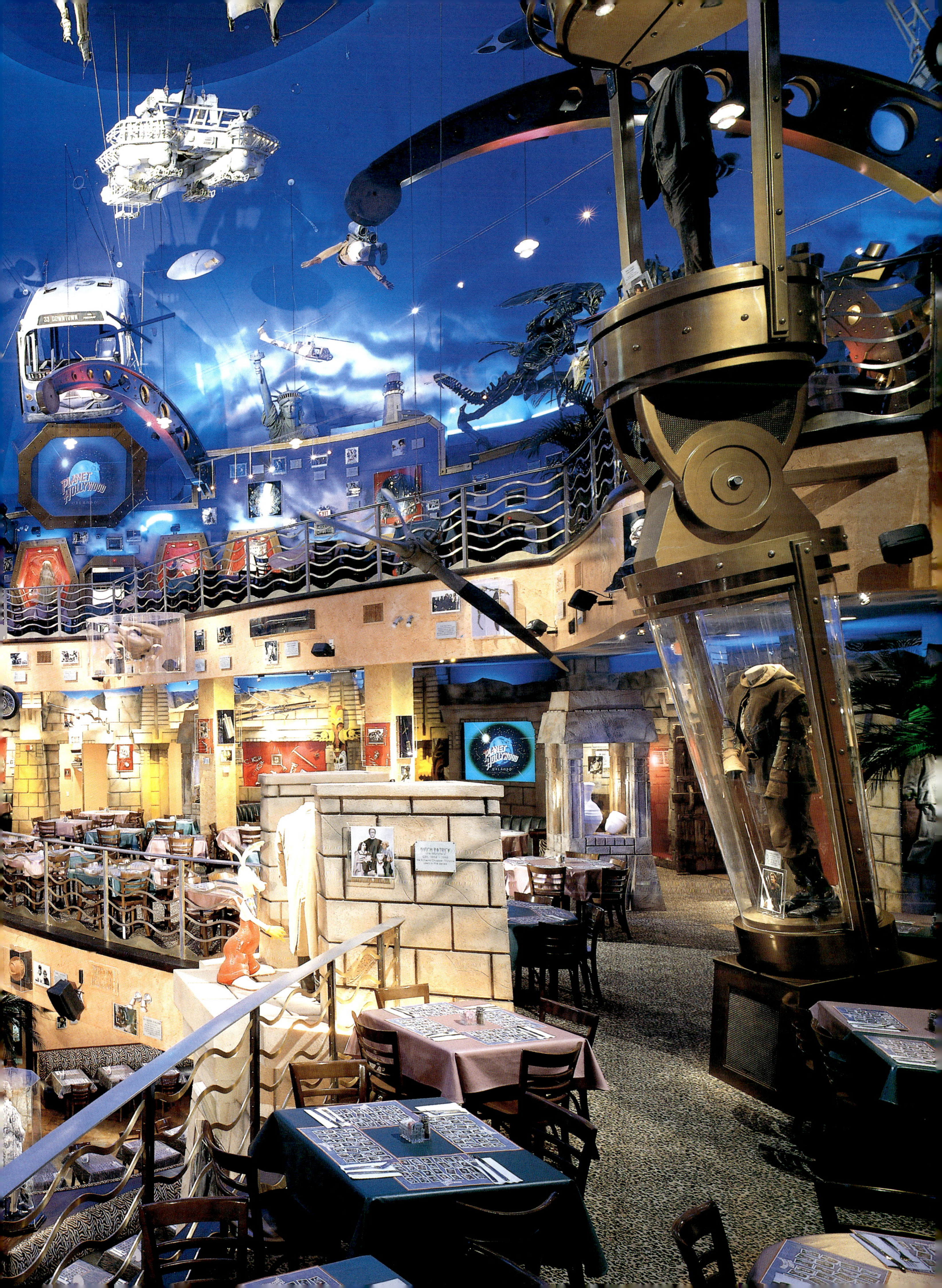
33 DOWNTOWN
PLANET HOLLYWOOD
ORLANDO

134

135

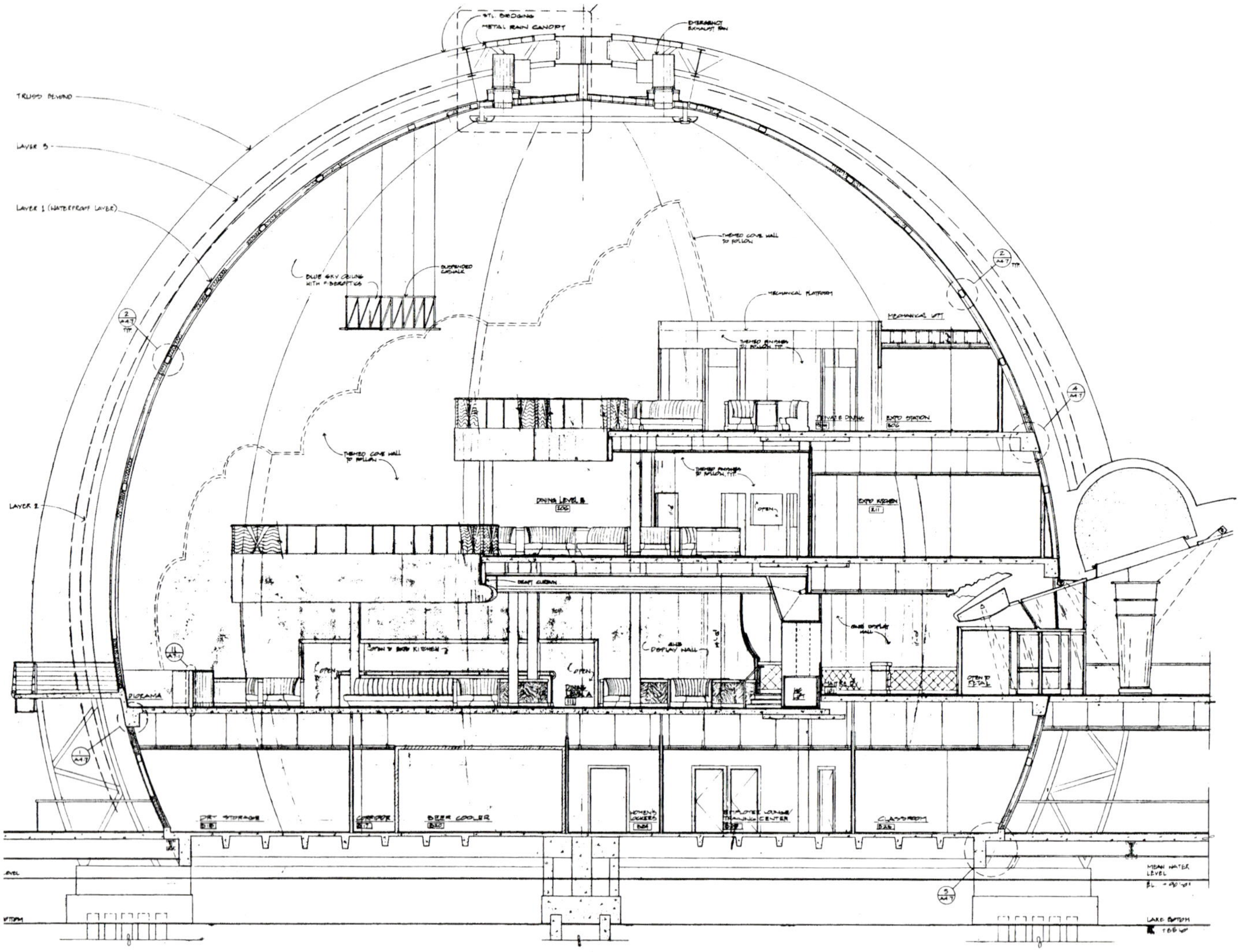

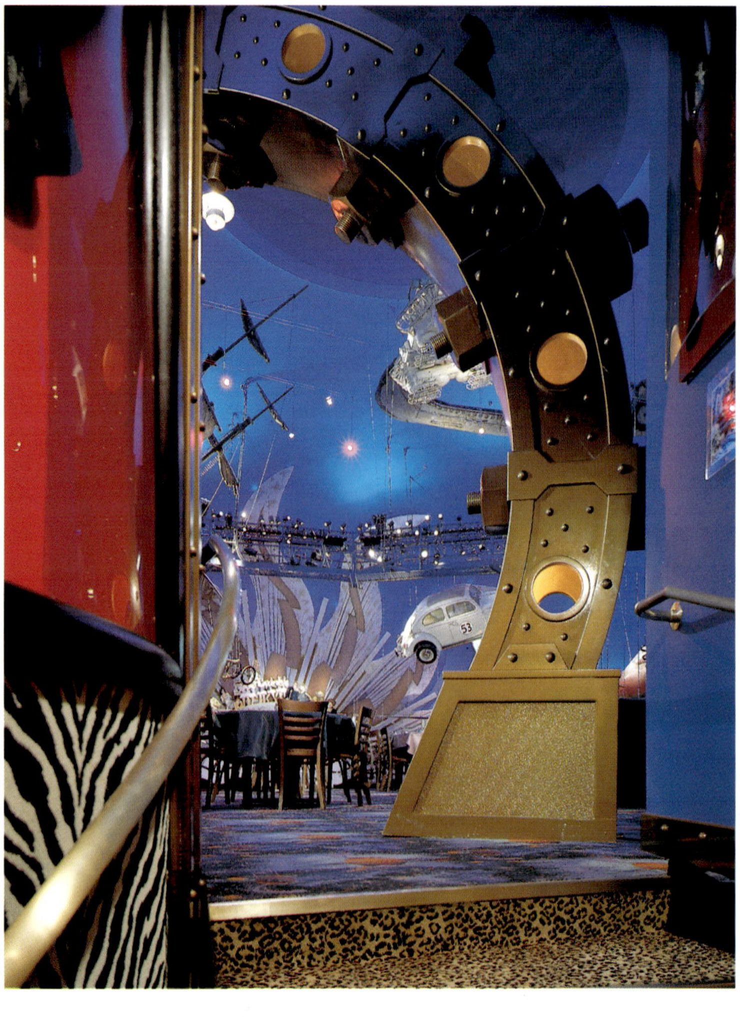

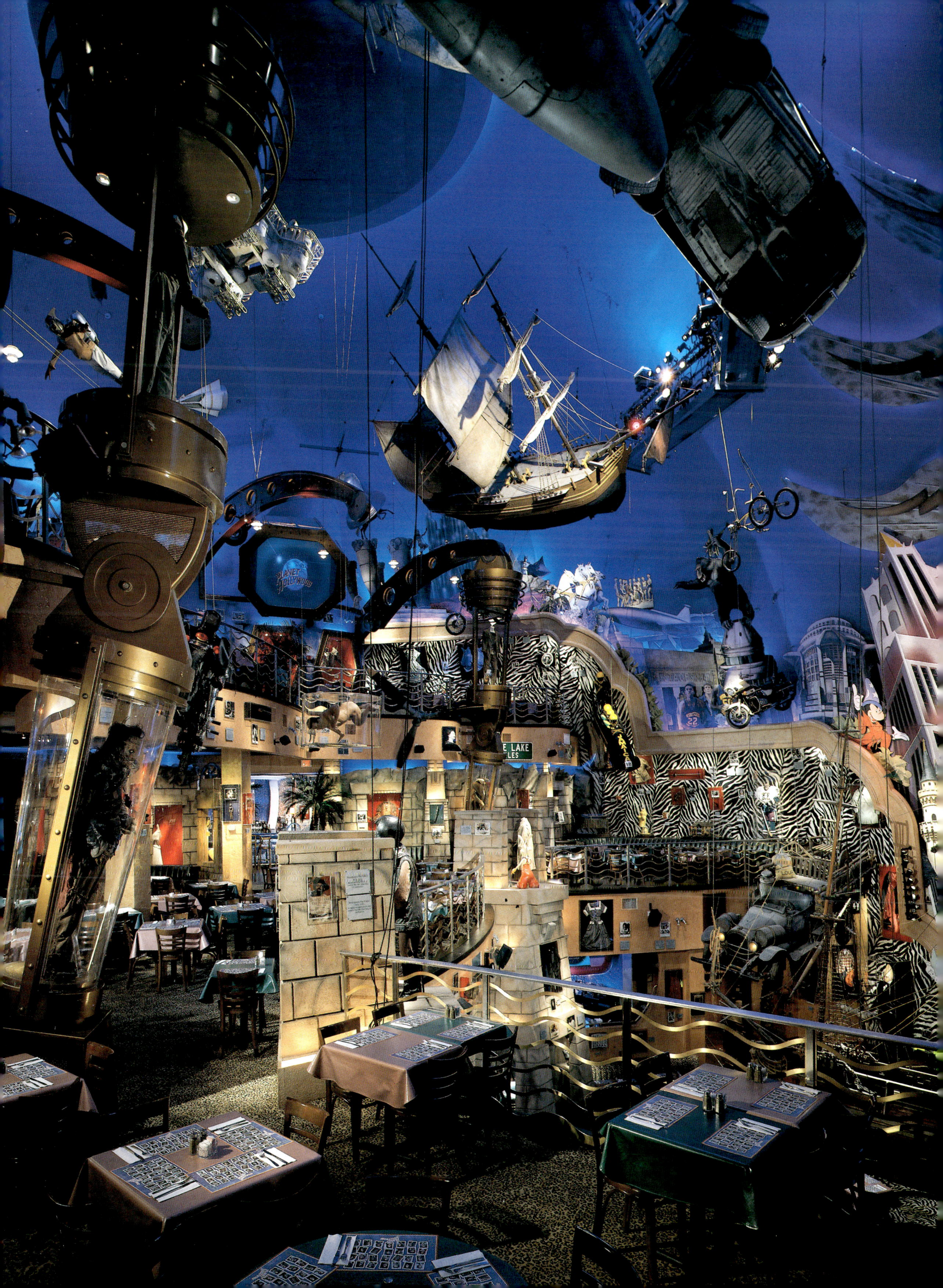

POIRET RESTAURANT

Ark Restaurant Corp. - Nancy Mah Weinstein Architect. New York, NY, USA, 1988

This contained and eclectic bistrot by the name of Poiret bestows the heart of Manhattan with the marvels of French cuisine in an informal, highly creative manner. From the street, the restaurant facade offers a strong visual landmark with an arrestingly colorful mosaic composed of fragments of glazed tiles arranged in huge rose patterns in shifting tones of red, yellow, and white. This is complemented by a checker pattern providing a figured base course that is emphasized by a profile made up of champagne bottle ends lodged in the wall. This upscale urban composition is topped by a fascia of blue tiling interrupted by a crowning design of vaguely colonial stamp. In this way the facade provides the basic image for the restaurant, alternating the mosaic idea and its vivid color scheme with a symmetrical arrangement comprising two set-back entrances and two central windows with striped awnings and sanded glass bearing the Poiret logo. The restaurant's interiors take up the floral refrain from the outside wall, albeit in a more subdued key, via a series of delicate painted roses combined with slender flowers on long stems (the work of Ron Wolfson, who was also responsible for the pattern designed on the parquet). A series of small vases arranged on the glass ledges at the entrance provide displays of cut flowers and perfumed roses, creating a pleasing floral backdrop. The interior has a regularly shaped plan with a stairway covered with a depressed vault, flanked by a lower space alongside. Hanging from the vault, whose springing line is marked by a delicate pattern on the wall, are two antique alabaster lamps on either side of a central five-armed candelabra that lights the ceiling. Halogen ambient lighting and diffusers are located on gesso wall-fittings matching the wall design. The pillars tinted in hues of yellow and red are the only strongly colored features, whose tones provide counterpoint to the black chosen for the traditional chairs, and the central pattern on the fine oak parquet floor.

Piccolo ed eclettico bistrot, Poiret porta nel cuore di Manhattan i sapori della cucina francese in modo informale e creativo. Sulla strada la facciata si propone come forte segno urbano con un coloratissimo mosaico composto da frammenti di lucide piastrelle che disegnano delle grandi rose rosse, fluttuanti in un degradare cromatico che lega il giallo al bianco, affiancate a una scacchiera usata come zoccolo figurativo di sostegno sottolineato dalla linea di coronamento in fondi di bottiglia di champagne incassati nel muro. Questa sorta di grande quadro urbano è concluso sulla sommità da una fascia di ceramica blu scura interrotta da un disegno di coronamento ad andamento vagamente coloniale. La facciata diventa così l'immagine del locale alternando alla figura del mosaico e ai suoi vivaci colori un impianto simmetrico con due ingressi laterali arretrati e due finestre centrali con tendine a righe e vetri sabbiati su cui è riportato il logo. L'interno riprende in modo più etereo il tema floreale dell'esterno sulle pareti decorate con una serie di raffinate rose dipinte insieme a fiori sottili dal lungo stelo (opera di Ron Wolfson, cui si deve anche il tappeto dipinto sul parquet). Una serie di piccoli vasi, posti su mensole di vetro di fronte all'ingresso, ospita una scelta di fiori e rose profumati, componendo una piacevole quinta floreale. L'interno si caratterizza come spazio regolare, con una sala coperta da una volta ribassata, affiancata da uno spazio laterale di altezza inferiore. Dal soffitto della volta, segnata sull'imposta da un bordo decorato con leggerezza, scendono due antichi lampadari di alabastro e uno centrale a cinque braccia che illumina il soffitto. Lampade alogene a luce indiretta sono collocate in appliques di gesso raccordate all'andamento delle pareti. I pilastri tinteggiati di giallo e di rosso si propongono come uniche forti presenze cromatiche contrapposti al nero scelto per le tradizionali sedie di legno, tonalità ripresa anche per la decorazione geometrica che segna la parte centrale del parquet di rovere.

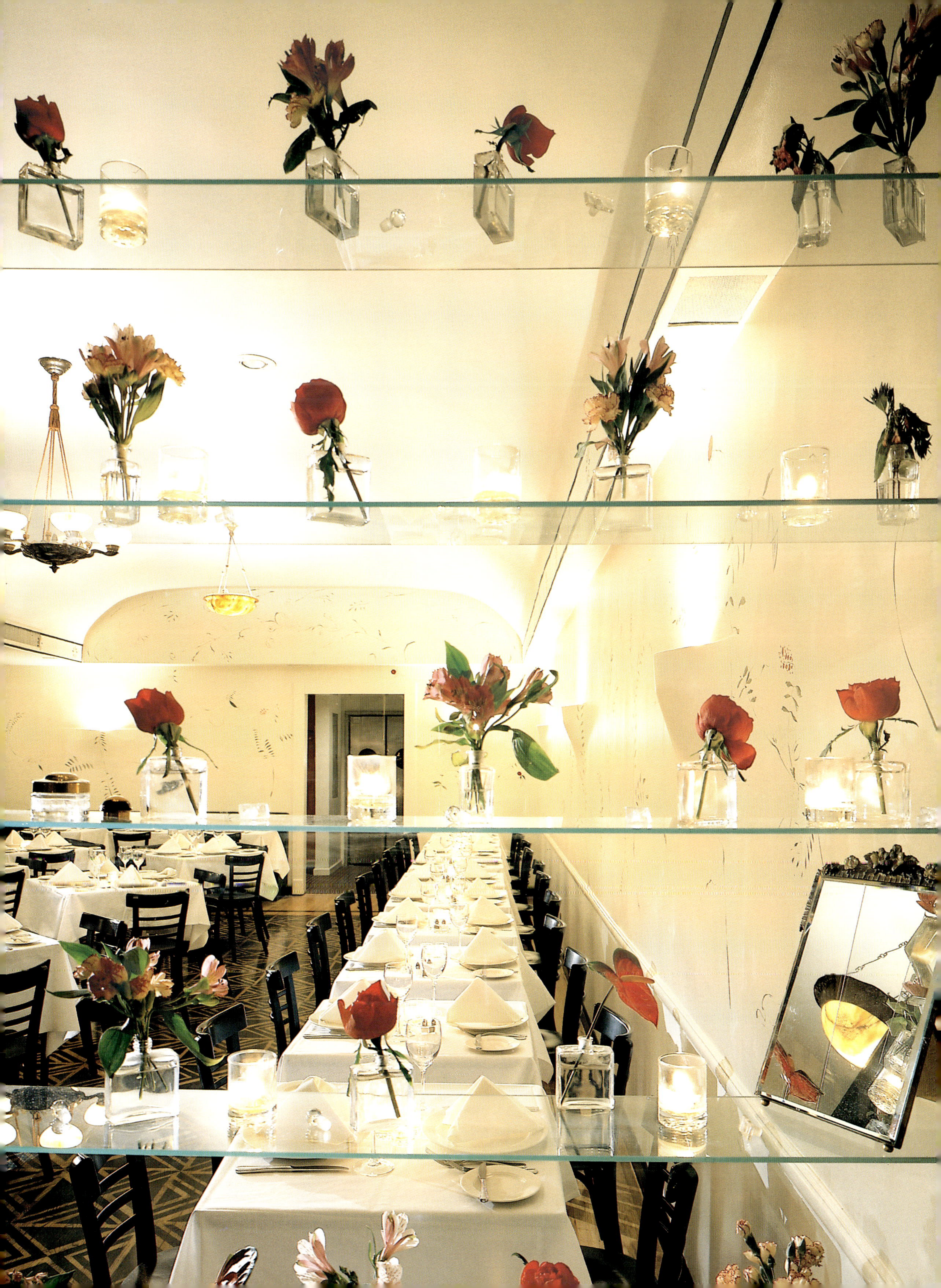

140

141

SAVANNAH RESTAURANT
Afuture Company - Alex Locadia, Giusi Mastro Architects. Miami Beach, FL, USA, 1997

Situated on the first floor of one of the numerous Art Deco buildings that dapple the area of South Beach, this restaurant has transfigured a capacious commercial space into a sophisticated and comfortable internal space. What one immediately notices are a playful use of deftly combined materials, a mindful selection of fittings and fixtures that involves mixing classics of Modern Movement furniture with new custom-made pieces, the carefully gauged lighting arrangement, and a soft, embracing color scheme. The actual space available to the architects was long rectangle, whose only front with openings was the entrance wall at one end, and the long walls completely blind. The keynotes of the design are the division of the single, open scheme into carefully controlled units that afford greater privacy and comfort. The entrance was tailored around the four structural pillars, which now occupy a central position; these have been clad in plaster to form sturdy white cylinders that end just short of the ceiling to reveal their core of timber cladding, a detail nicely picked out by the lighting set into the gap. The ceiling has an even pattern determined by the beams interrupted by the suspended disc, a visual device that gives weight to the piano zone below. A long bar counter runs the full length of the right-hand wall, while the wall opposite has been clad in horizontal slabs of Wisconsin stone, which are repeated on the pilasters of the entrance wall, underscoring the Country menu. The floor of Brazilian cherry is ranged with chairs and stools by Alvar Aalto, in pale wood with back and seat in woven cord. This little homage to modern furniture design is endorsed by the 1950s lamps designed by Poul Henningsen, which hang from the ceiling and reflect in the long glazed top of the bar counter. This deference to the past is given further emphasis by the custom-made furniture, such as the sofas and armchairs in the central area of the room, which offers a congenial little lounge space.

Ubicato al piano terreno di uno dei numerosi edifici Art Déco che caratterizzano la zona di South Beach, questo ristorante ha trasformato un ampio spazio commerciale in un sofisticato e confortevole spazio interno, giocato sull'uso di pochi materiali sapientemente accostati, su un'attenta selezione degli arredi che affiancano a classici del Movimento Moderno mobili su disegno, sull'uso calibrato delle luci e sull'impiego di tonalità morbide e avvolgenti. Lo spazio disponibile, di forma rettangolare stretta e lunga, presenta un unico fronte con aperture (la facciata d'ingresso) e i due lati maggiori completamente ciechi. La principale scelta progettuale è stata quella di dividere in zone distinte la grande superficie unitaria, calibrando i nuovi spazi per ottenere maggiore comfort e *privacy*. La sala d'ingresso è stata così ridimensionata in funzione dei quattro pilastri preesistenti, ora in posizione centrale. Questi sono rivestiti di gesso per divenire dei forti cilindri bianchi che nella parte terminale non raggiungono il soffitto denunciando la loro anima interna coperta di legno, sottolineata dalla luce posizionata nello scuretto ottenuto sulla sommità. Il soffitto è scandito dalla trama regolare data dall'andamento delle travi interrotta dal disco sospeso, episodio compositivo che sottolinea con forza la zona del pianoforte sottostante. I lati ciechi sono occupati da un lungo banco bar di legno sulla destra, mentre sulla sinistra l'intera parete è rivestita in conci orizzontali di pietra del Wisconsin, che proseguono sui pilastri interni di facciata, sottolineando il carattere Country del menù. Sul pavimento in legno di ciliegio brasiliano sono disposti sedie e sgabelli di Alvar Aalto, in legno chiaro naturale con schienale e sedute in nastro di corda intrecciato; un omaggio alla storia del mobile moderno cui si affiancano i lampadari degli anni '50 di Poul Henningsen, che scendono dal soffitto riflettendosi sul lungo vetro del banco-bar. A queste citazioni storiche si aggiungono gli arredi su disegno come i divanetti fissi e le poltrone della zona centrale del locale, proposta come accogliente *lounge*.

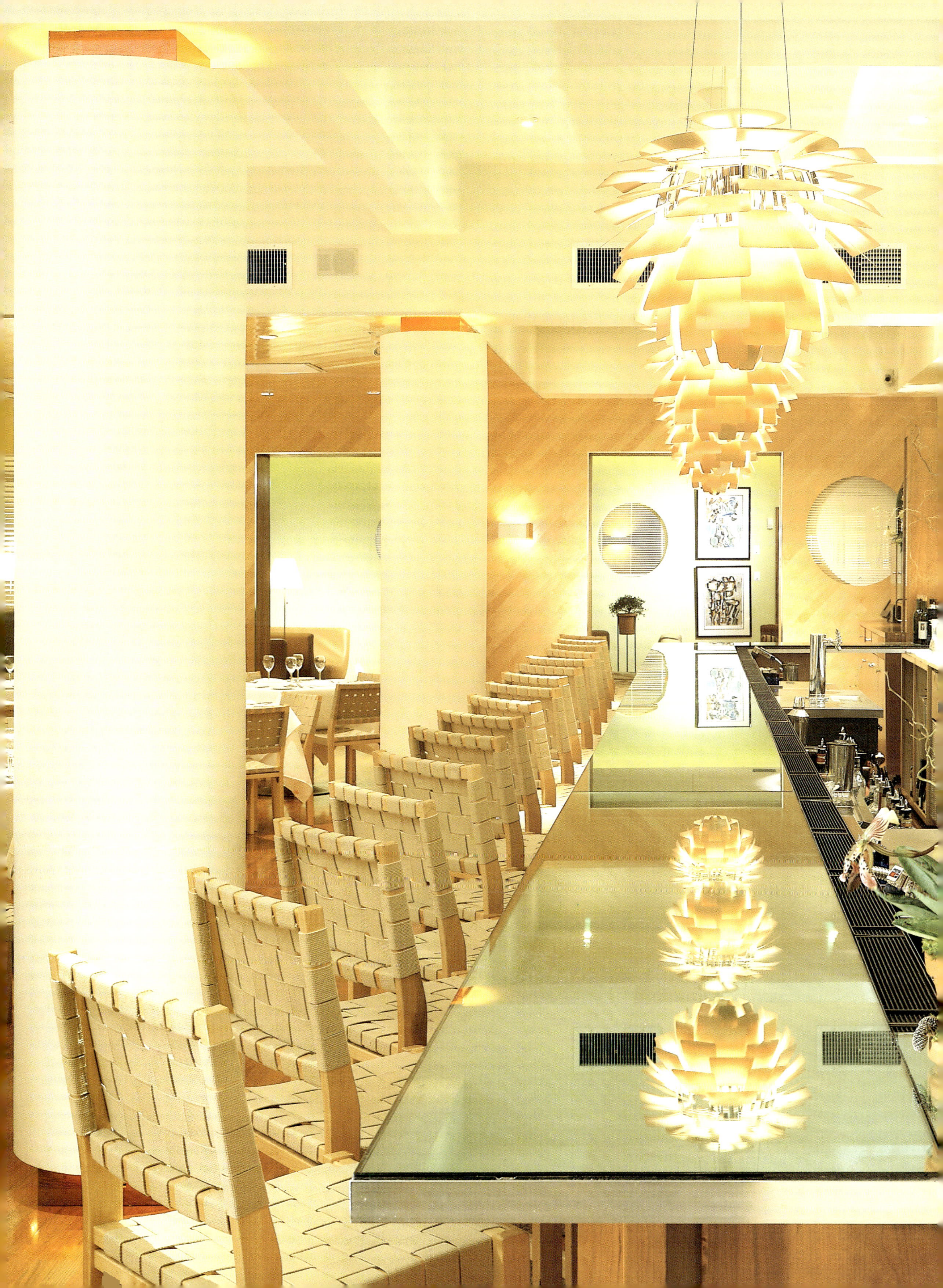

Facade / Facciata

Section / Sezione

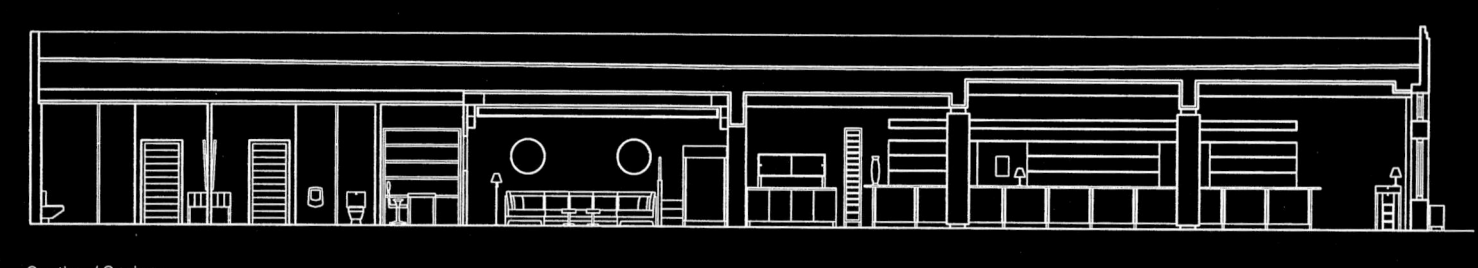

Section / Sezione

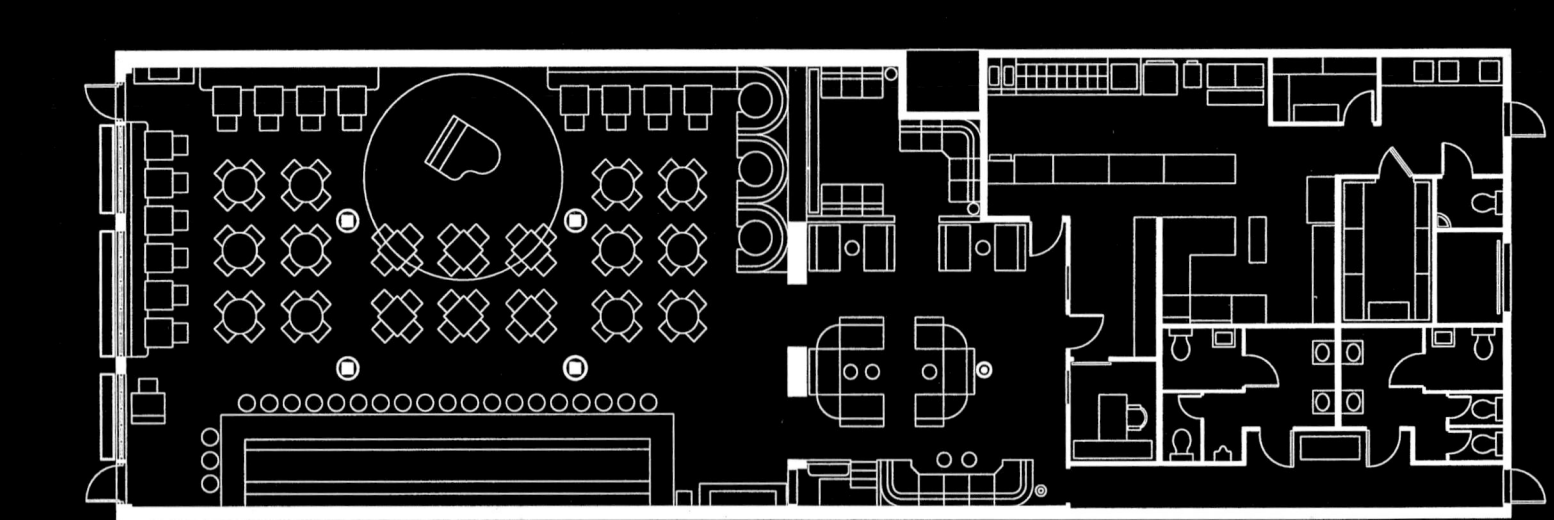

Section / Sezione

145

SCALINI RESTAURANT
Tony Chi Architect & Associates. Kuala Lumpur, MY, 1997

Nestled in the chaotic urban landscape of Kuala Lumpur in a building surrounded by a lush and flourishing garden, this restaurant proclaims its loyalty to the Italian cuisine right from its name, Scalini, meaning "steps." The ground floor of the building is slightly raised above the level of the garden. The steps of the title are positioned close to the access from the street, leading to the restaurant entrance via a boldly designed gateway of oxidized copper trimmed with a small marquee composed of glass panes supported by a neat steel frame. During the drier months the part of the garden closest to the building is used as an outdoor extension for luncheons. The interior is subdivided into distinct areas. On the right of the entrance lies a comfortable guest lounge alongside the service rooms and kitchens; on the left, overlooking the garden, a long narrow space offers a wood bar counter and tables with round green marble tops accompanied by custom-built upholstered chairs whose backrests are pierced by little holes and stars in a slightly orientalizing pattern. The ceiling is clad in panels of plain wood and punctuated by a series of ultra-simple light fittings forming luminous parallelepipeds positioned in checkerboard formation overhead. The display system for the bottles behind the bar offers a kind of filter for the second dining area, and consists of a series of partitions made of patterned glass panels held in a brass framework, allowing intervals for visual interchange between the two separate dining rooms of the restaurant. The floor plan is completed by an extra room that looks onto the garden. This is where we encounter inflexions and accents of Italy, which is evoked throughout the restaurant by large photographs of Italian scenery and townscapes. A coffered ceiling overhead nicely offsets the pattern of little squares of the parquet floor, while a system of cabinets in period style with glazed doors line the walls, filled with finest Italian wines.

In una costruzione circondata da un rigoglioso giardino, calato all'interno del caotico paesaggio urbano di Kuala Lumpur, è stato ricavato questo ristorante che già nel nome denuncia il suo menù dedicato alla cucina italiana. Il piano terreno della costruzione si trova in posizione rialzata rispetto al giardino. Gli scalini, da cui prende il nome il ristorante, sono posizionati in prossimità dell'accesso stradale per condurre all'ingresso caratterizzato da un forte portale di rame ossidato e da una pensilina composta da lastre di vetro lavorato sostenute da una studiata struttura di acciaio. Parti del giardino, in prossimità dell'edificio, sono utilizzate nelle stagioni meno umide come piacevoli zone per pranzare all'aperto. L'interno è suddiviso in vari spazi: sulla destra dell'ingresso è organizzata una confortevole *lounge* d'attesa affiancata a servizi e cucina, mentre sul lato sinistro, rivolto verso il giardino, uno spazio stretto e lungo ospita un banco bar di legno e dei tavolini con piano rotondo di marmo verde affiancati da sedie su disegno con struttura in legno e seduta imbottita e schienale traforato a piccoli fori regolari e a stelline di sapore orientale. Il soffitto, rivestito con pannelli di legno naturale, è interrotto da una serie di essenziali plafoniere, parallelepipedi luminosi posizionati secondo una studiata scacchiera. La soluzione dell'espositore bottiglie del banco bar si pone come elemento filtro tra prima e seconda sala del locale: una serie di bacheche composte da lastre di vetro lavorato sostenute da una struttura di ottone lasciano, nella loro successione, degli spazi liberi di collegamento visivo tra le due sale da pranzo. Un'ulteriore sala conclude la disposizione interna affacciandosi sul giardino. E' qui che troviamo figure e soluzioni che ricordano le atmosfere italiane, richiamate negli altri spazi del locale con grandi fotografie di luoghi e volti del 'Bel Paese'. Un soffitto a cassettoni sovrasta il pavimento di parquet disposto secondo un disegno a quadrotti, mentre un sistema di contenitori, rivisitazione di mobili in legno con ante vetrate del secolo scorso, copre le pareti ospitando le bottiglie di vino italiano.

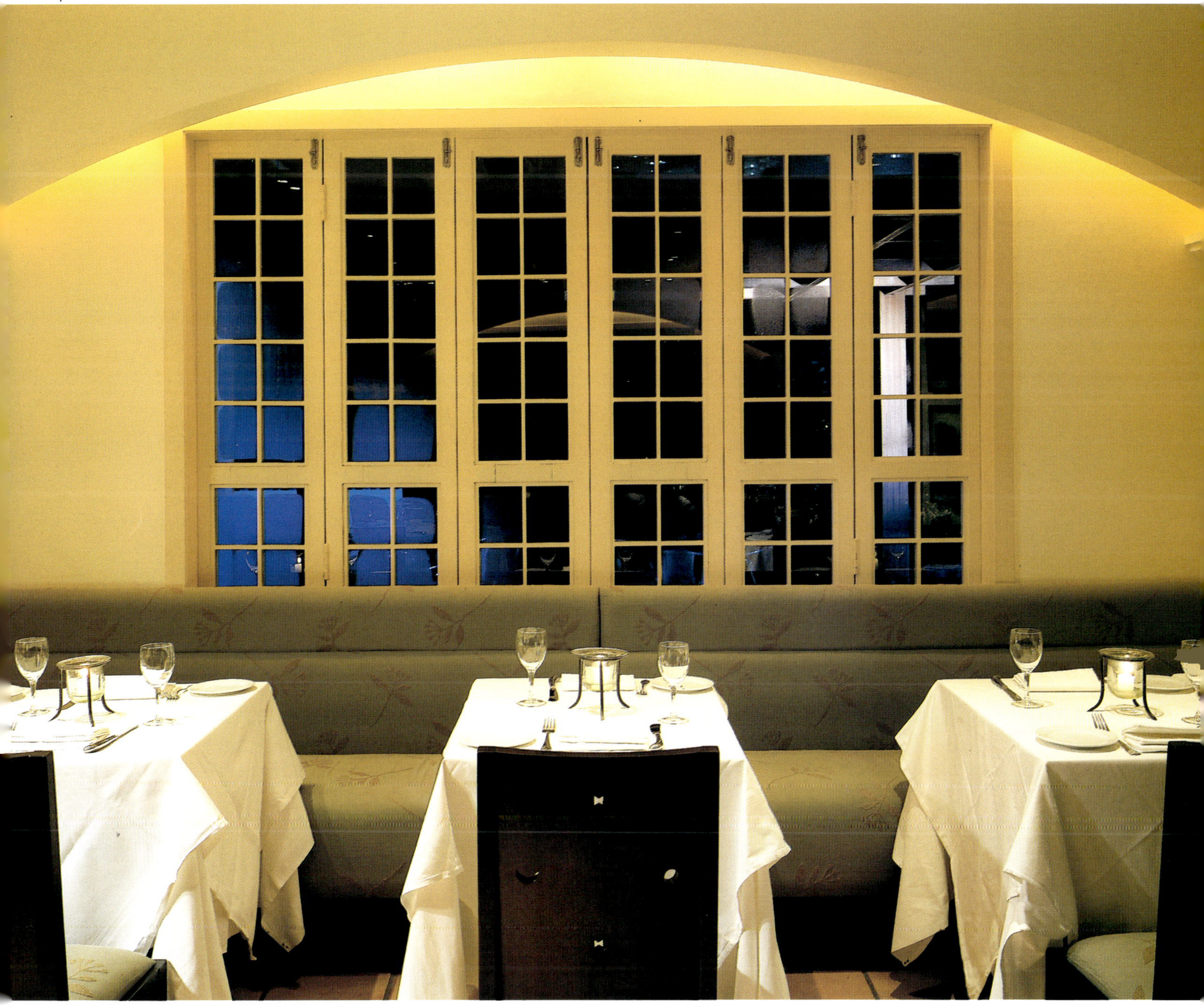

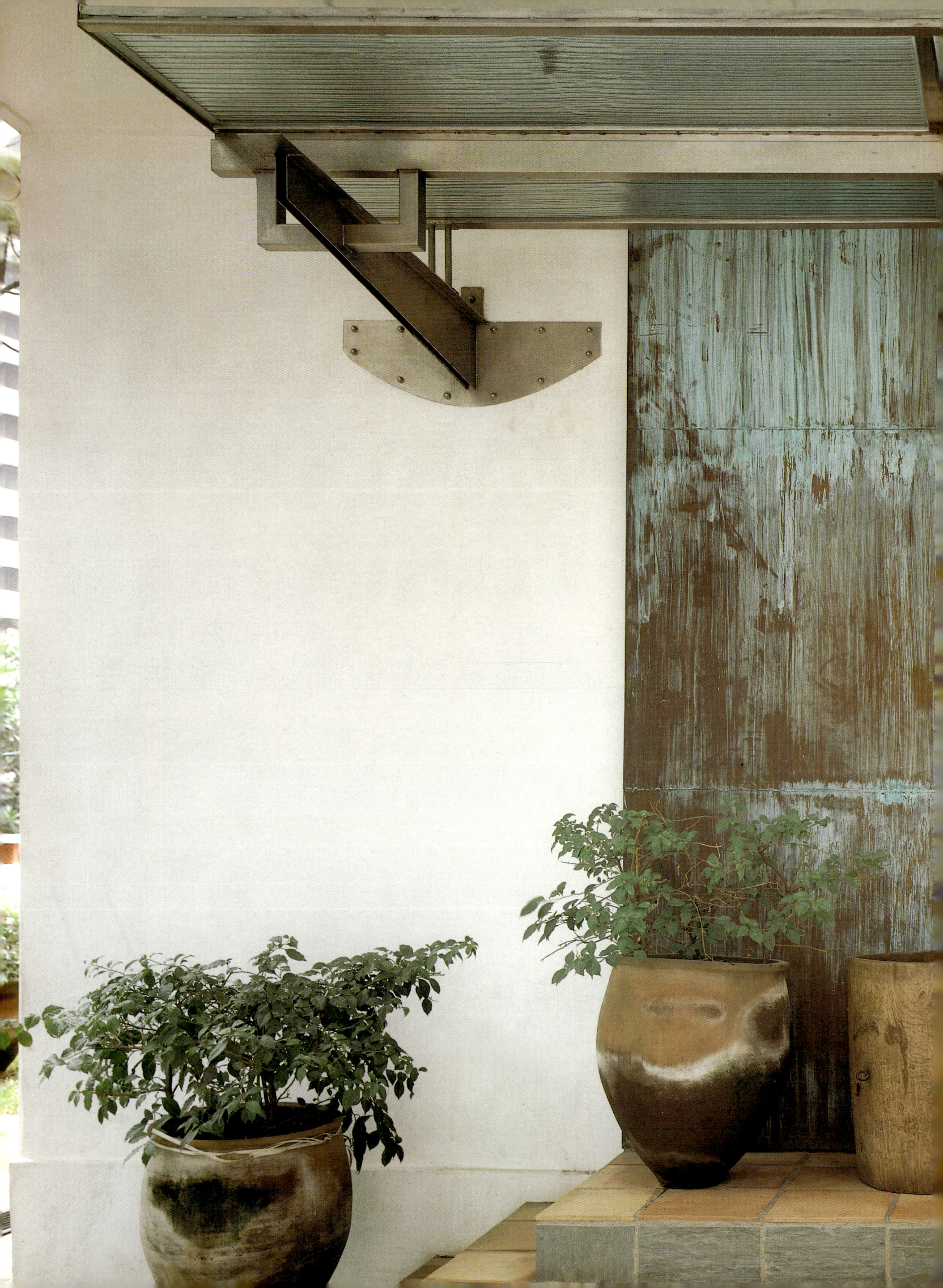

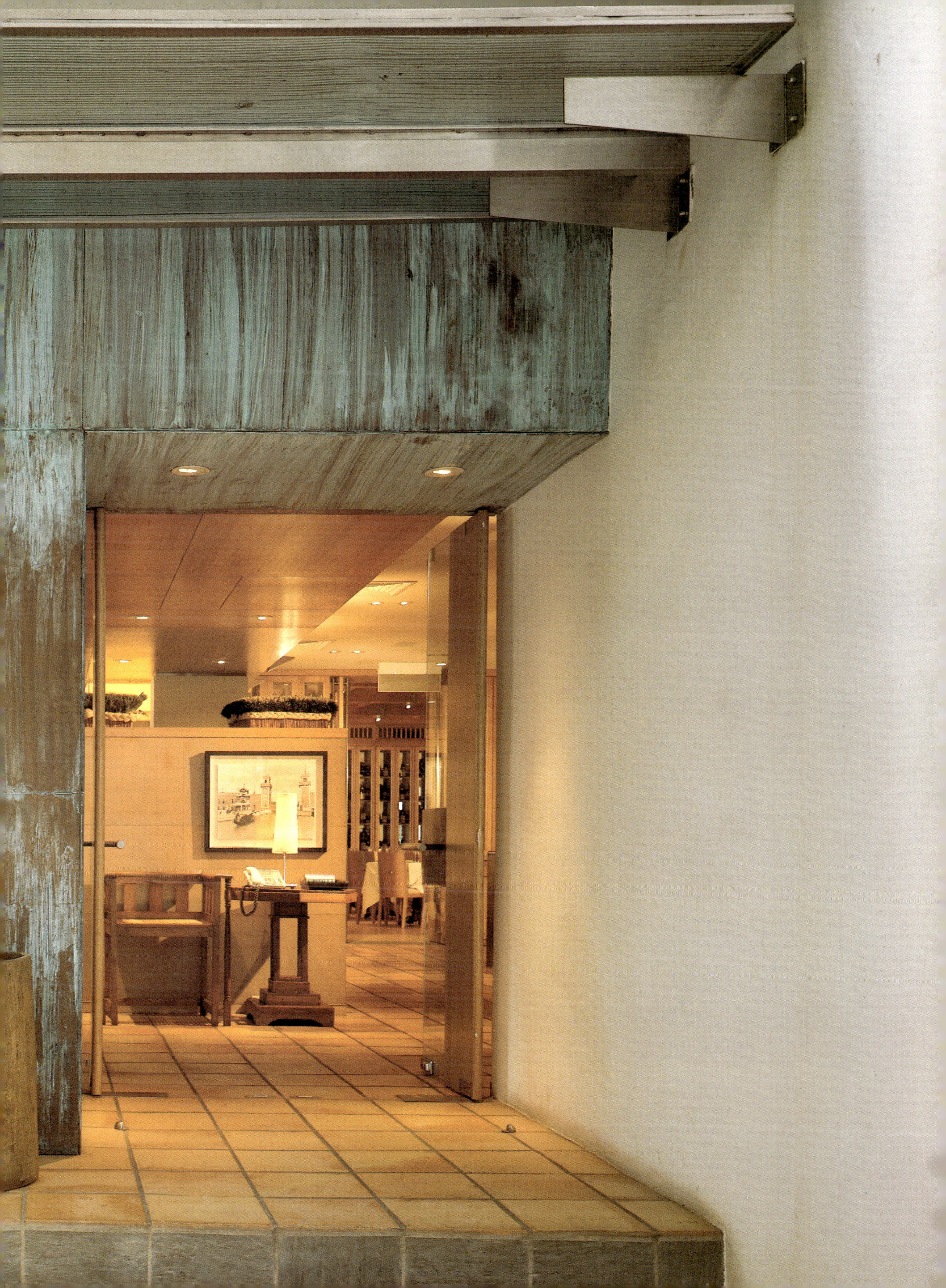

150

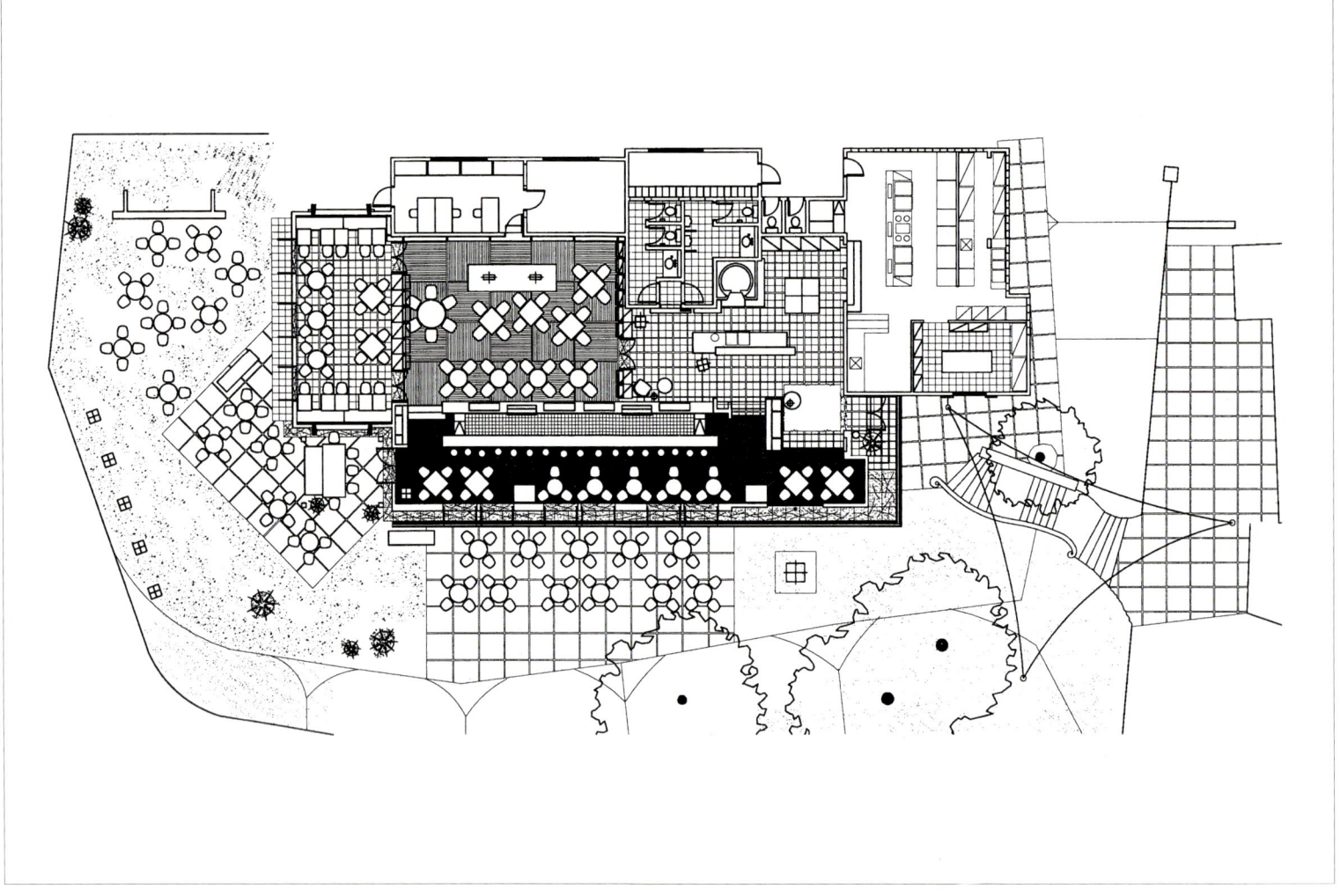

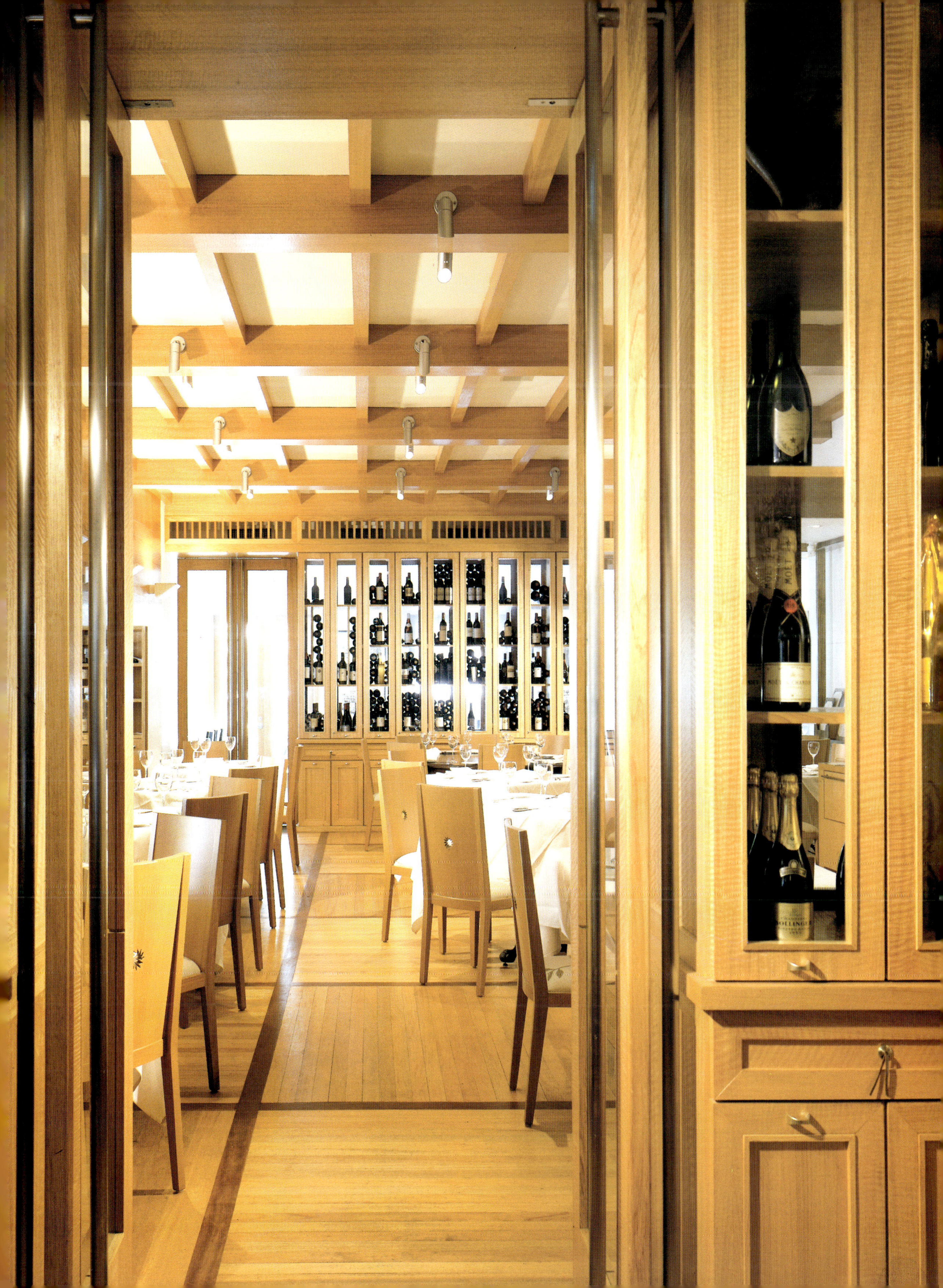

SEQUOIA RESTAURANT

Ark Restaurant Corp. - Bill Lalor Architect. New York, NY, USA, 1991

Built on Pier 17 of Manhattan's South Street Seaport, the Sequoia offers a superb view of the port, the Brooklyn Bridge, and the Statue of Liberty through its large full-height windows ranged across the main facades and through those with large wooden frames designed to capture picturesque views of the ships docked at the quays below. The décor and fittings are a creative reworking of the Manhattan style of the start of the century. Solid-looking wainscoting alternates with glazed white tiles. The floor is finished everywhere in dark granite, right from the entrance, past the long wooden bar counter with its striking corner columns, and beyond to the central dining area, which is designated by a raised level of parquet. The wood chairs of sleek, modern design are complemented by stools of a more classic design distributed along the front of the bar and around the small tables at the entrance lobby. Recessed downlighters in the ceiling and classical brass light fittings are carefully arranged throughout the interiors. Caissoned sections of ceiling are repeated here and there, embellished with a decorative band depicting sailboats that stand out against a deep sea-blue background. Seafaring is the second theme reiterated through the restaurant; the boats docked in the marina are complemented by little models in illuminated display cases or hanging from the ceiling; the smaller ones have been used to enhance the impact of the bar counter. Positioned beneath the crowning cornice and lit up with small but bright spotlights, the carefully assembled little model boats offer an unusual and charming array of marine imagery. Besides underlining the restaurants intimate connection the Manhattan's port, this decorative caprice nicely plays down the overall classicism of the interiors, which manage to evoke a by-gone atmosphere while avoiding the pitfalls of revivalism.

Costruito sul molo n°17 nel porto di New York City, il Sequoia Restaurant si caratterizza per la splendida vista del porto, del ponte di Brooklyn e della Statua della Libertà, offerti dalle ampie finestre a tutt'altezza che si sviluppano lungo le facciate principali e da quelle incorniciate da ampi profili in legno che sembrano trasformare in scene pittoriche le viste delle navi ormeggiate alle banchine sottostanti. La scelta compositiva per le soluzioni dell'interno si basano su una creativa rilettura dei ristoranti newyorkesi dell'inizio secolo. Massicce *boiseries* rivestono le pareti, alternandosi a piastrelle in ceramica bianca, mentre un pavimento di granito scuro copre l'intero locale dall'ingresso, con il lungo banco bar di legno segnato da forti colonnine angolari, sino alla zona pranzo centrale rialzata su una pedana in parquet. Le sedie in legno, di disegno essenziale e moderno, si affiancano agli sgabelli di forma più classica disposti lungo il banco bar e intorno ai tavolini della zona ingresso. Faretti ad incasso e classici lampadari di ottone sono disposti con attenta regia. Il soffitto di gesso a cassettoni, ripetuto in varie zone del locale, è arricchito da una fascia decorativa che disegna una serie di raffinate barche a vela che emergono dal blu marino. E' il tema della nave il secondo riferimento che troviamo ripetuto nel locale; alle barche ormeggiate nel porto si affiancano numerosi modellini di legno che riproducono navi del passato. Quelli di dimensioni maggiori sono posti in bacheche illuminate o semplicemente appesi al soffitto, mentre quelli più piccoli sono stati impiegati per arricchire la figura del banco bar. Posizionate sotto la cornice di coronamento e illuminate da potenti faretti, le piccole barche colorate, costruite con cura e attenta filologia, offrono un'inconsueta e divertente rassegna di memorie navali. Questa soluzione decorativa e progettuale, oltre a sottolineare il rapporto del ristorante con il porto, sdrammatizza con elegante ironia l'immagine classica e ricercata complessiva che, senza cadere nella pratica del revival, vuole ricordare atmosfere del passato.

153

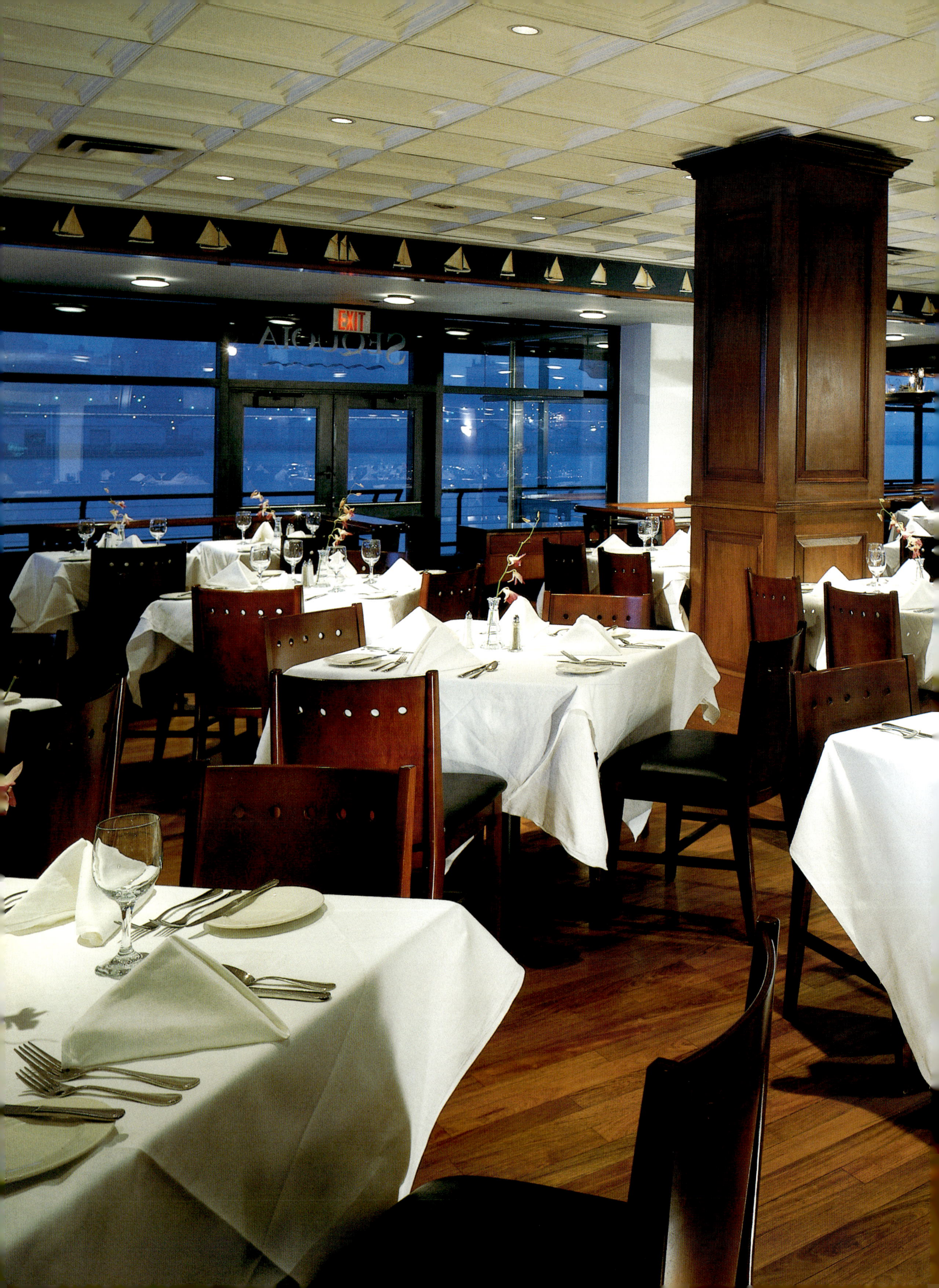
EXIT

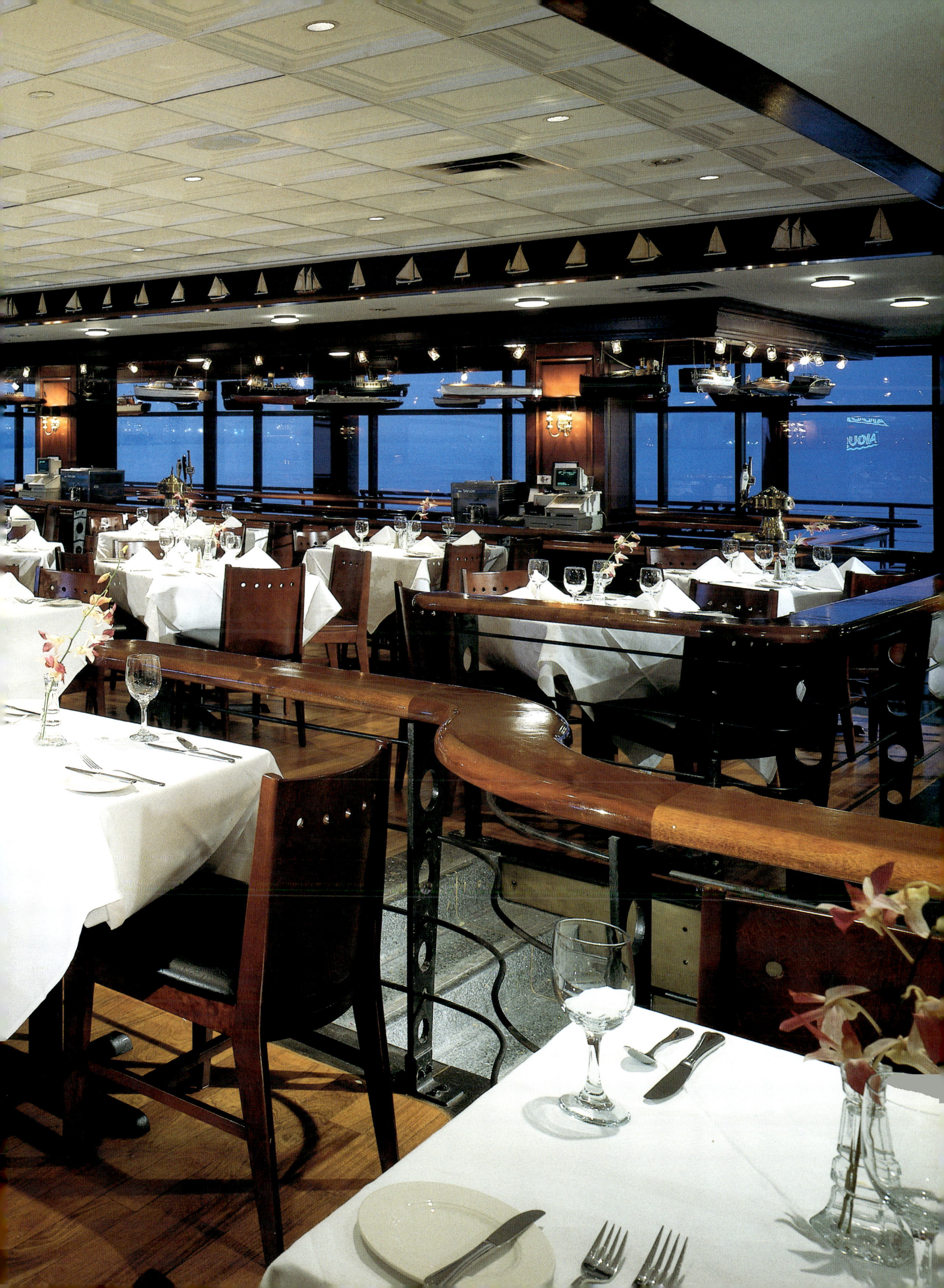

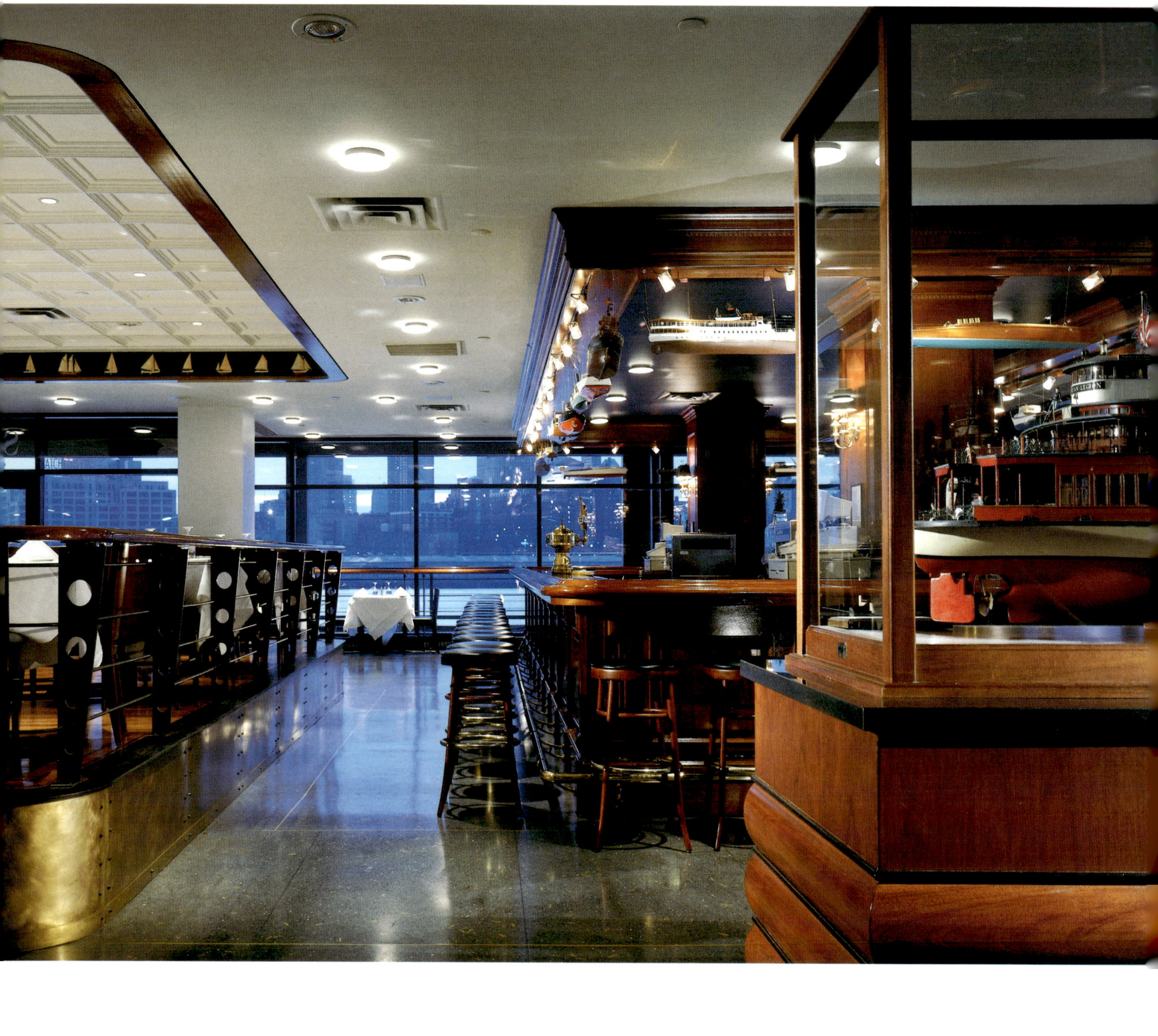

SI PIAZZA RESTAURANT
Haverson Architecture and Design. Charlotte, NC, USA, 1995

As its name suggests, this restaurant installed on the ground floor of a large new office tower that gives onto the street with large colorful windows, aims to recreate an urban space with a well-defined architectural image. The internal frontage are devised as stylized architectural settings with a variety of treatments of material and colors. The restaurant has two separate entrances, one on the street and the other from the building's entrance lobby. The former entrance is framed by two eye-catching stone stage flats at angles to each other to emphasize the perspective created by the ample, double-height doorway. The two facades simulate a double street frontage set with twin doorways surmounted by two windows with yellow awnings. The lobby entrance reiterates the idea of the double gateway, this time surmounted by two oculi with awnings in colored stripes. Both entrances project into the large circular interior, which is overlooked by a large balcony gallery. The mauve ceiling acts as a canopy for the composition of the spaces below, which are styled so as to recreate a small piazza. The scenery flats of the street entrance are enhanced by distinctive architectural devices, such as the little uneven, brick-colored facade, the geometrical design of the gallery balustrade, the central pillar with its earth-colored sheathing, girdled by a green shelve that doubles up as a dining table in the rush hour. Running around the circular wall of the piazza is a counter that changes function at intervals: now a bar, now a shelf, now a table. The circular tables of the ground floor are flanked by wood seats with a craquelé finish, which is also used for the gallery dining area. A large half-moon of metal and gilded fabric gleams suspended over the void, marking the piazza below, which is paved in various shades of granite laid in a lively geometrical pattern.

Ubicato all'interno del piano terreno di un nuovo grande edificio per uffici, scandito verso strada da una successione di colorate vetrate dal sapore vagamente déco, il Si Piazza, come già esprime il nome, si propone come uno spazio urbano rivisitato, caratterizzato da una studiata immagine architettonica. Le facciate interne sono proposte come stilizzate quinte architettoniche, trattate con diversi materiali e colori. Il ristorante è stato pensato con due ingressi, uno rivolto verso strada e l'altro aperto verso la lobby dell'edificio. Il primo ingresso si caratterizza per due alte quinte in pietra, sorta di riuscita soluzione teatrale che propone due fronti inclinati, a sottolineare la prospettiva creata verso la porta vetrata d'ingresso a doppia altezza. Le due facciate simulano dei fronti urbani nel disegno del duplice portale sormontato da due fori-finestre con tendine gialle. L'ingresso dalla hall dell'edificio ripete la soluzione del doppio portale, questa volta sormontato da due oblò con tende in aggetto a strisce colorate. Entrambi gli ingressi si proiettano verso il grande spazio circolare centrale su cui si affaccia la balconata del soppalco. Sotto un soffitto colorato di viola si sviluppano le soluzioni compositive chiamate a configurare l'interno del locale come una sorta di spazio urbano reinventato. Alle quinte dell'ingresso su strada si aggiungono così dei brani architettonici distinti, come la piccola facciata irregolare color mattone, il disegno geometrico della balaustra del soppalco, il pilastro centrale rivestito e tinteggiato color terra, circondato da una mensola verde usata anche come tavolo da pranzo nelle ore più affollate. Lungo il muro circolare della piazza è posizionato un piano continuo che diventa di volta in volta, banco bar, funzionale mensola di appoggio e tavolo per pranzare. I tavolini circolari del piano terra sono affiancati da sedie di legno decorate con trattamento *craclé*, impiegate anche per la sala da pranzo del soppalco. Una grande mezzaluna di metallo e tessuto dorato brilla e fluttua nel vuoto per segnare la 'piazza' sottostante, pavimentata con diverse tonalità di granito, posato secondo un movimentato disegno geometrico.

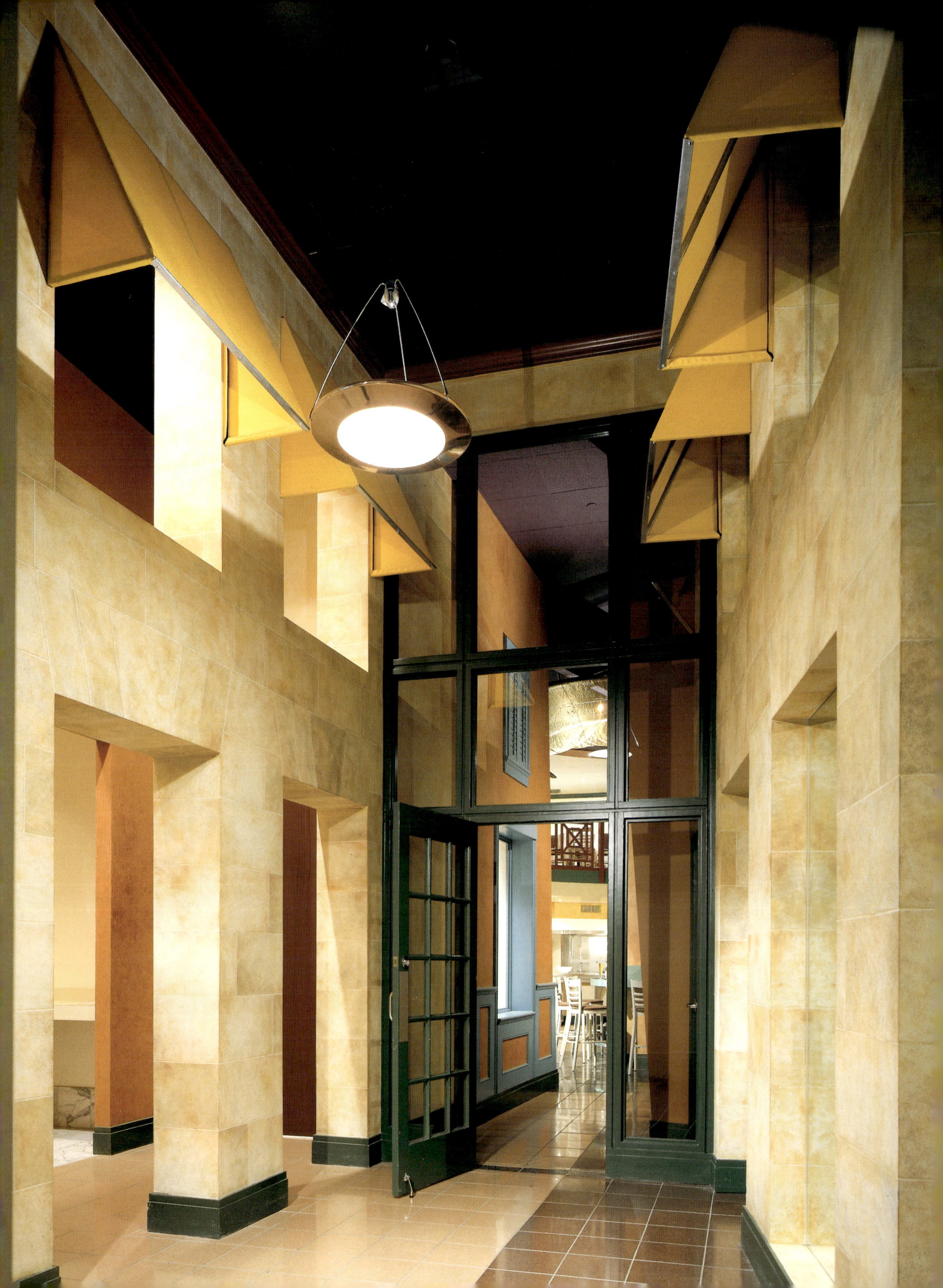

159

160

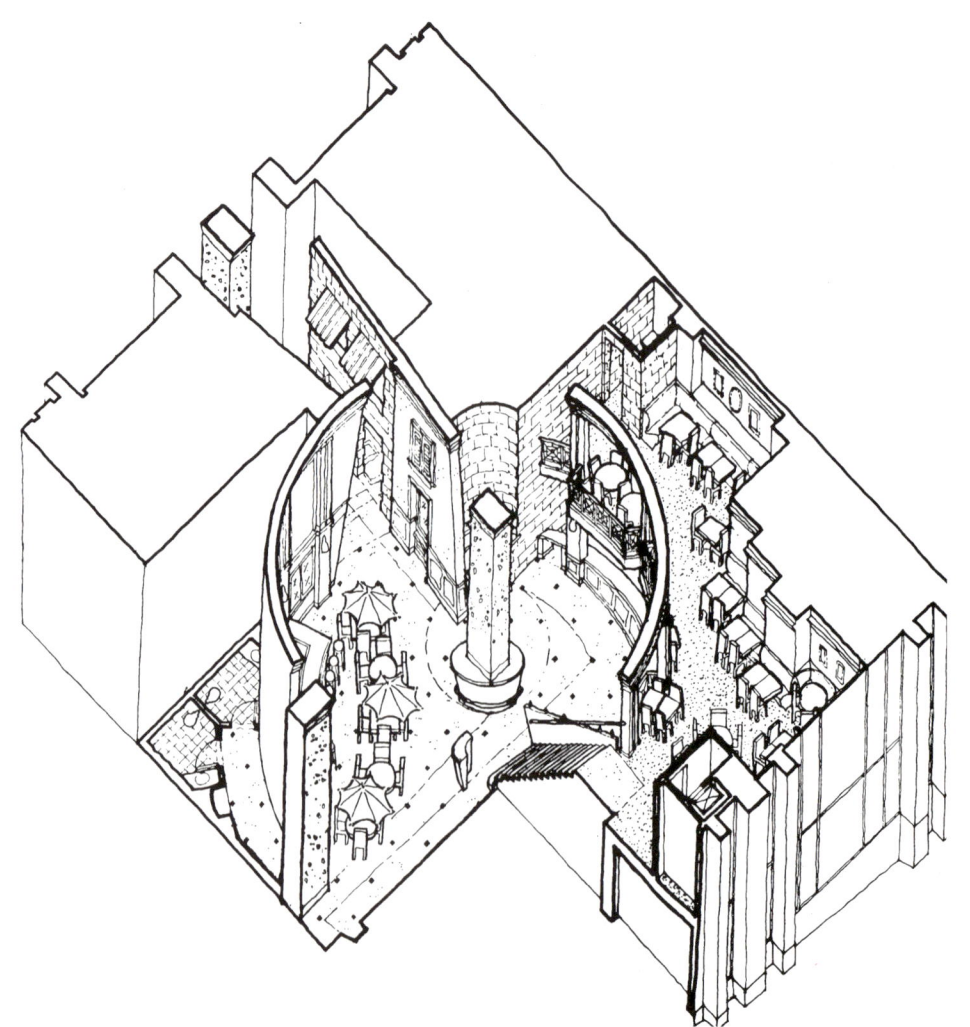

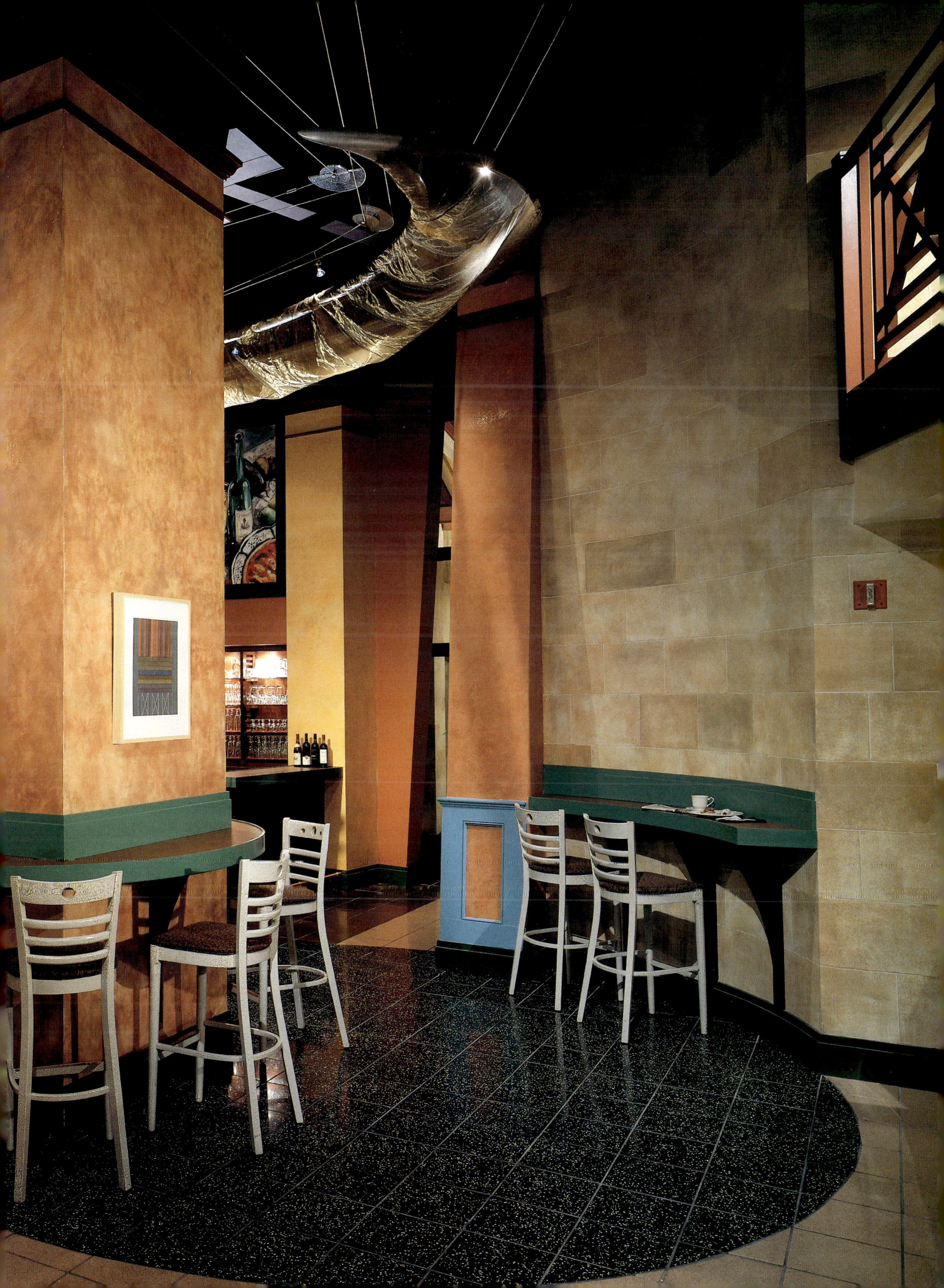

SPIGA RESTAURANTS

Haverson Architecture and Design. Scarsdale e Bedford, NY, USA, 1994 -1995

Bedford

With their colorful, welcoming interiors, the Spiga restaurants built in Greenwich and Scarsdale are like compact constructions in which colors, images, and patterns conspire in an imaginative reappraisal of the *trattoria*-type venue. The facades of both restaurants carry awnings spangled with stars and moons against a deep, night-sky blue, while a strong sense of rhythm is conferred upon the large, single-space interiors via the raised floor-levels and sections of false ceiling supported by a series of highly colorful pillars in the form of upturned pyramids, which are repeated throughout the space in a variety of hues. This clever use of color provides a snappy overall scheme of cohesion for the restaurant. The wall treatment includes rough exterior plaster and striated *veneziana* in strong, spry hues, employed variously to cover walls, small facade sections, arches, and cornices, all geared to emulate and pay tribute to the Italian piazza; the imaginative idea is reiterated in the pictorial sections of the ceiling, with its representations of towers, campaniles, and other Italianate architecture, surrounded by swirling cypresses – the epitome of the Mediterranean landscape. The overall impression one gets on entering the restaurant is a succession of ingenious compositions orchestrated with unerring creative flair. The Italian landscape features are complemented by a ceiling of glowing moons and constellations (recessed downlighters capped with colored filters), which rehearse the pattern of the awnings outside. A row of entryways offers a series of mini-facades that also resemble downscaled theater boxes jutting from the walls, housing cozy private dining units with fixed couches. The bar counter in both rooms is clad in wood with a diagonal checker pattern which also characterizes the perimeter wainscoting that covers the colored plaster areas of the lower band of walling, giving visual linkage with the carpets and tiling, which are alternated according to the function of the zone in question. Another classic feature of the Italian *cucina* is the pizza-oven, which is given pride of place in the restaurant scenario here: sheathed in a regular checker tile pattern or in chunks, and crowned with a broad band of copper round the top, the pizza-oven provides a boldly assertive visual element characterizing the entire venue.

Colorati e accoglienti ristoranti dedicati alla cucina italiana, gli Spiga costruiti a Greenwich e a Scarsdale si configurano come piccole costruzioni in cui si ripetono colori, immagini e motivi dedicati alla fantasiosa ricostruzione di un ambiente italiano. Entrambi i locali propongono sulle facciate delle tendine in aggetto decorate con stelle e lune che spiccano su un telo blu notte, mentre gli interni sono pensati come ampi spazi unitari movimentati da pedane e giochi volumetrici nel soffitto e da una serie di coloratissimi pilastri di forma piramidale rovesciata ripetuti in diversi colori. L'uso accattivante del colore appare subito come caratteristica dominante in questi vivaci locali; intonaco da esterno e stucco spatolato alla veneziana in tinte forti e accese sono impiegati per coprire pareti, piccole facciate, archi e cornicioni, che nel loro dinamico confronto tendono a configurare i ristoranti come libere rivisitazioni delle piazze italiane, ricordate anche nelle decorazioni pittoriche di parte dei soffitti, in cui troviamo torri, campanili e architetture circondate da svettanti cipressi, simbolo per antonomasia del paesaggio italiano. L'immagine degli interni si propone così come studiata successione di diversi episodi compositivi affiancati in modo creativo e divertito; ai paesaggi italiani riportati nel soffitto si affiancano cieli stellati con lune e stelle luminose (lampade a incasso con vetri colorati) che riprendono il motivo delle tende esterne; una serie di portali, proposti sia come piccole facciate, sia come palchi teatrali in scala ridotta, sono posizionati in aggetto lungo le pareti perimetrali per accogliere piccole salette riservate con divanetti fissi a isola. Il banco bar in entrambi i locali è rivestito in legno con il disegno a quadrotti ruotati in diagonale che caratterizza anche la boiserie perimetrale che copre i colorati intonaci nella prima fascia di collegamento con il pavimento in moquette e piastrelle, alternate secondo le diverse zone d'impiego. Immancabile nella tradizione della cucina italiana è però il forno della pizza che si propone come personaggio protagonista della scena interna. Rivestito di ceramica a quadrotti regolari, o a pezzi sbrecciati, con un'ampia fascia di rame impiegata come cornicione conclusivo, il forno diviene il forte segno riconoscibile di riferimento.

Bedford

Scarsdale

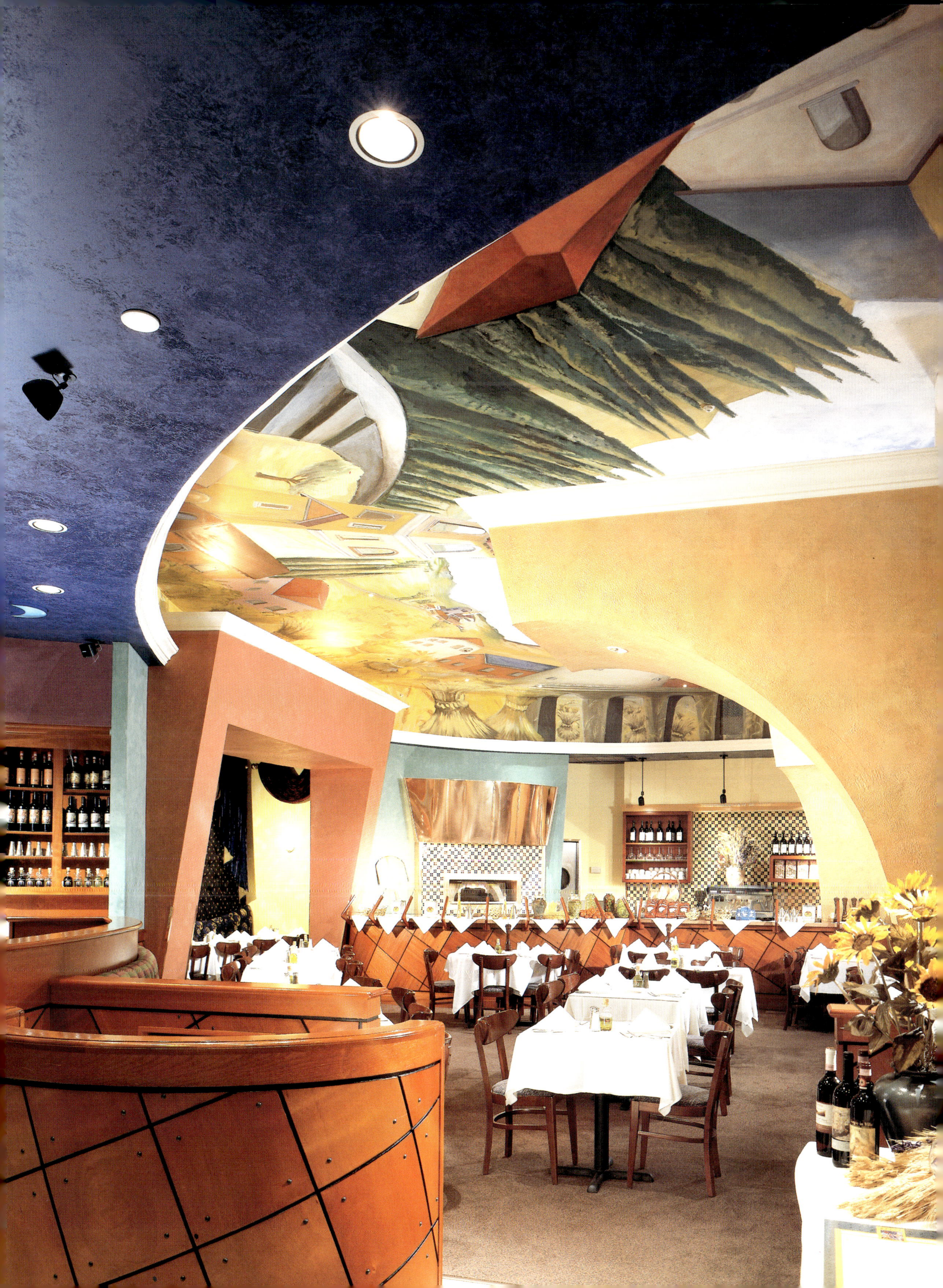

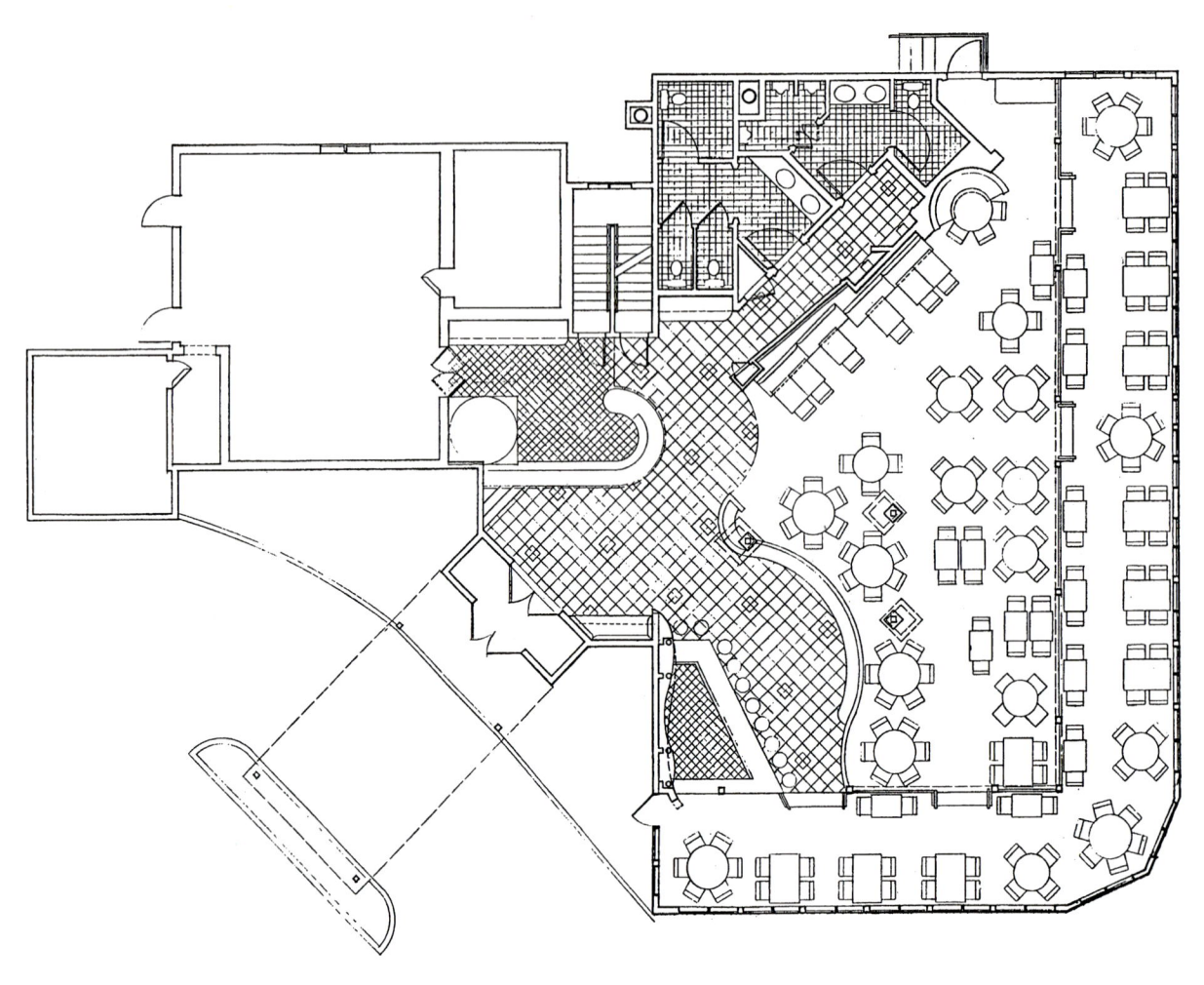

Scarsdale   Ground floor / Piano terra

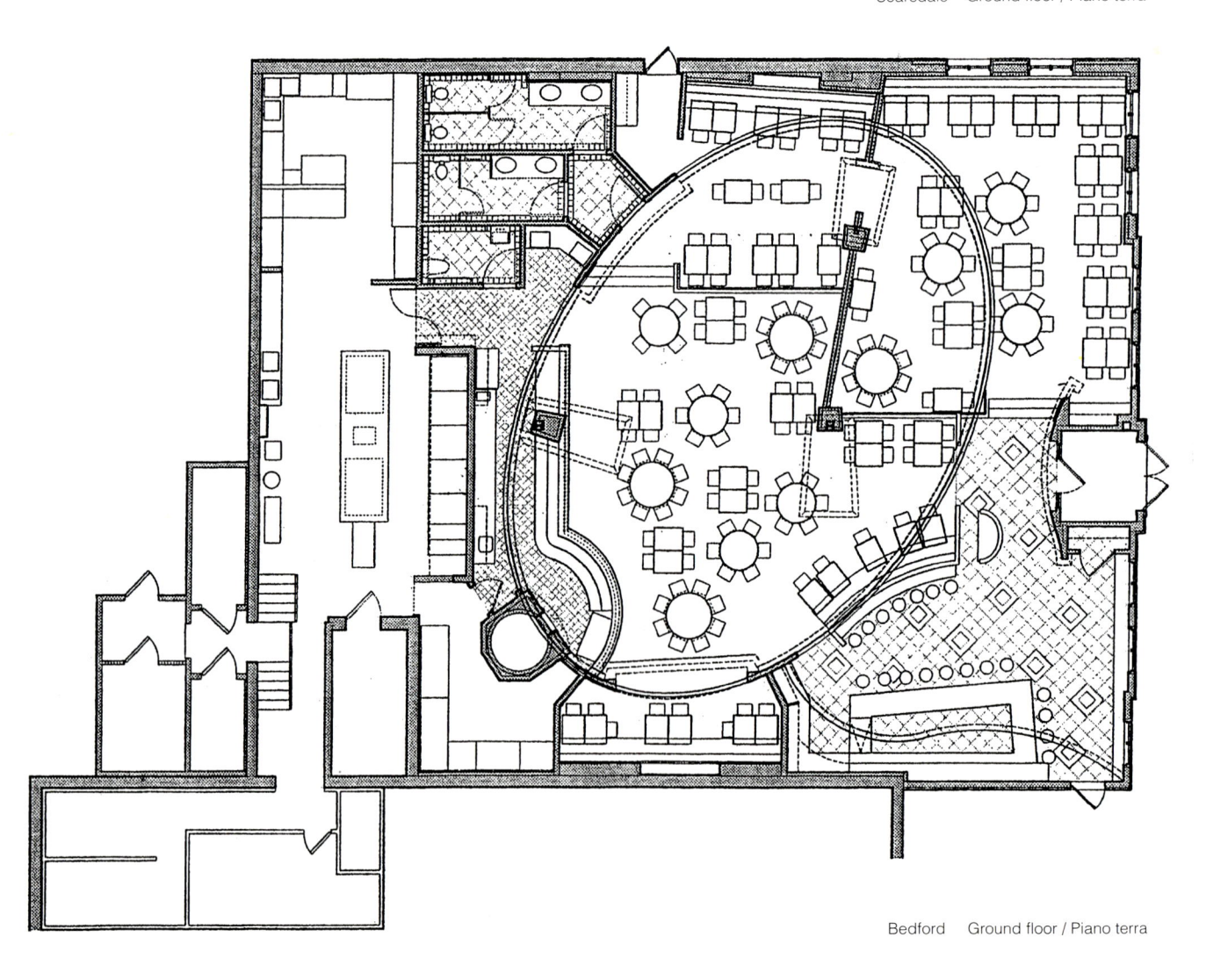

Bedford   Ground floor / Piano terra

Bedford

Bedford

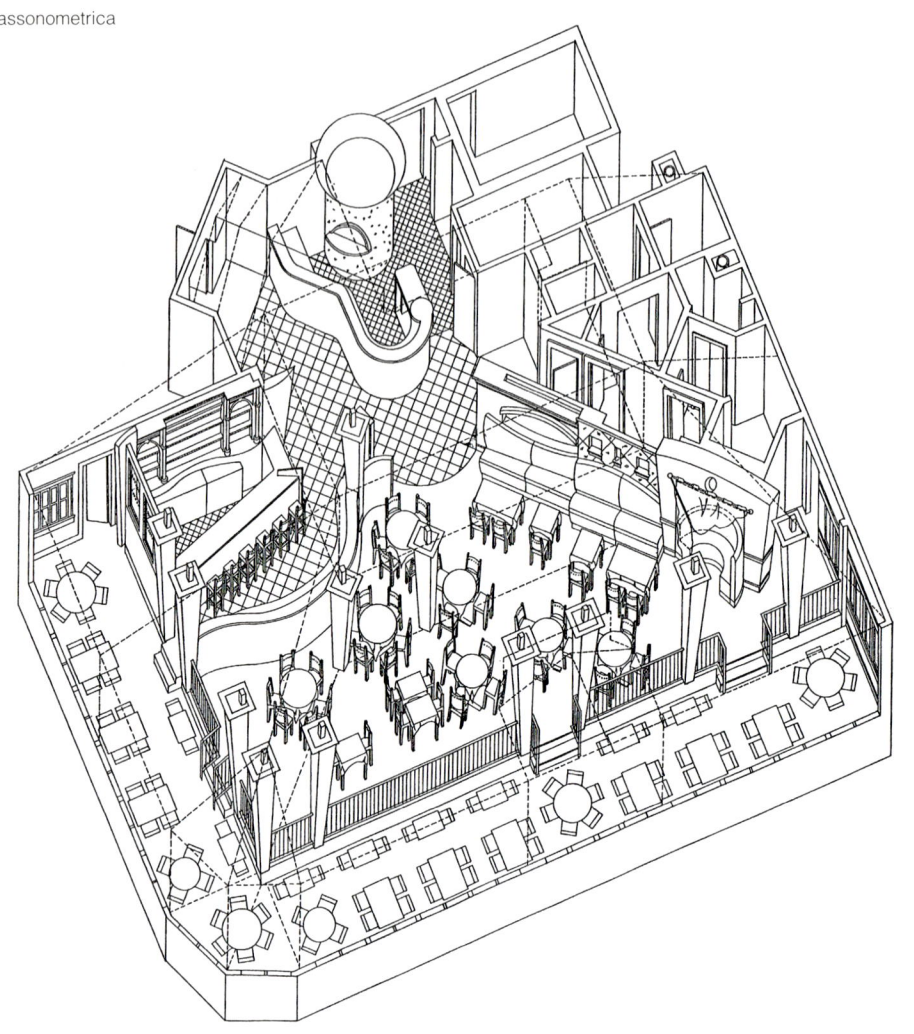

Scarsdale Axonometric view / Vista assonometrica

Scarsdale

Scarsdale

SYMPHONY CAFE'
Jeffrey Beers Architects. New York, NY, USA, 1989

The Symphony Café takes its tuneful name from the nearby Carnegie Hall, a concert venue that was installed inside a multipurpose complex built in 1891. The restaurant's designers have eschewed the revivalist approach and have instead created an elegant and congenial environment that transports the clientele back into the world of exclusive café-bars of the 1930s–40s, where theater-goers congregated after the evening show to exchange views and gossip. The restaurant has an L-shaped floor plan divided into two zones, with large windows lining the longer sides. The first area offers an entrance foyer and cocktail lounge, where a banded wood and brass counter occupies most of the available wall space, and along the window elegant round tables topped in green marble are complemented by 1800s-style seating made of wood, iron, and Vienna cane. The wall behind the bar is styled to resemble a facade (complete with central brass clock), which, where it faces into the dining hall, boasts floor-to-ceiling paneling of rectangular and square sections orchestrated by a slightly protruding geometrical grid, into which several small high windows are set at intervals, together with the service door into the kitchen. A large hatch cut into the wainscoting enables the dinner-guests to follow what goes on in the kitchen, emphasizing the spectacle of the chefs' dexterous preparations of the food. The windows along the facade are veiled by elegant white curtains which gradually increase in opacity toward the ground, so as to offer greater privacy for the diners. The dining room itself, slightly raised with respect to the entrance area, and separated from the bar by a light-weight railing in brass, extends toward the back lined with the large windows and a series of fixed couches upholstered in green leather. These fixtures are complemented by square tables with Thonet chairs arranged in the central area. In line with the kitchen opening, two custom-built service counters with screens in opaline glass sustained by a thick geometrical grille in brass, offer the main central feature, which is matched overhead by the centrally placed lighting finished in the same materials, giving a slightly Déco taste to the whole. On the back wall, a scenic perspective is created by a large mural representing the auditorium of the Carnegie Hall seen from the dress circle, as if to turn the diners into spectators.

Il Symphony Café deve il suo nome alla vicinanza con la famosa Carnegie Hall, costruita all'interno di un edificio multifunzionale nel 1891. Lontano da ogni revival, il Symphony Café riesce a configurare un'atmosfera elegante e accogliente che vuole rivisitare con calibrata creatività i ristoranti esclusivi e i caffè da 'dopoteatro' degli anni '30 e '40. La pianta a 'L' del locale, con i lati maggiori segnati da ampie vetrate, è stata suddivisa in due zone: la prima, disposta su parte del lato minore, ospita l'ingresso e la zona bar, dove un grande bancone in legno con fasce di ottone orizzontali copre quasi l'intera superficie disponibile, occupata lungo la vetrina da eleganti tavolini rotondi con piano in marmo verde affiancati da sedute dal sapore ottocentesco, in legno, ferro e paglia di Vienna. Il retro del bancone si configura come facciata interna (con tanto di orologio centrale in ottone) che risvolta nella sala ristorante proponendo una *boiserie* a tutt'altezza con pannelli rettangolari e quadrati scanditi da una griglia geometrica ordinatrice in aggetto, dove trovano posto anche delle piccole finestre superiori e la porta di servizio che conduce alla cucina. Questa è rivolta verso la sala tramite una grande apertura ricavata nella *boiserie* che permette agli ospiti di vedere i cuochi al lavoro, spettacolarizzando le fasi di preparazione dei piatti. Le vetrate di facciata sono schermate da raffinate tende bianche, che nella parte inferiore divengono più compatte e opache per garantire la privacy degli ospiti. La sala, rialzata rispetto alla zona d'ingresso e separata dal bar con una leggera ringhiera in ottone, si sviluppa verso il fondo organizzando lungo le vetrate una serie di divanetti fissi rivestiti in pelle verde. A questi arredi fissi si affiancano i tavoli quadrati con sedie Thonet disposti nella zona centrale. In asse con il vano aperto sulla cucina, due mobili di servizio su disegno, con quinte in vetro opalino sostenute da una spessa griglia geometrica di ottone, si pongono come elemento centrale della sala; episodio compositivo connesso con i lampadari centrali che riprendono gli stessi materiali secondo figure di sapore dèco. Sulla parete di fondo, conclude la prospettiva della sala un grande murale che rappresenta l'interno della Carnegie Hall visto dal palco, rendendo così protagonisti e 'attori' tutti i commensali.

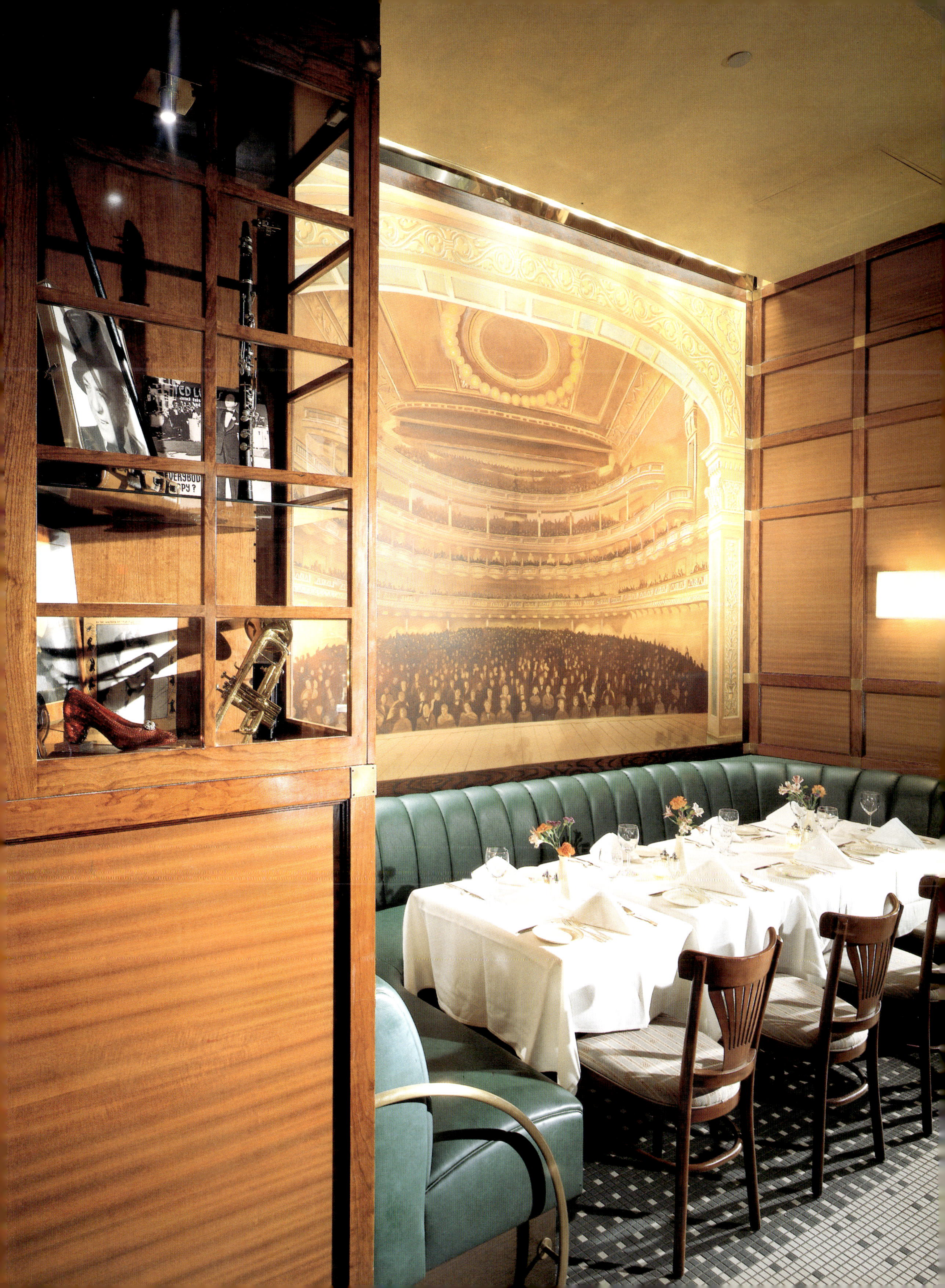

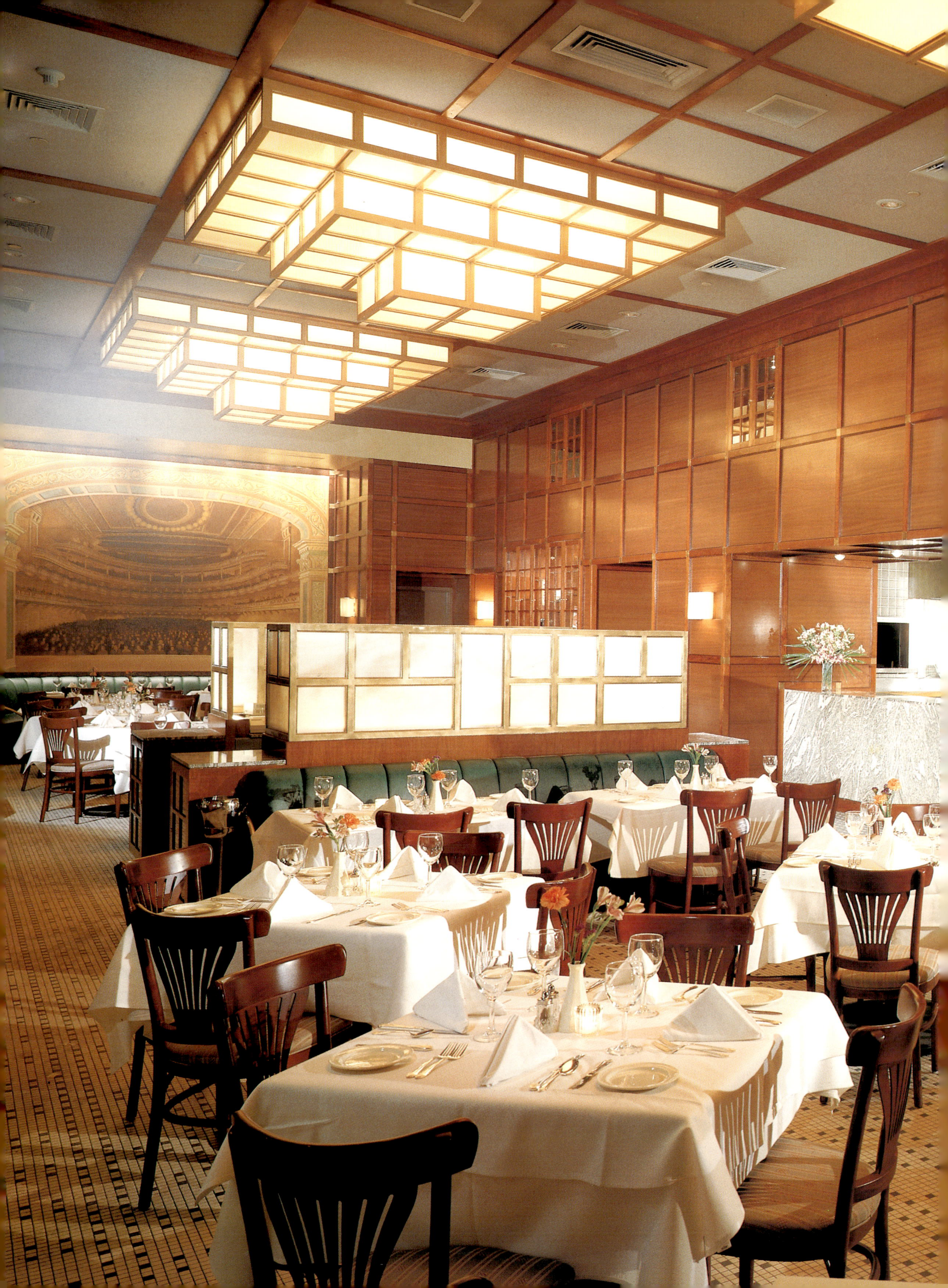

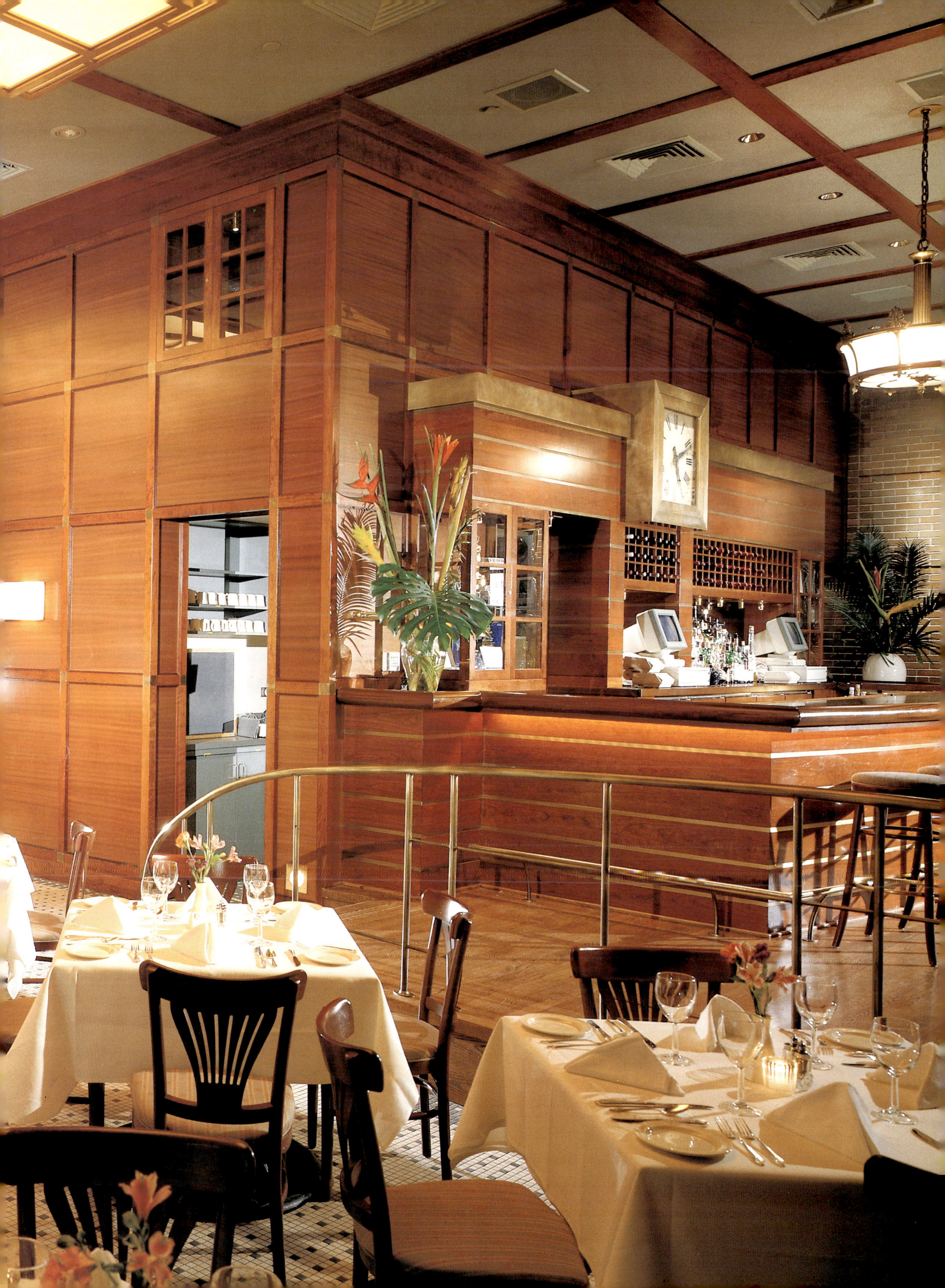

172

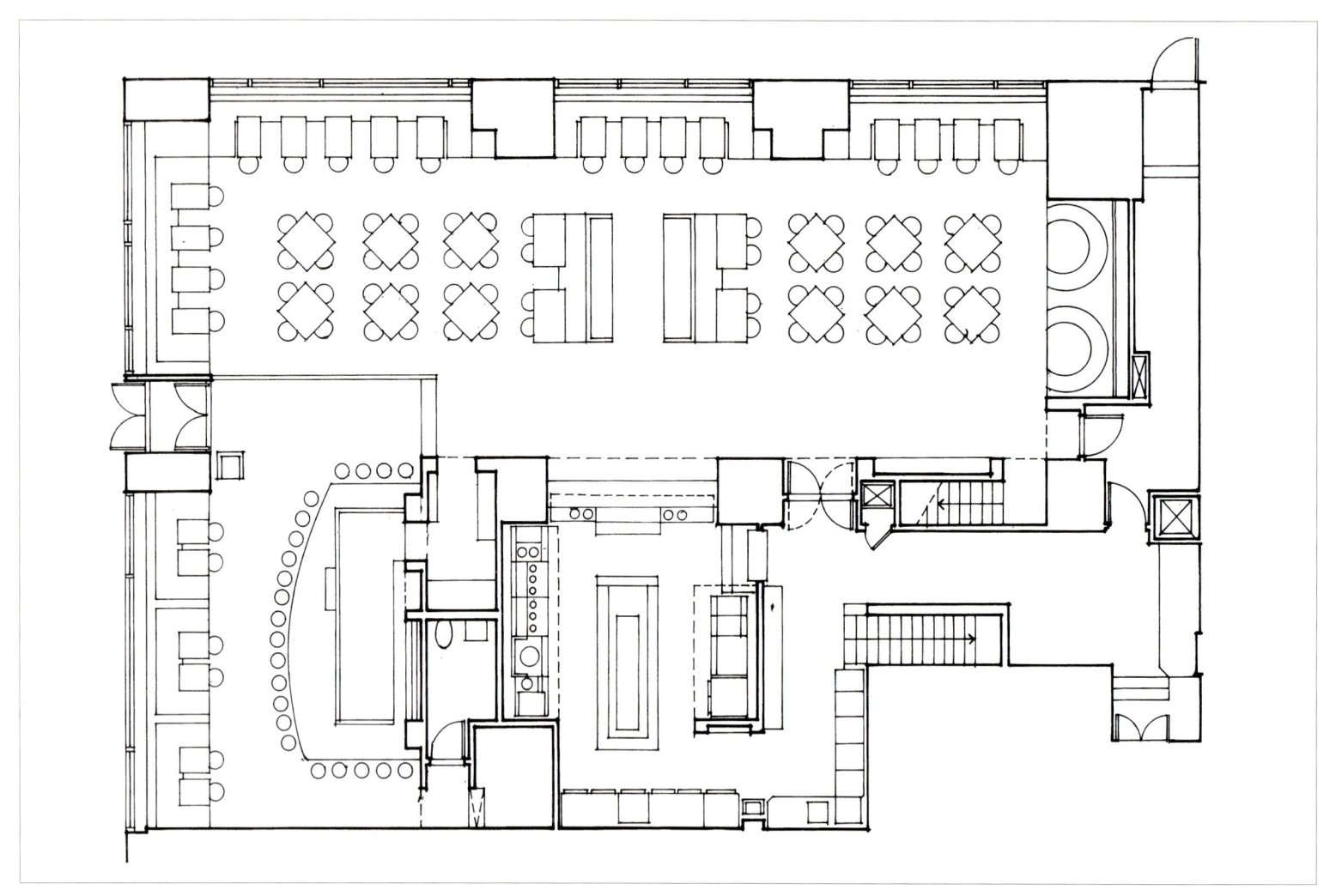

TAPIKA RESTAURANT
David Rockwell Architect. New York, NY, USA, 1995

Tapika is one of the winning "theme" restaurants invented by David Rockwell in a successful attempt to use interior design, brilliant decorative solutions and visual features to communicate the underlying culinary *persona* of the restaurant. The general scheme enhanced by other themes of a musical nature or associated in some way with the world of theater and sport. In this case, Tapika manages to express the atmospheres of the American southeastern states to which the menu is dedicated. We therefore find a conjugation of imagery borrowed from the cowboy's world, with its prairie landscapes, ranches and corrals, all used liberally to style the architecture of the restaurant's interiors. The simple L-shaped floor scheme is divided into a first area that accommodates the entrance foyer and a corner cocktail lounge, and in a dining room that extends the length of the premises, raised slightly above the entrance level and interrupted by a further central platform that lends a sense of movement and spatial variety to the whole. From the cocktail lounge one gets the cowboy feel immediately, with all its southeast state overtones. The perimeter earthred plaster walls have a striated finish that imitates the building techniques used in those states, while the windows are hung with curtains decorated with ethnic patterns and vertical planks painted red and white in imitation of the type of fencing used out west for delimiting paddocks. The large curved counter clad in leather is equipped with a row of stools with seats upholstered in mottled hide. Period photographs of ranches and cowboys are framed by metal silhouettes of men on horseback, a motif that is repeated along the crown of the bar, and again in negative on the partition screening off the restaurant area. This room is characterized by a raised central platform marked off by a low wall of plain wood which carries a series of marks made by branding irons, like those used for identifying livestock. Imposing their tone on the entire room are three large lamps hanging from the ceiling; the large discs of curved metal are punched with a series of stylized ethnic patterns which have their counterpoint on the end wall: a window filled with corn surmounted by a slice of clear blue sky, providing one more reference of the vast reaches of the West.

Tapika si colloca nel fortunato filone dei 'ristoranti a tema' progettati da David Rockwell nel riuscito tentativo di comunicare nel progetto d'interni, nelle brillanti soluzioni decorative e nelle figure della composizione complessiva, il carattere culinario del locale o un tema di riferimento, sia esso musicale, legato al mondo dello spettacolo o a quello dello sport. In questo caso Tapika vuole tradurre nella sua immagine le atmosfere degli stati del Sudest americani, cui il menù è interamente dedicato. Ecco allora che figure traslate dai ranch e dalle praterie, dal mondo dei cowboys, vengono reinventate e impiegate con creatività per definire l'architettura degli interni. La pianta del locale, a forma di 'L' regolare con ampie vetrine sui due lati maggiori, è divisa in una prima zona in cui sono posizionati l'ingresso e la zona bar, e in una sala ristorante che si sviluppa lungo il lato maggiore, rialzata rispetto all'ingresso e interrotta da un'ulteriore pedana centrale che ne arricchisce le caratteristiche spaziali. Già nel bar si coglie il carattere 'western', immagine della cucina del Sudest; i muri perimetrali sono trattati con un intonaco spatolato rosso terra che ricorda quello delle costruzioni di quegli stati, mentre le vetrine sono schermate da tende decorate con motivi etnici e da assi di legno verticali rosse e bianche che rivisitano il tema della staccionata di perimetro dei pascoli. Il grande banco bar in curva rivestito in cuoio è affiancato da una serie di sgabelli con sedute rivestite in pelo di cavallino maculato. Fotografie d'epoca di ranch e cowboys sono affiancate da una silhouette metallica di uomini a cavallo riportata in positivo come coronamento del mobile bar dietro al bancone e ritagliata in negativo nel paravento di lamiera che separa dalla zona ristorante. Quest'ultima si caratterizza per la pedana centrale segnata da una parete bassa di legno grezzo in cui sono riportate, come inconsueta decorazione, le autentiche marchiature a fuoco impiegate per i bovini. Tre grandi lampadari decorativi scendono dal soffitto caratterizzando l'intera sala; i grandi dischi di metallo curvati sono traforati da una serie di motivi etnici stilizzati che trovano nella decorazione parietale in asse sul fondo la loro conclusione compositiva: una finestra riempita di grano sormontato da uno spicchio di cielo blu, ulteriore richiamo alla ampie distese del Sudest.

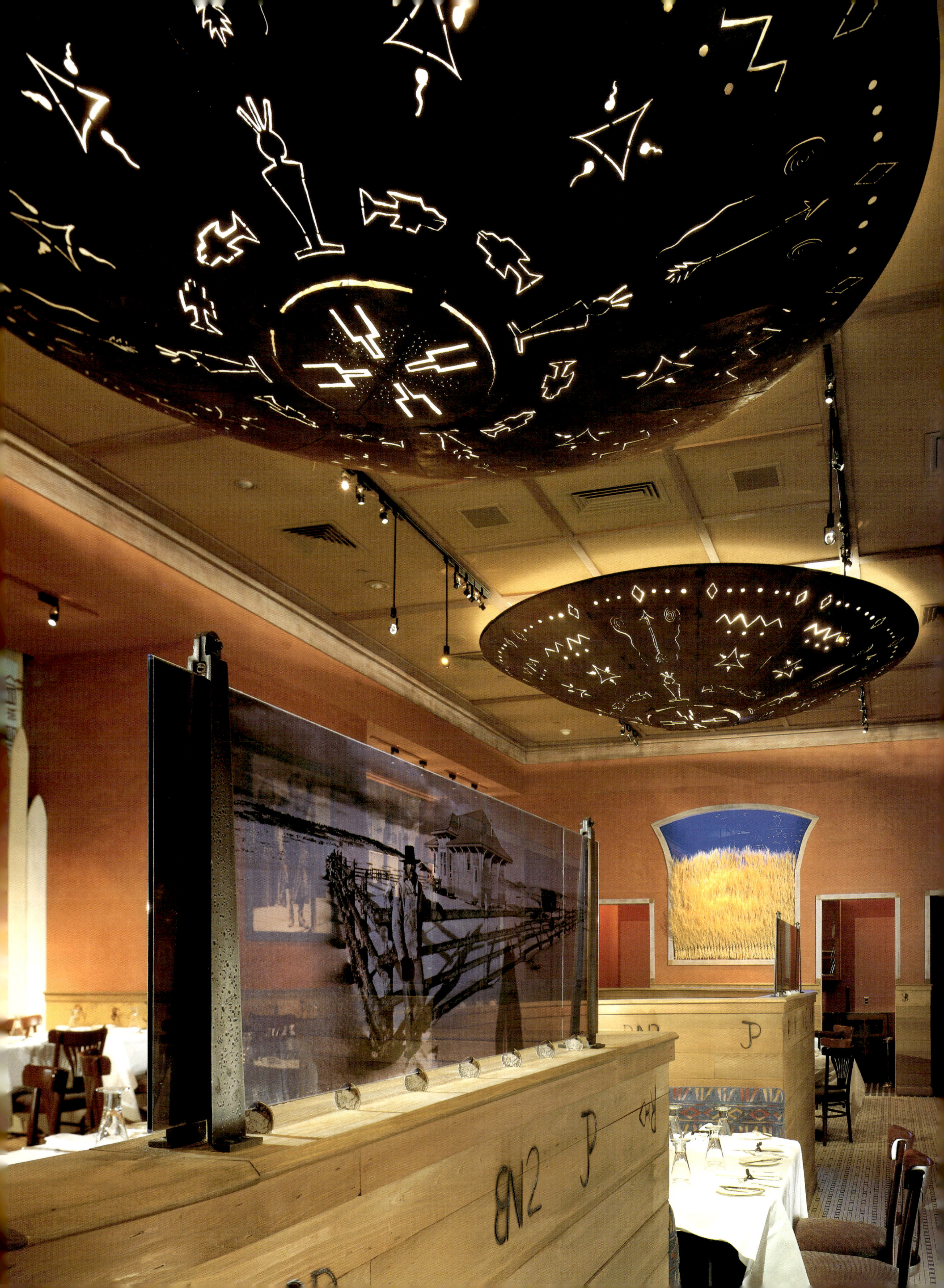

175

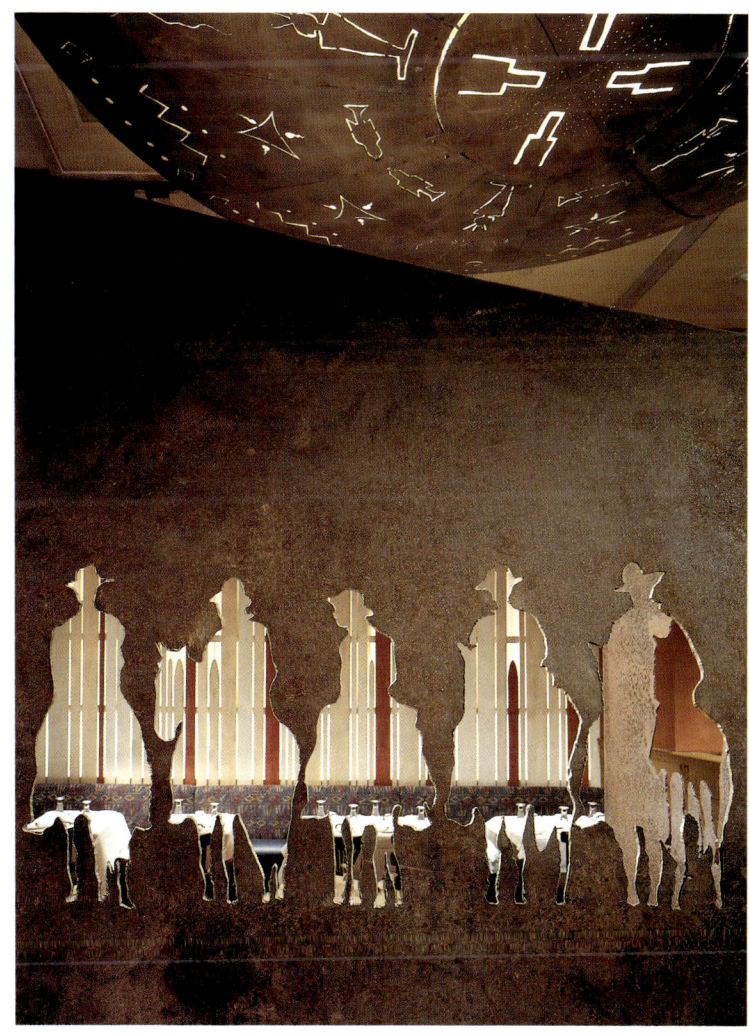

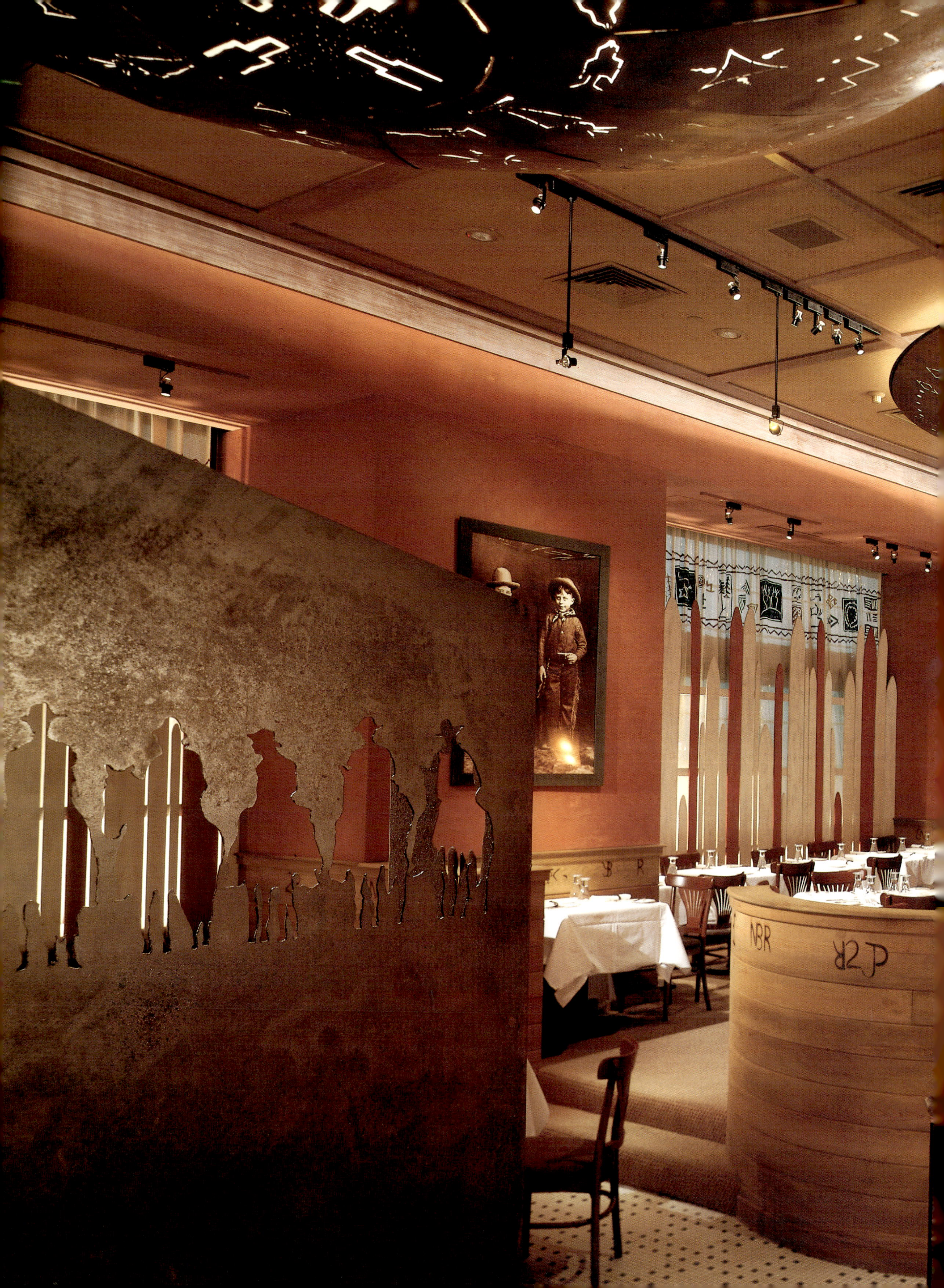
NBR

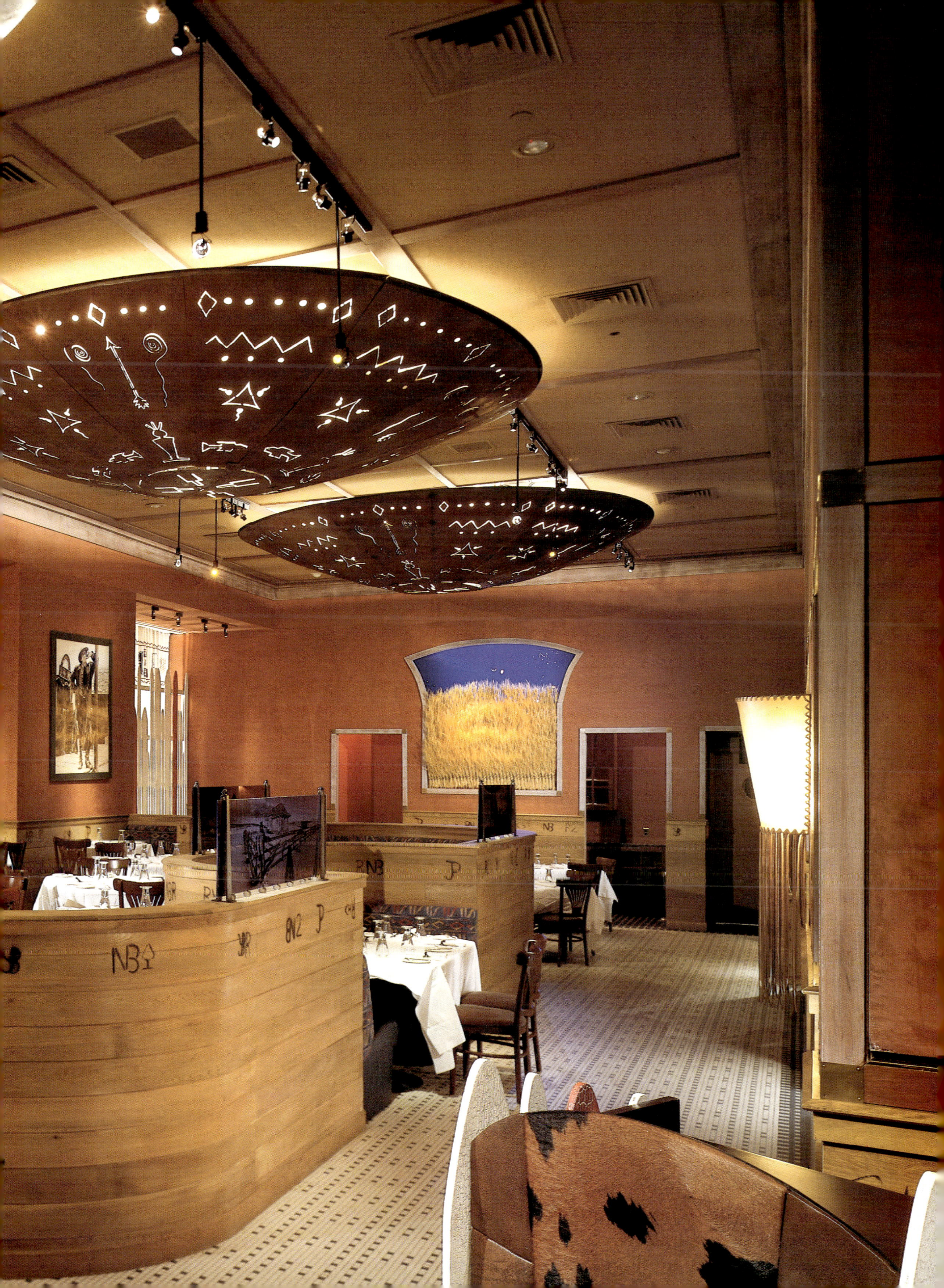

178

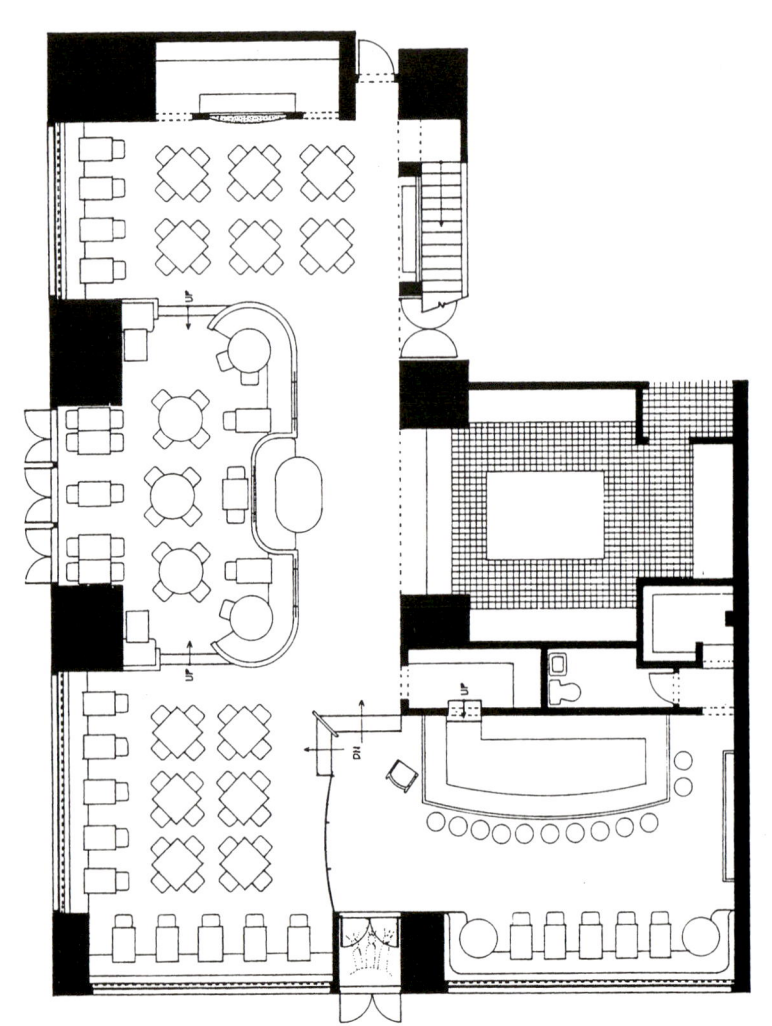

TATOU RESTAURANTS
David Rockwell Architect. Beverly Hills, CA e New York, NY, USA, 1990-1993

The restaurants in the Tatou chain, which have opened all across America, owe their success to their winning formula of a combined restaurant and music club with dance area, whose layout is ingeniously resolved at both architectural and decorative level. In order to give a suitable frame to the stage area where the blues bands play, the architect David Rockwell has borrowed several figurative and symbolic ideas from the opera houses of the southeast states and from Vaudeville. In the New York venue of the chain, the first in the series, the main dining hall faces inward onto a central stage, which is raised above the dining floor area, and framed by two female statues bearing lamps, heavy velvet curtains, and a stage curtain decorated with architectural designs. The theater atmosphere is further underscored by the bronze heads of satyrs repeated along the wood-paneled wall that cordons off the central area which, once the tables have been cleared away, can be turned into a danc-ing piste. Along the dividing wall are various items of period-style furniture, elegant seats upholstered in rich damascened fabrics. From the ceiling, which is framed by a heavy cornice and molding, hangs a large chan-delier typical of those found in opera houses. The Beverly Hills Tatou repeats this formula, but enhancing the décor with traditional west-coast ideas and symbols. While the facade of the restaurant may appear rather austere and slightly Déco, though lit up to great effect, once inside, beyond the cocktail lounge whose design follows that of the facade, the large central dining hall-cum-ballroom subscribes to the theatrical and stage-design atmosphere with its row of tall fake palm trees (a stock symbol of the Los Angeles landscape) with illuminated trunks (optic fiber) sprouting coconut-shaped lamps at the top. Drapes and wall-paper dress the perimeter walls, while the stage boasts a heavy backcloth of classic maroon velvet. The ceiling, too, is draped with fabric, and from its center hangs a voluminous crystal chandelier flanked by spotlights that project bands of colored light when the dining area is cleared of its tables, freeing the floor for disco dancing.

Beverly Hills

La serie dei ristoranti Tatou, aperti in varie città americane, deve il suo successo alla formula di ristorante-music club-discoteca brillantemente risolta dal punto di vista architettonico e decorativo. Per incorniciare adeguatamente il palco dove suonano le band di blues, David Rockwell ha preso come riferimenti figurativi e simbolici gli ambienti delle *Opera Houses* degli stati del Sudest e i palcoscenici del Teatro Vaudeville. Nel Tatou newyorkese, il primo della serie, la grande sala è rivolta verso il palcoscenico centrale, rialzato rispetto alla quota del pavimento e incorniciato da due statue femminili che sorreggono lampade abat-jour, da drappeggi di velluto di chiaro sapore teatrale e da un sipario decorato con motivi architettonici. Atmosfere teatrali sono sottolineate anche dalle teste di bronzo dei satiri ripetute sul muretto di legno che nella sala da pranzo definisce la zona centrale che, liberata dai tavoli, si trasforma in pista da ballo. Lungo il muretto divisorio sono distribuiti gli arredi in stile, eleganti sedie imbottite rivestite in tessuto damascato. Dal soffitto, segnato da massicci cornicioni e modanature, scende un grande lampadario in gocce di cristallo che ricorda quelli impiegati nelle *Opera Houses*. A Beverly Hills Tatou ripete la formula newyorkese, arricchendo la composizione interna con segni e figure californiane. Se la facciata del ristorante può apparire austera e vagamente dèco, anche se illuminata con maestria, nell'interno, dopo il bar in sintonia con le geometrie di facciata, la grande sala centrale-pista da ballo non rinuncia a configurare atmosfere teatrali e scenografiche con la serie di alte palme artificiali (la pianta-simbolo della città di Los Angeles) dai tronchi luminosi (fibre ottiche) e lampade-noci di cocco. Drappeggi e tappezzerie coprono le pareti perimetrali, mentre il palco ha come sfondo un classico drappeggio di velluto bordeaux. Il soffitto è completamente coperto da una grande tenda, dal cui centro scende un grande lampadario di cristallo affiancato dai faretti orientabili che proiettano fasci di luce colorati quando la sala da pranzo si trasforma in movimentata discoteca dal vivo.

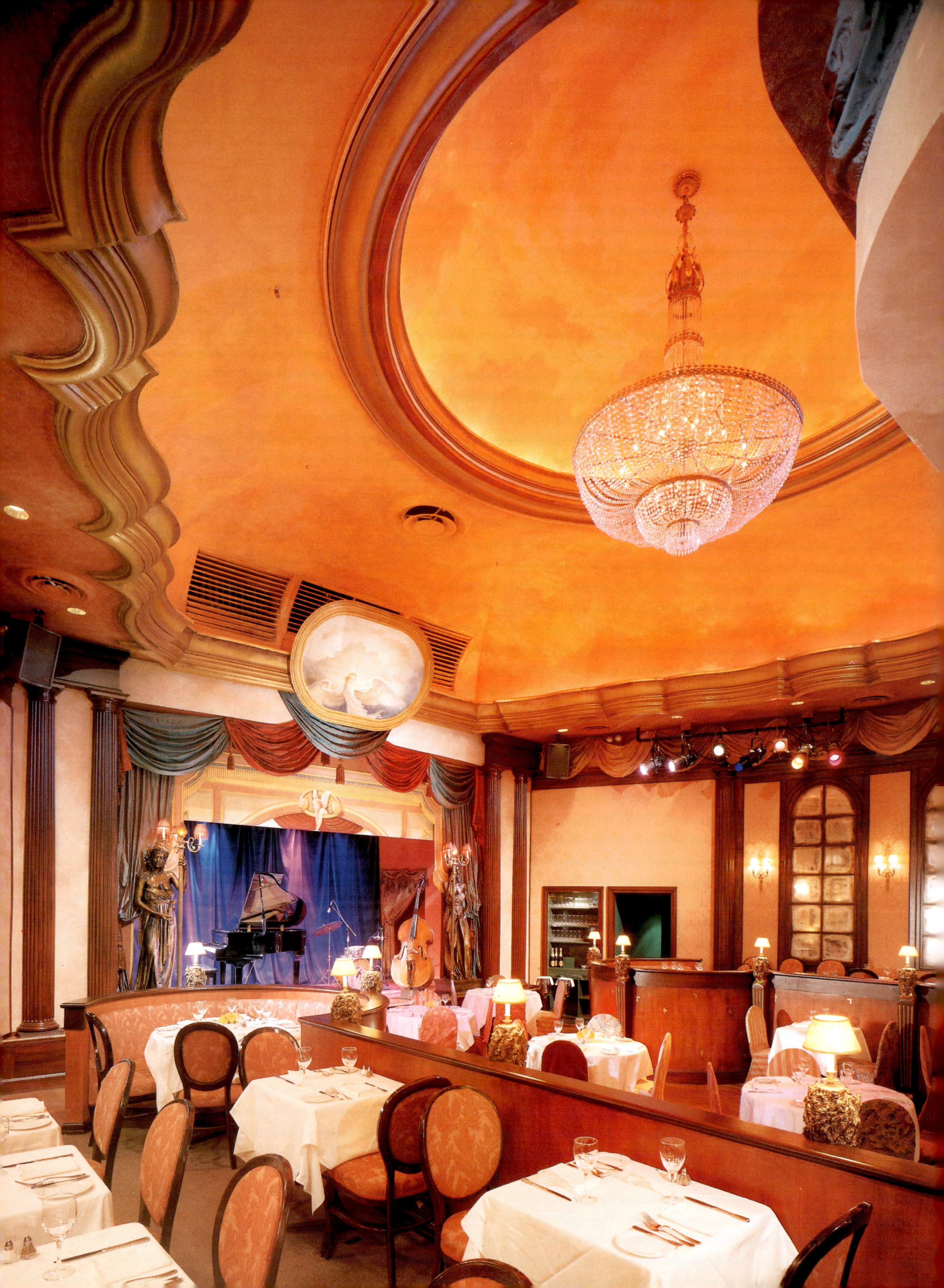

Beverly Hills

New York

182

Beverly Hills

New York

Beverly Hills

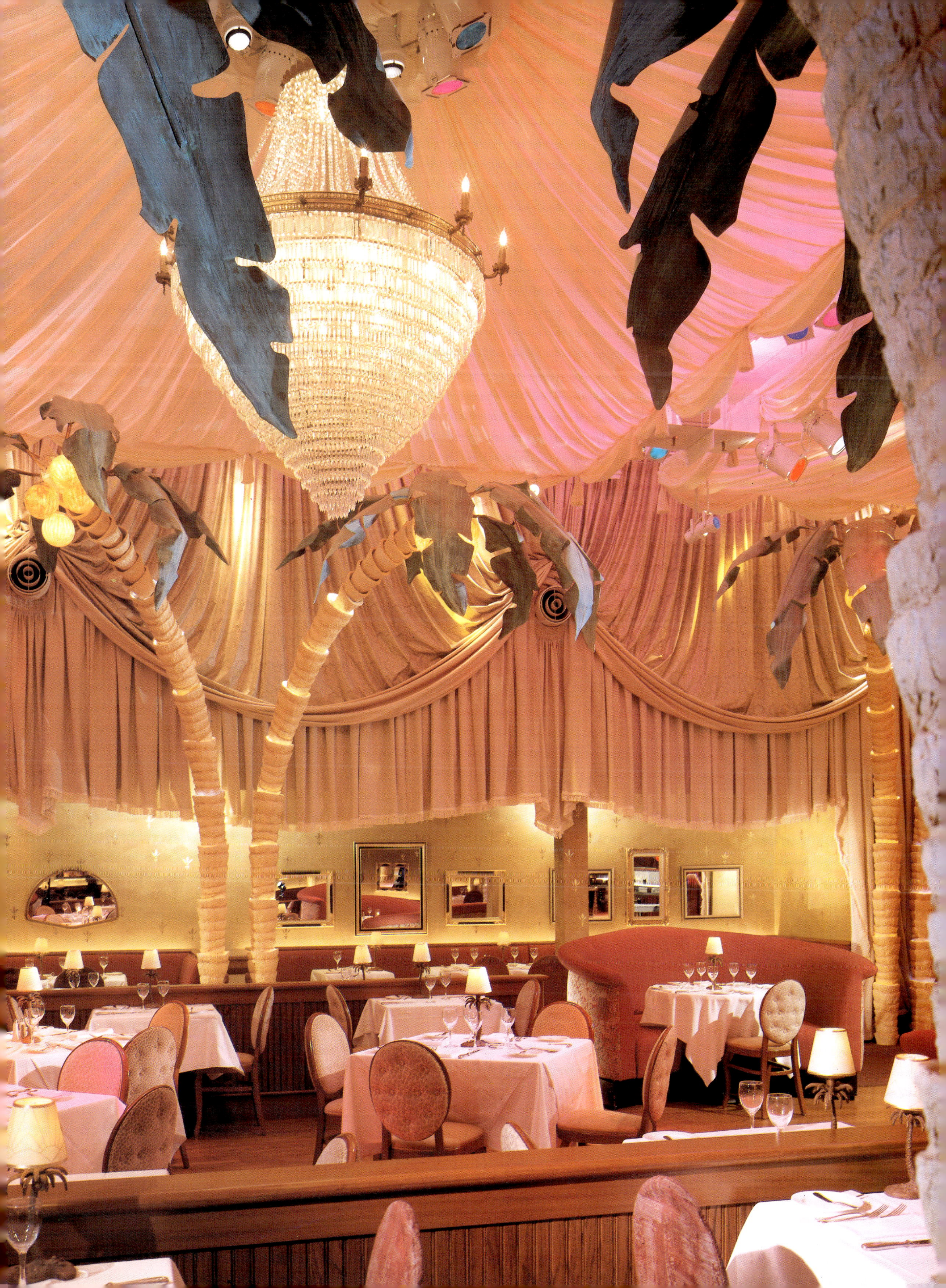

Beverly Hills

Beverly Hills　　　　　　　　　　　　　　　　New York

TORRE DI PISA RESTAURANT
David Rockwell Architect. New York, NY, USA, 1995

This distinctive chain of restaurants takes its title from the famous Tuscan *trattoria* in Milan run by Paolo and Marco Meacci, who decided to export their exclusive cuisine to the streets of New York. The compositional elements, imagery, and symbolism that David Rockwell has chosen as his means of establishing atmosphere in this new dining venue are all Italianate landscape features, as seen through the eyes of an architect from New York. The premises has a rectangular floor plan, with one of the shorter sides open onto the street, a feature that has been cleverly exploited for visual effect by emphasizing the scenic perspective this offers. A series of figurative and pictorial features associated with the Leaning Tower of Pisa and the imagery of the Metaphysical painter Giorgio de Chirico alternate along the left wall: a tilted frame echoing the Leaning Tower offers a kind of vitrine for a collection of Italian ceramics, standing out sharply against the wallpapered surface behind it, which is adroitly lit. The end of the room is characterized by a liberal variation on the Chiricoesque town square, creating an abstract architectural framework on reduced scale, complete with town clock high on a stylized tower that reaches up to the ceiling. A simulated building facade at the back is pierced by a central archway leading to the private smokers' room and exclusive dinner-party suite. On the left of the typically Italian street frontage that concludes the vista rises a raised platform that hosts a series of blue fixed couches positioned along the wall, flanked by the customized Marcia seats upholstered in velvet. A scaled-down building facade, complete with arches, tiles, and mosaic, marks the way through to the kitchens. The bar is stationed to the left of the entrance, conceived as a traditional Tuscan wine cellar, with fixtures and fittings to match. Alongside the counter, a wall has been faced with an intriguing collage of pictures, photographs, love-letters, votive picture cards, and street plans of various Italian cities. Fenced off at the start by two leather-clad screens hiding the access to the restrooms, the left wall opposite the series of imaginary townscapes offers a line of sturdy earth-colored columns that stand out against the blue wall and support the curved paneling of the lowered ceilings.

Il ristorante Torre di Pisa prende il nome dalla famosa omonima trattoria toscana a Milano, gestita da Paolo e Marco Meacci, che hanno voluto ripetere a New York l'offerta della loro cucina italiana. I riferimenti compositivi, le immagini e le figure che David Rockwell ha scelto per definire l'atmosfera di questo nuovo locale sono da ricercare nel paesaggio italiano, filtrato e reinventato dagli occhi di un architetto newyorkese. Lo spazio di forma rettangolare regolare, con un solo lato minore aperto verso strada, è stato sfruttato a livello scenografico nella sua profondità enfatizzandone la prospettiva finale. Una serie di episodi figurativi e pittorici legati alla figura della Torre di Pisa e alla pittura di Giorgio De Chirico si alternano lungo la parete di sinistra: una cornice pendente che rivisita la figura della Torre funge da elemento espositore per una collezione di ceramiche italiane, emergendo dalla tappezzeria del muro retrostante illuminato con studiata regia. Sul fondo, una libera reinterpretazione dei dipinti di De Chirico sulle piazze italiane, forma una serie di piccole architetture astratte con tanto di orologio luminoso sulla torre stilizzata che arriva al soffitto. Una facciata sul fondo, segnata da un'apertura ad arco centrale, si pone come ingresso alla saletta riservata per fumatori e per cene private. Sulla sinistra del fronte 'all'italiana' che conclude la prospettiva sul fondo si sviluppa una pedana rialzata che ospita i divanetti fissi posizionati lungo il muro perimetrale tinteggiato di blu che si affiancano alla sedie su disegno "Marcia" rivestite di velluto. Una facciata architettonica in scala ridotta con archi, piastrelle e mosaico segna l'accesso alla cucina. Il bar è posizionato a sinistra dell'ingresso, pensato come una tradizionale enoteca toscana in legno scuro e con arredi in stile. A fianco del bancone una parete è rivestita da un curioso collage composto da immagini, fotografie, lettere d'amore, santini e piante di città tutti italiani. La parete di sinistra, schermata inizialmente dai due paraventi in cuoio intrecciato che mascherano l'accesso ai bagni, fronteggia la serie di fantasie architettoniche ed è scandita da una serie di forti colonne cilindriche color terra che emergono dal muro blu per sostenere virtualmente i pannelli curvati del controsoffitto.

186

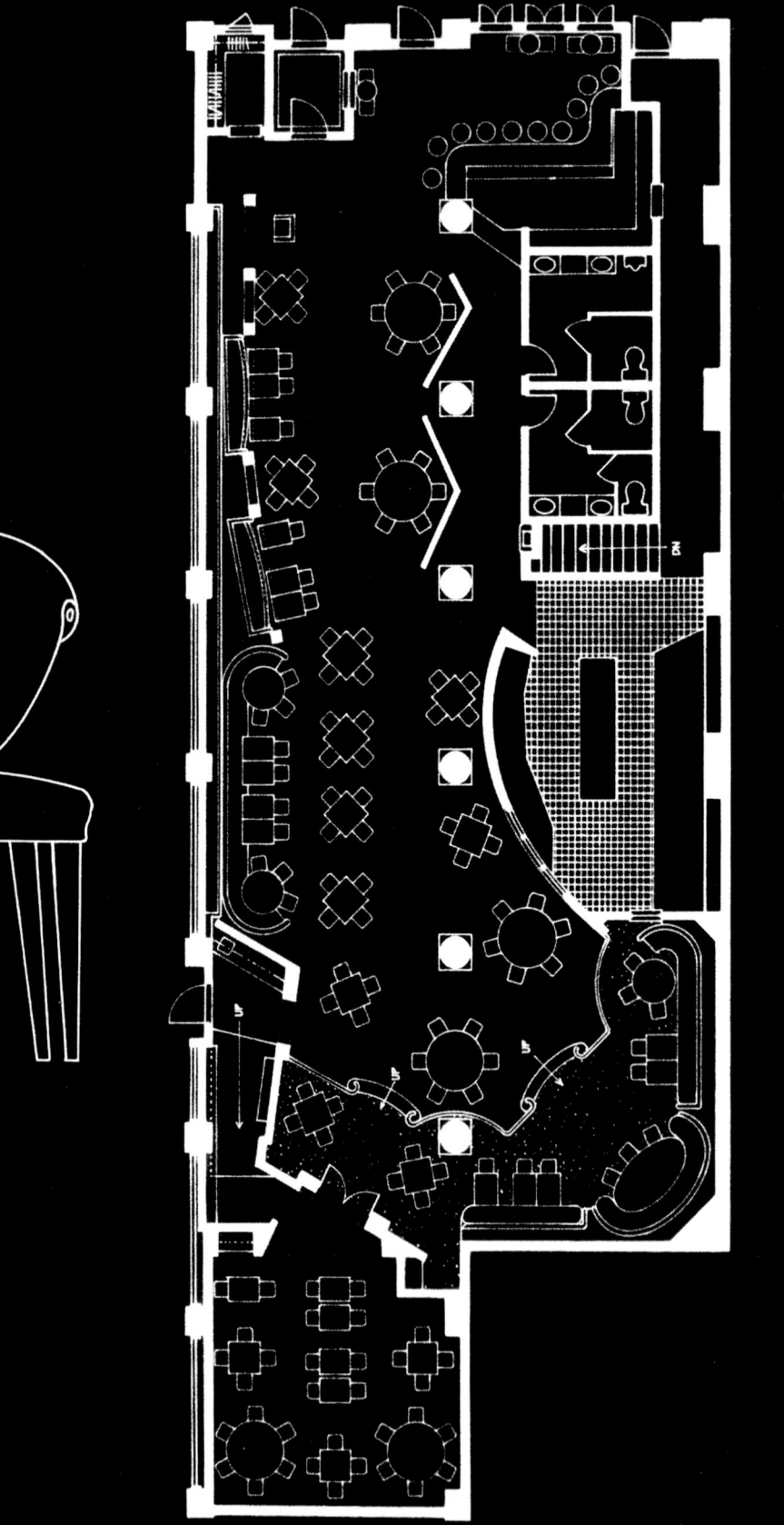

FRONT

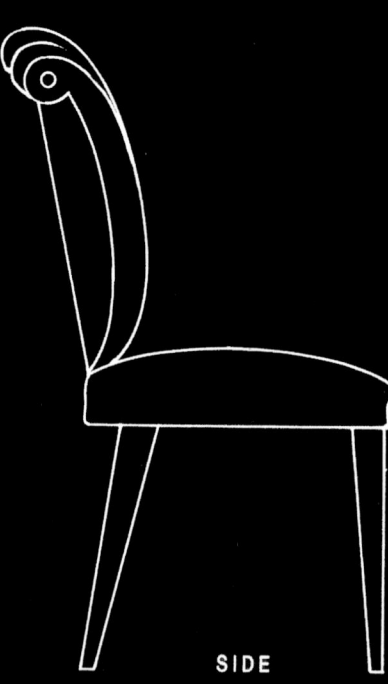

SIDE

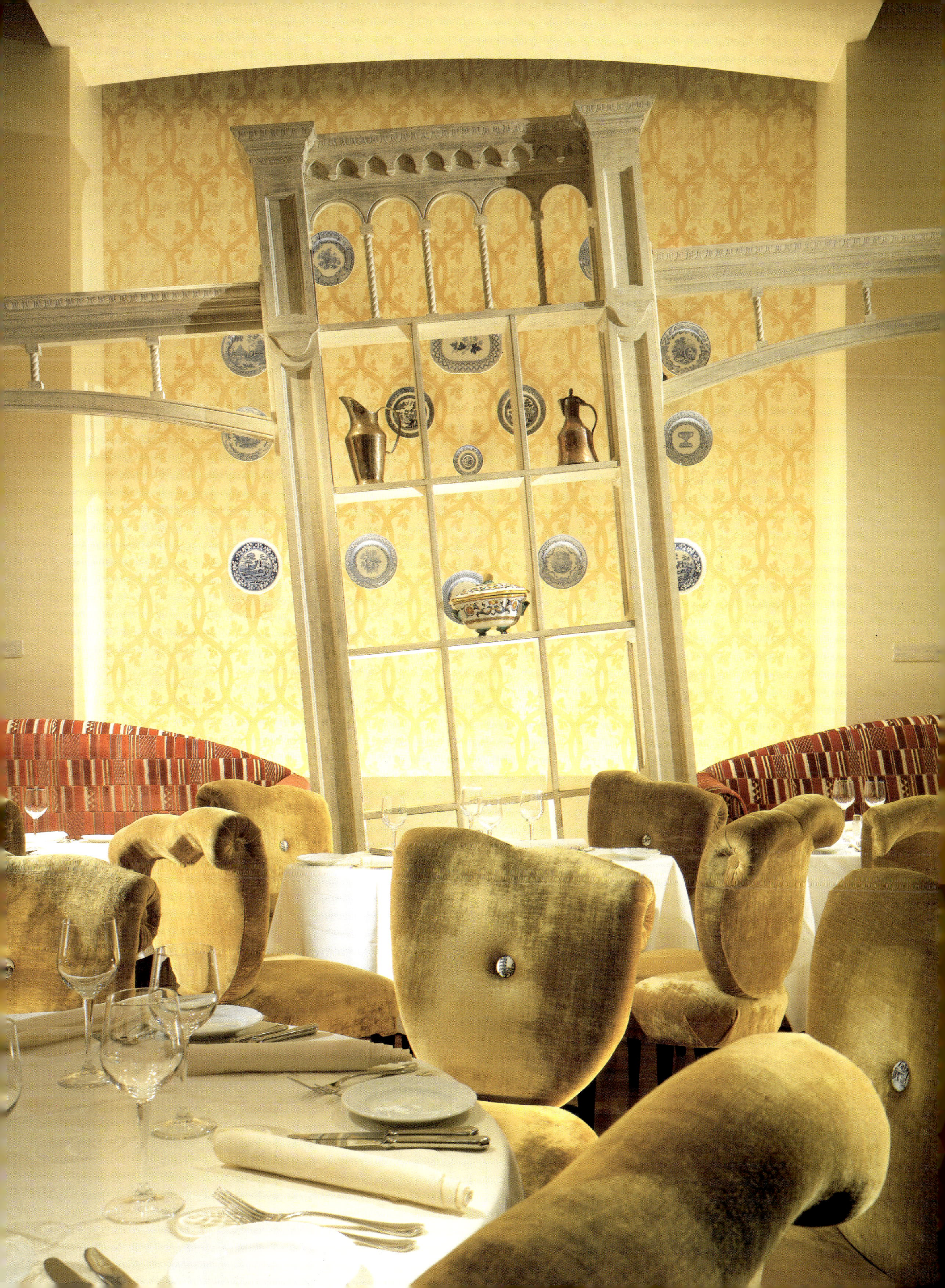

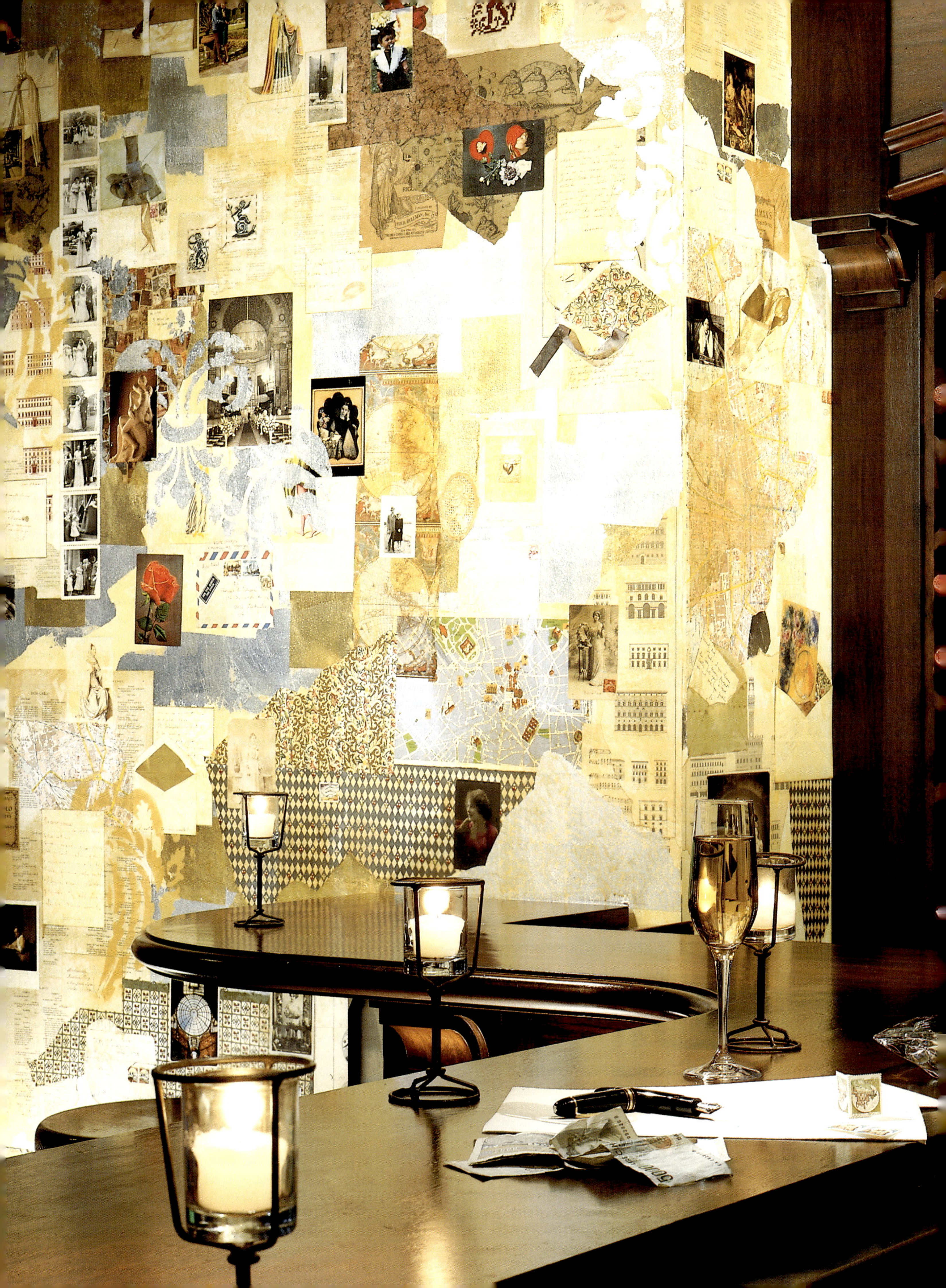

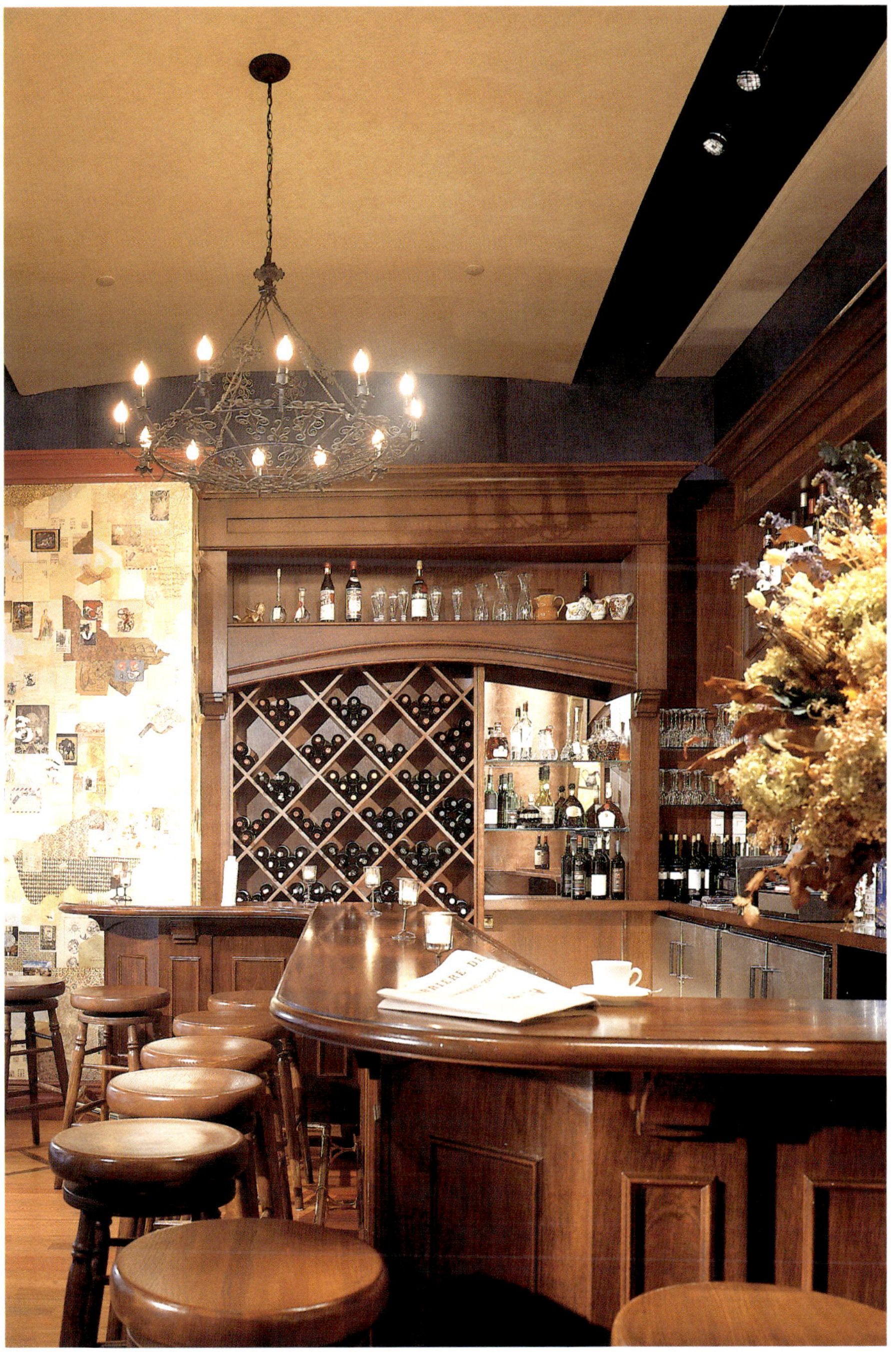

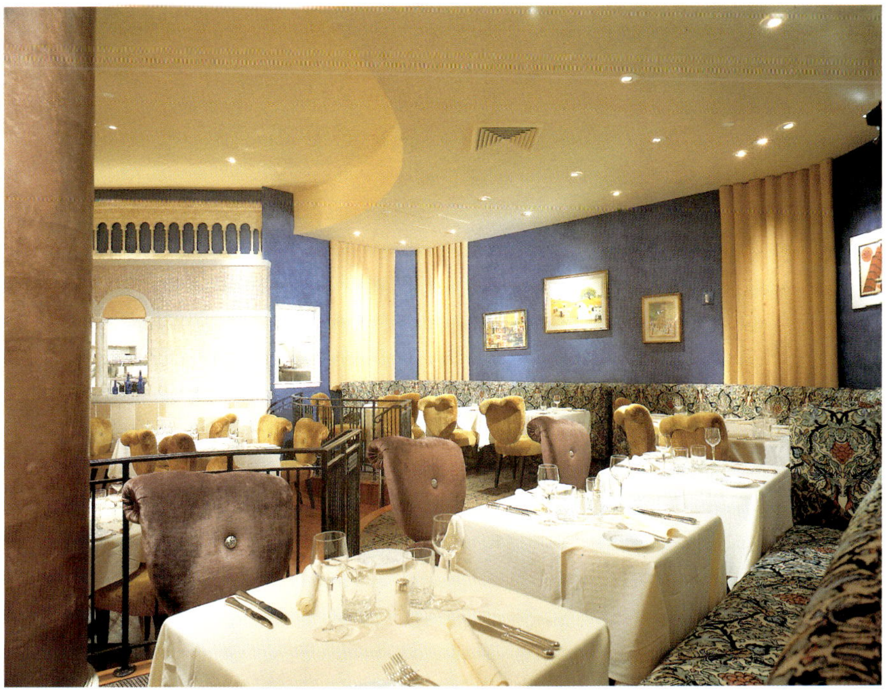

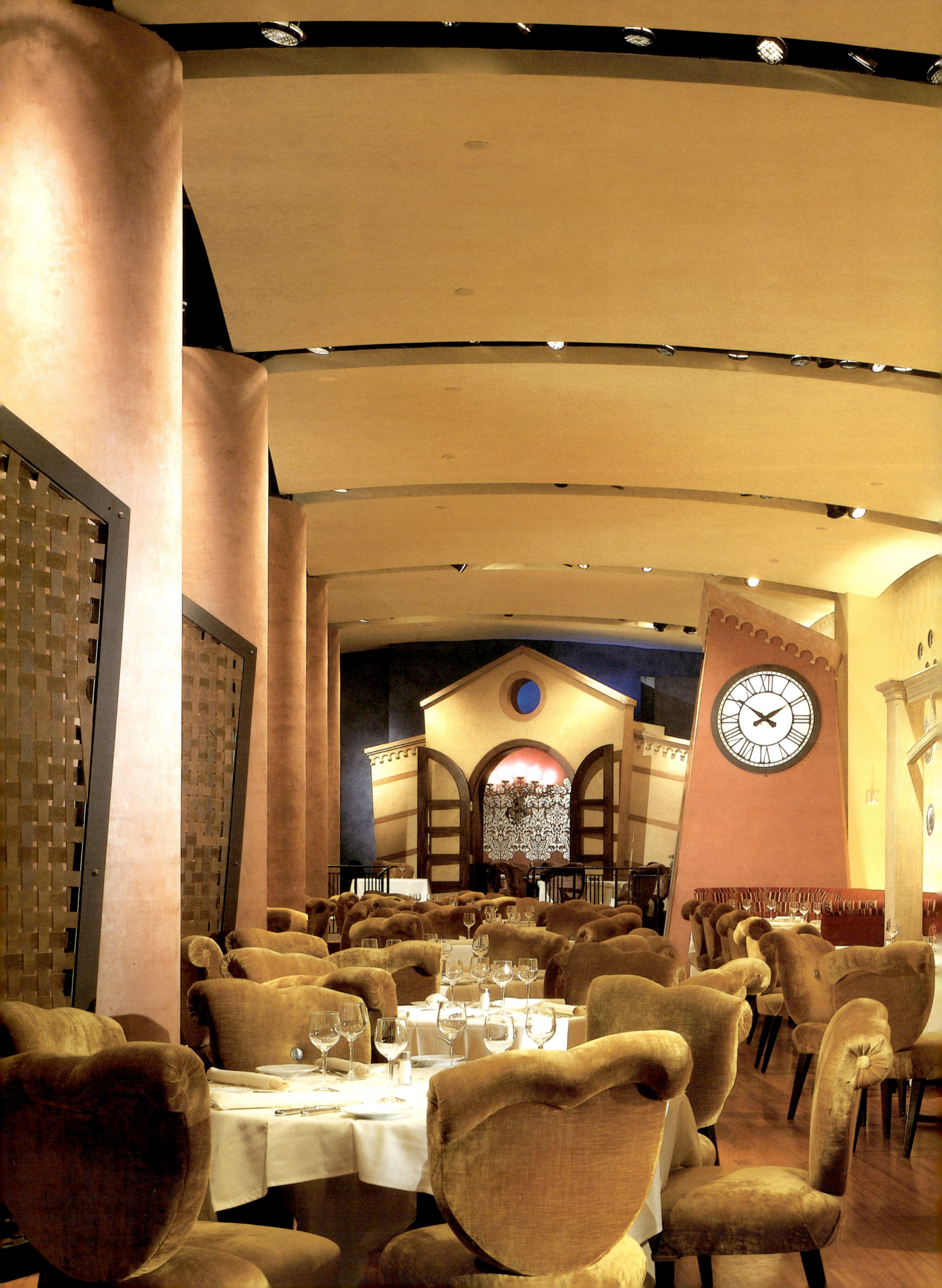

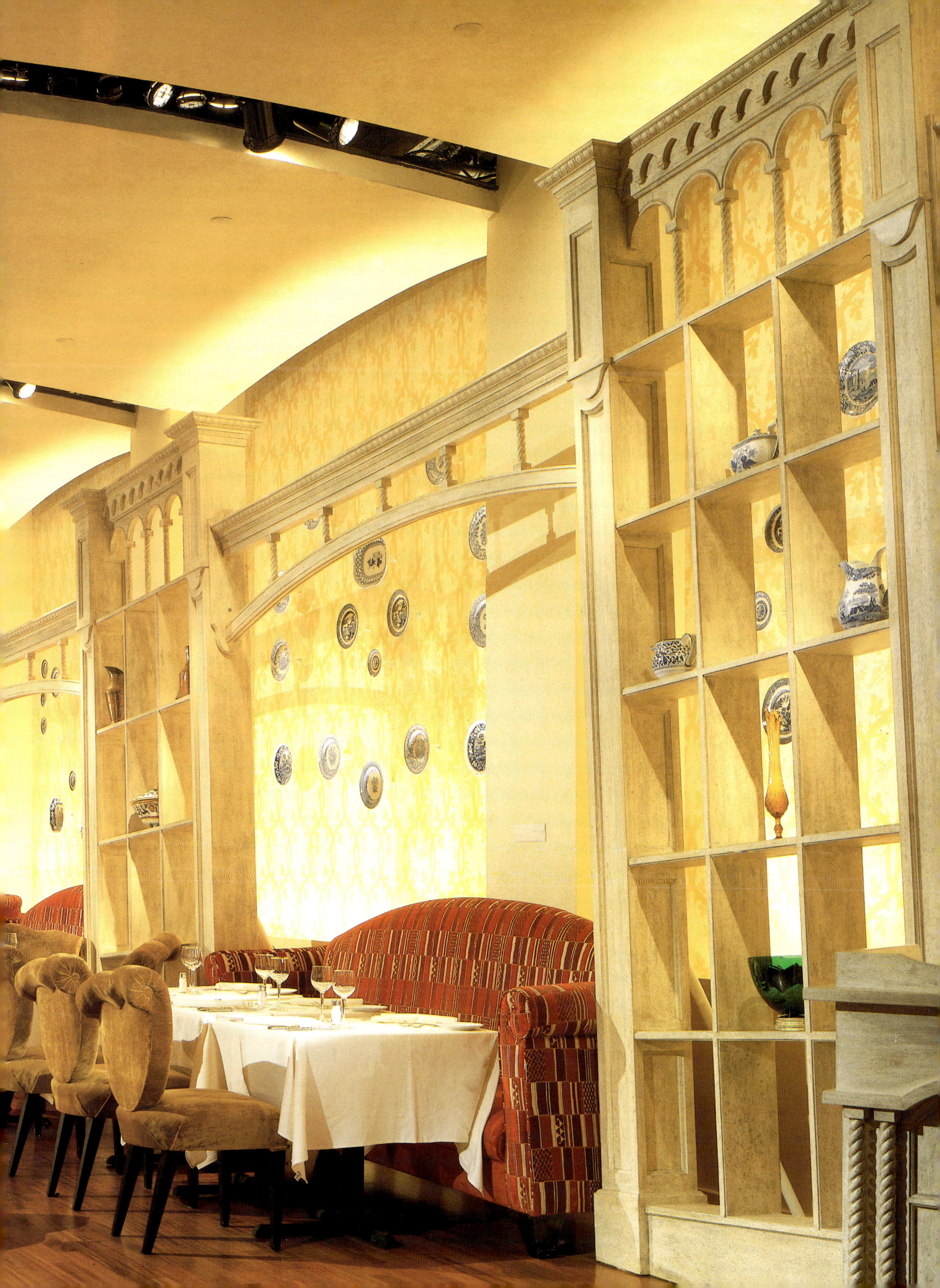

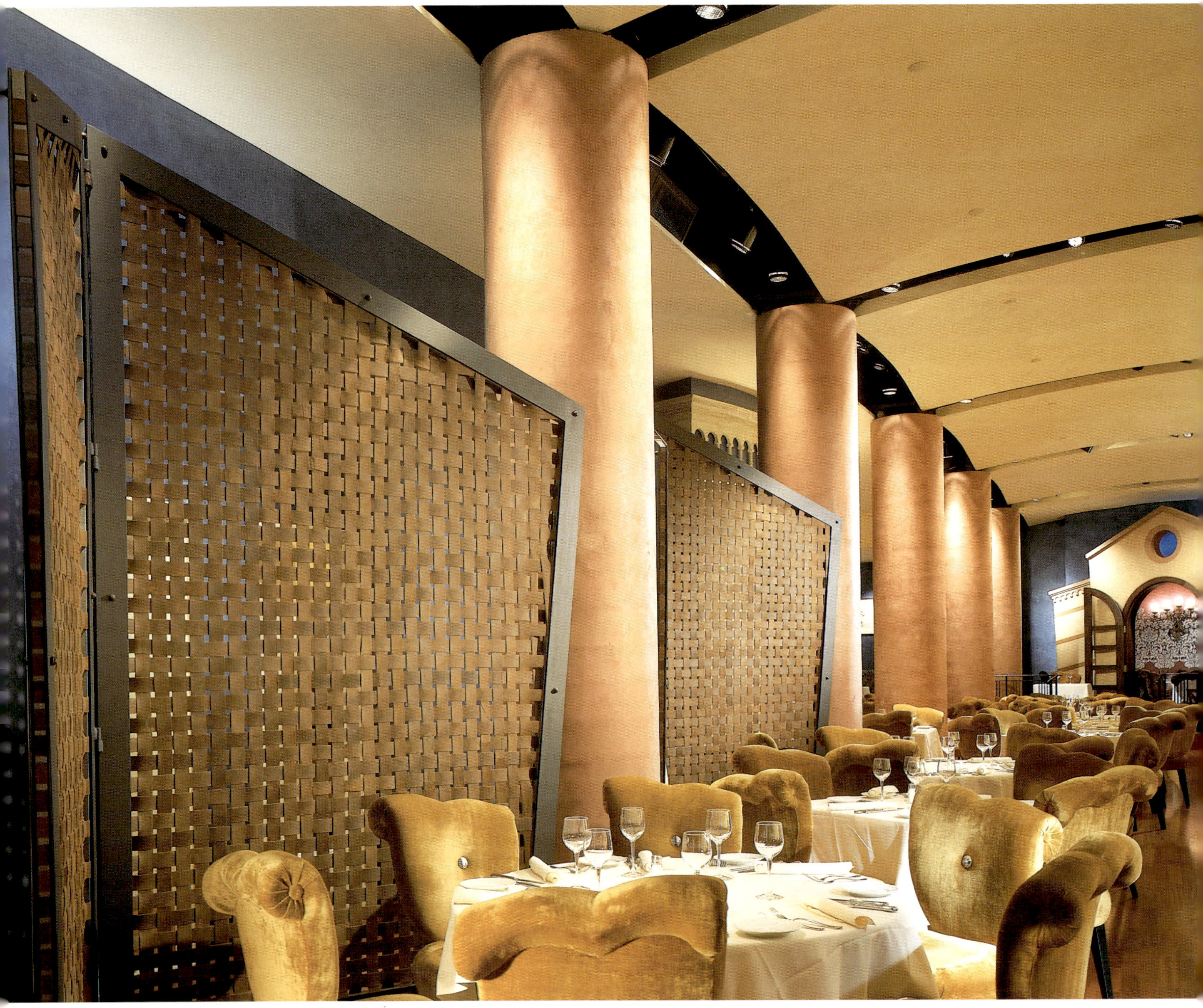

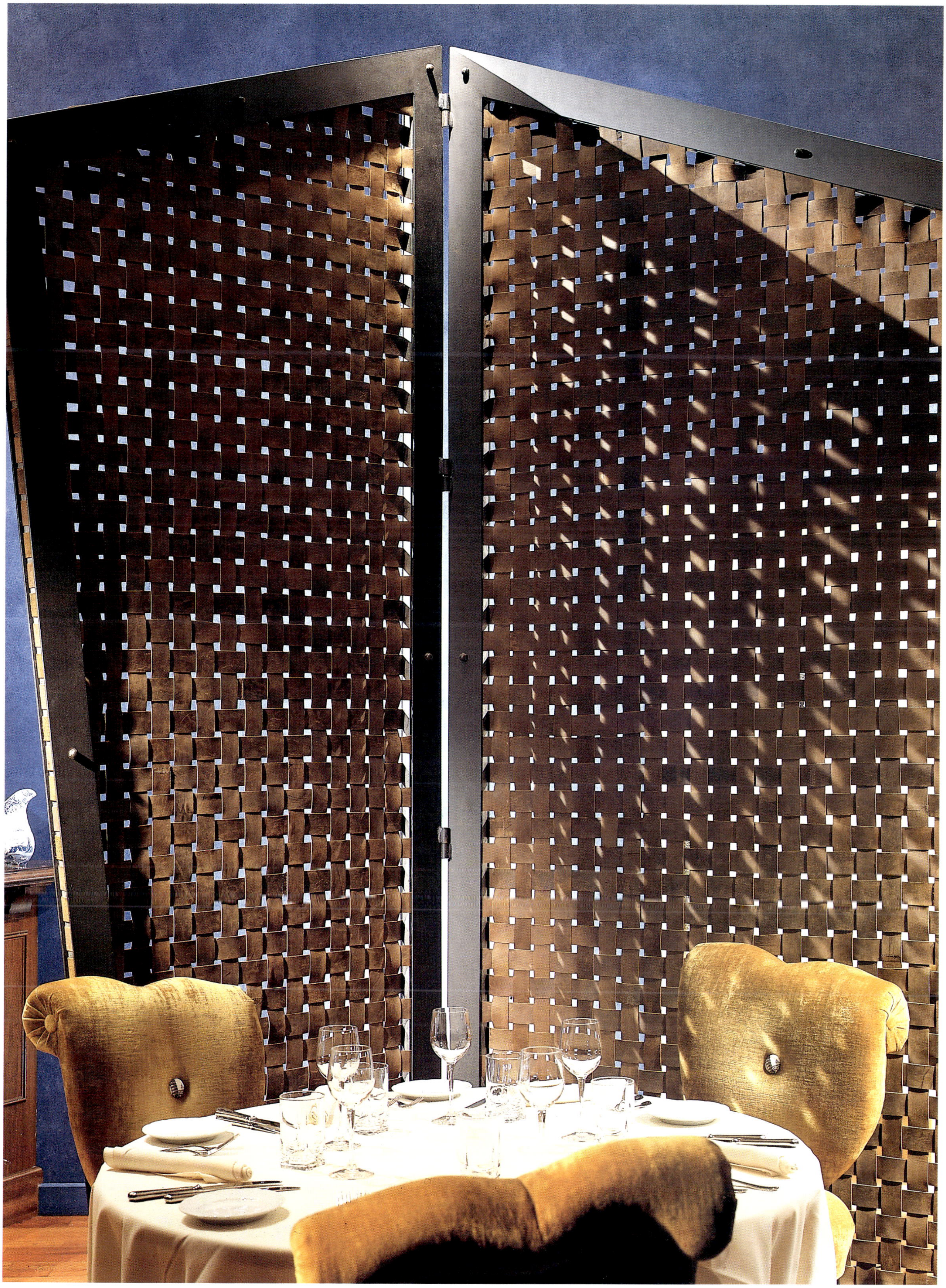

VILLAGE EATERIES RESTAURANT

Hardy Holzman Pfeiffer Associates. Las Vegas, NV, USA, 1997

In perfect accord with the compositive and thematic aspects of the building that houses the New York, New York Casino, which is an assembly of buildings symbolizing Manhattan (Brooklyn Bridge, Empire State, Chrysler, Statue of Liberty, all on a reduced scale), the Village Eateries complex occupies most of the ground floor of the hotel (around 3,000 sq. m) is a further homage to New York's distinctive cityscape, in this sophisticated simulation of the streets of Greenwich Village, Manhattan. Taking full advantage of the extra height offered by its ground-floor situation, the interior décor represents a line of street frontage four or five stories high that offers a hyper-realistic portrait of two city streets, all reproduced with the level of painstaking attention to detail typical of a film set. As at Universal Studios and in the finest scale models of a special-effects department, each of the materials reproduced in the model has been aged and weathered accordingly: the street asphalt and sidewalk slabs have been carefully enhanced with simulated stains and signs of wear. Rusted fire-escapes zigzag up building facades composed of various different materials (stone and brick, tiles and crumbling plaster, all reproduced in modeling gesso). The street frontage of this unusual multiple restaurant is decorated with neon signs, billboards with peeling advertising, shop windows all perfectly simulated, and scenes of domestic life seen through grimy yellow curtains. The eight restaurants that occupy the buildings have tables set out on the sidewalk, which are filled with the customary details of the New York cityscape, such as fire hydrants, parking meters, road signs, and street lamps fitted with the typical green plates marking the name of the streets, not to mention the trees, which are composed of pieces of dried oak branches trimmed with leaves of silk in a range of autumn colors. The false ceiling is made of dark blue metal panels, creating a sort of fake sky equipped with a sophisticated lighting system that changes in intensity according to the time of day, from the morning through to sundown, and then the night hours, when all across Greenwich Village the lights come on and the strains of music floats up from the various sidewalk cafés and bars, always packed with visitors.

In perfetta sintonia compositiva e tematica con l'edificio del "New York, New York Casino", composto dall'assemblaggio degli edifici simbolo di Manhattan (dal ponte di Brooklyn all'Empire State Building, dal Chrysler Building alla Statua della Libertà in scala ridotta) il complesso del Village Eateries, che occupa gran parte del piano terreno dell'albergo (circa tremila metri quadrati) si configura come ulteriore omaggio al paesaggio urbano newyorkese, nella sofisticata simulazione delle strade del Greenwich Village. Sfruttando al meglio l'altezza disponibile, è stata costruita una serie di fronti architettonici a quattro o cinque piani che nel loro composito e iper-realistico confronto definiscono due strade urbane, con un'attenzione quasi cinematografica nella ricostruzione della città vissuta. Come negli Universal Studios e nelle migliori scenografie del cinema, ogni materiale simula al meglio il proprio invecchiamento; asfalto e porfido di strade e marciapiedi sono attentamente ritoccati con macchie artificiali e tonalità differenti. Le scale di sicurezza in ferro battuto arrugginito si intrecciano sul disegno delle facciate composte da più materiali (pietra e mattoni, piastrelle e intonaci consumati, tutti costruiti in gesso decorato). I fronti stradali di questo inusitato pluriristorante sono arricchiti con insegne al neon, con cartelloni pubblicitari consunti, con vetrine perfettamente allestite, con scene di vita domestica simulate e protette da tendine interne lise e ingiallite dal tempo. Gli otto ristoranti che occupano gli edifici arredano le strade con i loro tavolini affiancati dalle tradizionali figure del paesaggio urbano newyorkese, come le prese dell'acqua antincendio, i lampioni e i segnali stradali, le colonnine a pagamento per il parcheggio dell'auto e i tradizionali cartelli verdi che indicano il nome delle vie, senza tralasciare la presenza degli alberi, costruiti con tronchi essiccati di quercia e foglie in seta dipinte secondo i colori della stagione autunnale. Il controsoffitto è in pannelli di metallo blu scuri, sorta di cielo artificiale dotato di un sofisticato impianto di illuminazione che cambia intensità secondo le ore del giorno, dal mattino sino ad arrivare al tramonto e alle ore notturne, quando nel Village si accendono le luci e si sente la musica uscire dai locali, sempre più affollati di visitatori.

195

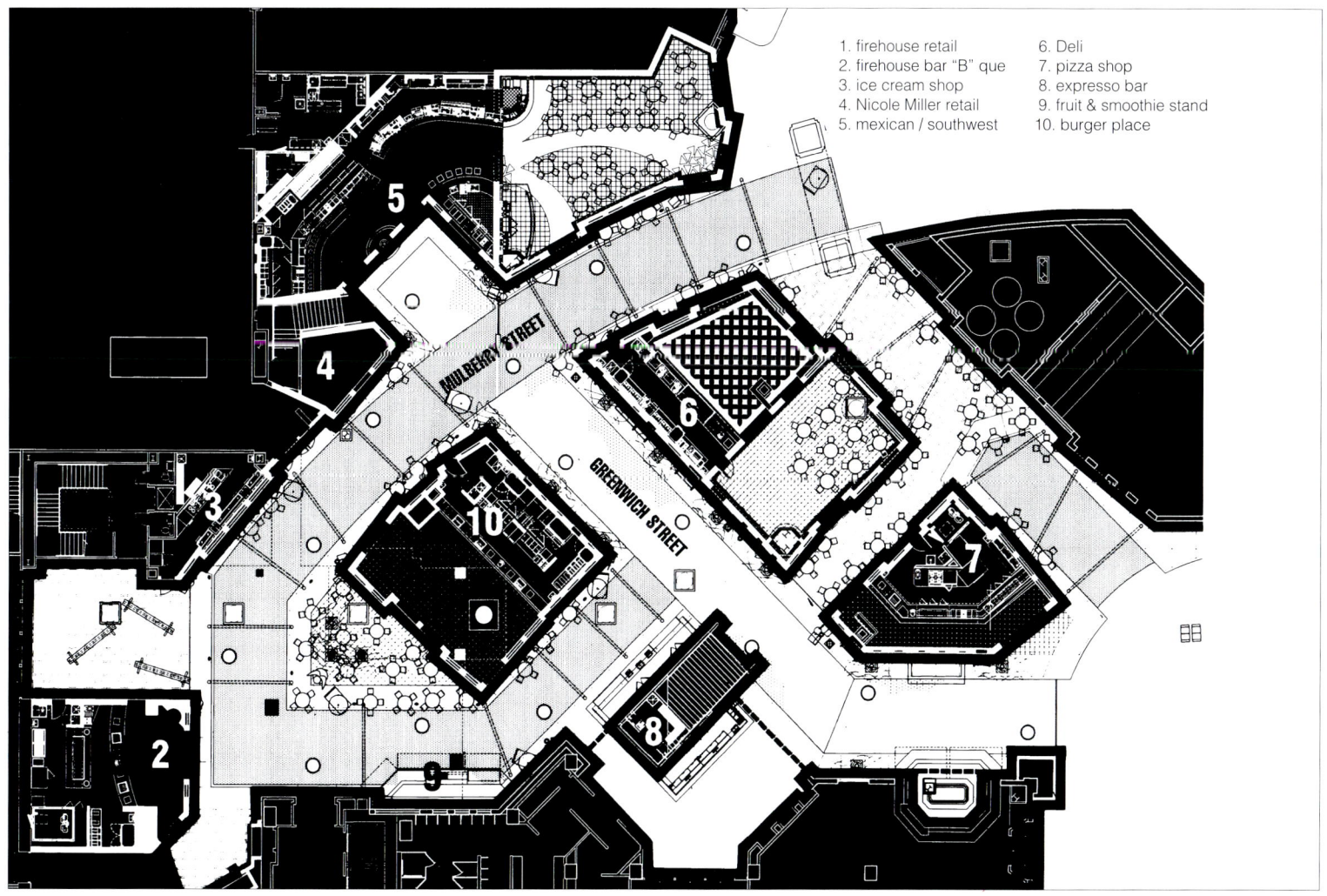

1. firehouse retail
2. firehouse bar "B" que
3. ice cream shop
4. Nicole Miller retail
5. mexican / southwest
6. Deli
7. pizza shop
8. expresso bar
9. fruit & smoothie stand
10. burger place

CKER
GONZALEZ
GONZALEZ
HARDWARE PAINTS
BROADWAY
ONE WAY
ROXY
TACO STOP

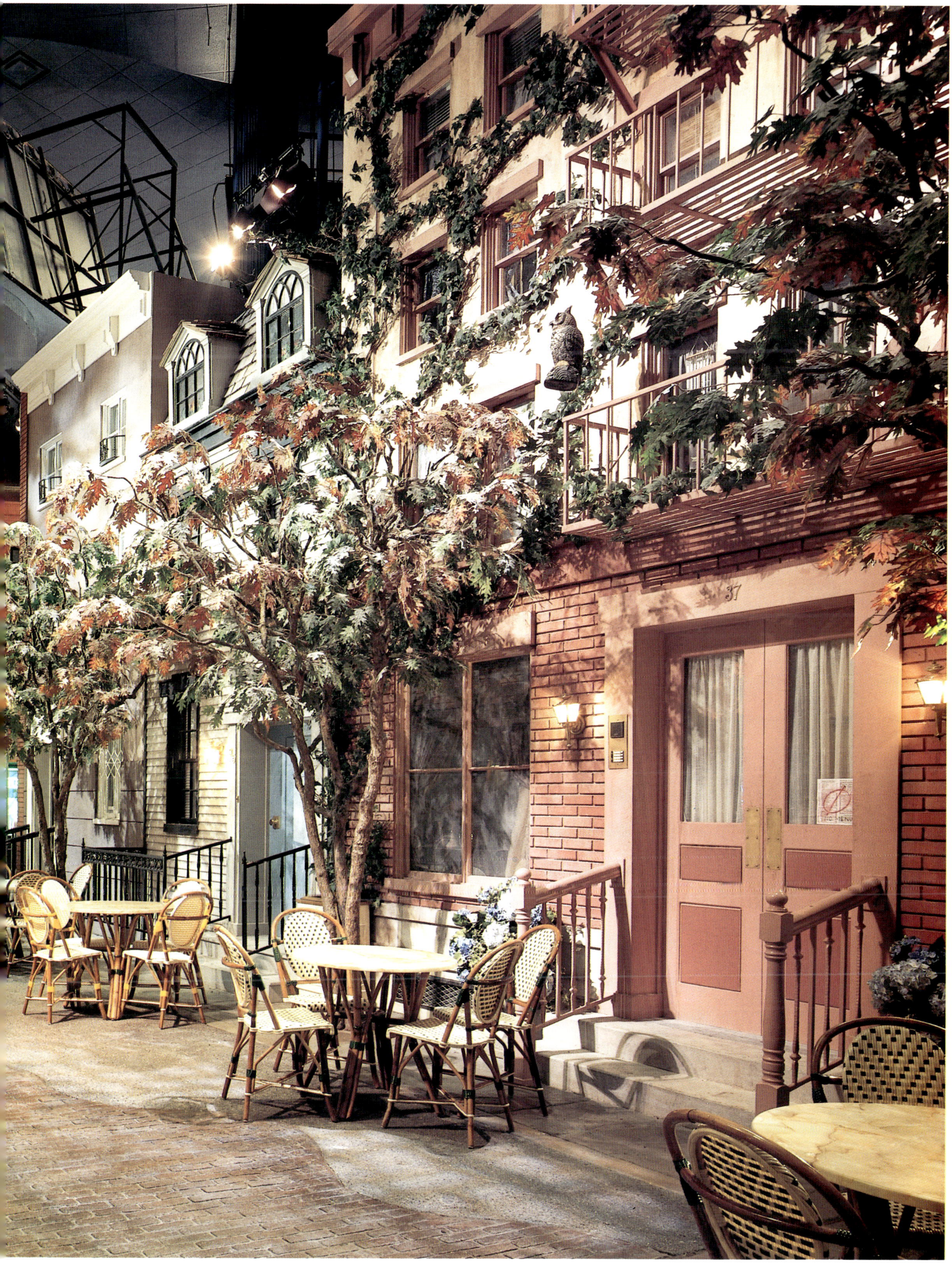
37

198

199

VONG RESTAURANT

Haverson Architecture and Design, David Rockwell Architect. New York, NY, USA, 1992

Entirely dedicated to the renowned Franco-Thai cuisine that has become the trademark of the master chef, Jean Georges Vongerichten, whence the name, the Vong restaurant has been faithfully fitted out with flair and elegance in an exclusive oriental style. In this project David Rockwell has ingeniously recreated a Thai interior, avoiding the pitfalls of mere copying and instead freely reinventing ideas garnered from the cultural universe and history of Thailand's architecture. First and foremost, the colonial ceiling fan – a stock feature of oriental interiors – has been transformed into a decorative floor-standing lamp with a wrought brass stem and wooden slats crowning the openwork sphere from which a soft, diffuse light emerges. This feature is repeated the full length of the wall, which is faced with an unusual collage composed of fragments of Thai pictures and postage stamps, matchboxes, gold leaf, and connects the entrance cocktail lounge with the main dining hall. Opposite this intriguing decorative device, a massive curved wall in lacquered wood hides the way in to the kitchens, thereby adding a feature of oriental interiors that has a long tradition, namely, the *screen*. In the dining room various elements orchestrate the space, lending a resonant and complex touch to the whole. At the bottom of the room, cordoned off by a green and red fence with tall vertical laths, lies the *tatami* area, set on a slightly higher level than the rest of the restaurant's wood floor, in honor of traditional oriental dining modes and manners. A large curved portal, with a gilded decoration of mosaic, leads into a small exclusive dining area, its entire surface clad in a colored quilted fabric. Another scenic portal in teak rises to ceiling height and carries a central horn of sanded luminous glass at its center, creating a striking visual framework. This dominant feature marks the entrance to the kitchens, and is screened off at one side by a panel of green wood with Thai-style openwork patterns. Hanging from the ceiling decorated with gold foil, studded with recessed downlighters, are a series of small glass lamps like rows of upturned tulips, creating a further homage to Thai culture and the traditional "Festival of Light."

Interamente dedicato alla celebrazione della cucina franco-thailandese dello chef Jean Georges Vongerichten da cui prende il nome, il ristorante Vong si configura come esclusivo ed elegante interno orientale. David Rockwell ha voluto in questo progetto creare atmosfere thailandesi senza però cadere nella dimensione della 'copia in stile', piuttosto reinventando liberamente alcune precise figure selezionate all'interno della cultura e della storia dell'architettura thailandese. Anzitutto il tradizionale ventilatore coloniale, simbolo di ogni interno orientale, è trasformato in lampada da terra decorativa con fusto di ottone lavorato e pale in legno di coronamento poste sopra la sfera traforata da cui esce una timida luce soffusa. Questo elemento è ripetuto lungo tutta la parete, rivestita da un inusitato collage composto da frammenti di immagini e francobolli thailandesi, scatole di fiammiferi, foglie d'oro, che collega l'ingresso-bar con la sala ristorante. Di fronte a questa riuscita invenzione decorativa, una massiccia parete in curva di legno laccato nasconde la cucina, come esplicito riferimento a una delle tecniche orientali più antiche. Nella sala ristorante diversi elementi scandiscono lo spazio definendo nel loro confronto la ricca figura complessiva. Sul fondo, cinta da uno steccato verde e rosso con alti montanti verticali, la zona del tatami, rialzata rispetto alla quota del pavimento di legno, si pone come omaggio alla tradizione del modo di pranzare orientale. Un grande portale in curva, dalle superfici dorate con fasce decorate a mosaico, ospita all'interno un'accogliente ed esclusiva zona pranzo rivestita su tutte le superfici con un tessuto colorato a quadretti. Un ulteriore portale architettonico inclinato in teak raggiunge il soffitto proponendosi come figura dominante segnata al centro dal sinuoso corno in vetro sabbiato luminoso. Questa forte presenza compositiva evidenzia l'ingresso alla cucina, schermata lateralmente da un pannello di legno colorato di verde e traforato secondo motivi thai. Dal soffitto, rivestito in foglia d'oro e dove sono collocati i faretti alogeni a incasso, scendono delle piccole lampade in vetro, pensate come luminosi tulipani rovesciati, ulteriore omaggio alla cultura Thai nella citazione del tradizionale "Festival delle Luci".

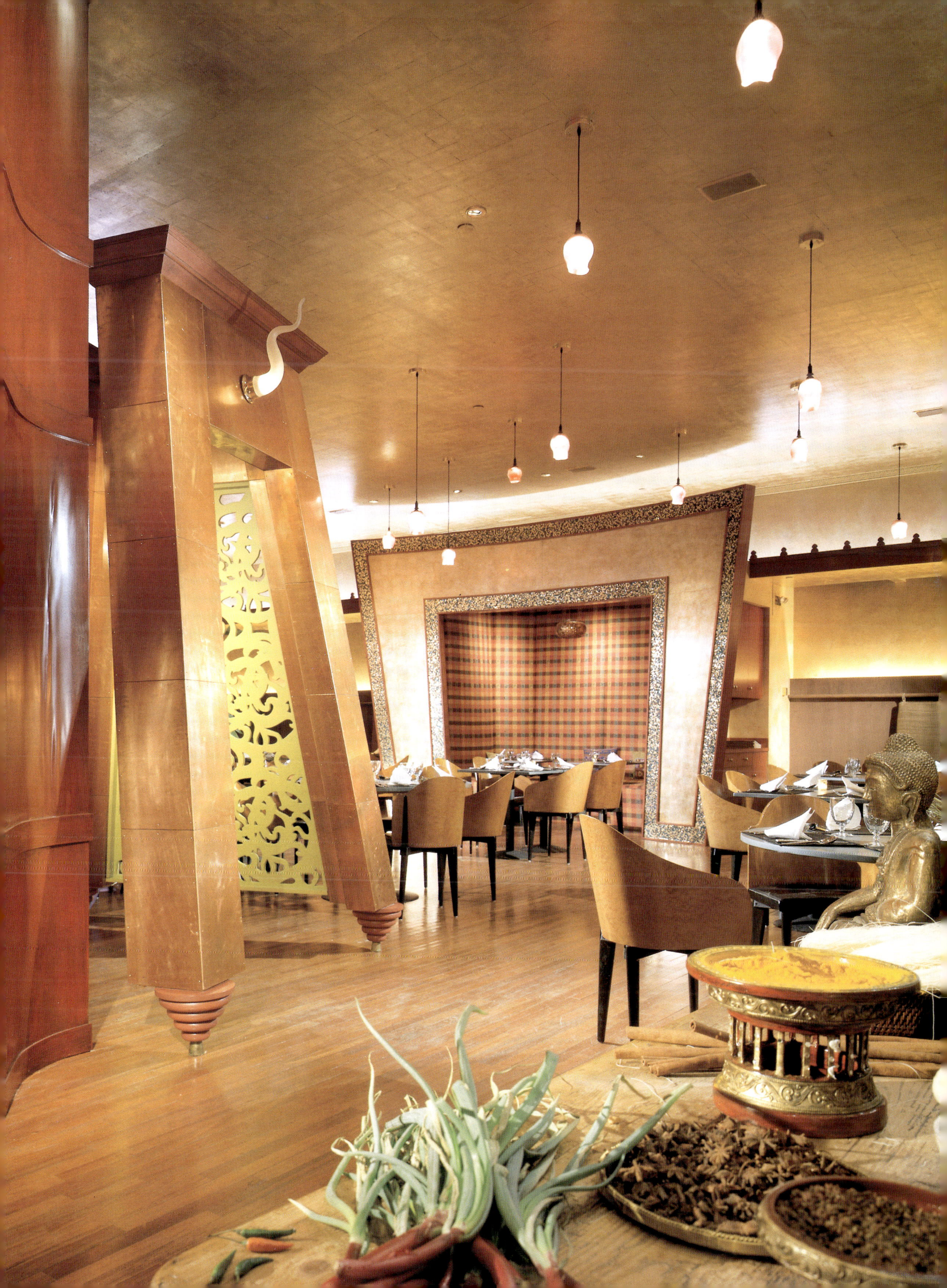

202

203

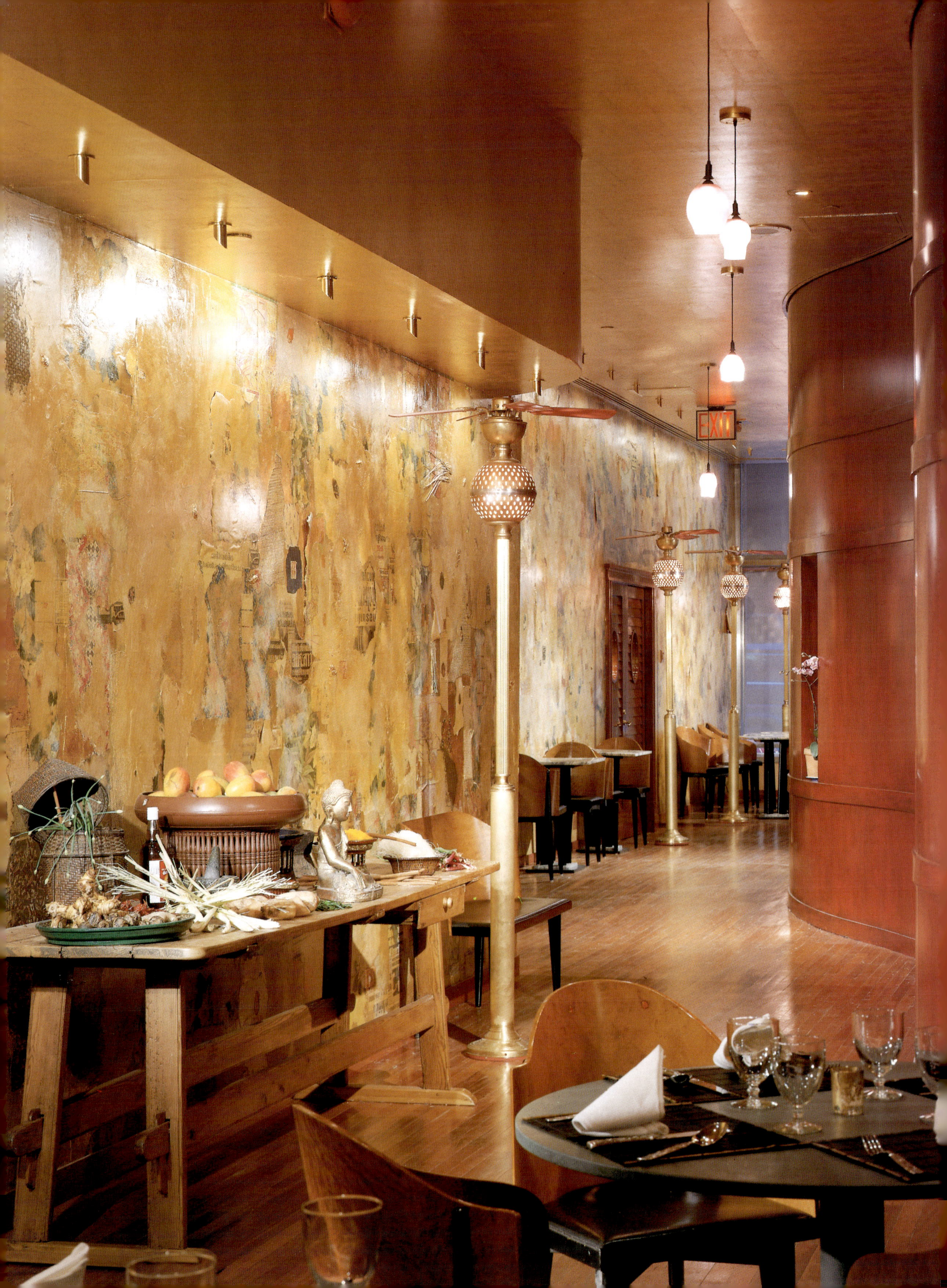
EXIT

ZIP CITY RESTAURANT
Fradkin Pietrzak Architects. New York, NY, USA, 1992

Installed in a spacious former factory building with a uniform rectangular plan with one of the short ends bordering the street, Zip City is a restaurant-cum-brewery that has earned wide renown for its own brand of beer, which is produced with all the requisite machinery on the premises, directly in view of the clientele. The main room had a characteristic vaulted ceiling supported by two rows of tall Corinthian columns in cast-iron, starting at the entrance and repeated the length of the inside, dividing the loft into three bays of equal width. The architects have kept these original features, exploiting the only open side of the space with a large tripartite window that looks onto the interior, and is screened at the center by a wooden partition; the upper section is composed of a gridwork of glazed squares. The cast-iron columns on the right have been partly encased in new partitions that hide the staircase leading down to the basement floor, where the large steel brewing vats are stored; they also partially screen the staircase up to the mezzanine floor, from where a private dining room looks down onto the main floor below. The columns along the left, which have been carefully conserved and integrated with the new scheme, prompted the design of the long horseshoe bar, with its two-tone wood top and riveted metal base. The counter develops around the columns, with scattered stools in black wood, occupying over half of the restaurant's floor space. The area on the right is arranged with dining tables along a projecting wooden wall that conceals the circulation route to the mezzanine. On the left, along an exposed brick wall, lies an area of fixed seating, consisting of a succession of cabin-like areas typical of the European public houses upon which the entire dining venue has been styled. The large wood counter therefore imposes itself as the keynote of the locale. Within its perimeter is a bar in plain wood stretching between the two first cast-iron columns, whereas the ensuing bay is occupied by high copper brewing vats, posing a striking visual feature that celebrates the traditional method of beer production.

Ricavato all'interno di un grande loft industriale a pianta rettangolare regolare con un unico fronte aperto sulla strada, Zip City è un ristorante-birreria caratterizzato dal fatto di produrre direttamente la birra, grazie all' attrezzatura tecnica necessaria, ricostruita con attenzione all'interno del locale. Lo spazio disponibile si caratterizzava per il caratteristico soffitto a volte ribassate affiancate in serie e per le due alte colonne corinzie in ghisa dell'ingresso, ripetute all'interno in doppia fila, dividendo così il loft in tre campate di uguale misura. Entrambe le caratteristiche originali sono state mantenute sfruttando l'unica apertura con una grande vetrata tripartita aperta verso il locale interno e schermata nella parte centrale da una parete di legno, con parte superiore vetrata secondo una fitta scacchiera a quadretti. La serie di colonne di destra è stata in parte assorbita dai nuovi tavolati divisori che nascondono sia la scala di discesa all'interrato, dove sono posizionate le botti di acciaio per la fermentazione della birra, sia quella di salita al mezzanino, in cui è stata organizzata una sala privata affacciata sullo spazio sottostante. Le colonne di sinistra, mantenute e valorizzate dalla soluzione progettuale, hanno invece suggerito la forma a ferro di cavallo del lungo bancone, con piano di legno a due colori e base in metallo rivettato, che si sviluppa al loro intorno, affiancato da numerosi sgabelli in legno nero, per più di metà dello spazio del locale. Sulla destra sono disposti i tavoli da pranzo, sotto la parete di legno naturale in aggetto, che maschera il passaggio al mezzanino. Sulla sinistra, lungo il muro in mattoni, è invece disposta la zona con le sedute fisse, che organizza una serie di posti a sedere 'a cabina', su modello delle birrerie europee dell'inizio secolo, cui l'intera atmosfera del locale fa riferimento. Il grande bancone di legno emerge così come elemento compositivo primario centrale. Al suo interno un mobile bar di legno naturale si sviluppa tra le prime due colonne in ghisa, mentre l'interasse successivo è occupato dagli alti cilindri di rame per la produzione della birra, conclusione scenografica che spettacolarizza un antico processo produttivo.

206

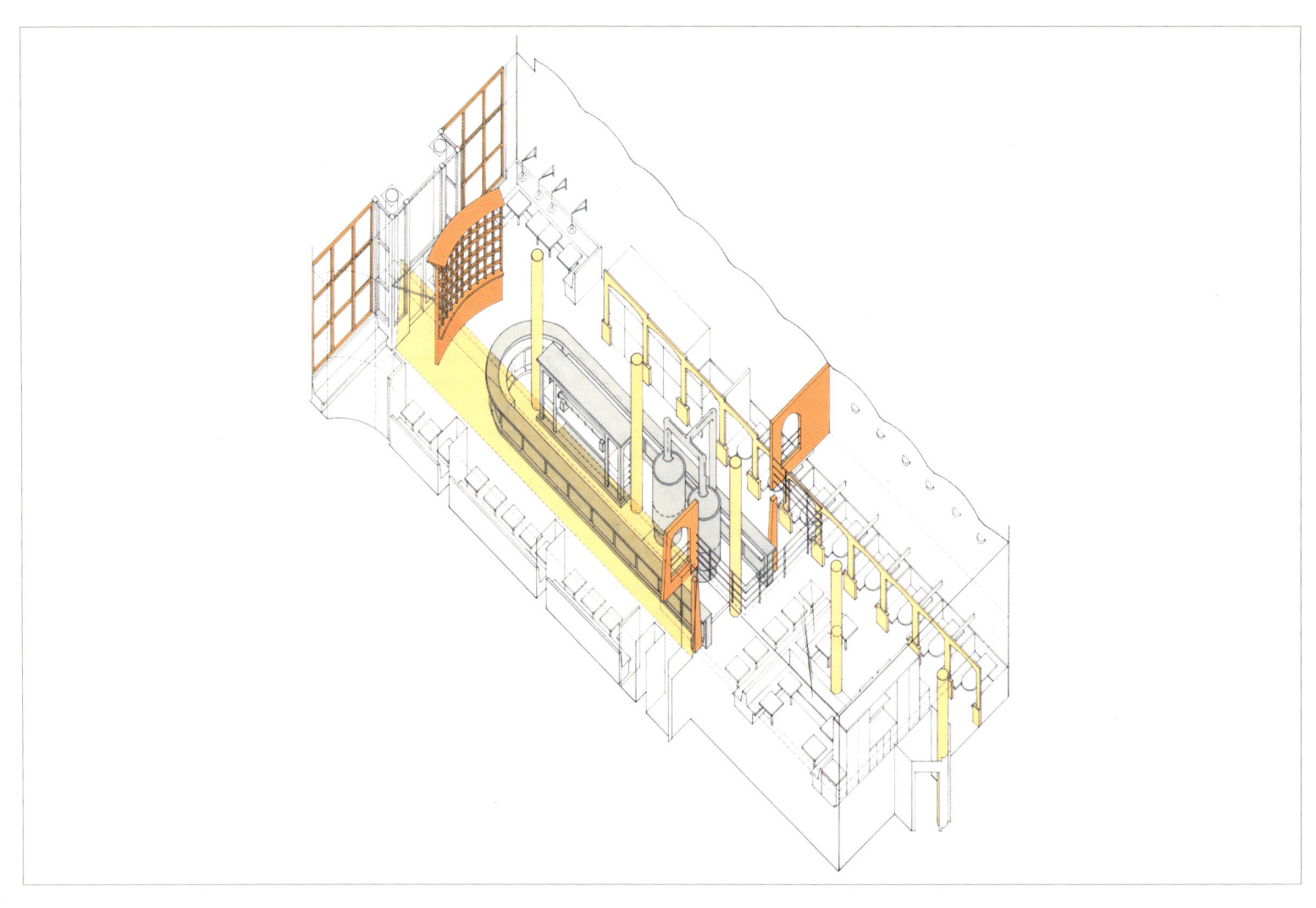

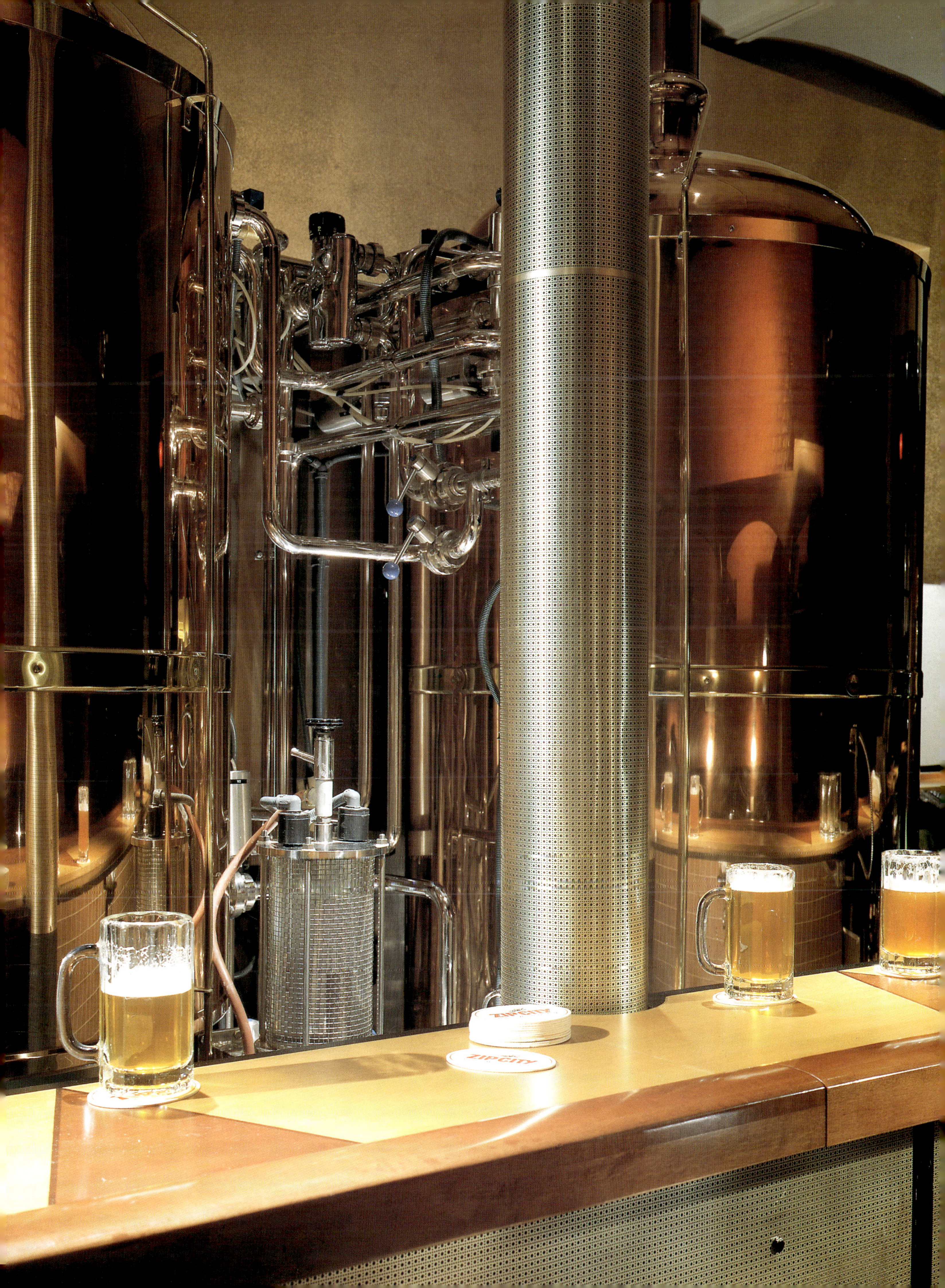
ZIPCITY
ZIPCITY

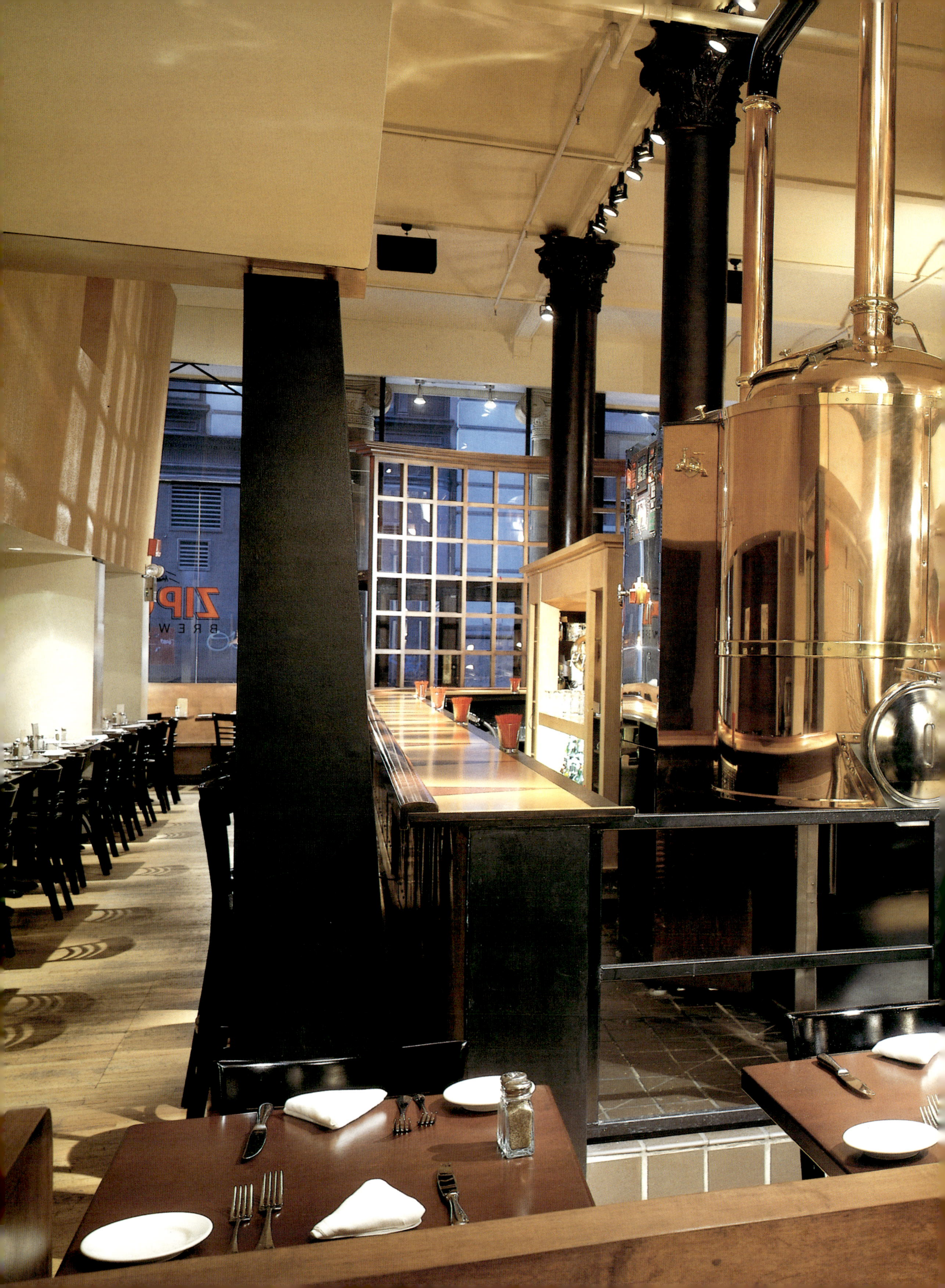

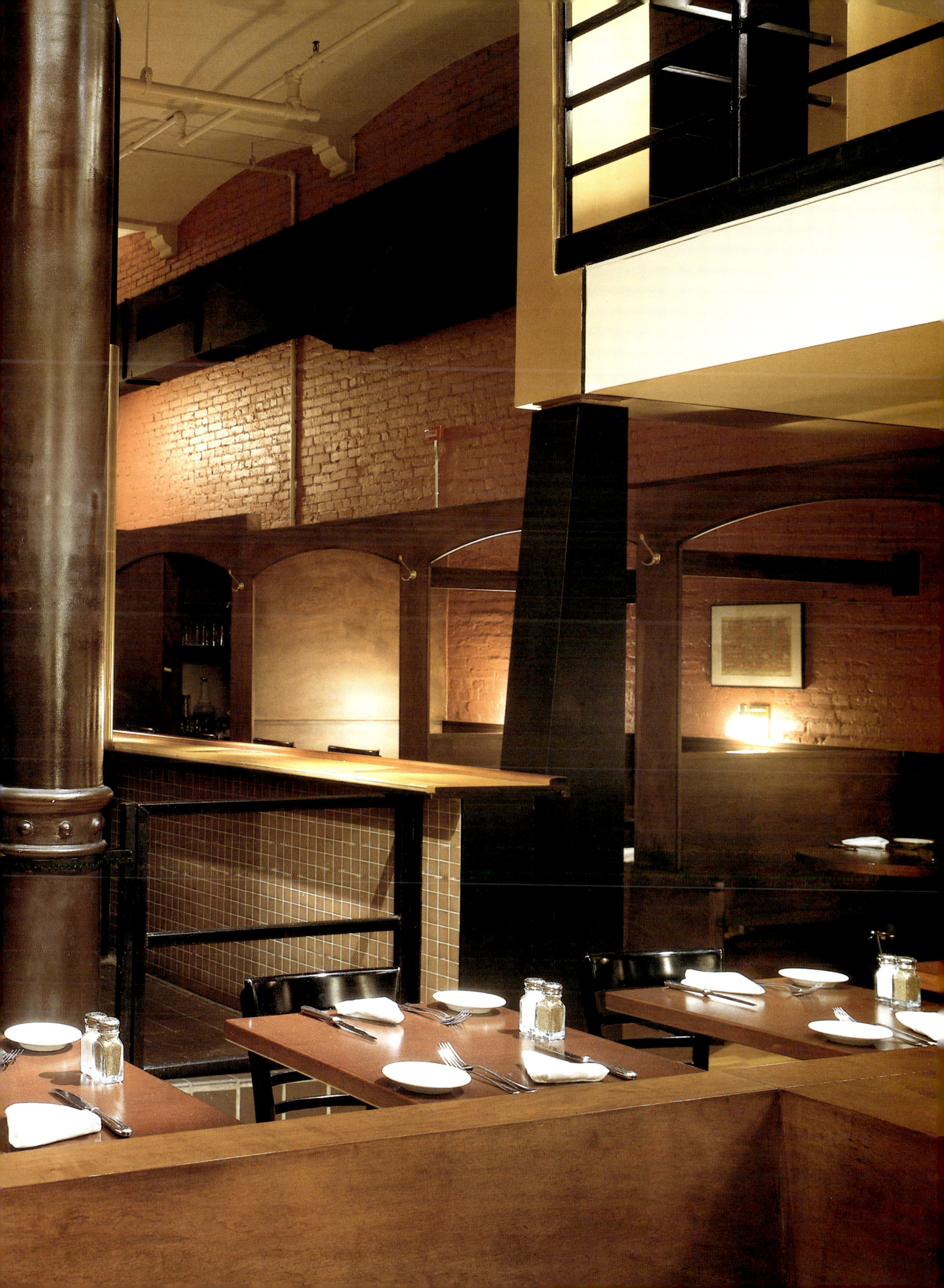

ZOE RESTAURANT
Jeffrey Beers Architects. New York, NY, USA, 1992

Located on the ground floor of a 19th-century building in SoHo, Manhattan, the Zoe restaurant is like a composite expression of the colors and imagination of the countless artists, painters, and sculptors who inhabit this ward of Manhattan, which is home of some of New York's most important art galleries. The original space, a factory loft with a characteristic central row of columns, offered a standard layout with a uniform oblong plan, long and narrow, with a single side along the street front and a corner area that was not accessible. The project has maintained the overall uniformity of the space, emphasizing the perspectival effect toward the back of the premises by means of a variety of special compositional, decorative, and functional features. The tiled floor, which offers a two-color pattern arranged in sets of squares framed in wood surrounds, covers the entire floor area and is echoed in the ceiling bulkheads, which are painted a complementary pink and recessed from the walls with ample rectangular cut-away sections around the pillars. These have been faced in irregular-shaped terracotta blocks producing a rough, sculptural effect, and are studiously lit, as is the perimeter wall on the left, which has been painted a variety of colors in abstract sections, creating a sort of permanent "picture" spotlit by the oblique lighting that deftly emphasizes the gap between wall and bulkheads. The foyer is arranged with a cocktail lounge with a handsome wood and marble counter over which hang atmospheric ceiling lights terminating in cones of colored glass. The dining room continues on from the bar with wood and marble tables along the painted wall, the first part of which is embellished with a tile mosaic surmounted by a horizontal light running the length of the wall, a device that also helps establish visual separation between the two different sections of surface treatment. The kitchens give onto the dining area, and are screened by a wood counter where guests can enjoy a meal diner-style. The counter also provides a perspectival backdrop to the room as a whole. The kitchens are equipped with an earth-colored wood-burning oven and a grill framed by a large gilded surround with geometric inserts repeated at intervals on a vast blue background.

Ricavato al piano terreno di un edificio del XIX secolo a SoHo, il ristorante Zoe sembra tradurre nella sua immagine complessiva le figure e i colori espressi dai numerosi artisti, pittori e scultori, che lavorano in questo quartiere della città, popolato come noto anche dalle maggiori gallerie d'arte. Lo spazio originario, un loft industriale segnato da una fila di pilastri centrali, proponeva la comune tipologia di forma rettangolare regolare, stretta e lunga, con un unico fronte aperto sulla strada e una zona d'angolo non accessibile. Il progetto ha mantenuto lo spazio nella sua dimensione unitaria, enfatizzando la prospettiva verso il fondo con diversi episodi compositivi, decorativi e funzionali. Il pavimento in ceramica gioca su due colori, disposti a formare una serie di quadrotti incorniciati e si sviluppa su tutta la superficie calpestabile trovando un eco nel controsoffitto ribassato, elemento complementare tinteggiato di rosa, staccato dai muri perimetrali e interrotto da ampie zone rientranti di forma rettangolare, ricavate in prossimità dei pilastri. Questi, rivestiti con conci di terracotta irregolari in curva, si pongono quasi come sculture 'd'arte povera', illuminate con studiata regia come la parete perimetrale sulla sinistra, colorata secondo partizioni geometriche astratte, sorta di grande quadro fisso valorizzato dalla luce radente che sottolinea il distacco tra muro e controsoffitto. Nell'ingresso è organizzata la zona bar con un raffinato bancone di legno e marmo su cui scendono delle suggestive lampade a cono di vetro colorato. La sala ristorante si sviluppa dopo il bar con i tavolini di legno e marmo disposti lungo la parete dipinta, rivestita per una prima porzione con un mosaico di ceramica sormontato da una lampada orizzontale continua, che funge anche da elemento compositivo divisorio tra le due diverse lavorazioni della superficie parietale. La cucina, aperta verso la sala ristorante e schermata da un bancone di legno dove poter pranzare secondo le modalità dei *diner*, si pone come conclusione prospettica del locale; è dotata di forno a legna color terra e grill incorniciato da un grande mosaico, composto da cornici dorate e inserti geometrici ripetuti secondo una disposizione regolare su una vasta superficie azzurra.

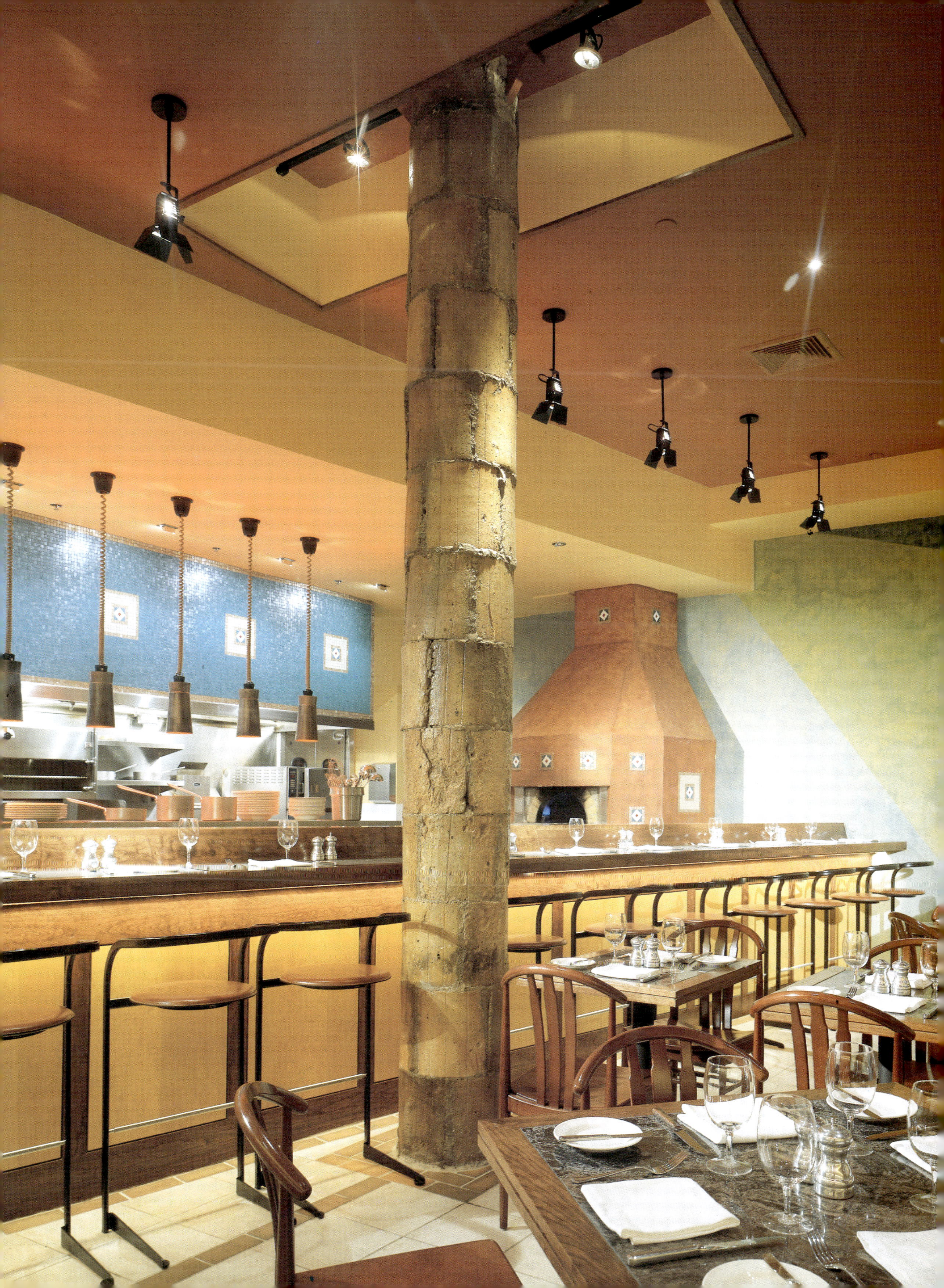

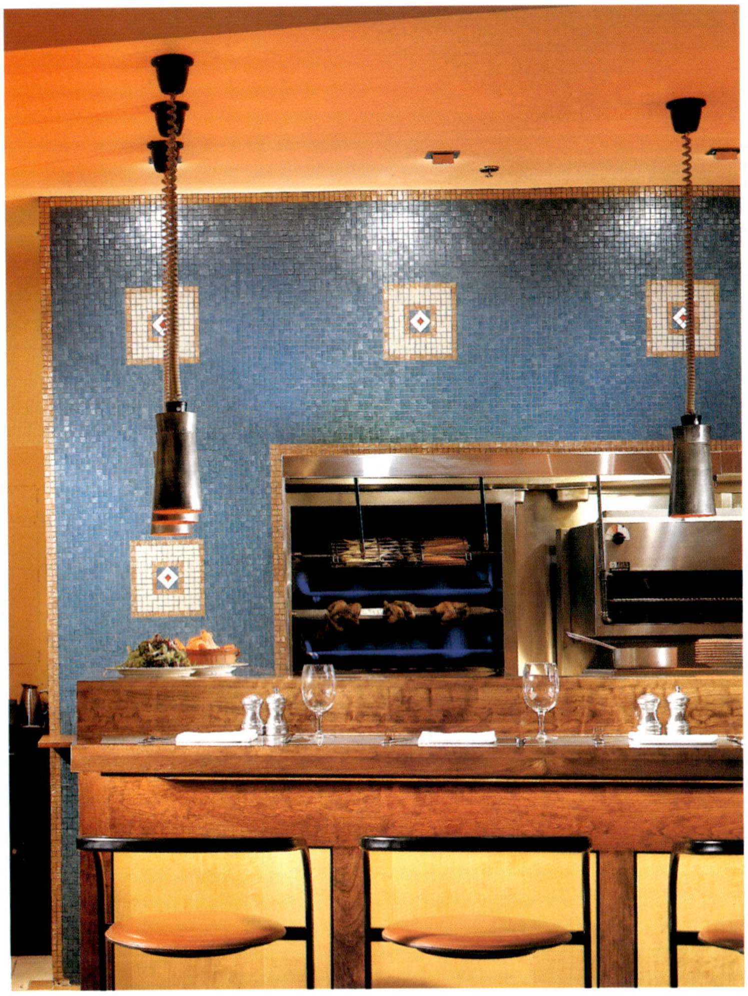

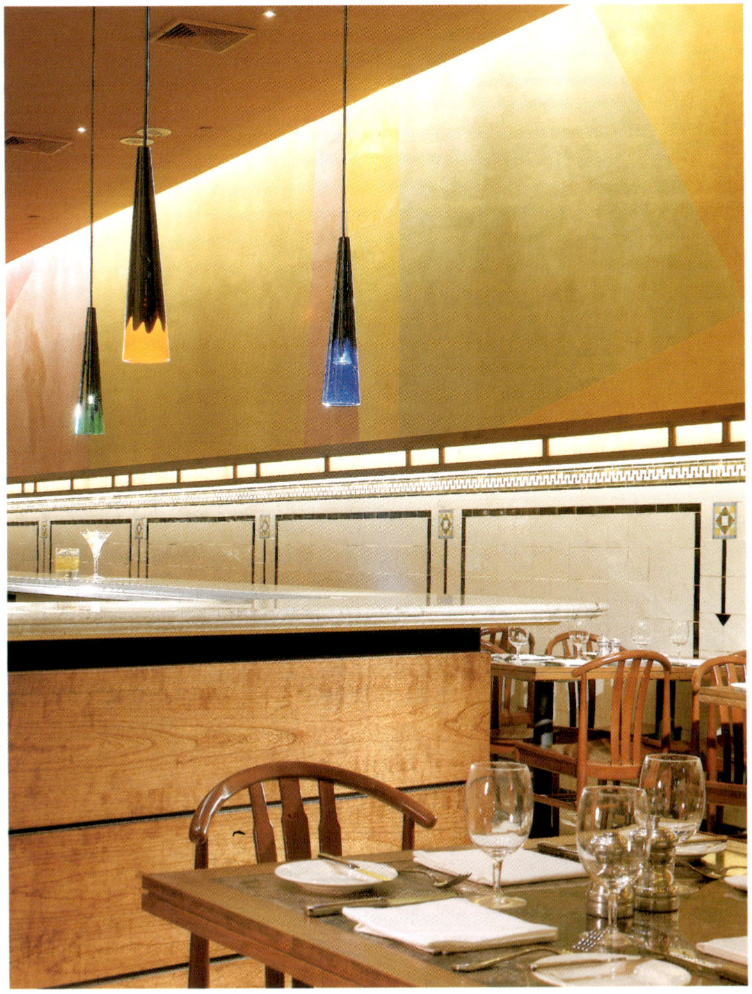

Section / Sezione

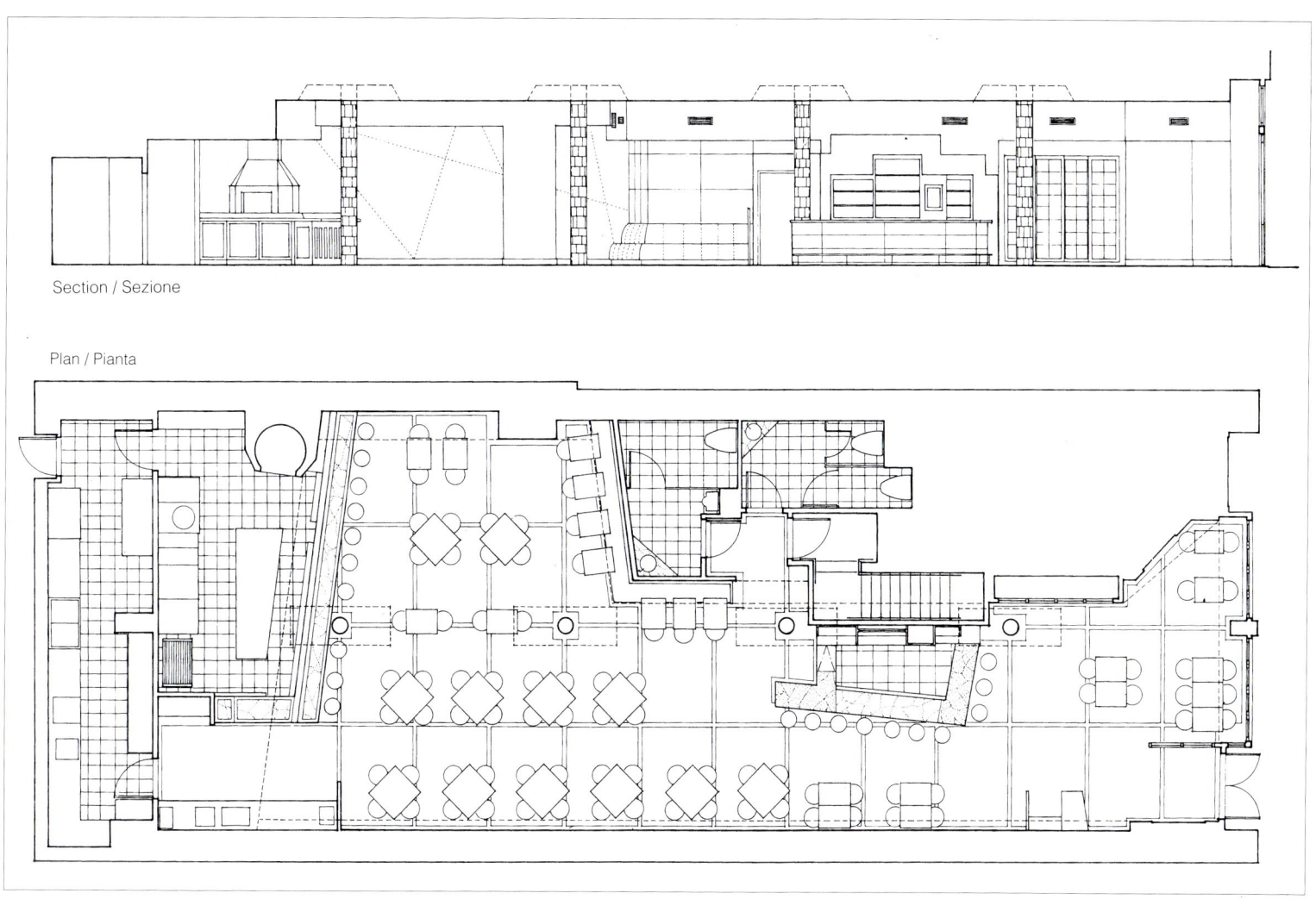

Plan / Pianta

SCHEDE TECNICHE
TECHNICAL DATA

150 WOOSTER RESTAURANT
Soho, New York, NY, Usa

Inside a found object (a parking garage in Soho).

This interior for a Brazilian restaurant presented an opportunity to investigate ways of generating formal arrangements and configurations of the "exotic" without resorting to direct representation.

The shapes, colors and materials have been selected so they play at least in two symbolic "registers": they are abstract minimal shapes and primary colors that propose a syntactic reading of the surfaces and at the same time recall Brazilian outdoor urban spaces. The syntax distorts the reading of the box by means of folded and overlapped walls suggesting an urban space. This is reinforced by the blue and yellow tile floor that refers to the sidewalks of Copacabana in Rio De Janeiro. In this strategy of montage, the elements make no claim to be real. For instance the disruption of scale and the size of the floor tiles result in an image that is familiar but slightly distorted, as if it were on a computer screen. But then we also synthesized the unseemingly compatible perceptions of Brazil our clients had, such us the 1950s Copacabana, of tropical juice stands, the Northeast of Brazil vernacular and Portuguese baroque.

The facade of the building including the rolling garage door was preserved, complete with graffiti. A steel and glass garage door was added behind the extant garage rolling door.

The materials used were 2"x2" color floor tiles. Stucco walls. Plywood for the Bar.

ALL STAR CAFE
New York's Times Square,
New York, NY, Usa

The Official All Star Cafe is a rich, fun-filled sports environment that provides the patron with a visceral sense of "being here." At each and every sporting event the patrons feel as if they're actually present, an experience that's enhanced from the feel of the glove-leather seats in the simulated raceway bar area to the prominently displayed sports memorabilia in the re-invented stadium. The simulated stadium environment is also filled with a surround of video screens.
Our design for this project takes the use of technology as entertainment to a new strata in its state-of-the art application of interactive TV and virtual-reality video.
An orchestrated and choreographed approach is additionally achieved by creating video segments that bookend and link the live sports feeds from the networks, cable channels, international satellites, and real-time celebrity interviews from throughout the restaurant.

Design Team
Principal: David Rockwell
Associate-in-charge: Ian Birchall, Chris Smith
Project Manager: Anne Corvi
Design Team: David Mexico, Jay Valgora
Interiors: Claire Baldwin, Lorraine Knapp, Lisa Pope
Staff: Mimi Kueh, Oswaldo Brighenti, Jeff Harris, Dan Kocieniewski, Tim Nanni, Martin Weiner
General Contractor: Tishman Interiors
Total Square Footage: 40,000 sq.ft

Product Manufactures/Suppliers
Banquette and Glove Seating; ArtCraft, Orlando, FL
Upholstery: Munrod, New York, NY

Floorcovering
Carpet: Custom sports carpet, USAX, Greenville, Mississipi - Custom playing field carpet: DESSO Carpets, Paoli, Pennsylvania
Hard: Hartco Wood Flooring, Knoxville, Texas
Resilient: No fault industries, Baton Rouge, Louisiana

Walls
Vinyl: Eial Interior Resource, New York, NY
Paint: Benjamin Moore, Pratt & Lambert
Specialty Painting: Modeworks, New York, NY

Custom Toilet Room Mirrors: Craft Services, Orlando

Bars, Doors & General Millwork/Wood work:
Superior Architectural, Forest Hills, NY

Memorabilia Display: Orlando Corporate Services, Orlando, FL.

Diorama: ASI, Jersey City, NJ

Maitre d'Stand, trusses & display cases: Unique Wood Designs, Altamonte Springs, FL

Interior & Exterior Signage: Custom Sign, Eldon, Missouri

Consultants
Structural Engineer: DeSimone, Chaplin and Dobryn Consulting Engineers, P.C. New York, NY
Mechanical, Electrical and Plumbing Consultant:
Robins Engineering, Little Silver NJ
Kitchen Consultant: Brass and Stainless, Dallas, Texas
Lighting Consultant: Focus Lighting, New York, NY
Audio-Video Consultant: Soundelux, Orlando, FL
Specification Consultant: Robert Schwartz & Associations Specification Consultants, New York, NY
Trusses & Cases: Unique Wood Design, Altamonte Springs, FL

AMERICA RESTAURANT
New York New York Casino
Las Vegas, NV, Usa

Size: 2000 mq
Owner: Ark Restaurants
Designers: Wayne Turett, Kirk Lenard
Collaborators: Simeon Siegel, Lewis Chu, Jin Suk, Sonja Moers, Anette Ponholzer

Consultants
graphic designer: Memo Productions Inc.
map designer: John Doepp
lighting designer: Fisher Marantz Renfro Stone (map and front dining)
lighting designer: Gary Gordon Design (billboard and ancillary dining)
kitchen designer: JRS Associates

Furnishings
metal: Modelsmith
seating: Chairs and Stools
banquettes: Amtrend Corporation
flooring: Western Tile (hardwood), Gibson Tile (terrazzo)

Project Description
Located in the recently completed New York New York Casino in Las Vegas, America is the third in a series of high-profile restaurants which originated in New York City by ARK Restaurants. One of several collaborations of the architect with ARK Restaurant Corporation, this was an attempt to create a restaurant that would be at home not only in the glitzy surrounds of Las Vegas, but in any contemporary setting. Roughly 21,000 SF with kitchen, this restaurant seats over 450 patrons. A huge free-standing bass relief map of the United States is the focus of the entrance and front room of America, each major city or historical site marked by a recognizable (and sometimes comic) symbol; it also serves as the backdrop for the rooms which spiral around the sides and back of this sculpture.
The architecture of the rooms is modern and spare, allowing images reminiscent of domestic travel to intrigue America's patrons: large metal billboards, enlargements of quintessential roadside postcards collected from a variety of landmarks throughout the country; a text wall of quotes taken from actual vacation postcards collected by the client. Elements within the construction (besides the restaurant's main feature) are also derived from the image of the American flag: the wall behind the gift shop, built of layered dark and light woods as the flags stripes; the terrazzo flooring and the density of evenly spaced suspended lamps in a black ceiling both reveal the flags stars.

BAANG RESTAURANT
1191 East Putnam Avenue
Greenwich, CT, Usa

The name "Baang," meaning in Chinese to bind or tie together, signifies the blending of French with Asian cuisine, and Asian interpreted design with whimsy. The innovative quality of the design makes you feel as if you're in Manhattan, and yet it also blends with a contemporary Greenwich lifestyle.
The kitchen, dining room, and bar area are all contained in one high-ceilinged room creating an intimate, social atmosphere where patrons are encouraged to eat, drink, people watch, and spend the evening. Ginger-root yellow, chili-pepper red, and leek green cover the walls, ceiling, and floor. Inspired by Asian pagodas and copper woks, 18 foot, copper mesh clouds rest atop four oxidized copper columns that also provide lighting. During warmer weather, the 12 foot, zinc-covered hangar door slides back, connecting the restaurant to the patio and creating a New York street cafe effect.

BEN'S KOSHER DELICATESSEN RESTAURANT & CATERERS
209 West 38 Street,
New York, NY, Usa

*A couple were dining out one evening
at the neighborhood kosher deli, when they
were amazed to have a Chinese waiter approach
to take their order. To their astonishment, the
suave Asian addressed them in perfect Yiddish.
When he left, they motioned to the
proprietor. "A Chinese waiter in a Jewish
delicatessen!" exclaimed the man. "And not
only that, but he speaks perfect Yiddish. How
come?" The proprietor looked around and put
his finger to his lips.
"Shhhh! he whispered. "He thinks
I'm teaching him English!"*

Three Yiddish jokes hand-stenciled in gold and a lively, Chagall-inspired ceiling mural dramatically highlight the refreshing new design at Ben's Kosher Delicatessen and Restaurant in the heart of New York City's garment district. A welcome departure from the long and cavernous space that once housed an old-fashioned wood-paneled dining room, the restaurant and catering hall, formerly known as "Lou G. Siegel's," has been imaginatively transformed into light and airy, seemingly more spacious rooms that convey a kind of merry, theatrical presence. Having gained celebrity status with the broadcast of Eddie Cantor's radio shows in the 1920s, Lou G. Siegel's had long been recognized as the eatery of choice among those who enjoy a strict kosher dining experience. Happily for many, the new menu has been expanded to include a more diverse kosher cuisine that features traditional delicatessen fare such as stuffed cabbage and potato kugel, as well as lowfat, nouveau selections such as Caesar Salad with Fresh Grilled Salmon Filet. Ben's Kosher Delicatessen Restaurant & Caterers is a full service restaurant that seats 225 people; it exudes a warm, welcoming and playful atmosphere, whether serving up a great pastrami sandwich, still considered sacred, a full-course meal, or lighter kosher delights.

A prominently lit canopy, running the full length of the exterior, rises above the main entry: we cure our own corned beef, our chicken soup cures everything else, the marquee proudly exclaims. An eye-catching, oversized clock, symbolizing continuity and a modern rebirth of fine kosher food, is incorporated into the signage overhead; and the facade, once closed in and heavily laden with travertine marble, has been expansively opened up for increased visibility. The extensive use of glass allows passersby to catch a glimpse of the deli functioning on one side, while viewing the bar and main dining room beyond on the other. Running the full length of the west wall, the delicatessen opens seamlessly to the main dining room on the opposite side. The once familiar long and narrow look of the main dining room appears proportionately squarer thanks to the skillful use of a folding partition wall. This device also serves to nicely delineate the two private dining rooms to the rear. Characteristic of the culture, a lighthearted poking-fun-at-oneself prevails in the humorous, slice-of-life Yiddish jokes that are hand-stenciled in gold in bands along the walls.

The interior of the restaurant celebrates the decorative arts with talented artisans having obviously played an important role in the design process. Savory foods and familiar, heartwarming objects artistically rendered in the terrazzo floor set the tone and atmosphere of the dining experience to come: the taste of fine wine flowing from an uncorked wine bottle as guests enter; the sound of music emanating from the strings of a violin at the bar; a freshly brewed cup of coffee at the breakfast counter and a characteristic kosher pickle at the deli queue. A decorative painting technique on the walls and soffits suggests the parchment on which Torahs were written. The antique texture and warm amber hue softly lend balance to the light and dark woods that alternate throughout the space.

Multi-colored, illuminated glass radiates in patterns at the face of the deli, bar and eating counters. The counter surfaces are hand-worked, gleaming stainless steel that catch the patterned light from colorful fixtures interspersed in seemingly random heights and spacing. Banquettes and booths reveal softly bowed backs with an upholstered chevron pattern in subtle food colors alternating between grape, cranberry and mango. The food colors are echoed in the multi-colored glass throughout the restaurant and take center stage in the striking Chagall-like ceiling mural in the main dining room.

The mural, alive with floating, dreamlike figures that represent everyday life in the New York garment and theater districts, the "old country," and Jewish culture and tradition, is one with its surroundings in a humorous, self-deprecating way. Eddie Cantor, for instance, is singing sour notes in the form of pickles; a bowl of matzoh ball soup is depicted larger than life; three conservative rabbis are gleefully standing on their heads; and the Empire State Building is swooning across the spiraling composition. Back-lit with warm fluorescent fixtures, the work of art is a softly draped series of panels that run between beams. Its surface is painted in a combination of semi-transparent acrylic and dyes applied in a variety of textures to create depth and brilliant color. "L' chaim!" the words painted across the mural read, representing a celebration of life, a good time, a good feeling and a good meal amidst a unique blending of traditional Jewish orthodoxy and a more progressive mode in dining.

Ben's Kosher Delicatessen Restaurant & Caterers speaks to living life to its fullest, an abundance of life and an enduring legacy found in laughter and lively conversation with friends while feasting on the kosher fare of one's choice in the comfort of familiar, visually rich surroundings.

Designer of operation
Jay M. Haverson, Principal-in-Charge; Carolyn Haverson; Michael Kaufman; Lisa Bianco; Nick Lios and Gina Librandi

Environmental Factors
Lighting:
The lighting of the main room is accomplished through a series of fixture types and varied colored lamp shades. The primary source of illumination is from a low-voltage rail system mounted to the main beams in the ceiling. The lighting is suspended from the tracks by stemmed fixtures of various heights. The main focus of the lights, which are a combination of MR-16 and MR-11 fixtures, is to light each table surface and also accent the architectural design features of the space.
A series of gently cascading mylar panels form a mural that is rear lit from a two lamp fluorescent fixture mounted in each coffer to create a luminous ceiling and evenly wash the entire dining area. In addition, each column is fitted with ornamental metal bracket bands trimmed with colorful glass that are rear lit with neon to create a strong visual feature.
The exterior lighting is contained within a substantial marquis sign that is internally lit with cool fluorescent strips silhouetting a humorous phrase mounted to the signage. Individual recessed fixtures light the underside of the canopy while the restaurant's brand and the original Lou G. Siegel's clock are internally lit with neon.

Sound System / Acoustics:
The sound system is fairly modest and consists of a series of ten high output recessed speakers mounted invisibly in the ceiling and soffits spread symmetrically throughout the room. The space has an acoustical ceiling tile panel system in back of the draped mural panels. Carpeted floors and substantial runs of banquettes help to quiet the main space. The ceiling breaks also minimize reflective sound. The delicatessen area has many smooth and hard surfaces and consequently is louder. Given the significant balance of soft and hard surfaces in the room and its openness to the delicatessen, the space is relatively quiet.

Mechanical:
The restaurant is served by a split forced-air HVAC system unit located in the ceiling of the kitchen. Air is distributed from the face of dropped soffits in the main space and in ceiling registers where there is a stamped metal lay-in ceiling. The open kitchen has a pair of balanced hoods that are served with 80% make-up air creating a negative pressure that pulls a small amount of air from the dining room inhibiting the migration of kitchen odors into the delicatessen and formal dining areas.

Furnishing list
Judges must know both the kind and manufacturer of each item in order to determine how effectively the furnishings suit the needs of the entry:
Number of seats: 227 Seats

Items
Furnishing item, Manufacturer name & address

Exterior Signage - Serola Signs, 110-01 14th Avenue, College Point, New York
Revolving Door - Crane Fulview Door Company (847.295.2700)
Storefront - Lynbrook Glass, 941 Motor Parkway, Hauppauge, New York 11788
Terrazzo Flooring - Durite, 524 East 72nd Street, New York, New York 10021
Delicatessen Cases - Federal Industries, 215 Federal Avenue, Belleville, Wisconsin 53508
Table Tops and Bases - Custom - Chairmasters, 200 East 146th Street, Bronx, New York 10451-5599
Banquettes - Custom- Chairmasters, 200 East 146th Street, Bronx, New York 10451-5599
Banquette Fabric Back - 1) Patterned - Artex Textiles Eden Sage Spice from Blumenthal, Inc., 979 Third Avenue New York, NY 10022. 2) Solid - Anzea Valetta, distributed by Silver Associates, 401 East 74 Street, New York, New York 10021.
Banquette Fabric Seat - Kravet Fabrics Matchless #16 - 225 Central Avenue, Bethpage, New York 11714
Bar Stools - Custom - Chairmasters, 200 East 146th Street, Bronx, New York 10451-5599Chair/Bar Stool Fabric - Nytek Specialties Majilite/Baby Ostrich - distributed by Evan Shatz, 16 Mt. Nimham Court, R.R. 3, Kent Lakes, New York 10512-9803
Carpeting - Custom - Patterson, Flynn, Martin & Manges, 979 Third Avenue, New York, New York 10022.
Track Lights - Custom - Patdo Lighting Supply, 25 South Main Street, Port Chester, New York 10573
Mural - Custom - Willem Van Es Design Studio, 222 West 23rd Street, New York,

New York 10011
Bartop/Deli Counter - Stainless Steel - Graffiti - Surface Design & Technology, P.O. Box 487, 32 Riverview Drive, Wayne, New Jersey 07474
Counter Stools - Custom - Chairmasters, 200 East 146th Street, Bronx, New York 10451-5599
Counter Seats - Nytek Specialties Majilite/Baby Ostrich - distributed by Evan Shatz, 16 Mt. Nimham Court, R.R. 3, Kent Lakes, New York 10512-9803
Banquette Lights - Custom - Patdo Lighting Supply, 25 South Main Street, Port Chester, New York 10573
Mirrors - Custom - Bendheim Architectural Glass, 122 Hudson Street, New York, New York 10013
Stenciling - Julie Lifton Schwerner / Citrus, Inc., 133 Highmount Avenue, Upper Nyack, New York 10906
Woodwork - Diamond Shapes - Chairmasters, 200 East 146th Street, Bronx, New York 10451-5599
Tin Ceiling - Align Design, 948 East 92 Street, Brooklyn, New York 11236
Column Lighting Glass - Kokomo Glass, P.O. Box 2265, Kokomo, Indiana 46904-2265
Columns (woodworking) - Bego Custom Built Furniture, 301 Walton Avenue, Bronx, New York 10451

BOHEMIA JAZZ CLUB
Takeo Kikuchi Building
3-17-25 Nishi Azabu, Minato-Ku
Tokyo 105, JP

Bohemia is one of three interiors created by Branson Coates for owner Takeo Kikuchi, whose boyhood dream was to own a jazz club. The club was planned in a classical way, with the focus of attention directed toward the stage. Utilizing an existing curved wall, Branson Coates raised the stage of the club and separated it from the main seating area by a sunken bar that also offers views of the musicians.
The club's bold syncopation of color, pattern and materials express visually the musical improvisations ad-libbed on stage. The atmosphere is that of a London Soho basement during that period of relaxed Brazilian Jazz, Astrid Gilberto, and airplane travel. The design exploits the artfully makeshift, with a Bruce McLean revolving hoarding behind the performers, and a riot of NATO figures and hoardings closing in on either side of it.

Area: sq.m. 190 (3 floors)
Team Design: Nigel Coates with Doug Branson assisted by Peter Sabara, Jeremy Pitts, Alan Mitchell, Anne Brooks
Furniture Design: Nigel Coates with Peter Sabara
Client: World Company, Tokyo
Project Coordinator: Shi Yu Chen, Mari Kida, Tokyo
U.K. Structural Engineer: Tim MacFarlane
Main Contractor: Shinnichi Construction Co. Ltd
Commissioned Artists: Tom Dixon, Andre Dubreuil, John Keane, Judy Levy, Adal Lowe, Bruce McLean, Mark Prinzeman, Peter sabara and Peter Thomas, Nick Welch, NATO: Catrina Beevor, Nigel Coates, Robert Mull, Matk Prinzeman, Carlos Villanueva

BRYANT PARK GRILL
Bryant Park
New York, NY, Usa

Interior seating: 180
Outdoor seating: 125
Square feet: 5,000
History
The conversion of park from urban blight needed private sponsorship to remain pristine and botanically bountiful. Hence a joint venture between the city, Bryant Park Restoration Corp., and Ark Restaurants Corps. Rent from restaurant provides the extra income needed for the park.
Materials
Tiger-striped satin wood-wall above banquet
Onyx and Bronze Bar
cast resin light fixture - above bar
Wenge floors in main dining room
Slate floor in Bar area
Hand tinted plaster walls
Bronze clad columns
Art work
Hunt Slolen - Bird Mural

CAFFE BONGO
Parco Part 1, Shibuya-Ku,
Tokyo 105, JP

Caffe Bongo is a Fellini-esque layering of fifties aluminum curves and leaning cast-iron columns, set in front of the decaying wall of a Roman basilica. The aircraft wing suspended above the two-story plate-glass window converts a hard concrete building into an urban stage.

Area: sq.m 264
Principal materials: aluminum sheet, concrete screed, reclaimed materials
Design Team: Nigel Coates and Doug Bransom assisted by Mike Tonkin, Alan Mitchell
Furniture Design: Nigel Coates with Peter Sabara
Furniture Manufacture: Rockstone
Client: Parco
Project Coordinator: Shi Yu Chen, Mari Kida, Tokyo
U.K. Structural Engineer: Tim MacFarlane, London
Commisioned Artists
Jasper Conran, Ron O'Donnell, Andre Dubreuil, Adama Lowe, David Phillips, Zaza Wentworth Stanley

CAN RESTAURANT
482 West Broadway
New York, NY, 10012 Usa

Seats: 70
Square Footages: Ground Floor 1475 sq.ft, Cellar 1665 sq.ft
Interiors Designer: Stomu Miyazaki/ ES Studio INC
Architect: WYS Partners
Artists: Jon Lewis, George Minot
Design concept
On the corner of West Broadway and Houston Street in Soho, a former boutique space was transformed into a multilevel hybrid cuisine. As a design concept for such a multi cultural cuisine, sociological and environmental subjects were chose to be explored rather than an application of ethnic ornamental motifs.
Origins of people and surrounding environments create our own culture. However those original cultures are often hybridized by political confrontation with other cultures, as a result, new culture is created. The French Vietnamese culinary art is no exception.
For this project, the metaphorical natural landscape and human factors were emphasized in the concept rather than emphasizing ethnic ornamental elements such as many other trendy ethnic restaurants had. As the result, the interior of Can serves neutral and serene atmosphere has long been awarded by many customers.
Project Description
Facade/Entrance:
Custom-made Curved glass
Earth-color stucco wall (w/pebble stones)
Brick flower pot
Clear entrance glass door (w/etched Logo)
The stucco wall representing mountain has embedded small pebble stones creating layered effect.
Corridor:
natural finished oak floor
Concrete floor embedded small pebble stones
Dry wall - eggshell/white
Whitewashed brick wall
handrail wrapped with rattan
Maitre's stand (stand top-ebonized wood with clear finish)
Triangular brick arch
The oak flooring represents land, concrete flooring represents river.
Bar Area:
Earth stucco wall (w/pebble stones)
Dry wall - egg shell/white
Spiral stair - natural finish oak
Handrail wrapped with rattan
Floor - green marble tile
Bar counter - ebonized wood with clear finish
Liqueur shelves - clear glass shelves & onyx back panel with lighting fixture behind.
The green marble flooring represents underground water. The onyx represents minerals.
Dining Area:
White washed brick wall w/built in light fixtures
Dry wall-egg shell/white
Sky light/clear glass, aluminum frame w/green patina
Frosted window w/natural branches artwork
2 windows - frosted wave patterns

Oak floor - natural finish
Rosed carpeted floor
Ceiling - eggshell/white
Handrail - wrapped with rattan

The brick & dry walls surrounding dining room were designed to be sculptural backdrop. Especially for the brick walls, we combined original brick walls and additional areas which housed lighting fixtures at three corners and a triangular arch, were built with old bricks to blend in. The surface treatment of the brick walls was such a dusty and messy job. The first, we painted the entire brick wall with white latex paint, then scraped off the paint partially using electric sanders. The final treatment was to wash the wall with watered-down and white paint so that the fine dust from bricks and white paint creates natural pinkish color.
The crumbling sections of the three corners of the brick wall housed light fixtures controlled by dimmers. This lights represent energy of rebirth from war.
The two large windows facing Houston Street, were frosted lower sections with wave patterns. Since always heavy traffic on Houston Street, it is not favorable view for dining experience. The frosted glass area covers it, upper portion of clear glass allows to see the street trees, sky and upper portion of architectural detail of the buildings at the other side of the street. At night from outside, passersby see mysteriously flickering shadow patterns on the frosted glass.

Art works
Permanent Wok:
1. Natural branches at the frosted window in the dining room by Stomu Miyazaki. Bleached branches, twigs.
2. Flower vase at a brick wall niche in the dining room.
Stratum by Stomu Miyazaki. Concrete, dyes, small pebble stones.
Temporary Work:
The white dry wall area at the corridor is a temporary exhibition space for young artists.
Young talented artists have a chance to show their art works every two month.
Curator: Stomu Miyazaki.

Furniture
The furniture used in Can was selected by its comfortable, style & color.

CHINA GRILL
60 West 53rd Street
New York, NY, Usa

Located in a prime area of Midtown Manhattan, on the ground level of the CBS Building also know as Black Rock. This city-block-wide location is a classy, downtown food loft in a classic, midtown skyscraper.

The 6,000-sq.ft restaurant seats approximately 180 people. The main dining area is comprised of a large exhibition kitchen which, indeed serves as an active stage for a number of chefs. The seating design was intentionally created on 3 different platforms. Mr. Beers feels people want to see and be seen thus creating better sight lines throughout
the restaurant. They also designed green lines to run along the floorboards to visually connect the block-wide restaurant. Within these lines he then stenciled passages from Marco Polo's travels in china which ties in with the East meets west concept of cuisine.

Note that not one element in this restaurant was from a catalogue. Each piece was creatively developed for this unique project. From a series of illuminated cloud like canopies to Oriental-kite shaped light fixtures suspended from the twenty-foot ceilings.

CHRISTER'S RESTAURANT
145 West 55th Street
New York, NY, Usa

Named for owner/chef Christer Larsson, Christer's (3,000 sq.ft) setting complements its Scandinavian and American fare by being a sophisticated take on the sort of rustic interior you'd expect to find in fjord country while reflecting the owner's desire for comfortable, unpretentious surroundings.
The compact entrance vestibule opens into a spacious front room and bar area occupied with groupings of white-napped wooden tables and a single grand banquette. Log ends set into white plaster walls, along with twig bar stools, add rusticity. Suspended from the ceiling, dozens of hammered-copper ovals shimmer like a school of fish swimming in sunlight.
The focus of the main dining room is a hefty stone fireplace with a decorative wooden mantel. Peeled logs form a dropped ceiling, while banquettes covered in blue plaid fabric recall the wool shirts of outdoorsmen. Vivid yellow, blue, orange, and green dining chairs add a shock of color. The second dining area, referred to as "the porch," has a bright, airy quality reminiscent of the seashore. Overhead, billowy swags of white sailcloth diffuse the flood of illumination from skylights.

FISHDANCE RESTAURANT
Kobe, Japan

The owners/operators are a large Japanese corporation. Their programmatic requests were that the building be an exciting place to dine, that it feel "informal" and "crowded," and that perhaps a fish be prominently incorporated into the design, relating to a preoccupation of the architect or to the waterfront location, or both. The proposed menu changed many times during the design period, all the way from Italian food to the final choice of seafood and Japanese specialties.
Located in a new public park along the Inland Sea, this restaurant has as its neighbors shipyards, cranes, docks, a reconstruction of a 19th century customs building and, at each end of the site, double-deck expressways. An adjoining warehouse, remodeled by the owners as a multi-purpose hall, actually extends under one of the elevated expressways.
In response to this urban/waterfront chaos, the restaurant took shape as three large simple objects: a copper-clad spiral "snake" form, a 70-foot high fish sculpture made of chainlink mesh, and a sloped-roof building clad in light blue metal with a clerestory tower. The spiral contains a bar and, winding above it, a *kushi-katsu* (deep fry) counter. The sloped-roof building houses the kitchen and main seafood dining area, with a bridge for the *teppan-yaki* (grill) on an upper level. All of the dining areas look through windows or glass walls at the fish.
The 8,500-sq.ft project was designed and construction was completed within a 10-month period, from July 1986 to April 1987.

Client: The World Company Ltd. and The City of Kobe
Area: 8,500 sq.ft.
Schedule: Begin Design: July 1986
Begin Construction: November 1986
Completion: April 1987
Cost: $3,000,000 (approximately, including fish sculpture)
Project team
Frank Gehry- Design Principal
David Denton- Project Principal
C. Gregory Walsh - Project Manager/Designer
Tom Buresh - Project Team
Edwin Chan
Dalia Jagger
Charles Dilworth
Sergio Zeballos
Fred Ballard
Mitchell Lawrence
Bryce Thomas

Associate Architect: Takenaka Komuten Co. Ltd.

Structural engineer: Takenaka Komuten Co. Ltd.
Mechanical/Electrical: M. Tanaka

MARKET AT NEWPORT RESTAURANT
Newport Tower, Newport Center
Jersey City, New Jersey, Usa

Size: 1800 mq
Owner: ARK Restaurants, Georgetown Properties
Designers: Wayne Turett, Stuart Basseches
Collaborators: Lewis Chu, Simeon Seigel, Esther Lee
Consultant List
graphic designer: Louise Fili
lighting consultant: Gary Gordon
kitchen consultant: JRS Associates
mechanical engineer: Reynaldo Prego
spec writer: Robert Schwartz and Associates
Source List
general contractor: Terry Higgins
metal fabricator: Modelsmith
cabinetmaker: Hudson Equipment
stucco (blue wall): Stucco Lustro Veneziano
linoleum flooring: Forbo
slate flooring: PM Cousins
murals: Anthony Russo
satellite dishes: Winrich
signage: Kaltech
computer menus: TTSS
banquettes/tables: Rollhaus Brothers
chairs: Jasper
table laminate: Abet Laminati
Project Description
Located in the base of Newport Office Tower in Jersey City, New Jersey, across

the Hudson from downtown New York City, The Market at Newport caters to the tenants from the office tower and surrounding buildings. It was built to offer a healthy and comfortable alternative to the fast food shops of the adjacent mall. The owner and operator of the restaurant, Georgetown Properties and ARK Restaurants, wanted a cafeteria-type operation without the corporate cliché stylings of the typical cafeteria with its steam pans, long service lines, and fluorescent lay-in ceilings.

The designers chose to expand upon the notion of the conventional cafeteria. Starting with the two elements common to all cafeteria facilities, the servery and the dining hall, and placing them back-to-back, their relationship has been slightly skewed by contrasting the two spaces and allowing some elements of each to overlap into the other.

The servery is festive, a low-slung metal mesh canopy giving it an intimate scale, colored carts and servery units displaying a variety of foods and items, menu monitors and signage arms advertising and locating regional cuisines. The 70' long servery line is unified and softened by a sinuous tray rail that invites customers to enter the procession at any point along the way. The materials are warm and simple: slate stone flooring, colored plywoods, limestone trays, raw metals. The lighting, a series of spots and floods as well as ambient food-enhancing fixtures, filters through the canopy, adding to the quality of light one might find in an outdoor marketplace.

By contrast, the dining hall is a destination, a calm, expansive, congregational space, separated from the servery by a distinct mediating element, a meandering blue stucco wall. The room, 60' wide by 100' long holding seating for 350 customers, is encompassed in landscape, either mural (depicting stylized farm scenes of planting and harvest) or view to the exterior (towards the New York skyline), and is sheltered by an array of metal satellite dishes which are uplit to give the room a warm, subtle cast of light. These, in combination with a crisscross pattern of lines and colors in the linoleum flooring reminiscent of ariel farm landscapes, gives the room an open outdoor feeling.

Contrast is a theme which is evident in other ways throughout the cafeteria, on various scales: colored plywoods are set against steel frames; the convex ceiling of the servery canopy overlaps the concave light dishes of the dining room; curvilinear forms of the servery line and ceiling contrast against the rectilinear confines of the project perimeter; primary colors bleed out of the servery into the subtle tones of the dining hall. It was the hope that by providing these oppositions, the archetype of cafeteria has been broadened to something more lively and user-friendly.

METROPOLE RESTAURANT
6-4-5 Roppongi, Minato-Ku
Tokyo, JP

Interior design project for the creation of a high class restaurant, the embodiment of the "Englishman's Club" abroad.

Area: 190 sq.m
Principal Materials: plaster, MDF, steel, mosaic, tiles, timber, floors
Site: an old garage

MIREZI RESTAURANT
59 Fifth Avenue,
New York, NY, Usa

The design of the restaurant was conceived as an upscale pan-Asian bistro and grill catering to an urbane clientele. The objective aesthetically was to create a sophisticated contemporary Asian setting without resorting to obvious oriental themes or motifs. By the use of indirectly lighting, balanced geometries, and natural finishes, the sensibility and mood were made distinctly Eastern. There are subdued accents and flourishes within this uncomplicated background, such as the eleven miniatures LCD monitors embedded in the walls. These monitors, connected to remote video players display changing still and moving images which uniquely evoke the culture of Asia without overpowering the elegance and simplicity of the space. The color palette consists of earthen and metal fones interspersed with the delicate glow of the monitors and other lighted features. Certain details evoke Asian elements such as the abstracted ridepaper screens made of acrylic and steel the chandeliers inspired by patterns of traditional Korean wrapping cloths, and the doorpull is a ring like the those on ancient gates. The vertical niches in the wall across from the bar are dimensional picture scrolls, and the suspended panel with lighted acrylic rods in the back dining area is reminiscent of water dripping from the eaves after a rain. The design incorporates the sense of touch as well as vision the doorpull is a heavy raw steel, the floor in entrance area is inlaid with rivet-fun stones which can be felt underfoot upon entering the restaurant, the tabletops are clad in copper a soft "warm" metal; the walls are smooth plaster.
Two story restaurant with full cellar
Lower Level (3'-4" or 1.02 meters below street level)
Upper Level (63'-2" or 1,88 meters above street level)

Materials and Furnishings
Floor:
Lower Level - pine heartwood plank stained ochre
Upper Level - random oak strip stained ochre
Ceiling: Painted pressed tin coffers, painted gypsum board
Furniture:
tables: copper clad table tops
chairs: beechwood chairs with upholstered seats
banquettes: upholstered banquette seats by SoHo Furnishings
Walls: artisan plaster by Art in Construction
Stair: red travertine slab treads and risers; steel handrails
Interior Structure: masonry walls, wood joist floors, steel beam at new stair opening

Artworks
Rear Dining Area:
diptych painting by Jung Hyang Kim "Petals and Thorns," 1996 Oil and Graphite on Canvas 60 x 80 inches courtesy of Art Projects International, New York
Private Dining Room:
painting by Kyung Lim Lee Untitled, 1996 oil on Canvas 40" x 48" courtesy of Sigma Gallery, New York
Bar: counter plaster with metal infill by Art in Construction; stool steel rod with upholstered seat by SoHo Furnishings

Lighting
chandeliers interiors illuminated opaline acrylic panels in a steel skeleton frame
Translucent walls: handmade paper hand-laminated onto acrylic panels set in steel framework.

MONKEY BAR AT THE HOTEL ELYSEE
60 East 54th Street
New York, NY, Usa

During the summer of 1994 we resurrected this 1930s and '40s hot spot. Frequented by such colorful legends as Tallulah Bankhead, Joe DiMaggio, Tennesse Williams, Marlon Brando, and Ava Gardner; the design solution entailed tapping into the collective memory we all have of '30s and '40s nightlife.
The new furnishing and material were carefully selected with the original design in mind. The installation of the original "monkey sconces," the restoration of Vella's original "monkey" murals, and the resurrection of large mirrors are intended to evoke and invoke the "naughty fun" and general insouciance of those earlier times. The famed mahogany bar has also been revived, as have the banana leaves stenciled onto the cobalt blue linoleum floor. The original Monkey Bar had no restaurant so the design of the new restaurant was achieved by combining a sense of New York today with nostalgic references to the original Monkey Bar. In the new restaurant, large scale murals depict New York skylines, while deep-toned woods and rich-red surfaces infuse this new space with the colors of Maxfield Parrish, the '30s style of a Fritz Lang movie, and the aura of New York as seen in the drawings by Hugh Ferriss.

Furnishing Items
Monkeys: Gem An Eye Arts, New York, NY
Railing: Mongik Company, New York, NY
Wood Floor: Christian Brothers
Upholstery Fabric: Krovet, New York, NY
Carpet: Paterson, Flynn, Martin & Manges, Inc. New York, NY
Aluminum Leafed Ceiling: Surfacing Arts (Cindy Fraley/Lisa Frank), New York, NY
Dining Chairs: Ted Boerner Furiniture Design, San Francisco, CA
Millwork: Concord Woodwork & Upholstery
Linoleum Floor: Forto Industries, New York, NY
Table Tops, Bases & Bar Stools: West Coast Industries Inc, San Francisco, CA
Glass Screens: Savittier Furniture Design, Wallington, NJ
Murals: Decorative Painting, Brookfield, CT

MOONSOON RESTAURANT
Sapporo, JP

Restaurant and Bar
Completed Interior

Client: Jasmac Corporation, Japan

Design Team: Zaha Hadid with Bill Goodwin, Shin Egashira, Kar Hwa Ho, Edgar Gonzales, Brian Langlands, Ed Gaskin, Yuko Moriyama, Urit Luden, Craig Kiner, Diane Hunter-Gorman.
Model : Daniel Chadwick
Consultants : Michael Wolfson, Satoshi Ohashi, David Gommersall.

Two Floors
total floor area : 435sqm

Designed: 07/90
Started on site: 02/90
Open to public: 07/90
Producer: Axe Co, Ltd. Japan
Publications
Architectural Design, No 87 1990
Ku'kan, No. 9 1990
Shotenkenchiku, Vol.35 No. 9 1990
The Japan Arctitect, No. 9 1990
Progressive Architecture, Feb. 1991
Arquitectura Viva, July-Aug. 1991
Domus, July-Aug. 1991
Schöner Wohnen, Aug. 1991
Diseño Interior, Sep. 1991

MOTOWN CAFE
at the New York New York Hotel & Casino
3790 S. Las Vegas Boulevard,
Las Vegas, NV, Usa

The exterior of Motown Cafe in Las Vegas is reminiscent of a world famous New York City musical landmark. Passersby viewing the Cafe will perceive it as the cornerstone of the magical Manhattan skyline created by the New York New York Hotel & Casino. Located on the strip, the facade of Motown Cafe features a dazzling, horizontal zipper sign that alternately announces "Motortown Revue Live," "Motown Cafe Moments," and a variety of acts currently performing at the restaurant along a wraparound canopy. Additional signage rises prominently in a vertical stanchion where "Motown Cafe" is again visibly displayed. This 50 foot tall icon has animated lettering that is sequenced to spell out the signage letter by letter and finally as "Motown Cafe."

Guests enter Motown Cafe directly from inside the Casino by going through a facade inspired by the great 1930s vintage theaters across the country where many Motown artists performed during the '60s and '70s. The theater marquee prominently displays MOTOWN CAFE MOMENTS LIVE in large block letters. Patrons walk under the marquee and are greeted on either side of the "building" facade by life-sized statues of The Supremes gesturing with outstretched arms "Stop In the Name of Love" and The Jackson Five playfully cavorting in the "A," "B," and "C" letters reminiscent of their famous album cover. Built-in video presentations accompany the statues on either side and attest to the mood of fun and celebration inside. Showcased in the center of the Cafe entryway is a retail display in the guise of a freestanding ticket booth set to display the Motown Cafe Moments in a recording session sporting the latest merchandise. The display serves to whet the appetite of guests who will later be enticed to "Shop Around" at the full service retail store situated to the right of the Motown Cafe entrance lobby rotunda.

The full service retail store to the right of the lobby is prominently positioned for maximum visual exposure and ease of customer access. Taking its name from the 1960 Miracles hit, "Shop Around," the shop features an extensive display of Motown merchandise and music in full view of visitors as they approach the main dining area. The shop is themed Motown "backstage" to give guests a glimpse of what it might be like to find themselves behind the scenes before or after a theatrical or television performance. Scenic backdrops and Motown artists graphics are viewed along a catwalk above the merchandise display. Brick walls with messages and sayings are small reminders of who was there. As current celebrities visit the Cafe, they will contribute their authentic signatures to the walls to commemorate their visit to the restaurant. The storefront opens directly into the Casino through the entry rotunda displaying Motown Cafe signage and merchandise set against large glass windows. The merchandise display cases are fun presentations of mannequins in the process of performing and playfully interacting with fans of all ages.

Patrons moving through the spacious, circular lobby are entertained by a large projected video presentation prominently set within the Shop Around store. Clips from classic Motown footage, celebrities and fans from Motown Cafe openings, and current music videos are featured. On the opposite side, a classic instructional tape featuring the famous Motown choreographer Cholly Atkins demonstrates "The Temptations' Walk." It is looped for patrons to follow the dance steps "mapped out" in a series of footsteps set in the Motortown Revue Map on the floor. This video is featured in a central display with classic Temptations costumes and vintage photos taken during dance rehearsal sessions.

The Motortown Revue Map highlights famous Motown touring areas that crisscross throughout the country and the world, such as Chicago, St. Louis, Indianapolis, Cleveland, Los Angeles, London, Tokyo, Hong Kong and many others. Motown's birthplace, Detroit, and main hub from which its music came, is centrally located in the entry rotunda where guests will queue; while New York City's placement is at the hostess stand at the beginning of the map, highlighted by the largest and brightest star. Las Vegas, another popular place where artists performed, is placed in front of a vignette statue display of the Four Tops shown in their 1965 Lincoln Continental with a backdrop of the Las Vegas skyline lit from behind. It's as if the group had stopped at a light and were greeted with cheers and waves from their fans. The Motortown Revue Map, originating at the entrance below the Casino entry, is strikingly set in terrazzo and leads patrons to the retail store, main dining and bar areas beyond.

A host or hostess in the center of the lobby rotunda, dressed in the style of classic Motown performance apparel, welcomes patrons as they enter. Guests can feel the energy emanating from the Twenty Grand main dining area and are drawn into the warm, colorful and dynamic atmosphere. Dramatically spinning overhead is the world's largest 45 r.p.m. record (slightly bigger than its counterpart in New York City), complete with the Motown label and song title "Reach Out, I'll Be There," performed by the Four Tops. The lobby affords visitors a wonderful, panoramic glimpse of the

Twenty Grand main dining space beyond; the spectacular Stairway to Success; performances of the Motown Moments who rove throughout the restaurant and appear at a number of locations, including the store, the main bar, the Diana Ross Room and in front of the piano merchandise boutique.

Although music can be heard throughout the lobby at entry, the electrifying sound of Motown is best appreciated as guests move into the Twenty Grand dining room which is situated on two levels. The Twenty Grand was conceived as a piece of living American musical history. The re-creation harks back to the legendary Detroit '60s lounge that featured many of the young and rising Motown stars. A step-down floor in the center of the space accommodates tables for seating during regular dining hours and comes alive later in the evening for dancing as furniture is removed and stored, leaving a traditional, wooden dance floor for well over 200 people. Tables along the periphery overlook the trapezoidal dance/dining area, and three sections of banquettes are distinguished by separate, distinctly hued color identities. One banquette, situated in front of the Main Bar, is low and freestanding so as not to mar the view of the stage, and the other two are warmly nestled against the walls on either side of the space. Replicas of costumes, a hallmark of Motown performers, and other appropriate artifacts in dramatically lit cases adorn the walls in back of banquettes and large floor-to-ceiling tableaux. The decor utilizes wonderful, oversized photographs of Motown artists, brightly colored materials and warm woods that recall the early 1960s. Performers on stage intermittently step down to move among the guests and then mingle throughout the restaurant. Patrons in this lively, hospitable setting will experience a warm feeling of inclusion and the sense that every day and night is a party at the Motown Cafe.

The Main Bar, with a view of the performers on stage, is designed as a classic '60s Harlem "blues club," with back bar tufted walls behind radiantly lit bottle risers and memorabilia presentation cases. The bar is further enhanced by a dynamic Motown video presentation, fun for guests to watch while waiting for their seats. The bar face is a channel tufting formed by colorful purple and gold metallic material, an example of vintage period construction. The bartop also glows with a glass chipped terrazzo surface comprised of a mixture of period glass colors.

The Stairway to Success, leading up to the mezzanine, is constructed of Motown's solid gold hit records and labels such as "Stop in the Name of Love," "I Heard It Through The Grapevine," "Shop Around," and "My Girl," among others. The stair treads are underlit translucent terrazzo using classic Motown purple and reds to symbolize the success of Motown's performers – no group of artists started with so little and achieved so much. Life-sized statues of the performers in various areas of the Cafe energize the space with their dynamic sense of presence: A young Stevie Wonder stands behind a microphone playing the harmonica in
the main dining room; Martha Reeves is seen singing in a curtained stage setting in the Twenty Grand dining room on the upper level; Boyz II Men are viewed in the process of walking off with multiple music awards next to the Piano Retail; and Gladys Knight and The Pips, facing Boyz II Men, appear singing at a full dress rehearsal. These evocative statues of groups and individual artists who sang and performed scores of singles and albums are the great treasures of Motown.
Having been directed up the Stairway to Success to either the Twenty Grand Bar or mezzanine seating, three elements are striking to patrons from the upper level: The ceiling of the main space is vaulted and coffered with infill provided by Motown Gold albums set one alongside the other in a pervasive pattern that shimmers and glows. The DJ/VJ booth is titled "Radio Motown" and is situated opposite the main marquee in prominent view of nearly everyone. The backdrop for the main stage is designed as a tableau featuring The Temptations statues singing into their classic four-prong microphone. Another central focus seen from above is a 16-cube video wall. Although the wall incorporates modern technology, it recollects the early days of Motown when families and friends gathered in their living rooms to watch TV. Again, the walls in this area are brightly rendered with purple, teal, gold and touches of cherry red, finishes that may at first appear mismatched, but it soon becomes clear that, like a mosaic, the

differing colors are separate pieces carefully woven into one whole, varied cloth.

The Marvin Gaye Lounge, entered from the upper level of the rotunda or directly from the elevator, is a private room used for conferences or special parties. It is distinctively decorated with plush finishes and has its own clear identity. The room is fashioned after the original Roostertail Lounge, known for its great view of the Detroit River, and its reputation as an elegant, plush lounge popular with the most successful entertainers and celebrities of 1960s Detroit. Motown performers and other luminaries would often be seen entertaining and having fun late into the night. This Lounge is certain to draw a similar type crowd as well as people from all walks of life who readily identify with the stylistic performers and inimitable Motown sound. Motown Cafe's Marvin Gaye Lounge is fronted with an etched glass wall featuring the score to the performer's hit song, "I Heard It Through The Grapevine," while the lyrics are famous Marvin Gaye song titles. The space is lavishly finished with twotone quilted banquette backs, a series of coffers in the ceiling and picture lights that highlight Marvin Gaye photographs during all phases of his rich career performing solo and with other Motown artists.

Motown Cafe at the New York New York Hotel & Casino in Las Vegas, like its flagship location in New York City, draws upon the rich history and cultural impact of the legendary record label that defined a style, a generation, even a way of life. The design is firmly rooted in the classic American architecture of the period – from the late 1950s to the late 1960s when Motown chalked up more than 110 Top Ten pop hits. It visually captures the excitement and the driving artistic energy of the Motown sound, imparting an authentic representation of Motown performers and a reliving of their success story to all those who visit. The atmosphere is warm, colorful, inclusive and dynamic.

Architecture and Interior Design
Jay M. Haverson, Principal-In-Charge; Carolyn Haverson;
David Jablonka, Project Manager;
Lisa Bianco, Interior Designer;
Michael Gonzaga,
Tim Koelle,
Michael Kaufman,
David Jimenez,
Barbara Vazquez,
Gina Librandi,
Nick Lios

Joe Kaplan; Kaplan Architectural Lighting
Lighting Designer
1901 Avenue of The Stars #1750, Los Angeles, CA 90067
David Brewer; Six Flags Theme Parks
Retail Consultant
26101 Magic Mountain Parkway, Valencia, CA 91355

Linda & Heather White; White Design
Interior Consultant
16925 Donna Ynez Lane, Pacific Palicades, CA 90272

Gary Peters; Peters Development Corp.
Construction Manager
119 Tatnic Road, Moody, ME 04054

Environmental Factors
Lighting:
The lighting of the restaurant is accomplished through a variety of fixture types dispersed over various spaces within the overall dining room and bar area setting. For dramatic effect each table is pinspot with MR-16 recessed fixtures. Neon lit coves are positioned throughout the ceiling space to create "horizons" that give the effect of space beyond. The neon is lit in a series of warm colors including tangerine, red, gold, bromide blue and lavender. The stage marquee and album art displays are illuminated in a cool fluorescent light temperature to present a contrasting and distinct color look as feature attractions. The lower level bar-face is lit from within using a continuous, warm white neon strip, as is the translucent terrazzo bar counter surface.

The main dining room ceiling is comprised of panels layered with polished brass LP discs that are edge lit from neon. The narrow beamed light is projected through holes in the center of the records to the main opening below. A series of base mounted lights spaced around the perimeter of the atrium opening uplight the ceiling and emblazon the reflective gold records.

The memorabilia and costume display cases are lit with warm, recessed fixtures from above and well lights at the base to highlight the artifacts in an even wash to provide the brightest illumination in the entire space. The statuary of Motown artists is lit theatrically from below from a base with recessed well lights gelled to create a mix of color over the bronze forms. Additionally, the features of the statues are grazed from above with a combination of adjustable, recessed MR-16 fixtures and canopy-mounted spot heads.

The exterior of the Motown Cafe is illuminated from a combination of fluorescent, neon, quartz and halogen lamp sources to create a variety of light colors on the surface of the building which is reminiscent of a period theatrical building such as Radio City Music Hall. This structure has a vertical blade sign that displays Motown Cafe in animated flashing red neon. The horizontal canopy is a polished aluminum with a blue neon banded wraparound marquee that includes a three tiered message board colorfully illustrating "Las Vegas Never Sounded So Good" and other catch phrases.

Sound System / Acoustics
The sound system is designed to create as even a coverage throughout all the public areas of the restaurant using both high and low frequency output. This is accomplished with recessed, open-backed ceiling mounted speakers to cover spaces under the lower ceiling areas and bracket-mounted three-dimensional units in the larger, open volumes of the atrium. Each speaker is spaced equally from the next to evenly distribute the sound. Sub-woofers are mounted in the face of the balcony to create a balance of bass tones. Audio and video controls are positioned in the DJ/VJ booth which is highly visible at the mezzanine level. Capturing the quality of the classic Motown sound is very important in the acoustical design of the space. To this end, the upper ceiling of the main space is coffered with acoustical panels set off the vaulting with a hanging system that uses resilient clips to absorb sound and reduce reverberation time. The 2500 layered discs also are designed to capture sound. All of the seating in the restaurant is upholstered to also reduce the amount of hard reflective surfaces. Several walls are also tufted in channeled upholstery for the same reason. The coffering of the ceilings at the underside of the mezzanine helps to contain sound as well.

Video Presentation
Visitors are greeted by pairs of stacked videos at the casino entrance into the Motown Cafe. The Shop Around at the front of the restaurant features a prominent stacked video cube presentation which is tied into the overall presentation of the restaurant. Individual monitors are placed strategically in the upper level dining areas and at both bars to feature the restaurant's video content. A large video cube is located at the lower level of the restaurant much like the family's television was set up in the living room of a home during the early 1960s so the viewing experience is collective and a gathering experience.

Theatrical Presentation
The performance areas designed for the Motown Cafe "Moments" are strategically placed throughout the restaurant on the main stage at the lower level, on the balcony of the Diana Ross room, by the bar at the second floor and in the merchandise store. Each area is fit with a camera that transmits images to the video system. The lighting is classic theatrical with color washes to backlight the performers and front lighting to enhance their dramatic presence.

Mechanical
The Motown Cafe was designed within the spatial parameters offered by the shell of the casino structure. The mezzanine floor was placed at a height to ensure the most available mechanical routing space and to maximize ceiling height. The system is comprised of chiller units mounted on the roof of the building that supplies air handlers with chilled water loops serving 5 zones. Air is delivered through a catwalk space above the mezzanine ceiling and through chases to the mezzanine below. The ductwork had to be carefully located to avoid a maze of other building mechanical systems and architectural treatments and to deliver proper air quantities at correct velocities. Ductwork is held to the perimeter underside of the mezzanine level to form drop-down soffits that also create a smoke curtain and cove lighting opportunities. Return air is pulled back to the air handling equipment via the open banquette bottoms on the second level, return air grilles and also through the open center of the 28' record spindle at the upper ceiling in the rotunda area.

Furnishing list
Number of seats: 671 Seats
Items
Furnishing item, Manufacturer name & address
Terrazzo Flooring - Roman Mosaic, 20445 Gramercy Place, Torrence, California 90501
Interior Signage - Young Electric Sign Company, 5119 S. Cameron Street, Las Vegas, Nevada 89118
Railings - John Bentley, Advanced Architectural Metals, 3950 West Ponderosa Way, Las Vegas, Nevada 89118
Statues - Custom - Studio EIS, 35 York Street, Brooklyn, New York 11201
Lower Level Carpeting - Custom - Axminster - by Patterson, Flynn, Martin & Manges, 979 Third Avenue, New York, New York 10022
Banquettes - Custom - DBK Upholstery, 366 Canal Place, Bronx, New York 10451
Banquette Fabric Back - Silver Associates, 401 East 74 Street, New York, New York 10021.
Banquette Fabric Back - Solid Color (along wall) - Anzea Neon Electric from Silver Associates, 401 East 74 Street, New York, New York 10021
Tabletops and Bases - L & B Empire from J.C. Sales Company, 480 Riverdale Avenue, Yonkers, New York 10705
Chairs - Custom Cherry Frame - L & B Empire from J.C. Sales Company, 480 Riverdale Avenue, Yonkers, New York 10705
Lower Level Bar Stool Back - Parfait - Silver Associates, 401 East 74 Street, New York, New York 10021
Audio/Video, See Productions, Las Vegas, Nevada

Ceiling Records - Swiss Services, Las Vegas, Nevada
45' Ceiling Record - Custom - Young Electric Sign Company, 5119 S. Cameron Street, Las Vegas, Nevada 89118
Lower Level Chair Back Fabric - 1) front of back - Anzea Jellybeans from Silver Associates, 401 East 74 Street, New York, New York 10021. 2) back of back - Dark Green/Light Green Squares, Zimmer & Rhodes, 41 East 11 Street, New York, New York

Lower Level Chair Seat - Red Zodiac with Teal Zodiac welt by Naugahyde, Frank Bella, 485-17 S. Broadway, Hicksville, New York
Album Art Lightboxes, Brian Chillington, Chillington Builders, 11 Ridge Road, Newton, Connecticut 06470
Curtains on Stage - Purple - Xanadu by Design Tex, 56-08 37th Avenue, Woodside, New York
Curtains on Stage - Gold - Metallic Holiday Gold by Circle Fabrics, 263 West 38 Street, New York, New York
Dance Flooring, Permagrain from Architectural Products Company, 53 Oak Hill Road, Southborough, MA
Upper Level Carpeting - Custom - Axminster - by Patterson, Flynn, Martin & Manges, 979 Third Avenue, New York, New York 10022
Upper Level Bar Stools - Custom Frame - L & B Empire from J.C. Sales Company, 480 Riverdale Avenue, Yonkers, New York 10705
Upper Level Bar Stool Seat - Teal Zodiac - Naugahyde by Frank Bella, 485-17 S. Broadway, Hicksville, New York
Upper Level Bar Stool Back - Ebony Parfait - Silver Associates, 401 East 74 Street, New York, New York
Upper Level Banquette Back Fabric - 1) front of back - Kravet Fabrics, 225 Central Avenue, Bethpage, NY 11714
2) back of back - Silver Associates, 401 East 74 Street, New York, New York 10021
Upper Level Banquette Seat - Naugahyde from Frank Bella, 485-17 S. Broadway, Hicksville, New York
Upper Level Banquette Top - Naugahyde Zodiac from Frank Bella, 485-17 S. Broadway, Hicksville, New York
Upper Level Chairs - Custom Frame - L & B Empire from J.C. Sales Company, 480 Riverdale Avenue, Yonkers, New York 10705. 1) Front of back - Appolinaire Gold by Robert Allen, 55 Cabot Boulevard, Mansfield, MA 2) Back of back - Dark Green/Light Green Squares, Zimmer & Rhodes, 41 East 11 Street, New York, NY
Upper Level Chairs - Seat - Teal Glitter with Gold Glitter welt by Naugahyde from Frank Bella, 485-17 S. Broadway, Hicksville, New York
Harlequin Wall Cover - Custom Checkers by Willem Van Es Design Studio, 222 West 23 Street, New York, New York 10011
Photo Framing - Frames and Art by Simone, 37 South Broadway, Nyack, New York 10960
Diana Ross Room Curtains - Dedar, Goccia 4201.007 - Jack Lenor Larson, 232 East 59 Street, New York, NY
Dining Table - Custom by White Design, Los Angeles, CA - manufactured by Galerkih Design, Gardena, CA
Big Chairs - Miss Emily Series by Frewill, 605 N. LaBrea Avenue, Los Angeles, CA.
Big Chair Fabric - Parkertex Oslo from Kneedler/Fauchere, 8687 Melrose Avenue, Los Angeles, CA
Sofas - Miss Emily Series by Frewill, 605 N. LaBrea Avenue, Los Angeles, CA.
Sofa Fabric - Parkertex Oslo fabric from Kneedler/Fauchere, 8687 Melrose Avenue, Los Angeles, CA

Carpeting - Wildebeast/Leopard by Shaw Industries from International Flooring, 451 N. Robertson Boulevard, Los Angeles, CA
Ceiling - Liquid Lame, 115992 White Gold by Dazian, 423 West 55 Street, New York, New York
Chandelier - Custom - White Design, Los Angeles, CA
Dining Chairs - Boullee Chair JM1000 by Frewill, 605 N. LaBrea Avenue, Los Angeles, CA.
Dining Chairs Fabric - Rodolph Victoriana VT 3385 Crimson Cloak D - from Pollack & Associates, 979 Third Avenue, New York, New York
Marvin Gaye Room Banquette Backs - Midtown #007 Apple, Maharam, 251 Park Avenue South, New York and Protocol Citron, Knoll Textiles, East Greenville, PA
Marvin Gaye Room Banquette Seats - Innovations LX Series, Lace 20402-Gold from Silver Associates, 401 East 74 Street, New York, New York 10021
Chairs - Custom - L & B Empire from J.C. Sales Company, 480 Riverdale Avenue, Yonkers, New York 10705
Chair Back Fabric - Apollinaire Charcoal by Robert Allen from J.C. Sales Company, 480 Riverdale Avenue, Yonkers, New York 10705.
Chair Seat Fabric - Lace Gold by Innovations from J.C.Sales Company, 480 Riverdale Avenue, Yonkers, NY 10705
Carpeting - Custom - Axminster by Patterson, Flynn, Martin & Manges, 979 Third Avenue, New York, NY 10022
Etched Glass - Custom - Image Construction, 5070 South Arville, Suite #12, Las Vegas, NV 89112
Retail Store Signage, Faux Brick Fixturing System, Display Cases - Rick Sciorci, Fixture Arts, Inc., McBean Parkway, Santa Clarita, CA
Stage Lighting - Halo Lighting

MOTOWN CAFE
104 West 57th Street,
New York, NY, Usa

The design team had as its starting point the rich history and cultural impact of the legendary record label that defined a style, a generation, even a way of life. The team conceived a distinct design or "identity" for the flagship New York location, the first of several Motown Cafes planned to open nationally and internationally, to be unique and immediately recognizable as Motown.

Situated on West 57 Street between 6th and 7th Avenues, the Motown Cafe dwells in what was once the Horn & Hardart Automat, built in the Art Deco style of the 1930s. Some interior spaces were selectively gutted, but features from the original structure such as the paneled ceiling, stepping pilaster columns and the wonderfully expressive glazed terracotta stairway connecting the main floor to the mezzanine were maintained.

The Motown identity is established immediately. A 20-foot-tall beacon resembling a radio tower rises from the roof.

Five-foot tall blazing letters (lit from within) and five radiant stars that proclaim "Motown" sit atop the parapet wall directly above the main entry. The glazed terracotta building facade and storefront has been restored to its original form with the addition of the revolving door and the new stainless steel canopy.

As much a celebration as a salute to the music and artists of Motown, the Motown Cafe design is composed of separate distinct areas of visual interest – reflecting the different elements of music, lyrics, production and artistry of the Motown sound. A series of vignettes make up a contrasting yet integrated visual whole, and are stylistically representative of actual places in the lives of the artists in their rise to fame. The basic visual design is firmly rooted in the classic American architecture of the period – from the late 1950s to the late 1960s when Motown chalked up more than 110 "Top 10" pop hits. The atmosphere is colorful, warm, friendly and dynamic.

The mood is established immediately on entering; the sound is distinctly Motown. A circular platform with "Motown" in classic block lettering with five stars is set into the floor in yellow letters on a field of blue terrazzo. A collection of Motown "icons" are visible on several different visual levels: life-sized statues of the Supremes in the foreground; the marquis and stage announcing "Motortown Revue Live Tonight" and an oversized nearly 30-foot spinning Motown single suspended from the ceiling above the stage. The key elements to the success of the Motown sound were style, movement, and sound.

At your feet is a map of the Motortown Revue, with such locations as Chicago, St. Louis, Indianapolis, Cleveland, and of course Detroit at the center marked with stars set into the terrazzo floor. This sense of journey continues as a Motown host or hostess, dressed in the style of classic Motown performance apparel, guides you toward your seat on either level, the bar or the shop.

At the left is the Motown Bar, curvilinear, streamlined and well crafted from materials of the early 1960s, including aluminum, stainless steel, glass block and blonde wood. Softening this image are a series of artifacts of the period and an informal display of candid photos of the Motown stars in their cars, as well as sheet music and classic Motown albums.

The main dining area is the design focus of the Motown Cafe. The colors are platinum, gold, ruby red, teal, charriols and "Motown blue." The world's largest 45-r.p.m. record, complete with Motown label, spins slowly above. A formal dining arrangement is avoided, with casual banquette seating serving to tie the space together. The lighting is a warm, indirect cove effect with pinspots highlighting memorabilia and album covers lining the perimeter of the open volume.

The Automat was inspired by the original Horn and Hardart Automat. This takeoff on New York's favorite diner of long ago also captures the humble beginnings and late night eateries of Detroit where Motown's now famous artists ate after practice and recording sessions. A wall permanently displays LPs, singles, and song titles from the top-of-the-charts heritage of the Motown sound.

The Roostertail Lounge was inspired by one of Detroit's hottest clubs of the era. The elegant, plush lounge can be closed off for private parties. The predominant colors are black, gold and dark burled maple. The walls are lined with a series of classic portraits of Marvin Gaye, the Jackson Five, Gladys Knight and the Pips, and Stevie Wonder and the Contours taken from the Motown archives.

Constructed of Motown's "solid gold" hit records such as "Stop in the Name of Love," "I Heard it Through the Grapevine," "Shop Around," and "My Girl" among others, a "stairway to success" leads to the mezzanine. The stairway symbolizes the success of Motown's performers – no group of artists started with so little and achieved so much. At the base of the stairs is a full-sized sculpture of the Supremes.

The Twenty Grand Bar/Lounge was conceived as a piece of living American musical history. The re-creation harks back to the legendary Detroit '60s lounge that featured many of the young and rising Motown stars. The distinct curvilinear fascia recognizable from the original club crowns the mahogany and red quilted bar below. The period green velour sofa-like banquette is a piece of furniture that "centers" this portion of the mezzanine. A young Michael Jackson statue peers over the railing in a playful way.

On the Mezzanine Lounge a multi-media gallery of video projection, sequencing slide presentations, line the walls of the banqueted perimeters of the upper dining area. Metallic cranberry red and patinaed silver leaf walls are the backdrop for a portrait gallery of the Motown artists in casual rehearsal and live performances at the Apollo Theater in New York.
The "rooftop" dining area looks over the Detroit that both echoes and evokes the urban roots of the Motown sound. The experience is further heightened by a skyline montage that creates a magical, nighttime "up on the roof" feeling. On hot summer nights urban dwellers without the benefit of air conditioning in bygone years would picnic and party on the roof.
A close-up view of the poster-plastered wall featuring original Motown acts at their original venues is composed to represent a typical wall from urban street life. Cable lights that call to mind electrical wires from street lighting sparkle against a deep blue ceiling.
Taking its name from the 1960 Smokey Robinson and The Miracles hit, "Shop Around," the two-story retail store selling Motown merchandise and music is located on the main floor and lower level. Access to the store is also available to non-diners from the main waiting area at the restaurant's entry and from a double door street entranceway. Blonde woods, black trim and terrazzo floors create a good contrast for merchandise display.

NOBU RESTAURANT
105 Hudson Street
New York, NY, Usa

Nobu remains one of the hottest restaurant spot in Manhattan. The high-ceilinged dining room seats nearly 100 at perimeter banquettes, the central sushi bar, and loose tables for four. The feeling of the decor is Nobu's native rural Japan. Floor-to-ceiling tree sculpture are made form birch tree trunks, rusted steel plates, and solid ashwood branches that also serve as lighting columns. A visual carpet of cherry blossoms was stenciled onto the beechwood floor. Framing the prominent sushi bar are custom sconces in the shape of dueling samurai swords. The bar itself is commodes of strongly back-lit pea-green onyx and a scorched wood top with details of bronze and plashed brass. Custom "chopsticks" barstools bask in the green glow. Their upright supports are huge black-lacquered chopsticks holding fish- patterned upholstered seats and backs. These elements play against abstracted sushi-shaped walls finished in handmade paper-like ceramic tiles, rusted steel, and a wall of one thousand, glossy up-lit, Japanese riverbed stones.
Window Treatments
Rods: John Saviteri Furniture, Wallington, NJ
Kimonos: Coyuchi Fabric, Pt. Reyes Station, CA
Tile: Elizabeth MacDonald, Bridgewater, CT
Shelves/trim: Mark Hill, Gilboa, NY
Sushi Bar: Mark Hill, Gilboa, NY
Pebble Wall: Madeworks, New York, NY
Trees, Screens, Sconces, Table Tops: John Saviteri Furniture, Wallington, NJ
Floor Stenciling: Julie Lifton Schwerner, Nyack, NY
Wall Plaster, Ceiling Finish: Vision in Plaster, New York, NY
Fabric Wall Panels:
Manufacture; Munrod, Pelham, NY
Fabric: Handwoven Studios, New York, NY
Booths: Mark Hill, Gilboa, NY
Cushions, Banquettes: Munrod, Pelham, NY
Fabric: Clarence House, New York, NY
Sushi Bar Chairs: John Saviteri Furniture, Wallington, NJ
Carpet: Masland, New York, NY
Installation: Patterson Flynn Etal, New York, NY
Bathroom Mirrors, Bathroom Trim, Radiator Covers: Mark Hill, Gilboa, NY
Chairs: Thonet, New York, NY
Copper Leaf Finishes: Madeworks, New York, NY
Front Door Glass: Bendheim, New York, NY
Front Door Handle: John Saviteri Furniture, Wallington, NJ
Accessories: James Griffini, New York, NY
Wall Paper: Anya Larkin, New York, NY

PLANET HOLLYWOOD
Walt Disney World
Orlando, FL, Usa

Lighting Designer: Focus Lighting in collaboration with Rockwell Group
Electrical Engineer: Rodin Engineering, Inc.
General Contractor: Welbro Contractors, Inc.
Structural Engineer: DeSimone, Chaplin & Dobryn
Duration of project: Fall 1993–December 1994
Name of client/client company: Robert Earl, President and CEO Planet Hollywood International, Inc.
Square feet: 30,000 sq.ft., three floors
Project's outstanding features
Sci-Fi Room
Adventure Room
Sky Room
Pool Bars
Diorama -the larges (the work curves around the interior surface)
A spherical interior - 110' in diameter
11 tons of hanging memorabilia
A rotating 26' long alligator
This project is most like a theater. The interior is reminiscent of atmospheric of the '20s – numerous balconies.
Materials, equipment, furnishing used in the project-supplier and address
Lighting: Focus Lighting, New York NY
Furniture and fittings: Banquettes: A.J. Munitz, ArtCraft
Flooring: Carpeting: U.S. Axminster, Couristan
Main Entry: Walls, ceilings, partitions: Glass tile: Dal-Tile
Textiles: Gilford, J.M. Lynne, Chris Stone, Schumacher
Main contractor: Welbro Construction, Orlando, FL
Consultants:
Audio-Visual Consultant: T.R. Technologies, New York, NY
Kitchen Consultant: Brass & Stainless Designs, Inc., Dallas, TX
Diorama Consultant: Modeworks, New York, NY

Associate-in-Charge: Carmen Aguilar
Staff: Tim Nissen, George Bennet, Michael Gonzaga, Erch Blohm, Mike Notaro, Tom Pedrazzi, Eve-Lynn Schoenstein, Alice Yu

POIRET RESTAURANT
474 Columbus Avenue
New York, NY, Usa

History
The objective was to convert the space from an old neighborhood Greek Diner to a warm eclectic French bistro with moderate prices.
Materials
Hand painted oak floor
Hand painted plaster walls and ceiling
Mosaic tile facade
Antique Alabaster pendent fixtures
Hand-sculpted plaster wall sconces
Technical Solutions
Because of its age, new structural supports were added dividing the room lengthwise into 2 sections, 1/3–2/3. This division was played up by erecting a high barrel vault in the larger area and a low flat ceiling in the small area, thus creating 2 distinct seating areas, as well as a bit of drama.
Art work
Hand painted walls and floor by Ron Wolfson.
Mosaic tile facade by Nancy Mah and Dan Bliere

SAVANNAH RESTAURANT & CABARET
427-433 Washington Avenue,
Miami Beach, FL 33139, Usa

History of Location
Built in the '20s or '30s as an Art Deco-styled commercial space, this location has had a variety of businesses housed within it, most recently a futon shop. The space was delivered to Savannah's owners bare and unattractive – concrete walls and ceilings and exposed metal columns and beams.
Square footages
Bar - 600
Dining Room - 1350
Main Lounge - 575
Marvin's Lounge - 135
Kitchen - 1000
Office - 60
Bathrooms - 300
Seating
Bar - 22
Dining Room - 112
Main Lounge - 23
Marvin's Lounge - 11
Total seating - 169
Concept

To create an environment that reflects the rural inspirations of Low Country Cuisine, the featured menu of the restaurant, but that is fused with the taste of the sophisticated urban international clientele that is prevalent in the South Beach area.

Special Features
The ceiling originally had two levels and several exposed beams. We used these features to divide the finished ceiling and accent the different areas of the restaurant. Some ceiling sectors are purely decorative and others functional in that they concealed the air-conditioning unit, lighting fixtures, and bar equipment (there is no basement in the space so all bar lines had to be run from the kitchen through the ceiling). The round suspended canopy ceiling, a signature feature of the restaurant, was designed to signify the stage area below it, as well as to house the necessary lighting needed for the stage.

Furnishings and Manufacturers
1. Bar
Artichoke Lamps Poulsen Lighting, Inc.
Bar Equipment American Food Equipment Company
Mirror and Glass South Beach Glass & Glazing
Standing Lamps at Rear Artemide
Sconces In-house fabrication
Standing Planter Hayes Company
Aalto-Inspired Barstools and Chairs In-house fabrication
2. Banquette
Banquette Fabric Westgate
Stone Coronado Products
Piano Yamaha
3. Lounge
Hardwood walls and floors National Wood Floors
Chair Leather Dualoy
Ceiling Fan Casablanca
Rug Stanton
Lounge Seats In-house fabrication
Cocktail Tables In-house fabrication
Metalwork Vigilant Design
Artwork South Art Gallery
4. Dining Room
Chandelier in Suspended Ceiling Artemide
Silverware Oneida
Glassware Libby
Plates Buffalo China
Frosted Candle Sleeves Luminaire
Table Lamps on Bar and Maitre d'Artemide
5. Restroom
Fixtures Kohler
Marble Tops Puma Marble
Vanities In-house fabrication

All lighting except where specified supplied by Lightolier

Wood for interior installations supplied by Whittelsey Wood Products

All paint throughout by Pratt & Lambert
Hardwood floors are Brazilian cherry

SCALINI
19 Jalan Sultan Ismail
Kuala Lumpur, My

Interior Design Team:
Tony Chi Principal Designer
David Singer Principal Lighting
Noel Bernardo Project Designer
Yolanda Constiniano Technical Support
Rafael Caceres Jr. Technical Support

Owner: Olympia Industries
Project Management: Restaurant Management Consultants Limited, Hong Kong
Engineering Management: Mascon Sdn, Bhd, Kuala Lumpur
Contractor: Perabot Van Hin Sdn Bhd, Kuala Lumpur
Graphic Design: Lilian Tang Design, Hong Kong
Table top Designer: Rene Ozorio, Hong Kong

Furniture List
Custom Light Fixture Arc Light Design, New York City
Stand Light Fixture LightCraft Sdn Bhd, Kuala Lumpur
Custom Door Van Hin Sdn Bhd, Kuala Lumpur
Table Base Falcon Product, Inc., Usa
Outdoor Parisian Table Smith Hawken, California
Fabric Donghia Textiles
B/W Photo Prints Romano Gallery
Barstool Jalex Sdn Bhd, Kuala Lumpur

Chair Jalex Sdn Bhd, Kuala Lumpur

SEQUOIA
Pier 17, South Street Seaport
New York, NY, Usa

History
Opened in 1991, overlooking NY Harbor, Statue of Liberty, Brooklyn Bridge. Views are a key element to work with.

Materials
Antique rowing skulls and bar
Model boats adorn bar
mahogany paneling and terrazzo floors complete the picture.

Art work
hand crafted boats after authentic designs

SI PIAZZA
Charlotte, NC, Usa

Project Description
The design objective was to create a multi-program restaurant space (including a bakery and catering kitchen) out of a series of underutilized areas in the lobby of an office building in downtown Charlotte. The end result is a perfect fit spatially and a memorable place that feels like a world transformed.

The defining concept of the restaurant begins in the adjacent space at the art gallery (lobby) entrance. Colors from the interior are brought forth in the canopies and menu boxes. The angled "street walls" that funnel into the restaurant are visually connected as well. The main space of Si! Piazza is a small courtyard or piazza at the end of the street into the lobby. The main bar, bakery and stair to the mezzanine all occupy the space.

It was a unique challenge to create a familiar looking, playful place connected to the circulation of the building and to fit a bakery, bar, restaurant and catering kitchen into one space. The strength of the design is in the spatial concept with its expression in color and material.

Environmental Factors
The lighting is designed as a series of layers to reinforce the architectural aspects of the space. Incandescent downlights and low voltage cable lighting with Halogen fixtures are distributed throughout the space with a deep purple ceiling backdrop. The balance of lamp color is flattering to the decor and the diners.

Sound is attenuated by a combination of acoustical ceilings at the upper level and fabric chairs and banquettes. The stairs and mezzanine level are carpeted where the primary seating is focused which aids in keeping the noise level lower.

The sound system is controlled at the bar area and consists of six surround sound ambient type speakers with two sub-woofer locations. The space is filled three-dimensionally with sound.

The HVAC system consists of a series of fan coil units linked to the condenser water loop provided by the office tower. There are 5 zones for maximum flexibility. The bakery and kitchen lines are exhausted from a hood and flue that rises five levels to the top of the parking deck. Comfort is maintained through the careful balance of ambient air in relation to the quantities exhausted in the kitchen.

The Lighting Wall at the Carillon Building
The idea of the lighting wall is to effectively block daylight from reaching two restaurants located within the interior space in order to create a separate world within.

In downtown Charlotte, North Carolina, zoning laws dictate that if you close a store front, you must create an architectural or artistic effect for the edification of passing pedestrians. Our solution was to design a wall of light.

Taking cues from the geometry of the office building's mullions, a colorful geometric stained-glass facade is created from custom designed opalescent glass panels that, when backlit at night, work as a spectacular, glowing street mural. A palette of 10 colors was used including cream, moss green, scarlet red, translucent yellow and mustard.

Encased in 10 bays that wrap around three sides of the downtown office building, the wall is backlit with warm fluorescent 20-watt strips at the top and bottom. Placed in a trough with reflectors, the fluorescents create an even wash of light that filters through the bright colors of the translucent wall to create a warm glow. A solid drywall partition 18 inches behind the wall allows access to the light troughs and helps to augment the reflective quality of the trough.

Furnishing item
Manufacturer name & address

Banquette - custom - Munrod Interior Upholstery, 629 Fifth Avenue, Pelham, NY 10803
Banquette Fabric - #12421 Color 519, Kravet Fabrics, 225 Central Avenue South, Bethpage, NY 11714

Chairs - Shelby Williams, 150 East 58 Street, New York, NY 10155
Bar Stools - custom - Shelby Williams, 150 East 58 Street, New York, NY 10155
Carpeting - STY.SAL, W. Weave Carpet; Patterson, Flynn, Martin & Manges, 979 3rd Ave., New York, NY*
Bar Top Linoleum - Town & Country Flooring, Inc., 14 East 38 Street, New York, NY 10016
Murals - Peter Grzybowski, 80 Varick Street 2D, New York, New York 10013
Decorative Painting - Peter Grzybowski, 80 Varick Street 2D, New York, NY 10013
Table Bases - L&B Contract Industries, Inc., Liberty Street, Haverstraw, New York 10927
Table Tops - James Mellin Contracting/Design, 33 Auldwood Road, Stamford, CT 06902
Table Umbrellas - Manufactured by Giati, Roger Arlington, 979 Third Avenue, New York, NY 10022
Canopy Fabric - Sunbrella #8602, #8603, #8610, Glen Raven Mills, Inc., Glen Raven, NC 27217
Canopy Manufacturer - Price-Davis Construction, 1800 East Boulevard, Charlotte, NC 28203
Lighting - Primo Lighting, 114 Washington Street, South Norwalk, CT 06854
"Moon" Shape - Acme Awning Company, Inc., 435 Van Nest Avenue, Bronx, NY 10460
"Moon" Fabrication - Munrod Interior Upholstery, 629 Fifth Avenue, Pelham, NY

Additional Vendors

General Contractor
Price-Davis Construction, Inc.1800, East Boulevard, Charlotte, North Carolina 28203, tel. 704.342.1025 fax. 704.358.8881

Kitchen Designer
Brass and Stainless Designs 3306 Borich Street, Dallas, Texas 75210
tel. 214.565.9655 fax. 214.428.8628

Decorative Painting / Murals
Peter Grzybowski, 80 Varick Street 2D, New York, New York 10013
tel. 212.219.8424 - fax. 212.219.8424

Banquette Fabrication
Munrod Interior Upholstery, Inc., 629 Fifth Avenue, Pelham, New York 10803
tel. 914.738.7128 - fax. 914.738.7134

Banquette Fabric
Kravet Fabrics, Inc.225 Central Avenue South Bethpage, New York 11714
tel. 516.293.2000 - fax. 516.293.2737

Table and Bar Top Material
Town and Country Flooring, Inc., 14 East 38th Street, New York, New York10016
tel. 212.679.0312- 718.409.1881 fax. 718.824.3571

Audio Design
New York Sound & Video Corp., 2525 Cruger Avenue, New York, New York 10467
tel. 718.655.6444 fax. 718.655.3281 fax. 212.689.0967

Tables
L&B Contract Industries, Inc., Liberty Street, Haverstraw, New York 10927
tel. 914.429.5700 - fax. 914.354.0323

Tabletop Fabrication
James Mellin Contracting/Design, 33 Auldwood Road, Stamford, Connecticut 06902 tel. 203.967.4211

Carpet
Patterson, Flynn, Martin & Manges 979 Third Avenue- D&D Building, New York, New York 10022 tel. 212.688.7700 fax. 212.826.6740

Chairs / Bar Stools (Custom)
Shelby Williams A&D Building, 150 East 58th Street, New York, New York 10155
tel. 212.888.9050

Lighting Design
Primo Lighting 114 Washington Street, South Norwalk, Connecticut 06854
tel. 203.866.4321 fax. 203.838.1612Hanging Moon Fabrication
Acme Awning Co., Inc., 435 Van Nest Avenue Bronx, New York 10460

SPIGA RESTAURANT
Scarsdale, NY, Usa

Project Description

The goal of this project was to imaginatively open up the interior of an existing space to create a memorable family-style Italian restaurant.
A fantasy Italian cityscape ceiling mural is the focus of the space and is punctuated with accent lights. Slashing, leaning columns frame the perimeter with wanted railings in between. A playful series of facade-like banquettes forms an angled wall which directs the eye into the room. Decorative finishes and other colorful surfaces intensify the surroundings, making the space feel festival-like. Other focuses of the interior include a strategically placed pizza oven, which is surrounded by a mosaic of cracked tiles, and the bar, salvaged from an earlier restaurant and embellished with upholstery and additional detail.

Environmental Factors
The lighting at Spiga is primarily a system of adjustable recessed halogen fixtures that light each table. Uplighting is provided onto the ceiling mural. Surface mounted specialty halogen fixtures accent the food display. A series of recessed star and moon fixtures with 15 watt quartz lamps are randomly spaced on the ceiling in the bar area. The lighting is designed to enhance the food presentation and be flattering to patrons. Acoustical impact is minimized by the space being completely carpeted. Chairs and banquettes are upholstered and the table are padded to absorb sound.
The sound system is controlled at the bar area and consists of six surround-sound ambient type speakers with two sub-woofer locations. The space is filled three-dimensionally with sound.

The HVAC system consist of two-package air-conditioning units with in-line heat coils provide air-conditioning and heating through a ducted system. The zoning is split between the upper and lower dining areas.

Number of seats: 175

Furnishing item
Chairs: Shelby Williams, New York, NY
Chair Seats: Mercury Cape Red, Donghia, New York, NY
Chairs Backs: Carnival Notte and Stellar Stripe Carina, Donghia, New York, NY
Custom Millwork: Robert Miller, Tarrytown, NY
Banquette Alcove Drap: Crushed Velvet Cardinal Red, A. Wimpfheimer and Brother, Inc. New York, NY
Banquette Alcove Wall Fabric: Marquette Black, HBF Textiles, Hickory, NC
Faux Finishes: Nofo Decorative Painting, New York, NY
Ceiling Mural: Tom Glisson, Wysong Company, New York, NY
Flooring: Patterson, Flynn, Martin & Manges, New York, NY
Table Tops: Custom, Robert Miller Tarrytown, NY
Table Bases: L&B Contract Industries, Inc. Haverstraw, NY
Pizza Oven Ceramic Tile: Susan Brown, Serpentile, New York, NY
Lighting: Primo Lighting, South Norwalk, CT

SPIGA RESTAURANT
Bedford, NY, Usa

The client's objective was to turn a cramped hum-drum space that formerly housed a cookie-cutter franchise eatery into an exciting 200-seat Italian "Fantasy" restaurant within tight budgetary constraints.
The design team's goal was to create a "playful" space making use of pictorial images and lighting to generate a sense of open air theater and a festival-like atmosphere that would transform dining into a memorable experience. First, the old restaurant gutted to create more open spaces to make full use of the available square footage. Then the infusion of light and color began.
The restaurant's dreamlike mood and identity are established from the beginning by using plum colored canopies (visible from the road), featuring a stars-and-moon cutout pattern, backlit and softly luminous in the night. Inside, a mannerist series of facade-like banquettes with glittering jewel buttons direct the eye into the room, and form a main focus. Decorative finishes and other colorful surfaces "intensify" the surroundings, making the space feel robust and "eventfull".
At the entry is the new bar, which was salvaged and remade from the pre-existing bar in the earlier space. Again, lighting is used as an architectural element in itself to create a sense of excitement and to define the space. The whimsical, almost magical recessed star and moon light fixtures with 15-watt quartz lamps designed by the firm and create by artisans for Spiga are set into the ceiling area in a random pattern over the bar. The bar and the restaurant are visually distinguished from one another while maintaining the feeling of openness and space that are an integral part of the restaurant's design. Beyond the bar are low walls with criss-crossing mahogany panels defining the space without visually blocking the view of the dining area. This area is further defined by a series of leaning arches that frame the perimeter of the dining area and conceal structural posts. canted railings run in between the arches. The angled arches flare out as they reach toward (but never touch) the ceiling and are topped with simple capitals. Venetian stucco and glazes in terra-cotta, burnt umber, and plum are applied to the column sheaths.

Total floor area; 5,500 sq.ft

Total capacity by tables: 200 seats

Principal Interior Constructions Materials by Manufacturer(s)
Wall coverings; faux custom paint
Paint: Benjamin Moore - Faux custom painting
laminate: Wilsonart
Dry wall; U.S. Gypsum
Masonry: Pizza Oven wall, Dal Tile Corp.
Flooring: Fritz Tile
Carpet/carpet tile: Bentley, Brighton
Carpet Fiber manufactures: Patterson, Flynn, Martin, Manges
Ceiling: Mural, Peter Grzybowski
Lighting fixtures. Patdo Lighting Design, Capri, Halo
Door hardware: Sclag
Glass:
Window frames: Pella Windows
Window treatments: Awnings, Cove Awning
Railings/screens/grill work: Post Road Ironworks
Principal Furnishings by Manufacturer(s)
Dining chairs: Falcon prod., Inc., Best Marketing reps.
Dining Tables: L+B Contract
Lighting fixtures: Hald + Capri, Patdo Lighting Design
Banquette/ built-in seating: Munrod Upholstery, David Kamm
Upholstery:
Chair seats: Momentum, Cathedral Orchid
Banquette Back: Donghia Textiles, First Edition
Banquette wall: HBF Textiles
Bar Face: J.M. Lynn Co, Inc.
Banquette Seat: Kravet Fabric Inc.
Banquette Swag Lining: Robert Allen Ametex Contract Fabrics
banquette Swag: A. Wimpfheimer + Bro. Inc.
Window treatment: John B. Arceri Windowscape
Architectural woodworking: Racanelli Construction
Planter, accessories: Heidi Nehlesen, Edelweiss Designs (Flower Arrangements)
Signage: Suprosigns
Logo Design: Carolyne Haverson, Haverson Architecture and Design P.C.
Structural Engineer: Desimone, Chaplin, Dobryn Engineers, Rod Gibble
Mechanical Engineer: ABM
General contractor, construction manager: Racanelli Construction Management; John Racanelli
Lighting designer: Patdo Lighting Design; Gary Novasel
Project team: Jay Haverson, Carolyn Haverson, Michael Kaufman, Andren Grace, Lisa Bianco, Debbie Olchowski.

SYMPHONY CAFE'
950 8th Avenue
New York, NY, Usa

The Symphony Café takes its cue from the nearby world-famous Carnegie Hall. The 4,500-sq.ft restaurant exudes rich warmth and sophistication with its dark mahogany panels and exposed brick walls. Hand-blown Italian amber light panels glow from the soaring 16' ceiling.
The concept of "stage" carries throughout the restaurant. The exhibition kitchen highlights the performance of the preparation of the American cuisine. The raised platform plays stage to the mahogany and bronze banded bar with glass enclosed shelves which house memorabilia from famous playwrights and musicians. Featured at the back of the restaurant is a floor-to-ceiling mural of Carnegie Hall, from the perspective a performer on stage. Elegant pine green banquettes and verde marble tables on mosaic tile flooring are the finale to the design of the space.

TAPIKA
950 8th Avenue
New York, Usa

Tapika replaces the former Symphony Cafe. Our design commission was to refurbish and reinterpret the character of the former restaurant. Owned and operated by the same people as the Monkey Bar and Restaurant, the Glazier's were confident of our ability to design a successful and unique environment for David Walzog's Southwestern cuisine.
Our design approach consisted of treating the space as two separate conditions: the inside or internal walls and the outside or perimeter walls. The inside condition, also defined by the former heavily wood-paneled walls, were sectionally obrey plastered in shadings of desert clay. The remaining wood, made of ash, was bleached, stained, and wire brushed to lighten and emphasize its texture. The exterior perimeter is in a fence motif that incorporates handpainted draperies and shields the patron from the garish lights flashing on Eighth Avenue. A seating platform break-ups the dining hall feel and divides the main dining area into thirds. The added wainscoting was treated to match the walls and has been branded with genuine branding irons obtained from a ranch in Texas.

TATOU RESTAURANTS
233 North Beverly Drive, Beverly Hills, CA, Usa
Beverly Hotel, New York, NY, Usa

Tatou, located on Beverly Drive in Beverly Hills, was inspired by the original Coconut Grove. Additional images of the Beverly Hills space came from sophisticated 1930s-style celebrity Hollywood nightclubs where the idea was "to see and be seen."
The main dining room, reminiscent of those 1930's hot spots, sports deep magenta velvet drapery behind a mahogany stage and gold and cream layered draperies on the side walls. Flanking the dance floor are four camel-backed banquettes appointed with a rich tapestry fabric on the outside and leafy burgundy fabric on the inside. The perimeter of the room is punctuated by ten custom-cast, patinated copper palm trees with fiber-optically lit trunks and bunches of glowing coconuts. Miniature custom-designed palm tree lamps complete the tropical image. The entire room is capped with a back-lit tented fabric ceiling.

Tatou has been a huge success in New York and for this reason is being expanded to new locations in Los Angeles, Aspen and Miami. Tatou has a unique concept in that it starts out as a supper club complete with a stage and blues band. As the night winds on, the center portion of the dining room is converted to a dance floor. The tables and chairs are stacked away and the room transforms into a highly kinetic disco with dance music and synchronized lighting experience. In the meantime, the private club is being separately operated upstairs. Our firm was instrumental in developing all facets of this concept, and worked closely with the owners from the very beginning.
The look of the restaurant is warm, comfortable and "lived-in" – reminiscent of Southern Opera House or Vaudeville Theater. Antique mirrors flank the raised platforms to the right and left of the main dining area. Satyr-headed newel posts line the parapet wall to reinforce the theatrical setting. Traditional pendant lighting and table lamps are combined with recessed fixtures and cove lighting to provide a full array of lighting sources. The main room is centrally oriented to the stage while the bar acts as an anteroom from main entrance.

TORRE DI PISA RESTAURANT
19 West 44th Street
New York, NY, Usa

After 37 years of owning and managing the famous Tuscan trattoria Torre di Pisa in Milan, Paolo Meacci and his son Marco moved to New York to open and manage the elegant New York Torre di Pisa.

The layout of the 160-seat restaurant is designed to provide a series of different dining experiences. After entering, the wall to the right re-creates a flattened rendition of the leaning tower of Pisa with a twist that consists of custom flocked wall paper behind a lacy latticework facade. Protruding into the space, the frame-like structure provides containment for the extensive collection of ceramics and pottery received many years before in Milan as artistic trade for food. Another stage set is an interpreted re-creation of De Chirico's cityscape clock painting. Additional items designed to enhance the futuristic-Italian-sojourn motif include petrified draperies, mosaic carpeting, and Doric white columns. A separate room was also designed for diners who smoke, and for private parties. And lastly, a wall made of Italian love letters adorns the cozy wine bar where people meet before they dine and where tasting events are held.

VILLAGE EATERIES RESTAURANT
at New York, New York Casino Hotel,
Las Vegas, NV, Usa

Floor
Bonamite (concrete) with integral stains and textured patterns made to simulate asphalt, sidewalks, brickwork and cobblestone.
Ceiling
Plateaus of painted 2x2 and 2x4 acoustical ceiling tile hung at different heights and separated by curvilinear sheet metal reveal
Furniture
Wood, stainless steel and wicker furniture, some with silk-screened elements
Walls
All walls are made of plaster, some simulated to look like brick and stone. Twenty different patterns were used with colored integrals and scenic-aging processes for final finish. Cast-iron buildings use wood component, moldings, cornices

and columns with painted finish and scenic aging. Wrought iron fire escapes have props to simulate differences in the facades. Lights (in the windows) on separate circuits illuminate different portions of the facades at different times.
Artworks
Murals by graffiti and scenic painters. Neon signage by specialty fabricator, other signs and props fabricated and installed by set design fabricators. Sound tracks were created in sound studios to accompany some of the windows and fire escape props. Billboards were fabricated for actual solicitation of advertising (such as DKNY).
Streetscape
Trees are made of freeze-dried oak tress with silk leaves. Parking meters, post office boxes with news dispenser and fire hydrants are clumped together at street corners. Stoops are constructed of concrete or wood with wrought iron ornamentation.

VONG RESTAURANT
The Lipstick Building
New York, NY, Usa

Vong was designed and named for the celebrated chef Jean Georges Vongerichten and his much-acclaimed French-Thai cuisine. The commission consisted of renovating a 3.000 square foot space that would contain a 125-seat restaurant and bar.
On entering, one sees an entire facing wall made of a golden collage created from fragments of Thai stamps, maps, newspaper, currency, matchbook covers, lemon-grass, boxing programs, train tickets, and protruding gold leafed seashells evoking the mysterious and dream-like feeling of the foreign, yet familiar. Inspired by Thai culture, we experimented with the central dining space by juxtaposing large-scale and traditionally Thai architectural elements. A tatami platform provides an exclusive dining room area. On another side of the room, a Thai-plaid dining alcove – dubbed the King's booth – is nestled into an oversized, curved screen of sparkling gold, green, and blue mosaics. The kitchen entrance is a gleaming copper portal with teak grilles. And lastly, hanging from the ceiling, tulip shaped, handblown pendant lamps cast glowing pink light to recall the Thai Festival of Lights.

ZIP CITY
3-5 West 18th Street
New York, NY, Usa

Site
6,600 sq.ft. in an eight story neo-Renaissance loft building the Ladies' Mile Historic District.
Program
Micro brewery and restaurant seating 200.
Basement
The basement contains a 700 sq.ft. lager cellar housing 20 storage and fermenting thanks that were custom designed built in Vienna, Austria, as well as spaces for mechanical equipment, food and liquor storage, malt storage, and offices.
Ground Floor
The brewhouse and tap system are surrounded by a 90 linear foot U-shaped bar seating 40. Banquettes, booths, and tables surrounding the bar seat 105. Food service is from a 750-sq.ft kitchen.
Mezzanine
The mezzanine, which overlooks the bar, seats 50 to 60 at tables and accommodates private parties, large parties, and overflow.
Design Concept
A modern interpretation of a traditional European brewpub for a distinctively New York space. The focal points are the copper and brass brewhouse, tap system, and maple inlay bar. The lighting, as well as other design elements highlight and emphasize these features.
Systems
Brewing Equipment: manufactured by Salm of Austria.
Tap System: custom designed by architect fabricated by Salm in Austria.
Technical Issues Mechanical
Brewing of beer occurs in exposed brew kettles in the center of the restaurant. this is accomplished by piping the brew to a remote gas fired boiler located in a rated enclosure in the basement – once heated, it returns to the brew kettle. This circulation occurs continuously.
Steam produced during brewing is brought into the basement where it is condensed and eliminated in the sanitary waste system.
Fermentation occurs in the Brewery Room in the basement which has a dedicated ventilation system.
Malt is stored in an explosion proof room with dedicated ventilation system.
Technical Issues Structural
New mezzanine connected to existing cast iron columns, with bolted collar connection.

Floor under brew kettles reinforced with steel beams to distribute load to structural frame.
Materials
Floor: Hardwood
Ceiling: Plastered brick arches – painted.
Walls: Painted brick, painted plaster. Tilted wall and arches: textured gold metallic paint.
Entrance Screen: Mahogany.
Bar: Maple, mahogany, birch, perforated metal screen, brass foot rail.
Beer Tap Island: Maple, glass, copper.
Brewhouse Area: Ceramic tile floor and walls.
Booths and Tables: Birch with mahogany stain.
Columns: Cast iron finished with epoxy paint.
Bar Stools and Chairs: Wood painted black.
Stairs and Mezzanine Railing: Painted steel.
Lighting
Mezzanine: Luna quarter-sphere, opal glass wall sconces by Lightolier with A19, 100W lamp on dimmers.
Bar Lighting: Tron 36 track fixtures with narrow spots by Lightolier with PAR-36, 75W lamps.
Banquette at Front: Nyhavn Pendant copper fixtures by Louis Poulsen with A19, 100 W lamps on dimmers.
Booth Lights: Wall-mounted brass and frosted glass fixtures by Sovereign Lighting with A19, 75 W lamps on dimmers.
Banquettes East Wall: Mini-adjustable gold downlights by Lightolier with MR-16, 50W lamps on dimmers.
Fixtures Under Mezzanine: Half-sphere opal glass fixtures by Lightolier with A19, 75 W lamps on dimmers.
Waitress Station Fixtures: Brass and opal-glass fixtures by Lightolier with 13W, 2 light compact fluorescent lamps.
Project Credits
The project was completed under the firm name Fradkin/ Pietrzak Architects. The office is now Fradkin Associates Architects.

ZOE RESTAURANT
90 Prince Street
New York, NY, Usa

Located in Soho, the center of New York's artists habitués and Historic Cat-Iron District, ZOE lies on the ground floor of a copper-topped, 19th Century landmark building. Recognizable by its facade of folding glass and wood doors, the interior of ZOE evokes somewhat of a timeless, European cafe atmosphere with such elements a s fourteen foot terra-cotta columns, original decorative ceramic and mosaic tiles, rich wood, inlaid stone and marble detail.
The concept for the restaurant was to create an exciting space that would blend creative American cuisine with the artistic neighborhood of Soho, here in New York. The 3000 SF restaurant seats approximately 125 people. The kitchen is a unique open design which encompasses a wood burning oven, large rotisserie grill and seating for twelve at the cherrywood and greenstone counter. The bar area is constructed of three different marbles, hand blown glass from Italy and cherrywood veneer. The walls and the colors of the restaurant are evocative of Native American blankets and basket weavings.
Source list
Architect & Interior Design - Jeffrey Beers Architects
Engineer - Michael F. Parlamis
General Contractor - Frank Parlamis Inc.
Graphic Design - John Kneapler
Decorative Painting - Nancy Kearing & Stefano Loffredo
Stone & Tile Installation - Stefano Loffredo
Marble & Granite - Fordham Marble Co.
Stone & Tile - Carminart Tiles
Tables - Custom by Jeffrey Beers Architects
Chairs - Shelby Williams Industries, Inc.
Bar Stools - ICF
Wine Rack - Kedco
Rotisserie & Oven - Renato
China - Villeroy & Boch
Sound System - Audio Design Associates
Computer System - Squirrel
Lighting Fixtures - CSL, DiBianco, Times Square

BIOGRAFIE
BIOGRAPHIES

Afuture Company
Alex Locadia, Giusi Mastro Architects
285 West Broadway,
New York, NY, Usa 10013
tel. 212-334-6477
fax 212-219-9114
E-mail: chris@afuture.com
Web site: WWW.afuture.com

Afuture Company was founded in 1994 by Managing Director Christopher Owles and Creative and Design Director Alex Locadia. Locadia, who began his career designing custom cars in Brooklyn, has amassed a body of contemporary work that runs the gamut from integrated sculpted speakers for Panasonic and futuristic Batman furniture for Warner Bros. Selected pieces are displayed in the permanent collection of the Musée des Arts Décoratifs at the Louvre. Among his commercial interiors are the designs for Match Uptown Restaurant and Tommy Boy Records.

Architect/designer Giusi Mastro, a co-founder of the Italian Bolidismo movement and a specialist in lighting, joined the Afuture team in 1995. Mastro, who was trained in architecture and industrial design at the University of Florence, has created both full- and limited-production furniture and accessories for Alessi, Elam, Fine Factory, Flavia, and Naos. She also designed the headquarters facade and several retail showrooms for the Italian lighting manufacturer Targetti.

Agrest & Gandelsonas Architects
740 Broadway New York, NY 10003
tel. 212-2609100 fax 212-2605661
E-mail: 74672.3300@CompuServe.COM

Diana I. Agrest, AIA
Diana Agrest is a practicing architect in New York City. She is a principal of Agrest and Gandelsonas, Architects and also has her own firm, Diana Agrest, Architect in New York City.
Diana Agrest has been involved in the design and building of projects in the USA, Europe, and South America, ranging from single family houses and interiors to buildings, urban design projects and master plans, since 1975 and has won awards for various projects. She is the Design Director of the Des Moines Vision Plan.
She is a Professor of Architecture at Columbia University and at the Cooper Union in New York City. She has taught at Princeton University, both as full-time faculty and as a Visiting Professor, and has been a Bishop Professor at Yale University. From 1972 to 1984 she was a Fellow at the Institute for Architecture and Urban Studies in New York, where she was also the Director of the Advanced Design Workshop in Architecture and Urban Form.
In 1992/93 she created and directed "Framing the City: Film, Video, Urban Architecture," a post-graduate course sponsored by New York University, The Rockefeller Foundation and the Whitney Museum.
Her work has been exhibited in museums and art galleries in USA, Europe and South America where she has also lectured extensively.
Both her work and writings have been widely published nationally and internationally in journals and books including Progressive Architecture, Architectural Record, Architecture and Urbanism, Architectural Design, Planning, Lotus, Oppositions, Architectural Digest, HG, Design Quarterly, etc.
She has published: The Sex of Architecture, Ed. Agrest/Conway/Weisman, Harry N. Abrams, 1996 - Agrest and Gandelsonas Works, Princeton Architectural Press, 1994 - Architecture from Without: Theoretical Framings for a Critical Practice, MIT Press, 1991 - A Romance with the City, The Work of Irwin S. Chanin, The Cooper Union, 1982
Diana Agrest received her Diploma Architect from the School of Architecture and Urbanism, University of Buenos Aires. She did post-graduate work at the École Pratique des Hautes Études and at the Centre de Recherche d'Urbanisme in Paris 1967–69. She is a registered architect in the State of New York, she is a member of the AIA and an American Citizen.

Mario Gandelsonas is a practicing architect in New York City. Since 1975 he has designed and built a wide range of projects including houses, interiors, urban buildings, master plans and urban projects. He has been a principal of Agrest and Gandelsonas Architects since 1979.
From 1971 to 1984 he was a Fellow at the Institute for Architecture and Urban Studies and the Director of Educational Programs. From 1973 to 1984 he was founder and editor of Oppositions. He is presently a member of the editorial board for Assemblage Magazine, published by MIT Press.
He was a fellow at the Institute of Architecture and Urbanism at the S.O.M. Foundation, Chicago from 1988 to 1990. He has taught at Yale, Harvard, the University of Illinois and the University of Southern California. He has lectured and given seminars at major American, European and Asian Universities. He is currently a Professor of Architecture at the Princeton University School of Architecture.
Since 1984 he has developed techniques for the formal analysis of American cities that served as a basis for a new concept of vision planning. He was the director of the Des Moines Vision Plan from 1990 to 1992 and he is currently developing a Vision Plan and Master Plan for Red Bank, New Jersey.
His articles and designs have been widely published in many national and international magazines and in several anthologies including Progressive Architecture, Architectural Record, Architectural Design, Lotus, Dolus, Design Quarterly, Space Design, A&U and Oppositions. His book, The Urban Text, SOM Foundation / MIT Press, 1991, presents a series of computer generated analytical urban drawings preceded by a collection of critical articles. The monograph Agrest and Gandelsonas, Works, Princeton Architectural Press, was recently published. The Order of the American City, Princeton Architectural Press, will be published in the Fall of l997.
Mario Gandelsonas completed his graduate studies at the School of Architecture and Urbanism, University of Buenos Aires and his post-graduate studies in Paris at the Centre de Recherche d'Urbanisme in 1967/68. He is a Registered Architect in the State of New York.

Associates LLC
Gene S. Park AIA & Min Yang AIA
11 West 30th Street
New York, NY, Usa
tel. 212-268-8118
fax 212 - 268-8079
E-mail minyang@associates.com

Gene S. Park AIA & Min Yang AIA formed their company in 1995 and now have offices with a staff of thirty in New York and Seoul, Korea. The firm's recent work include a broad range of architectural projects including master planning, large corporate facilities, industrial projects, resorts, restaurants, clubs, retail environments, and residences.

Gene S. Park, AIA
Education:
Massachusetts Institute of Technology, Master of Architecture, 1987
University of Illinois, Bachelor of Science in Architectural Design, 1983
Unite Pedagogique 3, Versailles, France 1983

Professional Experience:
1996–present AI Associates, Seoul, Korea, Principal
1995–present GPMY Architects, New York, NY, Principal
1989–94 Davis Brody & Associates, New York, NY
1988–89 The Architect's Collaborative, Cambridge, MA
1984–86 Woo & Williams, Cambridge, MA

Professional Affiliations:
American Institute of Architects
Registered in the State of New York

Min Yang, AIA
Education:
Tulane University, Bachelor of Architecture, 1987

Professional Experience:
1997–present AI Associates, new York, NY, Principal
1995–present GPMY Architects, New York, NY, Principal
1992–94 Architect Min Yang, New York, NY
1989–91 Arkiton, New York, NY
1987–89 Russo & Sonder, Architects, PC, New York, NY

Professional Affiliations:
American Institute of Architects
national Council of Architectural Registration Boards
Registered in the State of New York, New Jersey, Pennsylvania

Major Projects List
Master Planning Projects:
Cheju Island Resort Master Plan, Cheju, Korea
Young-dong-po Industrial Site Redevelopment Plan, Korea
Pusan Mixed-Use " I-Port" Development master Plan, Seoul, Korea
Posco Mixed-Use Building feasibility study

Architecture Projects:
VIPS family Restaurant, Seoul, Korea
Kim Residence, Tuxedo, New York
Park Residence, Canton, Ohio

Interior Projects:
Newave (lounge and club) New York, NY
Laparis Department Store, Queens, New York
Warehouse of London,(women's fashions) New York, NY
Mirezi Pan-Asian Bistro and Grill, New York, NY

Jeffrey Beers Architects
91 Fifth Avenue, Suite 801
New York, NY 10003
Tel. 212-352-2020
Fax 212-352-2195
E-mail SKSin NYC@aol.com

Established in 1986, Jeffrey Beers Architects is an architectural and interior design firm specializing in commercial property renovation including restaurants, clubs, retail stores and showrooms, as well as offices and residences. The cornerstone philosophy of the firm is to explore each project with respect to its own specific context, client and appropriate architectural expression. Jeffrey Beers Architects offers a unique dedication to creativity in interior design, utilizing artist/craftsman-created finishes and furnishings, custom lighting fixtures and furniture design, combined with a thorough understanding of the construction process.
The firm's founder and principal, Jeffrey G. Beers has extensive experience and an exceptional reputation in the architectural and interior design profession. After having received his architectural training at the Rhode Island School of Design, Mr. Beers extended his formal studies with a Fulbright Fellowship for International Architecture. Upon his return to the United States, he began a most valuable tenure with the world renowned architectural firm of I.M. Pei & Partners. Jeffrey Beers Architects is recognized as a leader in the architectural and interior design industry. Mr. Beers' work is widely published and has won several prestigious awards, including the Gold Key Award for Design Excellence. His most celebrated projects include China Grill New York City and South Beach, Saks Fifth Avenue, Pappagallo, Azure, Yobo and Zoe.

Branson Coates Architecture
23 Old Street
London EC1V 9HL
U.K.
tel. 44 171 490 0343
fax 44 171 490 0230
E-mail: ecstacity@dial.pipex.com

Current Commission
New gallery building
Shoreditch, London
Client: Geffrye Museum

National center for popular music
Sheffield
Client: Music Heritage Ltd

Design for British Expo pavilions Lisbon 98 and Hanover 2000
Client: Foreign and Commonwealth Office

Design for new renaissance theater
Gdansk, Poland
Client: Theatrum Gdansk

Exhibition design - look inside! new british public interiors
International tour 1997
Client: The British Council

Living bridges exhibition
International Tour
Client: The Royal Academy of Arts

Nigel Coates' concept house
Winner of Blueprint/Ideal Home Exhibition Competition
To be exhibited at Daily Mail Ideal Home Exhibition 1998
Midlands Arts Centre (Mac)

Competition winners for the appointment of an architecturally led design development at Cannon Hill Park, Birmingham.Client: Midlands Arts Centre (MAC)

Completed Projects

1985
Metropole Restaurant, Tokyo.

1986
Jasper Conran Shop, London.
Takeo Kikuchi Shop, Barber Shop and Bohemia Jazz Club, Tokyo
Caffè Bongo for Parco, Tokyo

1987
Ashiya Pavilion, Commercial Building, Ashiya (unbuilt)
Silver, Jewellery Shop, London
Jasper Conran Shop, Dublin

1988
Dunhill International Exhibition, London, Toronto
Jigsaw, Shop, Kensington, London
Jigsaw, Shop, Bristol
Katharine Hamnett Shop, Glasgow
Katharine Hamnett Shop, Sloane Street, London
Arca di Noe, Restaurant Building, Sapporo

1989
Jasper Conran Shop, Tokyo
Stonehenge Shop, Stonehenge, Salisbury
Situationist International Exhibition Centre Georges Pompidou, Paris
ICA London, ICA Boston
Hotel Otaru Marittimo, Otaru, Japan

1990
Hamnett Active, Tokyo, Japan
Nishi Azabu Wall, Commercial Building, Tokyo
Jigsaw Shop, Kings Road, London
Katharine Hamnett Shop, Tokyo
No Furs Shop, Habitat and Identitá Exhibition, Arezzo, Italy

1991
Taxim, Restaurant, Bar, Nightclub, Istanbul
Mayflower Golf Club, Japan
Jigsaw Shop, Brompton Road, London
Debating Chamber for weekly current affairs programme, La Cinq TV, Paris
Stage set for Laurie Booth's dance - Requiair

1992
Strategic Study, Liberty Regent Street
Jigsaw Shop, St Christopher's Place, London

1993
La Fôret and Nautilus Restaurants - Schiphol International Airport, Amsterdam
Invited Competition for Museum of Literature, City of Swansea
Strategic Study, Liberty Part II Consultancy on Cafe/Bookshop
Art Silo Building Tokyo
Liberty Tax Free, Terminal 3 Heathrow Airport
Perfumery Department, Liberty Regent Street
Liberty Bookshop and Cafe, Liberty Regent Street
Invited Participant for the Architectural Foundation's
Croydon Design Initiative Exhibition 1993

1994
Jigsaw Shop, Leadenhall Market, City of London
Far East Pilot Study, Katharine Hamnett
Jigsaw in Tokyo, Marui Department Stores
Kurt Geiger Shoe Department, Liberty Regent Street
Liberty Fashion Concept Room, Liberty Regent Street
Jigsaw Shop, Dublin
Jigsaw Menswear Shop, King's Road
Liberty Shop, Bromley, London
Jigsaw Shop, King Street, Manchester
Jigsaw Shop, Glasgow

1995
Jigsaw Menswear, Kensington High Street, London
Jigsaw in Tokyo II, Marui Department Stores
Liberty Shop, Stratford-upon-Avon
Liberty Shop, Fenchurch Street, London
Design for Exhibition Stand, Olympia Exhibition Halls, London
Feasibility study, Whitgift Car Park, Croydon
Design for Liberty Tax Free, Terminal 1, Heathrow Airport

1996
Jigsaw in Japan, Meiji Dori, Tokyo, Marui/Jigsaw
Shinjuku, Tokyo, Marui/Jigsaw

Jigsaw in Japan, Kashiwa, Tokyo, Marui/Jigsaw
New Bath House Department, Liberty Regent Street
Bargo Bar, Bass Taverns, Glasgow
Penhaligon's, Liberty Regent Street
Living Bridges - Bridging the City Exhibition, The Royal Academy of Arts, London
Design for Liberty Tax Free, Terminals 2 & 4, Heathrow Airport

1997
The Power of Erotic Design Exhibition, The Design Museum

Competitions and Awards
1990
Inter-Design Award for Contribution to Japanese Cities

1991
Invited Competition, Museum of Scotland, The Royal Incorporation of Architects in Scotland
1992
Winner, Invited Competition, New Gallery Building, The Geffrye Museum, London
Finalist, Invited Competition Museum of Literature, City of Swansea

1994
Finalist, BBC Design Awards
2nd Prize, Invited Competition, Luxury Highrise Apartments, Beirut
Competition, Cardiff Bay Opera House, Cardiff Bay Opera House Trust
International Port Terminal Design Competition, City of Yokahama

1995
Finalist, Invited Competition, Millennium Markers, London Borough of Richmond-upon-Thames
Winner, Invited Competition, National Centre for Popular Music, Music Heritage Ltd, Sheffield

1996
Thames Water Habitable Bridge Competition
•Financial Times Millennnium Bridge Competition

1997
Winners, Midlands Arts Centre (MAC)
Competition winners for the appointment of an architecturally led design development at Cannon Hill Park, Birmingham.

Tony Chi & Associates
20 West 36th Street
New York, NY 10018
Tel. 212-868-8686
Fax 212-465-1098

In today's business world one of the most powerful tools of communication is interior design. How a business presents itself and its products expresses that business' position in the market place. Tony Chi & Associates is committed to helping business establish their niche through spatial identity and trough packaging and graphics. Tony Chi believes in a personal approach, one that takes the client's needs into consideration. Tony Chi & Associates offers vertically integrated firm marketing, conceptual design, furniture, accessories and lighting design. This philosophy of incorporating all the client's objectives into a look that is uniquely the client's, offers greater visibility and impact something that is much needed in an over crowded business world. Tony Chi & Associates was established in 1984 to assist entrepreneurs to create restaurant trends in various market sectors. His present staff consists of twelve employees.

Tony Chi, principal of Tony Chi & Associates believes designers are here to serve the public, and must serve them well. In restaurant design we are selling a lifestyle, and performing art and artistic gestures that people enjoy. Chi finds the entailment pleasant, and in a restaurant situation people linger for an hour or two hours, and design environment romances their show. For this reason Tony finds the entertainment business irresistible.
Many newer trends have been credited it TC & An the most recent being Harvey Davidson Cafe prototype, and massive restaurants developments in Hyatt Recency Osaka, Japan, and currently developing Retail/Theme Restaurants and Theaters in a new business Tower, Graha Kuningan, Jakarta.
TC & A has taken a further interest in restaurant development by joining forces with the Hong Kong based company, Elite Concepts Ltd., in developing Asia top restaurants such as Tutto Bene – a slice of little Italy, Indochine 1929-a fine Vietnamese stylish restaurant, La Cité – French cafe society under cover, Cafe des Artist, Tokyo Joe – a sleek and minimal interior. Tutto Meglio -dark wood and white limn (Chi's favorite venue).
In Jakarta, Indonesia TC&A completed projects such as Empire Tower consisting of a trio of concepts: Empire Grille, a penthouse restaurant with a romantic vision of the past. Quantum Athletic Club, with is Bauhaus lines adding a modern twist, and the highly sophisticated Jalan Jalan, which is slated to be the premier entertainment center in Asia.
In Hotel Mandarin Oriental Jakarta, TC&A adds to his growing list of successful international projects Zigolini, an Italian Trattoria & Kafe Kafe, a Coffee Shop, and Tokyo Joe, Japanese Restaurant and Sushi Bar.
Additionally completed and on-going projects include the Chinese, Italian and Japanese restaurants in Melbourne, Australia, opening in May 1997; Paper Moon, Istanbul, a Italian trattoria in Turkey; Indian Jones, a theme restaurant in, India; and Scalini, a highly successful Italian restaurant in Kuala Lumpur, Malavsia.

Fradkin Associates Architects
920 Broadway, Suite 904
New York, NY 10010
Tel. 212-529-5740
Fax 212-529-5740

Bennet C. Fradkin, AIA, has designed a diverse group of commercial and residential spaces. He completed both interior and exterior architectural design for Zip City, Manhattan's first brew pub. He did the same for the Brooklyn Brewery, transforming a matzoth factory into a microbrewery, offices, and warehouse/tasting room. Renovation projects that present the opportunity to create a dialogue between new and old architecture are of particular interest.
Before forming Fradkin Associates Architects in 1986, he worked with haines Lunderberg Waehler and Cossutta & Associates on a wide range of projects, from corporate interiors to technically complex undertakings, such as biological research laboratories.
A graduate of Carnegie-Mellon University, Bennet Fradkin was born and raised in the New York area. He lives in Hastings-on-Hudson with his wife, a travel writer/editor, and their two daughters.

Jan R. Pietrzak has designed major projects with Skidmore, Owings & Merrill, Cossutta & Associates, and Roe/Eliseo in New York City. He is currently working with Skidmore, Owings & Merril in London.
Pietrzak and Fradkin worked together at Cossutta & Associates before collaborating on a series of projects such as Zip City. A graduate of the Warsaw Technical University, Jan R. Pietrzak studied Urban Planning at the École de Beaux Arts in Paris before coming to New York City. He currently lives in London.

Frank O. Gehry, FAIA
1520-8 Cloverfield Boulevard
Santa Monica, CA
tel.310-828-6088, fax 310-828-2098
E-mail: keithm@sunl.foga.com

Frank Gehry is Design Principal for the firm of Frank O. Gehry and Associates, Inc., which he established in 1962. Before founding the firm, Mr. Gehry worked with architects Victor Gruen and Pereira & Luckman in Los Angeles, and with André Remondet in Paris.
Raised in Toronto, Canada, Frank Gehry moved with his family to Los Angeles in 1947. Mr. Gehry received his Bachelor of Architecture degree from the University of Southern California, and he studied City Planning at the Harvard University Graduate School of Design. In subsequent years, Mr. Gehry has built an architectural career that has spanned four decades and produced public and private buildings in America, Europe and Asia. In an article published in The New York Times in November, 1989, noted architecture critic Paul Goldberger wrote that Mr. Gehry's "buildings are powerful essays in primal geometric form and... materials, and from an aesthetic standpoint they are among the most profound and brilliant works of architecture of our time." Hallmarks of Mr. Gehry's work include a particular concern that people exist comfortably within the spaces that he creates, and an insistence that his buildings address the context and culture of their sites.
His work has earned Mr. Gehry several of the most significant awards in the architectural field. In 1977 Mr. Gehry was named recipient of the Arnold W. Brunner Memorial Prize in Architecture from the American Academy of Arts and Letters. In 1989, he was awarded the Pritzker Architecture Prize, perhaps the premiere accolade of the field, honoring "significant contributions to humanity and the built environment through the art of architecture." In 1992, he received the Wolf Prize in Art (Architecture) from the Wolf Foundation. In the same year, he was named the recipient of the Praemium Imperiale Award by the Japan Art Association to "honor outstanding contributions to the development, popularization, and progress of the arts." In 1994, he became the first recipient of the

Dorothy and Lillian Gish Award for lifetime contribution to the arts. Mr. Gehry was named a Fellow of the American Academy of Arts and Letters in 1987, a trustee of the American Academy in Rome in 1989, and a Fellow of the American Academy of Arts and Sciences in 1991. In 1994, he was bestowed with the title of Academician by the National Academy of Design. Mr. Gehry has received honorary doctoral degrees from Occidental College, Whittier College, the California College of Arts and Crafts, the Technical University of Nova Scotia, the Rhode Island.
School of Design, the California Institute of Arts, the Southern California Institute of Architecture, and the Otis Art Institute at the Parsons School of Design. In 1982, 1985, and 1987-89, Mr. Gehry held the Charlotte Davenport Professorship in Architecture at Yale University. In 1984, he held the Eliot Noyes Chair at Harvard University. In 1996-97, he was a visiting scholar at the ETH Hönggerberg in Zürich, Switzerland. Mr. Gehry was elected to the College of Fellows of the American Institute of Architects (A.I.A.) in 1974, and his buildings have received over 100 national and regional A.I.A. awards.
Mr. Gehry's work has been featured in major architectural publications and in national and international trade journals, as well as in Newsweek, Time, Forbes, The Economist, Vanity Fair, Art in America, The Wall Street Journal, The New York Times, The Los Angeles Times, The Washington Post, Le Monde, L'Express, El Correo, and Frankfurter Allgemeine. Mr. Gehry's architectural drawings and models, as well as his designs for cardboard and bentwood furniture and his interpretations (in various forms and materials) of fish, have been exhibited in major museums throughout the world.

Frank O. Gehry & Associates
Frank Gehry established the architecture firm of Frank O. Gehry & Associates in 1962. Since that time, Frank O. Gehry & Associates has grown into a full service firm with broad international experience in museum, theater, performance, institutional, commercial and residential projects. The three principals of the firm, Frank Gehry, James Glymph, and Randolph Jefferson, work as a team in the development of all projects undertaken by the firm, with Frank Gehry working as Design Principal and James Glymph and Randolph Jefferson complimenting the work of Frank Gehry with their extensive experience in project management and in the development of technical systems.
At the heart of the firm's approach to design is a process which has developed over many years, in which the client is brought fully into the design process as part of the design team, making the design a true working collaboration between the firm and the client. The design process is based on extensive physical modeling at multiple scales. The models explore both the functional and sculptural aspects of the project in a medium understood by designers and laymen alike. Very early in the process, actual building materials and large scale mock-ups are employed to promote understanding of the design. Working simultaneously with materials and systems at the detail level and with the formal image at the urban scale, the project evolves in response to the programmatic and budgetary goals defined by the client. The combination of model building and mock-up capabilities, materials research, and the application of advanced computer systems and construction techniques allows Frank O. Gehry & Associates to develop designs, in a rational process, that reach beyond the traditional limits of architecture.
Located in Santa Monica, California, the architecture studio has a staff of over 65 people, which includes a group of senior architects who are highly qualified in project management and in the technical development of building systems and construction documents, as well as extensive model-making facilities and a model building staff capable of executing everything from scale architectural models to full size mock-ups. The firm employs a network of sophisticated computer aided design workstations in the development of projects and in the translation of design ideas into the technical documents required for construction. The firm uses CATIA, a 3-dimensional computer modeling program originally designed for the aerospace industry. This program is supplemented by more traditional 2-dimensional CAD programs.
Recent and current projects include: the Guggenheim Museum Bilbao in Bilbao, Spain; the Samsung Museum of Modern Art in Seoul, Korea; Pariser Platz 3, a mixed-use building adjacent to the Brandenburg Gate in Berlin, Germany; Der Neue Zollhof, an office complex in Düsseldorf, Germany; the Experience Music Project in Seattle, Washington; the Bard College Center for the Performing Arts in Annandale-on-Hudson, New York; the Vineyard Towers, a residential development in Dallas, Texas; the University of Cincinnati Center for Molecular Studies in Cincinnati, Ohio; the Team Disneyland Administration Building in Anaheim, California; the Nationale-Nederlanden Building in Prague, Czech Republic; the EMR Communication and Technology Center in Bad Oeynhausen, Germany; the Frederick R. Weisman Art Museum at the University of Minnesota in Minneapolis, Minnesota; the University of Toledo Center for the Visual Arts in Toledo, Ohio; the Vila Olimpica Retail and Commercial Complex in Barcelona, Spain; the Walt Disney Concert Hall in Los Angeles, California; the American Center in Paris, France; the EuroDisney Retail and Entertainment Center outside of Paris, France; the University of Iowa Laser Laboratory in Iowa City, Iowa; the Chiat/Day Office Building in Venice, California; the Vitra International Furniture Museum and Factory in Weil am Rhein, Germany; and the Vitra International Headquarters in Basel, Switzerland.

Zaha M. Hadid
Studio 9, 10 Bowling Green Lane,
London EC1R OBD, England
tel. 0171-253 4147
fax 0171-251 8322
E-mail: 101457.2237@CompuServe.COM

Zaha Hadid is a London based Architectural Designer whose work encompasses all fields of design, ranging from the urban scale through to products, interiors and furniture. Central to her concerns are a simultaneous engagement in practice, teaching and research, in the pursuit of an uncompromising commitment to modernism.
Hadid studied architecture at the Architectural Association from 1972, and was awarded the Diploma Prize in 1977. She then became a member of the Office for Metropolitan Architecture; began teaching at the AA with OMA collaborators Rem Koolhaas and Elia Zenghelis; and later led her own studio at the AA until 1987.
Hadid's academic concerns have continued to the present, with periods of visiting professorships at Columbia and Harvard Universities; and a series of Master Classes and lectures at various venues around the world. During 1994 she held the Kenzo Tange chair at the Graduate School of Design, Harvard University.
Since graduating, Hadid has been testing the boundaries of architectural design in a series of research based competitions. Her work was awarded wide international recognition in 1983, with a winning entry for The Peak, Hong Kong. This success was followed by first place awards for competitions in Kurfuerstendamm, Berlin (1986); for an Art and Media Center in Dusseldorf (1989); and for the Cardiff Bay Opera House (1994), home to Welsh National Opera and the National Museum of Wales, and the landmark building to herald the start of the new Millennium.
In parallel to her theoretical and academic work, Hadid started her own practice in 1979 with the design for an apartment in Eaton Place, London. This was awarded the Architectural Design Gold Medal during 1982. Other projects have included furniture and interiors for Bitar, London (1985); the design of two projects in Tokyo (1988); a Folly in Osaka (1990); and the interior for the Moonsoon Restaurant, Sapporo (1990).
In 1990 Hadid completed a Music Video Pavilion design in Groningen, Holland. She created the installation for "The Great Utopia" exhibition at the Guggenheim Museum, New York (1992) which was followed by the Pavilion for Blueprint magazine (1995) built for the 100th anniversary Interbuild exhibition in Birmingham.
In 1993, Hadid's fire-station for the Vitra furniture company opened to much public acclaim. In the same year, Hadid completed one of the last housing projects for the IBA - Block 2 in Berlin. Since 1989 various large scale urban studies have also been completed for harbor developments in Hamburg, Bordeaux and Cologne, leading to the prize winning Dusseldorf Art and Media Center project which was developed to detail design during 1992-93. More recently, Hadid has completed designs for competitions in Bad Deutsch Altenburg, Austria (1993); Copenhagen, Denmark (1993); New York (1995); Madrid(1995); and London(1996).
Hadid's paintings and drawings have always been an important testing field, and a medium for the exploration of her design. This work is widely published and has been shown internationally. Beginning with a large retrospective at the AA (1993), other major exhibitions have included the Guggenheim Museum, New York (1978); the GA Gallery, Tokyo (1985); the "Deconstructivist Architecture" show at the Museum of Modern Art in New York (1988); The Graduate School of Design at Harvard University (1995); and the Grand Central Station New York (1995).
Hadid's work also forms part of the permanent collection of various institution such as the Museum of Modern Art, New York, and the Deutsches Architektur Museum in Frankfurt.
Zaha Hadid continues to teach and practice. In 1996, her office completed the installation design for the Wishmachine, a major exhibition at the Vienna Kunsthalle, and her recent projects were featured at the Venice Biennale Masters pavilion. Ongoing projects include a housing project in Vienna and other projects in London.
Recent competitions include shortlisted finalist for the Victoria and Albert Museum's new Boilerhouse Gallery and the Luxembourg concert hall. The office is also joint winner of the Thames Water Habitable Bridge invited international architectural competition.
Zaha Hadid has been awarded the Sullivan Chair for 1997 at the University of Chicago School of Architecture and a guest professorship at the Hochschule for Bildende Kunste Hamburg. The San Francisco Museum of Modern Art will mount a major exhibition of her recent projects and competitions at the end of the year.

Hardy Holzman Pfeiffer Associates
902 Boardway, New York, NY, Usa
tel. 212-677-6030 fax 212-979-0535
811 West 7th Street, Losa Angeles, CA, Usa
tel. 213-624-2775 fax 213-895-0923
E-mail: ekubany@hhpa.com

Established in 1967, Hardy Holzman Pfeiffer Associates is a leading planning, architectural and interior design firm with offices in New York and Los Angeles. HHPA specializes in highly complex building types, primarily for public use. The firm offers a wide range of services including programming; site and master planning; architectural and interior design, documentation, and construction administration; historic renovation; and cost analysis.

Our professional and fully capable design staff of 124 people continues to be led by its three founding Partners: Hugh Hardy, Malcolm Holzman, and Norman Pfeiffer. They provide a high standard of personalized, responsive service for each client. They are directly involved in each project from initial design concepts through completion.

Highly respected for some of the country's most innovative architecture, HHPA is particularly well known for its work with buildings for public use. Over the past thirty years the firms has designed civic centers, performing and visual arts centers, libraries, educational facilities, retail facilities, restaurants, commercial headquarters, and a wide variety of buildings throughout the United States. The firm's clients include public and private institutions, corporations, private developers, as well as civic authorities.

Completed projects include the Cooper-Hewitt National Museum of Design (New York, New York); the Los Angeles County Museum of Art (Los Angeles, California); Riverbank West, a 44-story residential apartment tower with a retail base (New York, New York); the Willard Hotel Office and Retail Complex (Washington, DC); the restoration of New York's legendary Rainbow Room and reconstruction of the RCA Building's top three floors into the Rockefeller Center Club (New York, New York); new corporate headquarters for educational publisher Scholastic, Inc., (New York, New York); the Rizzoli Bookstore (New York, New York); expansion of existing facilities at the Dance Theater of Harlem (New York, New York); the Madison Civic Center (Madison, Wisconsin); Hult Center for the Performing Arts (Eugene, Oregon); Alaska Center for the Performing Arts (Anchorage, Alaska); restoration of the New Amsterdam and New Victory Theaters (New York, New York) in New York's historic 42nd Street district; the revitalization of Bryant Park and design of Bryant Park Grill (New York, New York); renovation of Windows on the World Restaurant at the World Trade Center (New York, New York); Middlebury College Fine Arts and Student Activities Centers (Middlebury, Vermont); a new temple and congregational center for Temple Israel (Dayton, Ohio); rehabilitation and expansion of the Los Angeles Public Library: Central Library (Los Angeles, California) and the New Haven Free Public Library (New Haven, Connecticut) among others.

Current work is equally diverse and includes Bridgemarket, a new marketplace beneath New York City's 59th Street Bridge; the renovation and expansion of the New York Stock Exchange; the Cleveland Public Library renovation and expansion (Cleveland, Ohio); a new Federal Building and Courthouse (Tucson, Arizona); a new Fine Arts Facility at California State University, Fullerton (Fullerton, California); a new four-year campus for Soka University of America (Aliso Viejo, California); the Columbus Performing Arts Center (Columbus, Georgia); Whitaker Center for Science and the Arts (Harrisburg, Pennsylvania) which includes a 600-seat theater, science museum and IMAX theater; the new San Angelo Museum of Fine Arts (San Angelo, Texas); renovation and expansion of Vassar College Libraries (Poughkeepsie, New York); renovation of Manhattan Community College Fiterman Hall; the new International Museum of Ceramic Art at Alfred University (Alfred, New York); and Rainbow Bridge, a new toll plaza and Administrative Building at the U.S. and Canadian border (Niagara Falls, New York).

Design Approach
HHPA's approach to buildings for public use blends concern for program accuracy and plan efficiency with an appreciation of the quality of its public spaces. Clear orientation and welcoming features are characteristic of this work. Combined with a proven ability in documentation and construction, the results are superiorly constructed buildings that make a spirited statement, simplify operation, and are practical to maintain.

HHPA's public projects have also been recognized for their efficiency and stature as well. From the movement of over 3,000 people in a six-story glass lobby on opening night at the Hult Center for the Performing Arts in Eugene, Oregon to the nearly 1,500-reader seat capacity at the Los Angeles Central Library, we understand the importance of accessible, functional spaces.

Our buildings are known for their responsiveness to program, appropriateness of solution, and compatibility with regional and local factors. We recognize good design comes from addressing a combination of unique program requirements and physical context requirements of each site. Rather than approach each project with an unwavering set of design principles, HHPA sees architecture as a way of enhancing and sustaining an environment that celebrates variety.

Guided by a process of inclusion, we can serve the goals of each project in differing ways: choosing an approach that is appropriate to the aspirations of each client as well as the context of each project.

For this reason, HHPA's work shows a variety of design characteristics which respond with uncommon specificity to the needs and imagery of each commission, whether new construction or historic renovation. No two HHPA projects have come to the same result. This varied aesthetic and planning approach, coupled with HHPA's inquiring attitude, is perhaps unmatched in present American architectural practices. It assures that each project receives the firm's full and fresh attention, leading to a result which is both appropriate and practical.

HHPA Recognition
Since our inception in 1967, we have been honored with over 100 national awards including Honor Awards from the American Institute of Architects (AIA) in 1976, 1978, 1979, 1981, 1983, 1994, 1995, 1996 and 1997; the Brunner Prize in Architecture by the National Institute of Arts and Letters (1974); the Medal of Honor by the New York Chapter/AIA (1978); as well as the prestigious Architectural Firm of the Year Award from the American Institute of Architects in 1981. In recognition of their significant contributions to the profession Hugh Hardy, Malcolm Holzman and Norman Pfeiffer were inducted into the Interior Design Hall of Fame in 1992.

HHPA also received the American Institute of Architects Urban Design Award for two consecutive years, in 1994 for Bryant Park, and in 1995 for the Los Angeles Public Library's Central Library. Named one of the top ten design achievements in 1993 by Time Magazine and awarded an AIA Honor Award for Urban Design in 1994, the restoration of New York City's Bryant Park has brought a new focus of activity to midtown and reestablished a favorite outdoor public space. Two restaurant pavilions carefully sited and designed by HHPA to blend harmoniously into the landscape offer the public enhanced refuge and enjoyment.

Awarded the 1995 AIA Honor Award for Urban Design, the rehabilitation and addition to the Los Angeles Central Library provides both a central cultural facility and related landscaping for public use in the midst of dense commercial development. As part of our master plan for the site, the new Maguire Gardens were created atop an underground parking garage.

HHPA has often been the subject of critical architectural evaluation. In 1992, Rizzoli International published a comprehensive retrospective monograph of the firm's work entitled, Hardy Holzman Pfeiffer Associates: Buildings and Projects 1967-1992, a celebration of twenty-five years of professional practice. In recognition of their significant contributions to the profession Hugh Hardy, Malcolm Holzman and Norman Pfeiffer were inducted into the Interior Design Hall of Fame that same year.

Aware that buildings should be designed to be enjoyed by everyone, HHPA's plans respond to the access and circulation needs of all users, including physically challenged visitors. We have been acknowledged leaders in this field since the Columbus Occupational Health Center in Columbus, Indiana was given the American Institute of Architects Bartlett Award for Providing Access and Usability for Handicapped Visitors in 1976, to our current work providing accessible facilities at New York's Lincoln Center.

Haverson Architecture and Design P.C.
289 Greenwich Avenue
Greenwich, CT 06830
Tel. 203/629-8300
Fax 203/629-8399

Haverson Architecture and Design Pc is an architectural and interior design firm located in Greenwich CT. The firm, including its two partners its two partners, Jay and Carolyn Haverson, is made up of staff of 21 professionals, specializing in restaurants, retail stores, office interiors and residence among other projects. Haverson Architecture and Design also provides graphic design identities for its architectural and interior design clients, including logotypes for restaurants and corporate clients, as well as menu designs and signage.

The firm's commercial work includes Si Piazza, a restaurant in Charlotte, NC; the LightingWall at the Carillon Building, also in Charlotte; Spiga Restaurant in Scarsdale and Bedford, NY; the new Lillian Auugdt Collections retail shop and Mediterranean Restaurant in Greenwich, CT; Arcadia Coffee Company in Darien, CT; Ben's Restaurant and Delicatessen in Manhattan; Motown Cafe in New York and the "Coney Island Emporium" and the second Motown Cafe both located ate the New York, New York Hotel and Casino in Las Vegas. The firm has also completed several exclusive residences in the metropolitan New York area. In addition, Haverson Architecture and Design has designed the Construction Fasteners offices and manufacturing plant in Reading, PA; the headquarters and group home for the Association for Retarded Citizens in Greenwich, CT and the offices for ESF Concepts for Children in Radnor, PA.

The latest projects in the design stage are a Bar/club in Caracas, Venezuela; the Harley-Davidson Cafe in Las Vegas; an apartment interior in the Trump International in Manhattan; and restaurant projects in Chicago and Miami for the New York Restaurant Group, as well as the third Motown Cafe in Orlando,

Florida.
While a partner in his former firm, Jay Haverson completed many restaurants, including Tatou in New York and Beverly Hills, Christer's, Vong, Hi-Life, the Mulholland Drive Cafe, and the first Planet Hollywood project in London, Chicago, Aspen, Washington DC, and the Mall of America, and the 12,000th Mc Donald's in a landmarked New Hyde Park, NY location. Carolyn Haverson developed many of the graphic identities on behalf of clients, and was involved with signage and other applications.
The Haversons have worked as members of the design team for the retail redevelopment of 42nd Street in New York, and have worked in a series of restaurants and entertainment projects at Disney World in Florida for the Disney Development Corporation.
Previous retail work includes the design of Morgenthal Frederics optical shop and Ilias Lalaounis Jewelry, both located on New York's Madison Avenue; and a new lobby and facade for 560 Seventh Avenue in the heart of New York's fashion district. Office space designs include Elite Model Management headquarters; the National Commercial Bank of Saudi Arabia, SICPA/Sectech headquarters, and offices of The Grief Companies, a clothing manufacturer.
Jay Haverson serves on he Town of Greenwich, CT Building Committee to oversee the design and construction of classroom additions to two of the town's elementary schools.

Lalor Design
William R. Lalor
46 Dawn Harbor Lane
Riverside, CT, Usa, 06878
Tel. 203/698-2462 - fax 203/698-1620

Mr. Lalor's love of the arts was fostered through tutoring and schooling in fine arts, painting, and music. His interest in art and design took a detour into food as not only an avocation but a vocation as well. His career in restaurants began at age thirteen as a dishwasher and busboy and continued through apprenticeship to the rank of chef, working as such while continuing to study art and design. The majority of Mr. Lalor's early design works were back of house, kitchen, and operational layouts of restaurants. Initially Mr. Lalor's full restaurant design projects came about due to a desire to translate his own unique ideas as a restaurant conceptualist. Many of his designs go beyond the traditional norm of restaurant architecture, the majority include strong thematic influences, meant to entertain and often expressed with a sense of humor. The ability to translate thematic concepts as well as traditional design has led to successful careers as a designer, chef and consultant. For fourteen years, he created with Ark restaurants, his concepts and designs included the Big Kahuma, Gonzales y Gonzales, Louisiana Community Bar and Grill, Mackinac Bar and Grill, Rodeo Bar, Sequoia-New York, Vanyon Road and many more. After leaving Ark, Mr. Lalor took a two year sabbatical traveling the world and enriching his depth of creative design and conceptual knowledge.
He has most recently conceptualized and designed City Grill, Canteen Cafe, and Noca Grill in NYC.

Nancy Mah
Interior Design
A division of Ark Restaurant
85 Fifth Avenue
New York, NY 10003
Tel. 212-206-8800
Fax 212-206-8845

Nancy Mah, born in Memphis, Tennessee studied at Bates College, University of Florence and Parsons School of Design. Jobs ranging from the Museum of Modern Art to Robert Isabell to David Rockwell lead her into interior design where she has worked as a designer since 1989. She has had projects appear in national publications such as Interior Design, Gourmet Magazine and Elle Decor. To date her work is mainly commercial but includes residences in New York, Florida, and Memphis.

Education:
1918-83, Bates College, Lewiston, Maine.
1983-84, University of Florence, Florence, Italy.
1987-89, Parsons School of Design, New York, NY.

Experience:
1984-85, Museum of Modern Art, New York, NY.
1989, Robert Isabell, Florist/Event Planner.
1990, David Rockwell Architect.
1993-94, Lee Harris Pomeroy Architect.

Ark Restaurants owns and operates 23 restaurants and manages 6 restaurants: 19 in New York City, four in Washington D.C.; three in Boston and one each in Rhinebeck, New York; McLean, Virginia, and Islamorada, Florida. The company also operates successful catering business in New York City and Washington D.C. and two wholesale and retail bakeries in New York City.

Stomu Miyazaki
ES Studio INC
2 Bronxville Road 2G
Bronxville, NY10708
Tel.-Fax 914/337-2660

1954 Born in Japan
1978 B.S. in Physics, Ninhon University in Tokyo, Japan.
1982 B.F.A. in Sculpture, California College of Arts & Crafts in Oakland, CA.
1982 Assistant at the Sculpture Dept in C.C.A.C.
1984 Architectural designer. SITE Projects INC, NYC.
1989 Established ES STUDIO INC, NY.
Exhibitions:
Percy West Gallery, CA.
Contemporary Art Gallery, MA.
International Design Center of New York, NY.
Boston Design Center, MA.
New York City Hall Park, NY.
Hal Bromm Gallery, NY.
The Applied Gallery, NY.
Sally Hawkins Gallery, NY.
Battery Park Korean Veterans Memorial Finalist Show, NY.
Tokyo Beam Building Gallery, Tokyo, JP.
The Gallery, MA.
Design works:
Restaurants, Private residence, Roof top garden, Display window, Residential Interior, Showroom interior, Night club Facade, Water front Parks, Furnitures.

Rockwell Architecture, Planning and Design, P.C.
5 Union Square West,
New York, NY 10003
Tel. 212-463-0334
Fax 212-463-0335

David Rockwell was born in Chicago, Illinois in 1956 and moved to Guadalajara, Mexico, at the age of ten. His mother was a dancer on the vaudeville stage which greatly influenced his love of theater and music and inspired his becoming an accomplished pianist. David earned his Bachelor's degree in Architecture at the University of Syracuse and went on to study at London's Architectural Association. The lure of Broadway brought David to New York City where he worked as an assistant for a Broadway lighting designer.
Rockwell Architecture, Planning and Design, P.C. is a full service design firm consisting of ninety design professionals. Best known for our entertainment architecture our highly dramatic architectural interiors such as Nobu, Vong, Monkey Bar, Tapika, and Torre di Pisa in New York City as well as nearly all the Planet Hollywoods on the planet, we're also internationally recognized for our residential, retail, mixed-use, and commercial projects.
Fundamental to our success is our design approach that implicitly insists on the uniqueness of each project as we maximize all opportunities for state-of-the-art interactions between technology, entertainment, and design. Our expertise in designing environments that combine high-end video technology, handmade objects, special effects, and fixtures and furniture made by specialized artisans into a unified whole is second to none. We have a proven track record of bringing highly unique and specialized projects in on-time and on-budget, and creating highly profitable projects for our clients.
For the past ten years much of our work has centered on entertainment architecture and the notion of "architecture as theater." The theatrical aspect of individuals proceeding through space is examined and emphasized by our focusing on the vital roles lighting, decoration, and special effects play in creating every 'set.' We also concentrate on designing environments that give the visitor, patron, or resident a feeling of being transported to another place in time. Most recently, having positioned ourselves to be on the cutting edge of technology, entertainment, and design, we've been experimenting with the role virtual reality plays in the design of environments and have as a result some very exciting projects on the boards.
Our client list includes such prestigious companies as: The Walt Disney Company, Planet Hollywood, CBS, Forest City Ratner, The Hahn Company, McDonald's, Marvel Comics, LCOR, Loews Hotels, The Related Companies, The Stanhope Hotel, The Sheldon Gordon Company, Caesars World, Sun International, and Sony Theaters.

Large-scale, mixed-use/entertainment projects include: New York City's Forty-Second Street Now! project; the World Trade Center Plaza Competition; Disney BoardWalk at Walt Disney World; Kids'Place and the proposed Caesars Forum III, both in Las Vegas. Madison Avenue retail shops include: Morgenthal Frederics Opticians at 61st and 74th Streets and Lalaounis jewelry at 63rd. High profile restaurant and club designs include: Nobu, Monkey Bar and Restaurant, Torre di Pisa, Tapika, Baang, Splash, Vong, Christer's, Le Bar Bat, Hi-Life, The Whiskey at the Paramount Hotel, and Tatou in Beverly Hills and New York City. Geographically, our projects are located from London and Dusseldorf to Jakarta and Shanghai. The recipients of numerous awards, our projects are also published and featured in: Crain's, Architectural Record, Interior Design, Interiors, New York Magazine, The New York Times, Interni.

Turett Collaborative Architects
86 Franklin Street
New York, NY, Usa 10013
E-mail info@turettarch.com

Turett Collaborative Architects was founded in 1984 by Wayne Turett. Established on the principle of creative design, it has grown into a multi-disciplinary practice with the ability to produce a range of design solutions from architecture and interiors to graphics and industrial products. TCA relies on client participation to direct and program all projects; the experienced staff then incorporates these principals into the development of the work, resulting in a product that is functional, creative, and current. Adherence to a budget and schedule, essential to a successful work, are also key in this process.

The current architectural project profile is comprised of commercial, retail, restaurant design, and corporate planning. Examples of recent projects include the design of America Restaurant Las Vegas (1997), The Grille Room Restaurant (1997), Hale and Hearty Soups at 3 locations (1997), The Atrium at 237 Park Avenue (1997), Tommy Boy Music offices (1992 & 1997), Priority Records offices (1993 & 1997), Penalty Recordings offices (1997), Newsbar's 4 locations (1992-1997), Majestic Theater renovations (1996), and Kenneth Cole Shoes at 4 locations (1996).

TCA has received numerous accolades and the projects have appeared in many domestic and international journals. The Market at Newport received Best Restaurant Award for 1996 and was nominated for Best Restaurant Award by the James Beard Foundation. Tommy Boy Music received Best Office Design of 1994 by Interiors Magazine. Newsbar received Best Coffee Bar from New York Press and Best Menu Design Award. Mr. Turett has also won the New York City Art Commission Award for Design Excellence for a newsstand located at 81st Street and Columbus Avenue and was also a finalist in the 1988 Newsstand Competition.

Wayne Turett RA
As principal of Turett Collaborative Architects, Wayne Turett meets directly with all clients to ensure that their needs are the primary focus in the formulation of design solutions. His presence on all projects in the office brings a similar language of form and invention to each of the works. His leadership role in the office makes him responsible for the overall coordination of all design and production efforts, as well as the general operation of the firm.

His projects have been gaining notoriety in the form of many journal publications, most recently in *Interior Design*, *Interiors*, *The New York Times*, *New York Magazine*, *Paper*, and *Metropolitan Home*. Besides the numerous awards that the office has won, Mr. Turett has also received a City Art Commission Award for Design Excellence for the design of a newsstand located in New York City. He also was a finalist in the Newsstand 88 Competition sponsored by the AIA and IDSA. His design for the Newsbar menu/bookmark won most imaginative category in the National Restaurants Association's Great Menu Design contest.

Mr. Turett has also designed furniture throughout his career. The "Dining Automator," was runner-up in the Design Explorations: 2001 Exhibition Competition. He has been invited on numerous occasions to participate in the Design Auction for the Cooper Hewitt Museum. His furniture has been incorporated into each project that has come through the office, and it is this attention to detail that makes the work particularly inventive, creative, and functional.

Prior to the creation of his own office, Mr. Turett was partner in the firm Turett Freyer Collaborative Architects. He has degrees in Architecture from the University of Illinois and Pratt Institute and is licensed to practice architecture in New York, New Jersey and Connecticut.

Stuart Basseches RA
As associate of Turett Collaborative Architects, Mr. Basseches is responsible for the inner-workings of the practice, from design through production and management. His 3 year collaboration with Wayne Turett has allowed a coupling of design directions, the products of which are projects which emphasize creative, contemporary solutions.

Before joining with TCA, Mr. Basseches was principal of Stuart Basseches Architect in New York City. The work produced in the office ranged from residential to small commercial work in the New York area. In 1994, he won a competition to erect a veteran's memorial in San Jose, California which is being unveiled in November 1997.

Prior to the creation of his own office, Mr. Basseches worked for Richard Meier Architect in New York and Paris. He was project designer for the Siemens Corporate Offices in Munich, Germany, and was staff architect for Canal+ Offices and Studios in Paris, France and Hypobank Offices in Luxembourg. Having tenured at Richard Meier he is uniquely familiar with the operations and coordination of larger buildings in both the United States and Europe.

Coupled with his architectural work at Turett Collaborative Architects, Mr. Basseches' more recent endeavors involve the design of a series of lighting fixtures for residential and commercial applications which are now in production. His lighting and photography has been exhibited at the Sculpture Center and other galleries in New York City.

Stuart Basseches attended the Massachusetts Institute of Technology where he received a Bachelors of Art in 1982, and later studied at the Yale School of Architecture where he received a Master of Architecture in 1987. He is a registered architect in New York.

Fotolito: Lorenteggio - Milano
Stampa: Grafiche Alma - Milano
Legatura: Pedrelli - Parma